Palgrave Studies in Literature, Culture and Economics

Series Editors
Paul Crosthwaite
School of Literatures, Languages and Culture
University of Edinburgh
Edinburgh, UK

Peter Knight
Department of English and American
University of Manchester
Manchester, UK

Nicky Marsh
Department of English
University of Southampton
Southampton, UK

This series showcases some of the most intellectually adventurous work being done in the broad field of the economic humanities, putting it in dialogue with developments in heterodox economic theory, economic sociology, critical finance studies and the history of capitalism. It starts from the conviction that literary and cultural studies can provide vital theoretical insights into economics. The series will include historical studies as well as contemporary ones, as a much-needed counterweight to the tendency within economics to concentrate solely on the present and to ignore potential lessons from history. The series also recognizes that the poetics of economics and finance is an increasingly central concern across a wide range of fields of literary study, from Shakespeare to Dickens to the financial thriller. In doing so it builds on the scholarship that has been identified as the 'new economic criticism', but moves beyond it by bringing a more politically and historically sharpened focus to that earlier work.

More information about this series at
http://www.palgrave.com/gp/series/15745

Nancy Henry

Women, Literature and Finance in Victorian Britain

Cultures of Investment

For George + Susie —
with thanks for all your
support in 2018!
Nancy
12-15-18

palgrave
macmillan

Nancy Henry
University of Tennessee
Knoxville, TN, USA

Palgrave Studies in Literature, Culture and Economics
ISBN 978-3-319-94330-5   ISBN 978-3-319-94331-2   (eBook)
https://doi.org/10.1007/978-3-319-94331-2

Library of Congress Control Number: 2018949352

© The Editor(s) (if applicable) and The Author(s), under exclusive license to Springer International Publishing AG, part of Springer Nature 2018
This work is subject to copyright. All rights are solely and exclusively licensed by the Publisher, whether the whole or part of the material is concerned, specifically the rights of translation, reprinting, reuse of illustrations, recitation, broadcasting, reproduction on microfilms or in any other physical way, and transmission or information storage and retrieval, electronic adaptation, computer software, or by similar or dissimilar methodology now known or hereafter developed.
The use of general descriptive names, registered names, trademarks, service marks, etc. in this publication does not imply, even in the absence of a specific statement, that such names are exempt from the relevant protective laws and regulations and therefore free for general use.
The publisher, the authors and the editors are safe to assume that the advice and information in this book are believed to be true and accurate at the date of publication. Neither the publisher nor the authors or the editors give a warranty, express or implied, with respect to the material contained herein or for any errors or omissions that may have been made. The publisher remains neutral with regard to jurisdictional claims in published maps and institutional affiliations.

Cover credit: Heritage Image Partnership Ltd/Alamy Stock Photo

This Palgrave Macmillan imprint is published by the registered company Springer Nature Switzerland AG
The registered company address is: Gewerbestrasse 11, 6330 Cham, Switzerland

ACKNOWLEDGEMENTS

First the money. I am grateful to the National Endowment for the Humanities for a fellowship that allowed me to write the better part of a book I have been thinking about for many years. The English Department at the University of Tennessee and the Hodges Better English Fund have provided money for travel to archives and conferences and for research assistants. Heads of Department Chuck Maland, Stan Garner, and Allen Dunn were unfailingly supportive. Business Manager Judith Welch managed the money and made it all happen. The Office of Research at UT provided summer research assistants and foreign travel money through the SARIF grant program. The Tennessee Humanities Center funded the Nineteenth-Century British Research Seminar, where I presented work and also enjoyed a thriving intellectual community. For her work at the THC, I thank Joan Murray. I also thank Alan Rutenberg for his encouragement and practical help with grant applications.

I am especially grateful to those who read complete drafts of the manuscript in its various forms, providing invaluable insights along the way: Graham Handley, Kat Powell, and George Robb. Those who read individual chapters also contributed incisive comments: Dermot Coleman, Silvana Colella, Anne Mayhew, and Talia Schaffer.

I have presented work from this book at too many conferences to mention. For inviting me to present talks related to my research, I thank especially Shalyn Claggett, Iris Goodwin, Francis O'Gorman, Clare Pettit, Leah Price, Angela Runciman, and Frederik Van Dam.

I wish to acknowledge my colleagues at UT, especially Misty Anderson, Amy Billone, Gerard Cohen-Vrignaud, Amy Elias, Nancy Goslee, Martin Griffin, Hilary Havens, Mary Papke, and all the members of the Nineteenth-Century British Research Seminar. I also thank librarian Chris Caldwell for his assistance in matters of research.

Other colleagues who have been especially important to this book over the years include: Tim Alborn, Jen Hill, Aeron Hunt, George Levine, Chris Looby, Maura O'Connor, Mary Poovey, Janette Rutterford, Cannon Schmitt, and Carolyn Williams.

The Dickens Universe has been a source of unending intellectual energy and so I thank John Jordon for organizing the universe, as well as my roommates and other friends over the years, especially Jim Adams, Jonathan Grossman, Tricia Lootens, Teresa Mangum, Jennifer McDonnel, Meredith McGill, Elsie Michie, Helena Michie, Catherine Robson, Ellen Rosenman, Rebecca Stern, and Robyn Warhol.

I am thankful to all of my current and former students at UT on whom I tested out ideas about women and money. I thank especially Katie Burnett, Allison Clymer, Kat Powell, and John Stromski.

Late in the game, Lila Stromer stepped in as a copy editor and accomplished amazing things. At Palgrave Macmillan, I thank Allie Bochicchio Troyanos, Rachel Jacobe, and Ben Doyle.

I thank my friends for their support of various kinds that cannot be measured: Jean Levenson, Jeannie Obie, Tom Cooper, Theresa Profant, Michael Kenik, Michelle Kenik and the spinners, Nancy Maland, Rosie Allen, Nick Shah, Ritula Shah and Graham and Barbara Handley.

Finally, though they cannot read and don't know about money, my animals teach me new things every day. So thank you Angus, Fiona, Annie, and Q.

Contents

1 Introduction — 1

2 Women Investors in Fact — 29

3 Investment Cultures in Dickens, Trollope, and Gissing — 53

4 Elizabeth Gaskell: Investment Cultures and Global Contexts — 85

5 George Eliot: Money's Past and Money's Future — 139

6 Charlotte Riddell's Financial Life and Fiction — 179

7 Margaret Oliphant, Women and Money — 225

8 Conclusion — 267

Index — 277

Abstract

This book defines the cultures that emerged in response to the democratization of the stock market in nineteenth-century Britain when investing provided access to financial independence for women. Women's experiences as investors complicate notions of separate domestic and public spheres as they contributed to local, national, and global economies. Victorian novels represent those economic networks in realistic detail and are preoccupied with the intertwined economic and affective lives of characters. Analyzing evidence about the lives of real investors together with fictional examples, including case studies of four authors who were also investors, Henry argues that investing was not just something women did in Victorian Britain; it was a distinctly modern way of thinking about independence, risk, global communities, and the future in general.

Keywords Women · Finance · Economics · Capitalism · Investment Biography · Victorian novels

CHAPTER 1

Introduction

[A] woman can take part in the government of a great empire by buying East India Stock.
—Barbara Leigh Smith Bodichon, *A brief summary, in plain language of the most important laws concerning women: Together with a few observations thereon*

In 2016, eight years after the start of the 2008 financial crisis, with stock market values climbing into record territory, two contributions to the early twenty-first-century American culture of investing marked the place of women in that culture. First, former Wall Street CEO Sallie Krawcheck founded an investment company, Ellevest, which promised to transform the investing experience of women and took as its motto: "Invest Like a Woman: Because Money is Power."[1] Second, the film *Equity* (2016) focused on women as traders on Wall Street; it was also written, produced, directed, and largely financed by women[2] (see also Ryzik 2016). Neither of these developments should be remarkable, but in fact both were. While women are more active than ever as investors, they are still relatively scarce as major players on Wall Street. Ellevest's bold claims to usher in a new financial era by targeting women's investment needs and *Equity*'s exploration of the complex problems faced by women in the high-stakes financial arena seem surprising and new.

Together, they offer a glimpse of the ways women are investing and how women investors are being represented in the twentieth-first century.

How did we get here? What is the history of women's role in financial markets? Why is gender a relevant category for thinking about investing today and in the past? These questions are among those that this book seeks to address through an exploration of how nineteenth-century British women authors invested and how investing women were represented, particularly in realist fiction.

In addition to the visibility of women investors in popular culture, scholars have taken an interest in the history of women's investment practices. Two groundbreaking works look at the role of women as investors in eighteenth-century Britain and nineteenth-century and twentieth-century America. Historian Amy Froide (2017) argues that "the financial independence of unmarried women, as well as married women's rights to separate property, allowed women to participate in and further England's Financial Revolution" (2). She shows that "Englishwomen's participation in early modern capitalism fits into, as much as it challenges, the economic history of women" (2). Historian George Robb (2017) argues that "Victorian women were active investors and shareholders, that contemporaries were well aware of this, and that there was much comment about the phenomenon, most of it negative" (2017, 1). What is missing from the portrait emerging in these works is an account of women investors in the nineteenth-century British economy and broader culture.

Women, Literature and Finance in Victorian Britain: Cultures of Investment takes a historical perspective on the role of women investors in the literature and culture of Victorian Britain, a role that, though appearing in plain sight in histories, biographies, and fiction, has nonetheless remained invisible to literary critics, possibly because, like the women behind the film *Equity*, Victorian women did not always make the condemnations of capitalism that literary critics especially seem to value. Novels by Elizabeth Gaskell, Charlotte Brontë, George Eliot, Charlotte Riddell and Margaret Oliphant raise the question: Is it possible to like money without liking greed? In their writing, and in their lives, these women pursued investing as a unique means of empowerment that increased their inherited or earned wealth. The women in this alternative history of capitalism were not traders on the London Stock Exchange (that would not be possible until 1973). Rather, they were either passive or active investors and, in rare cases, speculators. They confronted a set of cultural prejudices against their participation in the market, but took advantage of their legal right to invest, whether on the stock exchange or in private companies. Like today's more liberated women, they faced sexual entanglements with spouses, lovers, and advisors, as well as domestic obstacles in the forms of fathers, brothers, and children. In this respect, the decisions Victorian women made about how to invest their capital were simultaneously public and private, and novels in particular explore in detail the complex ways in which public and private spheres overlapped.

This book argues, first, that female investors were ubiquitous in Victorian fiction, reflecting a reality that has only recently attracted the attention of historians and critics. The fact that investing was open to women, as other avenues to wealth and power were not, meant that female authors' treatment of investing and capitalism in their writing was not characterized by the same types of critique that appear in William Makepeace Thackeray's *The Newcomes* (1853–1855), Charles Dickens's *Little Dorrit* (1855–1857) and *Our Mutual Friend* (1864–1865), Anthony Trollope's *The Way We Live Now* (1875) and *The Prime Minister* (1876) and George Gissing's *The Whirlpool* (1897), among many others. It argues, second, that paying attention to the lived experiences of women investors, including the lives of authors who contributed to financial fiction in the Victorian period, reorients our perspective both on the lives of women and on the history of capitalism.

Inheritance, investment, speculation, prosperity, and failure were hallmarks of the British middle-class experience during the late eighteenth and nineteenth centuries, and it is no wonder that these are all common features of nineteenth-century novels. Such mixed consequences of the volatile economy during the financial and industrial "revolutions" are at the heart of this book: Wealth was created and dramatically lost, and the domestic and economic spheres of society were inseparable. Many nineteenth-century novels introduce scenarios involving the inheritance of wealth, often amassed through global economic networks. Novels also present ethical questions arising from past and present commercial and financial practices. While novelists were uniformly critical of greed and the commodification of human life, which capitalism seemed to encourage, if not demand, many male and female authors were also investors who profited from expanded investment opportunities at home and abroad. Their experiences as local and global investors who represented investment cultures to their readers are crucially relevant to this study.

Women, Literature and Finance in Victorian Britain contributes to literary criticism, the cultural history of finance, and biographical or life writing studies. It revises how we think about financial history by focusing on women and by recasting the trajectories of women's lives as a set of financial events, conditions, and decisions, which are at least as important as the parallel domestic landmarks of marriage and childbirth. Like other forms of financial transactions, such as buying property, investing capital in private companies or government securities was (and is) simultaneously a public and a private act. The cultures of investment permeated familial relationships; at the same time, family dynamics influenced investing behaviors. Domestic and more broadly social concerns were interwoven with economic and financial concerns, a reality reflected in Victorian literature generally and emphasized particularly in fictional narratives by women authors.[3] I argue that, just as the financial and domestic spheres were inextricable from each other, so too were Victorian literary and financial cultures, and therefore they must be studied together in order to provide a more complete understanding of both.

The tradition of viewing Victorian culture as characterized by separate, gendered spheres has a contentious history. Leonore Davidoff and Catherine Hall's (1987) influential *Family Fortunes: Men and Women of the English Middle Class, 1780–1850* posited that the men and women in the extended networks of the families they studied were subject to an emergent separate sphere ideology that did not exist in earlier periods. Their thesis was both embraced and challenged in subsequent historical work (see Colley 1992; Vickery 1993). Davidoff and Hall responded to their critics in a revised edition (2002), explaining that their book "ends with the beginnings of the deconstruction of 'separate spheres' partially, at least, through nascent feminism" (xvii). "The feminism of the mid to late nineteenth century," they argue, "was built on a sense of grievance and it was women's sense of their exclusion from the public sphere and its consequences which led to their demand for entry to education, the professions and citizenship rights" (xvii). This observation refers to women's collective sense of exclusion and desire for inclusion. "Investor," by contrast, was not a collective, political identity around which women could organize. Even before the emergence of mid-to-late nineteenth-century feminism (and then alongside of it), the personal decisions women made about their money had a public impact. This is why in 1854, proto-feminist Barbara Bodichon (1854) wrote that shareholding was one of the few forms of political power available to women, who could "take part in the government of a great empire by buying East India Stock" (4).

Debates over *Family Fortunes* particularly and separate spheres generally are ongoing. Kathryn Gleadle (2007) points out that subsequent research (including her own) into women's political participation, for example in antislavery and anti-corn law campaigns, has "enhanced our understanding of the complexities of female experience and helped us to more fully appreciate the instability of the public/private binary" (775). Susie Steinbach (2012) defends *Family Fortunes* against its critics. She argues that for Davidoff and Hall, "separate spheres ideology was not a rigid set of rules internalized as natural and adhered to unquestioningly. Rather, separate spheres were in the process of being constructed, rife with internal contradictions, and frequently challenged (both overtly and covertly)" (830). She further contends: "Far from being independent of one another, the public and private spheres were mutually constitutive, materially as well as rhetorically" (830).

There seems to be a consensus at this point that a notion of separate spheres obtained, but that for an accurate understanding of Victorian culture, we must recognize complexities. Gleadle's *Borderline Citizens* (2009) splits the public sphere into the public and the parochial, suggesting that the parochial is an area in which the public and private spheres overlapped and in which women had unexpected influence. She writes: "Scholars of gender history have criticized the division of individual experience into the dichotomized departments of 'private' and 'public.' We now have much more sophisticated understandings of the blurrings and interdependence of these two notions, and are more sensitive to the multiple—and some sometimes contradictory meanings—which they may have held for contemporaries" (17). Her claim that "women's sense of involvement in an imperial nation ... could be rooted in their confidence as economic agents (as shareholders of the East India Company, for example)" (262) is born out by historians who focus on women investors.

This book builds on and expands research into the role of women investors that both implicitly and explicitly challenges notions of separate spheres precisely because such research attends to the ways in which investing is simultaneously private and public. The novels and case histories of individual investors discussed in the following chapters establish that when it comes to investing, public and private spheres were inextricable, and the distinction itself is unhelpful to our understanding of how women contributed to nineteenth-century investment cultures.

By the very nature of investing, women could participate in local, parochial, national, and global economies. Froide (2005) demonstrates that unmarried women were essential contributors to civic life in the early modern period: "Urban singlewomen could also be independent, knowledgeable, and prosperous property holders and creditors, as well as upstanding citizens who had much to contribute to their localities" (153). Focusing on women investors in government securities in the first half of the nineteenth century, David Green and Alastair Owens (2003) show that while investment choices were a matter of personal finance for individual women, their capital was crucial to underwriting national and imperial projects: "The social position of these single women was at odds with the central tenets of the ideology of separate spheres" (512).[4] In exploring, "the demographic and geographical importance of single middle-class women, and the range of wealth they possessed," Green and Owens argue that in the nineteenth century, "female wealth was of crucial importance to the expansion of the British state" (512).[5]

The chapters that follow trace the emergence of nineteenth-century British women as investors—passive and active, failed and successful— as they appear in the historical record and in fiction. Investing, whether conservatively in the Consols (consolidated government debt) or more aggressively in the stock market, was an economic activity that was open to single women and, increasingly over the century, to married women. I emphasize the economic role of real and fictional women as shareholders in publically traded companies as well as their identities as investors in private companies and various forms of government debt.[6] Starting in the eighteenth century, the prospect of money reproducing itself appealed to the working classes that sought to increase their wages and financial security.[7] Yet the numbers of working-class investors and the amounts they invested remained small. The majority of women discussed here had excess capital to invest, both inherited and earned. They range from wealthy heiresses and the upwardly mobile middle class to widows and never-married women without other sources of income.

Nineteenth-century financial markets were surprisingly democratic: One man's or woman's money was as good as another's when it came to financing speculative ventures for profit. Single women enjoyed the same legal rights as men to conduct business and invest their money, but, until 1870, a woman ceased to exist legally after she married. If widowed, she resumed legal rights to her own money. In the eighteenth century, women invested in the Consols and in Royal chartered companies, such as the South Sea Company, the Royal African Company, the East India Company, and the Bank of England. They were also investors in family businesses, local shipping ventures, real estate (at home and in the colonies), and mortgages. Before 1833, women were investors in West Indian sugar plantations and were entitled to compensations paid out by the government after the abolition of slavery.[8]

Throughout the nineteenth century, women became more numerous and influential as investors in shipping, insurance, and joint-stock companies financing canals, railroads, and banks, as well as a wide range of foreign and domestic bonds and securities.[9] Robb (2009) writes: "The industrial economy of the Victorian period was fundamentally different from the mercantile economy of the seventeenth and eighteenth centuries, and women could participate in it in ways that have largely gone unstudied" (120). As more people invested, women's livelihoods were linked to national and global economies, whether through their own investments or those of their family members. The financial lives of Victorian women involved family networks, insolvent men, abrupt reversals of fortune, and the pains of bankruptcy, a fate worse than—and sometimes leading to—death.

Until recently, we knew little about nineteenth-century women as investors, but pioneering archival work by historians Josephine Maltby, Janette Rutterford, Mark Freeman, Robin Pearson, James Taylor, David R. Green, Alastair Owens, Nicholas Draper, Helen Doe, Jehanne Wake, and others has revealed the presence of female shareholders in all forms of public and private companies and has prompted conversation about the social significance of this presence. Over the course of the nineteenth century, women comprised between 5 and 20% of the investing public. Seeking to answer previously unasked questions about the extent of women's involvement as shareholders, Maltby and Rutterford (2006b) show that, in contrast to married women before the Married Women's Property Acts of 1870 and 1882, spinsters and widows held shares with the same rights as men: "Indeed, although women did not gain the right to vote for governments until 1919, they were generally allowed to vote in annual general meetings" (227).[10] Freeman et al. (2011) elaborate that if a woman held the requisite number of shares in a joint-stock company, she "was eligible to stand as a candidate for the boards of most companies" (94). She could canvas and vote for board members and stood to profit or lose from her investments.

Beyond establishing and exploring the existence and representation of women investors, this study is unified by a set of interrelated subjects and themes that emerge from an investigation of local, national, and global investment cultures. These subjects include the entwined histories of slavery and insurance and the ethical problems attending money that was inherited, earned, and invested. I am interested in how these economic histories leave traces in all aspects of cultural production, such as architecture and public monuments, and especially how they might be encoded, that is when not specifically addressed, in nineteenth-century literature. In other words, I am concerned with how Victorians thought about money's past, present, and future. Rather than accepting that all novelists were anticapitalist critics, I show that women writers who were also investors had a complex relationship to the monetary dimension of familial and other personal relationships and that fiction by women authors examines these complexities while simultaneously gesturing to the broader, global economic contexts of everyday lives within England.[11]

Elizabeth Gaskell's first novel, *Mary Barton: A Tale of Manchester Life* (1848), provides an example of these themes and of my approach to uncovering them. Critics and biographers have observed that Gaskell wrote the novel, which contains painful domestic scenes including several deaths of children, to distract herself from grief over the death of her infant son. It is less often remarked that she drew on visits to her relatives, the Hollands, a prominent business family in Liverpool. It is also rarely noted that Gaskell used the proceeds from *Mary Barton* to make her first major investment of £1500 in the St. Katharine Docks in London, which twenty years earlier had been the subject of controversy for the destruction of a historic neighborhood and displacement of residents required for its construction. *Mary Barton* contains no heiress investing in a textile factory, as Margaret Hale does in Gaskell's *North and South* (1854–1855), no woman ruined by her investments in a failed bank like Miss Matty in *Cranford* (1853a), and no one defrauded of life insurance shares, as Thurstan and Faith Benson are in *Ruth* (1853b). But it does gesture to global commercial and financial networks, encoding a history of war, slavery, and abolition through allusions to the Liverpool Exchange building, the Nelson Monument and a ship named after the abolitionist John Cropper.

Reading Victorian novels within the context of women's financial activities and the authors' situations within financial networks helps to reveal what has remained hidden or coded. Women were neither physically nor mentally confined to a domestic sphere. The female authors I consider had diverse geographic, economic, and affective experiences that included strong regional ties and identities maintained after migration and relocation to urban centers. Gaskell grew up in Cheshire, visiting her father in London and eventually settling in Manchester. George Eliot lived in the Midlands until moving to London at the age of thirty. Charlotte Riddell emigrated from Ireland to London, and Oliphant moved from Scotland to London via Liverpool. All traveled extensively and had familial connections that made broader economic networks part of their domestic lives. They set their novels in various locations and all wrote about the West Indies and America, directly or indirectly considering the implications of internal British economies that relied on slavery.[12]

The history of slavery in relation to British capitalism seemed to require careful coding in fiction, but it lies behind the cotton mills of Gaskell's *North and South*, Rochester and Bertha's Jamaican past in Charlotte Brontë's *Jane Eyre* (1847), Mrs. Davilow's inherited fortune in George Eliot's *Daniel Deronda* (1876) and the demoralization of Kirsteen's father in Oliphant's *Kirsteen* (1890), to cite only a few examples.[13] I combine economic history and biography to help make visible what has remained hidden in literary texts to argue that women were embedded in global economic networks and that women authors were self-conscious about those networks when reimagining the historical contexts that informed their realist fiction.

George Eliot famously wrote in the finale to *Middlemarch* (1871–1872): "For there is no creature whose inward being is so strong that it is not greatly determined by what lies outside it" (785). Male and female authors created heroines whose lives are defined by social and economic connections and determined by economic opportunities. For example, Gaskell's Mary Barton Wilson emigrates to Canada; Florence Dombey Gay follows her husband to China in Charles Dickens's *Dombey and Son* (1846-1848); and Lucy Snowe in Charlotte Brontë's *Villette* (1853) establishes her career as a teacher while awaiting her fiancé M. Paul's return from Guadeloupe, where he traveled to oversee a plantation (for its female owner). While these heroines make economic decisions in conjunction with their husbands, others of all social classes invested to supplement their limited earning capacity.

From her earliest works, Eliot introduced minor female characters who are investors, including Mrs. Patten in "The Sad Fortunes of the Reverend Amos Barton" (1857b), the tenant farmer Mrs. Hartopp in "Mr. Gilfil's Love Story" (1857a) and Mrs. Glegg in *The Mill on the Floss* (1860), who invests in mortgages and speculates in her nephew Tom Tulliver's trading ventures. In *Middlemarch*, after committing to marry Will Ladislaw, the heiress Dorothea Brooke declares, "We could live quite well on my own fortune—it is too much—seven hundred a year—I want so little—no new clothes—and I will learn what everything costs" (Eliot 1871–1872, 762).[14] As we will see, Gaskell, Charlotte and Emily Brontë, and Eliot, as well as Dickens, Thackeray and Trollope, were all investors in the modern stock market. Riddell and Oliphant were partners in their husbands' (failed) businesses. All were active in the financial sphere beyond their participation as authors in the literary marketplace.[15]

Fundamentally, investing means that money will work for you rather than you working for money. There is a complex history of moral skepticism about money reproducing itself in Western culture, from Christian objections to usury through nineteenth-century critiques of capitalism by men such as Karl Marx, Thomas Carlyle, and John Ruskin.[16] By the mid-nineteenth century in Britain, however, investing in joint-stock companies, the Consols and foreign government bonds had become an accepted practice across social classes. In their writings, political economists, financial journalists, and novelists sought to establish a distinction between investment—which fueled a thriving economy—and speculation, which resembled gambling. These efforts were at least partially successful. As investing became a respectable part of everyday life, it provided opportunities for upper- and middle-class women, even offering some working-class women the chance to augment their limited incomes.

I combine archival research about how women managed their money with an examination of how male and female authors represented investing spinsters, widows, and wives in fiction of the Victorian period (1837–1901), with glances back to the eighteenth century and Regency period (1811–20) and forward to the early twentieth century. I use the plural "cultures of investment" in my subtitle to reflect the social changes that occurred throughout the nineteenth century, as well as to emphasize that when investors made personal decisions about money, they became contributors to distinct but interconnected local, national, and global economies. This focus on investment allows me to look at how various individuals and groups wrote about the financial dimension of their lives and how their experiences differed along the lines of gender, marital status, class, and geographical location. I argue that investing was not just something women did; rather, it was a distinctly modern way of thinking about independence, risk, global communities, and the future in general.

Novels by Thackeray, Charlotte Brontë, Dickens, Trollope, Gaskell, Eliot, Riddell, Oliphant, Gissing, and others reflect the active role taken by women as investors on the stock exchange and in public works and private ventures. Victorian novels are preoccupied with the intertwined economic and affective lives of their characters. Specifically, marriage and inheritance plots explore the financial dimensions of relationships among husbands, wives, parents, and children. In addition to their dealings in the literary marketplace, Victorian authors often invested the money they earned from their writing. The Brontës lost money in the "railway mania" of the 1840s; Gaskell complained about the diminishing dividends paid on her shares in the St. Katharine Docks; and Eliot began her career as an investor with £2000 of shares in the Great Indian Peninsular Railway. The experiences of women authors are particularly important in exploring the role gender played in nineteenth-century attitudes toward investment and the representation of finance capitalism in fiction. They all relied on male advisors: the Brontës on their publisher George Smith, Gaskell on her Holland cousins, and Eliot on her friend and future husband John Walter Cross. Riddell and Oliphant were less fortunate in their advisors and fended for themselves when struggling to pay off the debts of their husbands.[17]

Mary Poovey (2003) stresses the uneven development of financial institutions, arguing that both fiction and nonfictional writing, especially financial journalism, helped to explain the workings of the financial system to the public. She argues that financial writing "needs to be viewed as part of a discursive system in which Britons constructed ideas about finance and money alongside the system of finance itself" (5). While Poovey's invaluable collection of financial writing contains no contributions by women, some of the selections provide insight into women's influence. For example, Poovey includes D. Morier Evans's (1819–74) recounting of a childhood story that amounts to a primal scene of financial knowledge. When Evans noticed his father sharing information about the rise and fall of stocks with his mother, he began asking her questions: "I was informed of the nature and importance of the money market, the position and interest-bearing capacity of the funds, and promised, if were a very good boy, a trip with my father to take his dividends" (quoted in Poovey 2003, 306). It was his mother who gave him an account of "the Government connection with the Bank, the rise and progress of the Debt, and the differences between Consols, paying three per cent. and Long Annuities returning almost six" (306). Information provided by his mother made a lasting impression and influenced what became a preoccupation throughout his life as a financial journalist. This anecdote illustrates a thread running throughout this book: Many women possessed knowledge of money matters that amazed their contemporaries when it came to light through their writing. For example, critic John Ashcraft Noble (1885), reviewing Charlotte Riddell's novel *Mitre Court*, refers to her "fearful and wonderful knowledge of matters financial." Others, most notably Margaret Oliphant, almost compulsively denied any such knowledge even when constructing elaborate financial plots.[18] The knowledge displayed by women like Mrs. Evans, Emily Brontë (an avid investor), and Riddell continues to surprise us today, making it all the more important to recover the contexts of their financial experiences.

Poovey (2009) also argues that the increase in available shares starting in the early nineteenth century "marked the beginning of what eventually became a culture of investment in Britain" (40). In referring to the cultures of investment, I expand the category that Cannon Schmitt and I introduced in our collection titled *Victorian Investments* (Henry and Schmitt 2009). Historians and critics have offered other formulations to describe the pervasiveness of investment as a cultural practice. The volume *Show Me the Money: The Image of Finance, 1700 to the Present* (Crosthwaite et al. 2014) focuses on visual images and encourages us to conceptualize an atmosphere of investment: "Finance—money, investment, credit, debt—is the air we breathe" (1). Peter Knight (2016) refers to the American "culture of the market" (18). The Capitalist Studies Manifesto argues that capitalism is a "process": "Institutions, history, and cultural context shape the specific form that capitalism assumes in any given place at any particular moment" (Ott and Milberg 2014). These attempts to define a culture, atmosphere, or process of investment reflect the need to think about investment capitalism as a broadly cultural—not merely economic—phenomenon.

Such recent work is part of an evolving field of writing about economics and finance in relationship to literature and culture. Economic criticism is a thriving area of enquiry. Classic works on money and Victorian literature by John Vernon (1984), John Reed (1984), Norman Russell

(1986), Barbara Weiss (1986), Patrick Brantlinger (1996), and others preceded the publication of *The New Economic Criticism* (Osteen and Woodmansee 1999), a landmark in the field. Subsequently, collections such as Francis O'Gorman's *Victorian Literature and Finance* (2007) and Henry and Schmitt's *Victorian Investments* (2009) have contributed to interdisciplinary approaches that bring together literary critics and historians. Poovey's *Genres of the Credit Economy* (2008) shows the interdependencies of nineteenth-century writing about finance and what we now define as Literature, providing an archaeology of how Literature came to be defined as what was not economic or financial. Other critics who attend closely to Victorian political economy include Regenia Gagnier (2000), Gordon Bigelow (2003), Claudia Klaver (2003), and Catherine Gallagher (2006). Works devoted to women, gender, and economics include Deanna Kreisel's *Economic Woman* (2010), Elsie Michie's *The Vulgar Question of Money* (2011), Jill Rappoport's *Giving Women* (2011) and Lana Dalley and Jill Rappoport's *Economic Women* (2013).[19]

Women, Literature and Finance in Victorian Britain draws on this substantial body of criticism to show how Victorian social, legal, political, familial, and ideological conditions permitted women to participate in the expansion of the greatest economy the world had ever seen, encompassing both formal and informal empires. It argues that this context is essential for understanding how women investors were represented by male authors and how female authors wrote about the cultures of finance generally. Women had speculated since before the formalized stock market began in 1801, and middle-class women had invested in family businesses throughout the eighteenth century. The cultural phenomenon of women investing in the nineteenth century was surprisingly common and generally tolerated, despite the inevitable social critique and satire of their activities by male authors like Thackeray, Dickens, Trollope, and Gissing, which might seem to undermine their emergence as financial actors. On the whole, however, these critiques did little to prevent women from taking advantage of investment opportunities; rather, they only increased the visibility of women investors and naturalized their presence.

Business historians have observed that women were legally able to deal in the market simply because "no one had thought to exclude them" (Laurence et al. 2009, 4). Their money was good on the Stock Exchange, and, like men, women braved the risks of financial downturns and crashes. Limited liability legislation in 1855, 1856, and 1862 expanded investment opportunities generally, and the hard-fought battle over married women's property rights reflected women's desire to participate in investment opportunities. The Married Women's Property Act of 1870 encouraged women to invest because the law protected assets in the form of shares (Combs 2005; see also Holcombe 1983; Shanley 1989).[20] I place women at the center of an account of nineteenth-century global capitalism and demonstrate their importance in the investment cultures that emerged as opportunities for investment expanded through the related processes of industrialization, financialization, colonialism, imperialism, and global trade. By welcoming women, the stock market began a process of democratization that would accelerate at the end of the nineteenth century and into the twentieth.

In their writings about financial subjects, women authors were particularly aware of the troubled past and historical legacy of capitalism, but perhaps because of their status as outsiders to the processes conducted primarily by businessmen—even as they were growing in numbers as investors—their critiques tended to be different in nature from those of their male contemporaries. Expanding investment opportunities allowed them to increase their wealth and participate in enterprises from which they were otherwise excluded; therefore, they were less likely to make criticism of capitalism per se central to their writing, however much they deplored greed and financial corruption. Women writing about capitalism within the context of their limited but important involvement as investors means that their fictional representations were often more subtle and complex than those of male writers.

In addition to emphasizing the role of women in this larger story of capitalist development, I explore the financial lives of individual women who were also authors and show how their life experiences informed their fiction, which in turn influenced how readers understood these widening investment cultures. This version of capitalism's development refocuses attention on the economic lives of women in general and women authors in particular, but not only in relation to their publishing careers. Many Victorian authors struggled with financial problems complicated by their relationships to financial advisors and male partners, among them Ellen Wood, Catherine Gore, Charlotte Brontë, and Mary Elizabeth Braddon. I offer four case studies of the lives and writings of women who were financial investors beyond their contributions as authors: Elizabeth Gaskell, George Eliot, Charlotte Riddell, and

Margaret Oliphant. I consider how each of these women wrote about money, economics, and finance in ways that contributed to Victorians' understanding of modern capitalism.

In sum, this book argues that women played a central role in nineteenth-century local, national, and global economies because of how they invested their capital. The female investor was familiar to Victorians and widely represented in realist fiction. Both real and fictional women investors complicate models of separate public and private, as well as financial and literary spheres. It also argues that the history of women's financial lives is as important as the romance or marriage plots through which their stories are usually told. Together, these arguments challenge more familiar narratives of capitalism and culture in which women's exclusion is assumed. It thus offers new and revised perspectives on the relationship of finance, literature, and the lives of women.

I begin by establishing two important contexts for the following case studies. The first context is the historical presence and influence of women investors throughout the nineteenth century; the second is the representation of women investors and the cultures of investment generally in works by male novelists, particularly Thackeray, Dickens, Trollope, and Gissing. Next, case studies reveal the details of four women authors' lives and examine how their personal financial experiences are interwoven in their fiction, which in turn became part of the broader cultures of investment. The contextual chapters and case studies are unified by a set of interlinking themes, among them global commercial and financial networks, volatile economies, the business of insurance, material culture (commodities, architecture, engineering projects), as well as the legacy of slavery and the moral dilemmas attendant in inheriting, earning, and investing money.

Chapter 2, "Women Investors in Fact," shows that in the eighteenth century, women were voting shareholders in the East India Company and Bank of England. Later, the 1856 Companies Act and the 1862 Consolidation Act expanded opportunities for investing in publicly traded shares by limiting the liability of shareholders. The Married Women's Property Acts of 1870 and 1882 brought married women into the market as independent investors. This chapter discusses patterns of women's investments in government securities, canals, docks, and banks, as well as in domestic, foreign, and colonial railways; it sets the stage for my literary analyses and supports my argument that female authors' personal experiences of gaining independence through investing moderated their critique of capitalism in contrast to that of their male contemporaries. But, first, we must see the nature of those critiques and the popular fictional types against which women's writing implicitly protested through complex plotting, characterization, and moral inquiry.

Chapter 3, "Investment Cultures in Dickens, Trollope, and Gissing," focuses on how influential male authors of the period represented women investors in order to establish a point of reference for subsequent chapters on female authors. In *Vanity Fair* (1847–1848) and *The Newcomes* (1853–1855), Thackeray represented female investors in the East India Company with ironic skepticism about their power as voting shareholders. Trollope introduced various types, including the widow of business Mrs. Van Siever in *The Last Chronicle of Barset* (1866–1867) and the timid investing spinster in the eponymous *Miss Mackenzie* (1865). Trollope doubted whether Miss Mackenzie understood the relationship between increased interest and impaired security, thereby epitomizing a notion that women did not grasp the fundamentals of investing. Dickens railed against the American worship of dollars in *Martin Chuzzlewit* (1842–1844) and the regime of shares in *Our Mutual Friend* (1864–1865). Yet in Dickens's *Dombey and Son* (1846–1848), Sol Gills invests successfully and Harriet Carker offers her invested wealth to support the bankrupt Mr. Dombey and his estranged and disgraced wife Edith. Strongly influenced by Dickens and Trollope, Gissing focused on lower-middle-class women investors in *New Grub Street* (1891) and *The Odd Women* (1893). His novels explore the ambiguities of the New Woman's place in society, suggesting that limited financial empowerment did not always lead to independence. Dickens's *Little Dorrit* (1855–1857), Trollope's *The Way We Live Now* (1875), and Gissing's *The Whirlpool* (1897) are known for their sweeping critiques of the financial system. There is no comparable work by a woman author.

After showing that women investors were highly visible in Victorian literature and culture generally, I tighten the focus to explore in detail the financial lives and writings of four authors. Chapter 4, "Elizabeth Gaskell: Investment Cultures and Global Contexts," investigates the financial networks that influenced Gaskell's early life, including the business activities of her extended family in relation to the financial plots in *Mary Barton* (1848), *Cranford* (1853), *Ruth* (1853b), *North and South* (1854–1855), *Sylvia's Lovers* (1863), and *Wives and Daughters* (1864–1865). I discuss Gaskell's investments in docks, railways, and real estate to demonstrate that her critique of capitalism was complicated by the investments on which she depended to support herself and her daughters. Shifting the critical and biographical focus away from Manchester and toward Gaskell's rich explorations of other communities such as Liverpool, Wales, and Whitby, I emphasize the importance of familial economic networks to her identity and in her fiction.

Investing women such as the Dodson sisters in *The Mill on the Floss* (1860) appear throughout Eliot's fiction, and the problem of how best to use money is central to her plots. In *Middlemarch* (1871–1872), Dorothea Casaubon laments to Will Ladislaw: "My money buys me nothing but an uneasy conscience" (350). Chapter 5, "George Eliot: Money's Past and Money's Future," considers the ethics of inheriting money perceived to be tainted by a corrupt past and the choices that Eliot's characters face when considering how to invest for the future. It situates *Middlemarch* and *Daniel Deronda* (1876) in the context of the investment cultures of Eliot's late career, specifically her relationship to her financial advisor and future husband, the merchant banker John Walter Cross. Building on my *George Eliot and the British Empire* (Henry 2002) and Dermot Coleman's *George Eliot and Money* (2014), I pay particular attention to Eliot's uniquely progressive portfolio of diversified investments, overseen by Cross, which put her at the forefront of modern investing practices.

Chapter 6, "Charlotte Riddell's Financial Life and Fiction," discusses the most important financial novelist of the Victorian period, known in her time as the "novelist of the City" for works such as *George Geith* (1864)[21] and *Austin Friars* (1870). Yet, today Riddell remains one of the most forgotten of once-popular Victorian novelists. I provide new information about Riddell's personal financial troubles—which may be traced back to her mother's financial distress as a young woman in Liverpool—and the lawsuits in which she was involved following the bankruptcy of her husband, a failed inventor and businessman in London. I argue that Riddell's unique perspective on business ethics in her novels is a result of her own financial entanglements.[22]

Chapter 7, "Margaret Oliphant, Women and Money," shows that Oliphant was beset by financial problems and anxieties throughout her adult life, and that these troubles are reflected in the economic plots of her fiction. Oliphant grew up in Liverpool, and her first three novels were set there. I focus on these forgotten works, as well as on her short stories and better-known novels such as *Hester* (1883) and *Kirsteen* (1890) to show the ways in which she complicates representations of women and money. Oliphant treats the subjects of slavery's legacy, life insurance, and the struggles of women to achieve financial independence, evincing a distinctly ambivalent attitude toward new opportunities for women that situate her in the same context as her late nineteenth-century contemporaries Riddell and Gissing.

Chapter 8, "Conclusion," looks to the role of women investors from the 1890s to the early twentieth century. The tradition of Victorian writing about women investors continued with authors such as E.M. Forster and Edith Wharton, who write about the *rentier* class in Britain and America, even as Modernist authors sought to distance themselves further than their Victorian predecessors from the business class and the stock exchange.[23]

After its premier and a set of perceptive reviews recognizing its significance, the 2016 film *Equity* faded, seemingly without making a major impact. In a central scene, investment banker Naomi Bishop (Anna Gunn) assures a room full of women that it is okay to like money: "Money doesn't have to be a dirty word." At the end of the film, public attorney Samantha Ryan (Alysia Reiner), who has been investigating Bishop's IPO, repeats this line as she branches out into the private sector. These striking lines did not become iconic, like the declaration of Gordon Gekko (Michael Douglas) in the film *Wall Street* (1987): "Greed is good."[24] Rather than a condemnation of capitalist excess, the aptly titled *Equity* focuses on the particular problems of women in the financial world, including the sexual and reproductive politics that embroil its ambitious female characters. The failure of this movie to have the kind of impact that damning portraits of Wall Street that focus on men have had may be due to its status as a small, independent film, but its reception also has to do with our culture's unwillingness to recognize the complicated role of women in the world of business and finance capitalism (see Bianco 2016).

In this respect, *Equity*'s relationship to Wall Street may be likened to Margaret Oliphant's novel *Hester*'s relationship to Anthony Trollope's *The Way We Live Now*. *Hester* is a novel about the complex familial and sexual dynamics that face Catherine Vernon, a female banker, and Hester, her young cousin. The novel shows that women can be successful in the world of finance and applauds that success even as familial complexities undermine it. In contrast, *The Way We Live Now* is a scathing condemnation of male financiers and, by implication, the system of British finance. It has been taken up as a moral tale for modern times and has become canonical. *Hester*, in contrast, is little known outside of academic circles that recognize its boldness and originality as a representation of women and finance. The failure of the film *Equity* to register with critics and audiences has its equivalence in the failure of critics to explore the existence and significance of women investors in the Victorian period.

This study of women investors has relevance to our own investing culture. It is a common observation that modern capitalism is characterized by "abstraction." Yet, nineteenth-century business dealings retained and depended on relationships of family, friends, marriage, trust, and personal networks (see Finn 2003; Hunt 2014; Knight 2016). Our current distance from the companies in which we invest our money is a condition that began with the Victorians, who purchased shares, held the script, and received dividends paid by a company without necessarily knowing or caring how that company operated. Gaskell's and Eliot's respective holdings in St. Katharine Dock shares are interesting examples, if in fact they knew about the controversies that had attended the construction of these docks in which they later invested.

Contemporary actions such as boycotts and divestment have their nineteenth-century antecedents, for example, in Quaker merchants' refusals to invest in the opium trade and in women's organized boycotts of West Indian sugar. I have found little evidence that Victorian novelists examined the behaviors of the companies in which they purchased shares in terms of what we would call "ethical investing."[25] They invested to increase their incomes and enhance their financial security. Nonetheless, as this book will show, Victorian novels offer a unique window into how nineteenth-century thinking about money generally and investing particularly evolved—a conflicted legacy that we have inherited and from which we continue to learn.

NOTES

1. Ellevest.com, https://www.ellevest.com. Accessed 6 April 2018.
2. *Equity*, directed by Meera Menon (2016, Broad Street Pictures).
3. My methodological approach of emphasizing life writing as a form of financial history differs from that of much economic literary criticism, though my study of authors' financial lives has something in common with, and is indebted to, Smith (1968), James (2003), Coleman (2014), and Colella (2016).

4. Green and Owens' title—"Gentlewomanly Capitalism?"—invokes the seminal work of Cain and Hopkins—*Gentlemanly Capitalism and British Imperialism* (1999). See also Beachy et al. (2006).
5. Further challenges to the idea of separate spheres from a financial perspective have appeared in Phillips (2006), Froide (2017), Barker (2017). For a challenge to separate spheres in a Victorian literary context, see Lootens (2017), who calls on readers to "Suspend Separate Spheres!" (12).
6. The place of women as wage earners and consumers has been more extensively studied. For women as consumers, see Copeland (1995), Rappaport (2000), Finn (1996), Sanders (2006), and Walkowitz (2012).
7. In his study of the South Sea Bubble of 1720, Balen (2003) writes: "Even women were able to invest, the pace of change on the stock market exceeding the capacity of the law to rule against their doing so. Many of the women at the Princess of Wales's court were speculators, and at the other end of the social scale the women at Billingsgate market were said to talk of nothing else but buying and selling South Sea stock" (105).
8. Draper (2010) has found that the majority of small-scale slave owners listed in the records of those compensated in the 1830s were female (204). The author Matthew (Monk) Lewis (1775–1818) left his Jamaican estates to his sisters (43).
9. For the differences between the Royal chartered companies and the new joint-stock companies of the nineteenth century, see Alborn (1998). Alborn (2009) shows that life insurance directly contributed to the popularity of investing and the concept of mitigating risk over the long term (12).
10. Maltby and Rutterford's (2006a) special issue of *Accounting, Business and Finance History* (now known as *Accounting History Review*), devoted to "Women and Investment," gathers both broad surveys of women's roles as investors and case studies from British and colonial contexts. Collections such as *Women and Their Money* (Laurence et al. 2009) and *Men, Women, and Money* (Green et al. 2011) introduce groundbreaking research upon which this book draws.
11. Delany (2002), for example, claims that English literature has been "largely hostile to commerce and industry" (14). He notes that literary critics have "a history of sympathy for the organicist hostility to commerce" (15). Blake (2009) writes: "There are some signs of an increased 'tolerance' of capitalist economics and less 'knee-jerk recoil' from the commercial and industrial cast of the times" (29). Nevertheless, literary criticism published following the 2008 economic recession seems to have lost that tolerance and recoiled again from capitalist excesses as represented in Victorian fiction. Delany (2002) also observes that the material basis of *rentier* wealth and "prestige values" has always been a "veiled

and devalued presence" in English fiction (15). His work focuses on Trollope, Gissing, James, and Conrad. I take his project of exploring the veiled presence of prestige values further by introducing the perspectives of female novelists.
12. Armstrong's (1987) influential argument that the domestic was separate from the financial and that women were excluded from "direct access to political and economic machinery" (40) has been challenged on several fronts, and this book contributes to revising the assumption of women's exclusion from the economic sphere.
13. Lee (2010) has argued that Gaskell's novels encode nineteenth-century slave narratives.
14. Dorothea and her sister have £700 a year each. Shrimpton (2007) calculates the equivalence of this income as "£52,000 each in the early 1830s, where the book is set, £5400 in 1871" and that "this would be the produce, in 4% Consols, of a joint fortune of £35,000 (or £2.6m)" (33).
15. For women in the literary marketplace, see Gallagher (1994), Peterson (2009), Delany (2002), and Coleman (2014).
16. Shrimpton (2007) and Delany (2002) trace this history of hostility toward money from Aristotle and the New Testament to nineteenth-century England.
17. For public perceptions of investors, see R. Michie (2011).
18. Gleadle (2009) notes the habit of women to deny knowledge of politics: "These repeated denials of female political aptitude were part of the process through which ascendant gender ideas were upheld" (2).
19. Additional works of note include Houston (2005), Stern (2008), Blake (2009), Wagner (2010), Çelikkol (2011), Courtemanche (2011), Kornbluh (2014), Hunt (2014), Knight (2016), and Bivona and Tromp (2016).
20. Dolin (1997) argues that "the routine execution of the Married Women's Property law is felt as a powerful institutional undercurrent, in these texts and in Victorian fiction more generally, and the growing mood of discontent surrounding their reform breaks out as elements of textual disruption and resistance" (2).
21. *George Geith of Fen Court* was originally published in 1865 (and under the pseudonym F.G. Trafford); however, the copy I used in my research includes no publication date. For this reason, I leave it as no date.
22. Colella (2016) has revitalized Riddell's reputation. My discussion of Riddell concentrates on aspects of her life and work not covered by Colella.
23. While nineteenth-century novelists such as Thackeray, Dickens, Trollope, Gaskell, the Brontës, and George Eliot supplemented their income from writing with investments, early twentieth-century Modernists reversed this order. Delany (2002) notes: "Vanessa Bell, Leonard and

Virginia Woolf, Duncan Grant, J.M. Keynes, and E.M. Forster all worked obsessively (and used that work to supplement their income from investments)" (131).
24. *Equity*, directed by Meera Menon (2016, Broad street Pictures); *Wall Street*, directed by Oliver Stone (1987; Twentieth Century Fox).
25. This way of thinking was evident by the early twentieth century. As E.M. Forster wrote of his university education: "In came the nice fat dividends, up rose the lofty thoughts, and we did not realize that all the time we were exploiting the poor of our own country and the backward races abroad, and getting bigger profits from our investments than we should" (quoted in Delany 2002, 135).

REFERENCES

Alborn, Timothy. 1998. *Conceiving companies: Joint-stock politics in Victorian England*. London: Routledge.
———. 2009. *Regulated lives: Life insurance and British Society, 1800–1914*. Toronto: University of Toronto Press.
Armstrong, Nancy. 1987. *Desire and domestic fiction: A political history of the novel*. New York: Oxford University Press.
Balen, Malcolm. 2003. *A very English deceit: The secret history of the South Sea Bubble: The world's first great financial scandal*. London: Fourth Estate.
Barker, Hannah. 2017. *Family and business during the Industrial Revolution*. Oxford: Oxford University Press.
Beachy, Robert, Béatrice Craig, and Alastair Owens (eds.). 2006. *Women, business and finance in nineteenth-century Europe: Rethinking separate spheres*. Oxford: Berg.
Bianco, Marcie. 2016. "Equity" is a feminist Wall Street film that finally nails what it's like for women in power. *Quartz*, August 30. https://qz.com/768108/equity-is-a-feminist-wall-street-film-that-finally-nails-what-its-like-for-women-in-power/. Accessed 5 Apr 2018.
Bigelow, Gordon. 2003. *Fiction, famine, and the rise of economics in Victorian Britain & Ireland*. Cambridge: Cambridge University Press.
Bivona, Daniel and Marlene Tromp (eds.). 2016. *Culture and money in the nineteenth century: Abstracting economics*. Athens, Ohio: Ohio University Press.
Blake, Kathleen. 2009. *Pleasures of Benthamism: Victorian literature, utility, political economy*. Oxford: Oxford University Press.
Bodichon, Barbara Leigh Smith. 1854. *A brief summary, in plain language of the most important laws concerning women: Together with a few observations thereon*. London: J. Chapman.
Brantlinger, Patrick. 1996. *Fictions of state: Culture and credit in Britain, 1694–1994*. Ithaca, NY: Cornell University Press.

Brontë, Charlotte. 1847. *Jane Eyre*, ed. Margaret Smith. Oxford: Oxford University Press, 2008.
———. 1853. *Villette*, ed. Margaret Smith and Herbert Rosengarten. Oxford: Oxford University Press, 2008.
Cain, P.J., and A.G. Hopkins. 1999. *Gentlemanly capitalism and British imperialism: A new debate on empire*. London: Longman.
Çelikkol, Ayşe. 2011. *Romances of free trade: British literature, laissez-faire, and the global nineteenth century*. New York: Oxford University Press.
Colella, Silvana. 2016. *Charlotte Riddell's city novels and Victorian business: Narrating capitalism*. New York: Routledge.
Coleman, Dermot. 2014. *George Eliot and money: Economics, ethics and literature* (Cambridge studies in nineteenth-century literature and culture). Cambridge: Cambridge University Press.
Colley, Linda. 1992. *Britons: Forging the nation 1707–1837*. New Haven, CT: Yale University Press.
Combs, Mary Beth. 2005. "A measure of legal independence": The 1870 Married Women's Property Act and the portfolio allocations of British wives. *Journal of Economic History* 65 (4): 1028–1057.
Copeland, Edward. 1995. *Women writing about money: Women's fiction in England*. Cambridge: Cambridge University Press.
Courtemanche, Eleanor. 2011. *The "invisible hand" and British fiction, 1818–1860: Adam Smith, political economy, and the genre of realism*. Basingstoke: Palgrave Macmillan.
Crosthwaite, Paul, Peter Knight, and Nicky Marsh. 2014. *Show me the money: The image of finance, 1700 to the present*. Manchester: Manchester University Press.
Dalley, Lana L., and Jill Rappoport. 2013. *Economic women: Essays on desire and dispossession in nineteenth-century British culture*. Columbus: Ohio State University Press.
Davidoff, Leonore, and Catherine Hall. 1987. *Family fortunes: Men and women of the English middle class, 1780–1850*. London: Hutchinson.
———. 2002. *Family fortunes: Men and women of the English middle class, 1780–1850*, rev. ed. New York: Routledge.
Delany, Paul. 2002. *Literature, money and the market*. New York: Palgrave Macmillan.
Dickens, Charles. 1842–1844. *The life and adventures of Martin Chuzzlewit*, ed. Margaret Cardwell. Oxford: Oxford University Press, 2009.
———. 1846–1848. *Dombey and son*, ed. Alan Horsman. Oxford: Oxford University Press, 1984.
———. 1855–1857. *Little Dorrit*, ed. Stephen Wall. London: Penguin, 2003.
———. 1864–1865. *Our mutual friend*, ed. Michael Cotsell. Oxford: Oxford University Press, 2009.
Dolin, Tim. 1997. *Mistress of the house: Women of property in the Victorian novel*. Aldershot: Ashgate.

Draper, Nicholas. 2010. *The price of emancipation: Slave-ownership, compensation and British society at the end of slavery*. New York: Cambridge University Press.
Eliot, George. 1857a. Mr. Gilfil's love story. In *Scenes of clerical life*, ed. Thomas A. Noble, 65–166. Oxford: Oxford University Press, 2000.
———. 1857b. The sad fortunes of the Reverend Amos Barton. In *Scenes of clerical life*, ed. Thomas A. Noble, 3–64. Oxford: Oxford University Press, 2000.
———. 1860. *The mill on the Floss*, ed. Nancy Henry. Boston: Houghton Mifflin, 2004.
———. 1871–1872. *Middlemarch*, ed. David Carroll. Oxford: Oxford University Press, 2008.
———. 1876. *Daniel Deronda*, ed. K.M. Newton and Graham Handley. Oxford: Oxford University Press, 2014.
Finn, Margot. 1996. Women, consumption and coverture in England, c.1760–1860. *Historical Journal* 39 (3): 703–722.
———. 2003. *The character of credit: Personal debt in English culture, 1740–1914*. New York: Cambridge University Press.
Freeman, Mark, Robin Pearson, and James Taylor. 2011. *Shareholder democracies? Corporate governance in Britain and Ireland before 1850*. Chicago: University of Chicago Press.
Froide, Amy. 2005. *Never married: Singlewomen in early modern England*. Oxford: Oxford University Press.
———. 2017. *Silent partners: Women as public investors during Britain's financial revolution, 1690–1750*. Oxford: Oxford University Press.
Gagnier, Regenia. 2000. *The insatiability of human wants: Economics and aesthetics in market society*. Chicago: University of Chicago Press.
Gallagher, Catherine. 1994. *Nobody's story: The vanishing acts of women writers in the marketplace, 1670–1820*. Berkeley: University of California.
———. 2006. *The body economic: Life, death, and sensation in political economy and the Victorian novel*. Princeton, NJ: Princeton University Press.
Gaskell, Elizabeth. 1848. *Mary Barton: A Tale of Manchester Life*, ed. Edgar Wright. Oxford: Oxford University Press, 1998.
———. 1853a. *Cranford*, ed. Elizabeth Porges Watson. Oxford: Oxford University Press, 2011.
———. 1853b. *Ruth*, ed. Nancy Henry. London: Everyman, 2001.
———. 1854–1855. *North and south*, ed. Angus Easson. Oxford: Oxford University Press, 1998.
———. 1863. *Sylvia's lovers*, ed. Nancy Henry. London: Everyman, 1997.
———. 1864–1865. *Wives and daughters*, ed. Angus Easson. Oxford: Oxford University Press, 2009.
Gissing, George. 1891. *New Grub Street*, ed. Steve Arata. Peterborough, ON: Broadview, 2008.

———. 1893. *The odd women*, ed. Arlene Young. Orchard Park, NY: Broadview, 1998.

———. 1897. *The whirlpool*, ed. Gillian Tindall. London: Hogarth Press, 1984.

Gleadle, Kathryn. 2007. Revisiting "Family fortunes": Reflections on the twentieth anniversary of the publication of L. Davidoff and C. Hall (1987) "Family fortunes: Men and women of the English middle class, 1780–1850" (London: Hutchinson). *Women's History Review* 16 (5): 773–782. https://doi.org/10.1080/09612020701447848.

———. 2009. *Borderline citizens: Women, gender, and political culture in Britain, 1815–1867* (British Academy postdoctoral fellowship monographs). Oxford: Oxford University Press.

Green, David R., and Alastair Owens. 2003. Gentlewomanly capitalism? Spinsters, widows, and wealth holding in England and Wales, c.1800–1860. *Economic History Review* 56 (4): 510–536.

Green, David R., Alastair Owens, Josephine Maltby, and Janette Rutterford (eds.). 2011. *Men, women, and money: Perspectives on gender, wealth, and investment 1850–1930*. Oxford: Oxford University Press.

Henry, Nancy. 2002. *George Eliot and the British empire*. Cambridge: Cambridge University Press.

Henry, Nancy, and Cannon Schmitt (eds.). 2009. *Victorian investments: New perspectives on finance and culture*. Bloomington: Indiana University Press.

Holcombe, Lee. 1983. *Wives and property: Reform of the Married Women's Property Law in nineteenth-century England*. Toronto: University of Toronto Press.

Houston, Gail T. 2005. *From Dickens to Dracula: Gothic, economics, and Victorian fiction*. Cambridge: Cambridge University Press.

Hunt, Aeron. 2014. *Personal business: Character and commerce in Victorian literature and culture*. Charlottesville: University of Virginia Press.

James, Simon J. 2003. *Unsettled accounts: Money and narrative in the novels of George Gissing*. London: Anthem Press.

Klaver, Claudia C. 2003. *A/moral economics: Classical political economy and cultural authority in nineteenth-century England*. Columbus: Ohio State University Press.

Knight, Peter. 2016. *Reading the market: Genres of financial capitalism in gilded age America*. Baltimore: Johns Hopkins University Press.

Kornbluh, Anna. 2014. *Realizing capital: Financial and psychic economies in Victorian form*. New York: Fordham University Press.

Kreisel, Deanna K. 2010. *Economic woman: Demand, gender, and narrative closure in Eliot and Hardy*. Toronto: University of Toronto Press.

Laurence, Anne, Josephine Maltby, and Janette Rutterford (eds.). 2009. Introduction. *Women and their money 1700–1950: Essays on women and finance*. London: Routledge.

Lee, Julia Sun-Joo. 2010. *The American slave narrative and the Victorian novel*. New York: Oxford University Press.

Lootens, Tricia. 2017. *The political poetess: Victorian femininity, race and the legacy of separate spheres*. Princeton, NJ: Princeton University Press.

Maltby, Josephine, and Janette Rutterford (eds.) 2006a. Editorial: Women, accounting, and investment. Special issue. *Accounting, Business and Finance History* 16 (2): 133–142.

———. 2006b. "She possessed her own fortune": Women investors from the late nineteenth century to the early twentieth century. *Business History* 48 (2): 220–253.

Michie, Elsie. 2011a. *The vulgar question of money: Heiresses, materialism, and the novel of manners from Jane Austen to Henry James*. Baltimore: Johns Hopkins University Press.

Michie, Ranald. 2011b. Gamblers, fools, victims or wizards? The British investor in the public mind, 1850–1930. In *Men, women and money: Perspectives on gender, wealth, and investment 1850–1930*, ed. David Green, Alastair Owens, Josephine Maltby, and Janette Rutterford, 156–183. Oxford: Oxford University Press.

Noble, John Ashcraft. 1885. Review of "Mitre Court." *Academy*, December 5.

O'Gorman, Francis (ed.). 2007. *Victorian literature and finance*. Oxford: Oxford University Press.

Oliphant, Margaret. 1883. *Hester*, ed. Philip Davis and Brian Nellist. Oxford: Oxford University Press, 2009.

———. 1890. *Kirsteen: The story of a Scotch family seventy years ago*. London: Everyman, 1984.

Osteen, Mark, and Martha Woodmansee. 1999. *The new economic criticism: Studies at the interface of literature and economics*. London: Routledge.

Ott, Julia, and William Milberg. 2014. *Capitalism studies: A manifesto*, April 17. http://www.publicseminar.org/2014/04/capitalism-studies-a-manifesto. Accessed 5 Apr 2018.

Peterson, Linda H. 2009. *Becoming a woman of letters: Myths of authorship and facts of the Victorian market*. Princeton, NJ: Princeton University Press.

Phillips, Nicola. 2006. *Women and business: 1700–1850*. Woodbridge: Boydell Press.

Poovey, Mary. 2003. *The financial system in nineteenth-century Britain*. New York: Oxford University Press.

———. 2008. *Genres of the credit economy*. Chicago: University of Chicago Press.

———. 2009. Writing about finance in Victorian England: Disclosure and secrecy in the culture of investment. In *Victorian investments: New perspectives on finance and culture*, ed. Nancy Henry and Cannon Schmitt, 39–57. Bloomington: Indiana University Press.

Rappaport, Erika Diane. 2000. *Shopping for pleasure: Women in the making of London's West End*. Princeton, NJ: Princeton University Press.
Rappoport, Jill. 2011. *Giving women: Alliance and exchange in Victorian culture*. New York: Oxford.
Reed, John R. 1984. A friend to Mammon: Speculation in Victorian literature. *Victorian Studies* 27 (2): 179–202.
Riddell, Charlotte. (F.G. Trafford, pseud.). 1864. *George Geith of Fen Court*. London: Frederick Warne and Co, n.d.
Riddell, Charlotte. 1870. *Austin Friars: A novel*. London: Hutchinson.
Robb, George. 2009. Ladies of the ticker: Women, investment, and fraud in England and America, 1850–1930. In *Victorian investments: New perspectives on finance and culture*, ed. Nancy Henry and Cannon Schmitt, 120–142. Bloomington: Indiana University Press.
Robb, George. 2017. *Ladies of the ticker: Women and Wall Street from the gilded age to the Great Depression*. Urbana-Champaign: University of Illinois Press.
Russell, Norman. 1986. *The novelist and Mammon: Literary Response to the world of commerce in the nineteenth-century*. Oxford: Oxford University Press.
Ryzik, Melena. 2016. Where women run Wall Street. *New York Times*, July 11, 24, https://www.nytimes.com/2016/07/24/movies/equity-women-wall-street.html. Accessed 6 Apr 2018.
Sanders, Lise. 2006. *Consuming fantasies: Labor, leisure, and the London shopgirl, 1880–1920*. Columbus: Ohio State University Press.
Shanley, Mary Lyndon. 1989. *Feminism, marriage, and the law in Victorian England, 1850–1895*. Princeton, NJ: Princeton University Press.
Shrimpton, Nicholas. 2007. Money in Victorian literature. In *Victorian literature and finance*, ed. Francis O'Gorman, 17–38. Oxford: Oxford University Press.
Smith, Grahame. 1968. *Dickens, money, and society*. Berkeley: University of California Press.
Steinbach, Susie. 2012. Can we use "separate spheres"? British history 25 years after "Family fortunes". *History Compass* 10 (11): 826–837. https://doi.org/10.1111/hic3.12010.
Stern, Rebecca. 2008. *Home economics: Domestic fraud in Victorian England*. Columbus: Ohio State University Press.
Thackeray, William Makepeace. 1847–8. *Vanity fair: A novel without a hero*, ed. Diane Mowat. Oxford: Oxford University Press, 2008.
———. 1853–1855. *The Newcomes: Memoirs of a most respectable family*, ed. D.J. Taylor. London: Everyman, 1994.
Trollope, Anthony. 1865. *Miss Mackenzie*, ed. A.O.J. Cockshut. Oxford: Oxford University Press, 1992.
———. 1866–1867. *The last chronicle of Barset*, ed. Sophie Gilmartin. Harmondsworth: Penguin, 2002.

———. 1875. *The way we live now*, ed. Francis O'Gorman. Oxford: Oxford University Press, 2016.

———. 1876. *The prime minister*, ed. Nicholas Shrimpton. Oxford: Oxford University Press, 2011.

Vernon, John. 1984. *Money and fiction: Literary realism in the nineteenth and early twentieth centuries.* Ithaca, NY: Cornell University Press.

Vickery, Amanda. 1993. Golden age to separate spheres? A review of the categories and chronology of English women's history. *Historical Journal* 36 (2): 383–414.

Wagner, Tamara. 2010. *Financial speculation in Victorian fiction: Plotting money and the novel genre, 1815–1901.* Columbus: Ohio State University Press.

Walkowitz, Judith. 2012. *Nights out: Life in cosmopolitan London.* New Haven, CT: Yale University Press.

Weiss, Barbara. 1986. *The hell of the English: Bankruptcy and the Victorian novel.* Lewisburg, PA: Bucknell University Press.

CHAPTER 2

Women Investors in Fact

What a great good fortune it is that Mrs. R. did not invest the money as I advised and did my own.
— William Makepeace Thackeray

In April 1857, William Makepeace Thackeray gave a public lecture to raise money for the widow of his friend, Angus Bethune Reach. Upon presenting Mrs. Reach with £75, he advised her to invest it in "a good American security which pays 8 or 9 per cent."[1] His advice to the widow, however, was ill-timed. In August 1857, the collapse of overhyped US railway and insurance companies precipitated an international financial crisis. By October, the effects were being felt in London, Liverpool, and Glasgow (see Alborn 2010; Evans 1859; Shakinovsky, n.d.). On November 1, Thackeray wrote to the Baxters, his American friends, confessing that he had been afraid to write earlier because of the panic. He took a lighthearted attitude in describing the impact on himself and his daughters since, "all the American savings were gone to smash" (Thackeray 1945b, vol. 4: 55). Apparently, Mrs. Reach did not take the financial advice of the novelist. On November 29, Thackeray wrote to Octavian Blewitt: "What a great good fortune it is that Mrs. R. did not invest the money as I advised and did my own" (quoted in Cross 1985, 113). His investments included shares and bonds in the Michigan Central and New York Central Railways, which were certainly affected

© The Author(s) 2018
N. Henry, *Women, Literature and Finance in Victorian Britain*,
Palgrave Studies in Literature, Culture and Economics,
https://doi.org/10.1007/978-3-319-94331-2_2

by the crisis of 1857. But he held on to them, and after his death, his daughters sold them at a profit (Thackeray 1945a, Vol. 3: 275).

We do not know why Mrs. Reach failed to take Thackeray's advice, but it is tempting to think that it had something to do with his own financial history. His family fortune had been lost in 1834 in the failure of an Indian agency house; subsequently, he lived in a "chronic condition of insolvency" (Weiss 1986, 15). Or perhaps Mrs. Reach had read Thackeray's *The Newcomes* (1853–1855) in which the multinational Bundelcund Bank of Bengal's subscribers in London include several women who follow the advice of Colonel Newcome, but, like him, lose their money when the bank fails. We can only hope that Mrs. Reach found a safe investment for her £75 during those turbulent economic times.

With his personal and financial links to India and the USA, Thackeray's life and writing illustrate the mid-Victorian practice of investing in global stocks and bonds, as well as the representation of global finance, including panics, in fiction. We may tend to think of Victorian authors primarily as critics of speculative bubbles and satirists of greedy financiers who used bank failures and personal bankruptcies as plot devices, but many of them were affected by the economic instability that characterized their age and plagued their contemporaries. Thackeray's misguided advice was honest, but as George Robb (2009) observes: "While the corporate economy welcomed capital investments from women, it offered them little protection from unscrupulous promoters and managers" (120). Real women such as the widow Mrs. Reach and Thackeray's daughters, like the fictional characters in *The Newcomes*, were investors in a volatile financial market and struggled to negotiate the information and advice available to them in order to find safe investments for their capital and protect their financial well-being.

The experiences of real-life investors—about which we are learning more and more through the research of historians—provide essential contexts for our understanding of fictional investors and the broader cultures of investment, which grew increasingly diversified over the course of the Victorian period. The crisis of 1857 has been called the first global financial crisis (Kindleberger and Aliber 2005; Shakinovsky, n.d.). Within provincial, urban, and international cultures, famous novelists and impoverished widows alike found opportunities and dangers through investments that connected them to growing domestic, colonial, and foreign economic networks. Investing men and women experienced the highs and lows of nineteenth-century markets, facing questions about how much risk they were willing to take with their money. While continuing to accept (or reject) advice from male advisors, women increasingly took control of their financial lives, sometimes gaining and at other times losing as a result of their investment decisions. In their writing, realist novelists showed common people encountering the material and moral realities of global trade and finance. Authors faced the same financial conditions as those of their readers, but novels are unique in their capacity to explore the practical, ethical, and psychological problems posed by investing in an unstable economic climate. To gain the fullest possible understanding of the role women investors played in the Victorian cultures of investment, we need to look at how real women invested as well as how their entry into financial markets as investors and speculators was portrayed in fiction.

Thackeray, Trollope, Dickens, Riddell, Oliphant, and Gissing were among the novelists based in London who incorporated the experiences of London investors into their narratives. Riddell in particular focused on financial activities within the City of London. The Brontë sisters (investors living in Yorkshire), Gaskell (an investor living in Manchester), and Eliot (an investor living in London) drew from, and contributed to, a context of global economic networks for their novels and stories set outside of London—in Yorkshire, Lancashire, and the Midlands. They all created characters whose lives were remote from the financial center but were no less touched by aspects of global finance, as symbolized in public monuments and architecture, and embodied in the commodities of everyday life such as cotton, sugar, tea, coffee, tobacco, and opium. London is the setting for many financially themed novels, and London has received most of the attention from critics writing about literature and finance. But the Victorian cultures of investment encompassed "provincial" cities as well, particularly Liverpool. A surprising number of authors had familial connections to the second seaport in the kingdom, which also plays a role in their fiction, as later chapters will show.[2]

This chapter establishes how real women invested their money, providing essential context for discussions of how male and female authors represented women investors and financial cultures generally in fiction. It shows the presence of nineteenth-century women investors throughout Great Britain with an emphasis on their investment practices and on the transatlantic and global nature of their investments. These contexts are important for demonstrating that while Victorian fiction represented women investors in ways that reflect the experiences of real women, it also had recourse to a set of literary types, including the timid spinster, the business widow, the heiress, and the financier's daughter. Through an examination of these types, read against the reality of investing women, we can see the ideological complexities of male and female Victorians' responses to the role women played in the expanding financial markets that increasingly defined the cultures of investment. I argue that, while each author approaches the subject differently, in general the plots of domestic novels by women were self-consciously embedded in global economies and that women writers often provided critiques of commodity and financial markets that were more subtle and complex— sometimes even covert and coded—than those of their male contemporaries. Possible reasons for the tendency of women novelists to embrace the opportunities of investment capitalism while also criticizing its abuses include, on the one hand, their personal reliance on local and global financial markets in the form of stocks and bonds as a supplement to their income from writing, and, on the other hand, their awareness that women who were not successful novelists depended on such investments to secure their financial independence.[3]

Men too relied on such investments; they invested in much greater numbers and in greater amounts than women, often on behalf of not only themselves but also of their wives, daughters, and female dependents. Yet the position of female investors was different from that of men because professional careers such as the military, church, law, medicine, civil service, and politics were not available to them. As we will see, women could participate in some commercial activities, particularly family businesses, but for the noncommercial middle class, investing was a uniquely unrestricted entrance to the financial sphere of Victorian society. A surprising number of women chose to take advantage of their freedom to invest, complicating our perception of the limitations on women's involvement in the public sphere generally. This chapter focuses on those women who were not novelists but rather members of the relatively privileged upper and middle classes who had excess capital and who found outlets for that capital in a range of investment opportunities that were newly opened up to them by increasingly democratized cultures of investment. These included joint-stock companies, especially banks and railways (domestic, colonial, and foreign), shipping, docks, foreign government bonds, and a range of other local and global securities.

The types of women represented in fiction reflect categories recognized in property law. Single women and widows enjoyed much the same freedom as men to own their own property and to trade, lend, invest, and speculate. Historians have called attention to the problem of focusing on married women when generalizing about the economic disabilities of early modern and nineteenth-century women. Examining the early modern context, Amy Froide (2005) points out that at least one-third of urban women were single in the period she covers (1550–1750). She argues for the importance of establishing "singlewomen" as a category of historical analysis and decentering marriage as the norm in social, economic, and cultural terms. In the early modern period, single women reveal the importance of kinship and that "spouses and children did not always form the most important connections in women's lives" (7).[4] As we will see, these observations hold true for the nineteenth century, and Victorian novelists were mindful of the marital and legal status of women when exploring their financial situations.

The most common form of investment for women, and the one most familiar to readers of Victorian novels, was in the Three Percent Consolidated Annuities, also known variously as the Consols, the funds, and the three percents. These securities were a permanent loan to the government: "In return for their cash, fund holders received an annual yield equal to a fixed percentage of the nominal value of the loan which varied depending on the type of fund that had been purchased" (Green and Owens 2003, 520). Picking up on a phrase that was used as early as 1752, Benjamin Disraeli famously referred to the "sweet simplicity of the three percents" in his novel *Endymion* (1880) because of the reliable dividend this form of investment provided (II:227). Women formed a significant and growing proportion of fund holders, rising from 34.7% in 1810 to 47.2% in 1840: "one in three individual investors in the national debt in 1810 was a woman, and the proportion increased to almost one in two by 1840" (Green and Owens 2003, 524–5). These figures show that women were not "on the margins of property ownership, trapped within the limited confines of a private domestic world, but at the centre of a system of public finance that provided the government with revenues for imperial expansion and warfare" (525). By 1840, "spinsters funded almost 19 per cent of the national debt, and widows were responsible for a further 13 per cent" (528).

Throughout the eighteenth and nineteenth centuries, married women were also active in commerce. They invested their money in the businesses of male family members both in provincial towns and in London. They ran their own businesses or took over businesses after the death of a husband. Anne Laurence (2008) notes the "existence of the right of *femme sole merchant* (or *femme sole* trader) in London and some provincial cities" (31). This exceptional right enabled a woman to run her own business without her husband incurring liability for her debts and seems to have been used "more as a mechanism to protect against possible bankruptcy than as a means to allow married women commercial freedom" (31).[5]

Although the emphasis of this book is on investors, it is important to recognize an overall commercial and financial climate that was more favorable to women than is generally acknowledged. This climate produced diverse cultures of investment in London and in provincial towns, none of which divide easily into separate gendered spheres. Kathryn Gleadle (2009) writes, "Within local communities, women's economic standing was paramount both to the scope and nature of their activities and also to contemporaries' perception of them" (126). In *Enterprising Women and Shipping*, Helen Doe (2009) shows that married women often found ways around laws restricting their financial activities (16). Her findings also prove that existing laws were not always enforced, leaving women free to act as financial agents in ways not appreciated by historians who focus on the laws themselves rather than on empirical evidence of how women actually acted. She examines women investors in shipping, demonstrating that married women who lived in port cities often conducted business while their husbands were absent for long periods of time on ocean voyages and that neither married nor single women were constrained from owning shares in ships: "Before the first Married Women's Property Act in 1870, married women were not held back from holding shares in ships despite the restrictions of the legal system" (31). Her book contributes important information about women investors outside of London in diverse maritime subcultures between 1780 and 1880.

Without doubt, men dominated commercial and financial cultures, but women were often silent, or at least quiet, investors in local and global ventures. Women contributed capital to the construction of the Liverpool docks (Longmore 2008, 163). The Liverpool and Manchester Railroad (opened in 1829) had 40% female shareholders, many of them local (Freeman et al. 2006, 270). In the 1850s, a high proportion of proprietors in the Liverpool Bank were women (Anderson and Cottrell

2008, 611). In the late eighteenth century, Samuel Holland, Elizabeth Gaskell's uncle, with his partners Michael Humble and Nicholas Hurry (major players in the Liverpool shipbuilding industry), invested in the extensive Herculaneum pottery works in Toxteth on the shore of the River Mersey near Liverpool (Chapple 1997, 170; Checkland 1971). John Gladstone, the successful Liverpool businessman and father of future Prime Minister William Gladstone, managed the affairs of his wife's two unmarried sisters, "placing their slender resources in the Herculaneum pottery in Liverpool and in shares of the ship *John Sand* trading to the West Indies" (Checkland 1971, 81). Such local businesses were a natural outlet for women's capital. In *The Herculaneum Pottery: Liverpool's Forgotten Glory*, Peter Hyland (2005) reprints the investor records. In the list of proprietors for 1806, Anna Hird of Liverpool was the only woman out of twenty-eight proprietors, but the list for 1828 includes more women, as well as John Gladstone, who was investing for his wife's sisters. Of the twenty-seven proprietors on this later list, four were women: Jane Sarah Case (wife of Thomas Case), Elizabeth Holt, Susannah Humble (daughter of Michael Humble), and Bridget Jolley (gentlewoman) (191). These records show that in the early decades of the nineteenth century, women were investing their capital in the ventures of male family members and that married and single women were proprietors in this relatively small local company.

Joint-stock banks that were opened in the 1830s were viewed as suspicious and risky, but many women were initial subscribers. Gentlewomen, or spinsters, wives, and widows, "comprised between 72 and 100 per cent of the female shareholders" (Newton and Cottrell 2009, 117). The numbers of women investors increased over time as this form of investing became more accepted and was no longer perceived as risky. Those who did invest in the early days were rewarded with high dividends. By 1836, dividends reached between 6.5 and 12.5%.[6] For example, Mary and Agnes Hodgson, single women living in Liverpool, made investments of £1775 and £1525, respectively, in the Bank of Liverpool (120). By 1856, 30% of shareholders in metropolitan joint-stock banks were female (122). Investors at this time were "primarily unmarried women or widows who had sufficient wealth and were risk averse to investing in equity" (123).

The *Centenary Book of the Liverpool Stock Exchange* (1936) includes an anecdote about Mrs. Barton, a widow, who held shares in the London and North Western Railway Company in the joint names of herself and her son, Thomas Barton. Between 1874 and 1886, Thomas sold various amounts of stock without his mother's knowledge, forging her signature and paying her regular dividends to avoid detection. When his fraud was exposed in 1886, Thomas fled the country. Mrs. Barton sued the railway company and got back her stock (29). As we will see, this real-life incident recalls the plot of Gaskell's *Ruth* (1853b), in which Richard, Mr. Bradshaw's son, defrauds the naïve minister Thurstan Benson and his sister, Faith, through exactly the same method of forgery: selling the shares but personally continuing to pay dividends to disguise the sale. A similar cover-up of the sale of Betsey Trotwood's shares occurs in Dickens's *David Copperfield* (1849–1850). The *Centenary Book* illustrates the presence of women investors on the Liverpool Stock Exchange and the dangers of fraud by family members; ultimately, however, it emphasizes Mrs. Barton's power to recover her losses.

Permanent public debt was established in 1693; the Bank of England was established in 1694 to manage that debt; the three percent consols were set up in 1749 (Michie 2001, 18). Joint-stock companies emerged in the seventeenth century and secondary markets followed to trade in their securities. In "Women in the City," Carlos, Maguire, and Neal (2009) analyze the investment activity of women in the Bank of England and in the Royal African Company in 1720. Using shareholder records, they establish that women were active managers of their investments who showed acumen in their decisions during a volatile market (the period of the South Sea Bubble) and that overall, women made profits. While men always outnumbered women as investors, in aggregate women were actually more successful than men in making profits on their investments in these markets (see also Carlos et al. 2006).

The mid-eighteenth century saw a spike in women's participation in the London Stock Exchange. In the 1750s, women comprised 32% of East India stockholders. Their numbers then declined so that between 1818 and 1830 they represented around 17% (Freeman et al. 2009, 99).[7] After this dip in the early nineteenth century, the number of women shareholders increased throughout the rest of the century for a combination of reasons: more single women were seeking an income; watershed legislation limiting shareholder liability was passed in 1855, 1856, and 1862; and a wider variety of low-risk shares of lower denominations became available (see Newton et al. 2009).[8] Freeman et al. (2006) argue that it took "nearly a century for female investment to recover the relative importance that it had enjoyed in the great chartered trading companies of the early eighteenth century, though of course the absolute numbers of women shareholders and their range of holdings were far greater by the 1840s than they had ever been before" (272). This spike may be attributed to a general expansion of investment options attendant upon the construction of railways. Railway securities became the most important investment option for women, after government bonds and bank shares. In general, these public works projects began to replace traditional investments in the Consols, real estate, and mortgages. Later, the Married Women's Property Act of 1870 may have led women to prefer financial investments to real property (see Combs 2005; Laurence et al. 2009, 9).

By the mid-nineteenth century, women were well established as voting shareholders in the East India Company: 899 ladies—that is, more than half of the 1765 voters—had voting rights as members of the Court of Proprietors, and these ladies canvassed actively for the election of other members (Robson et al. 1990, 46). This is particularly remarkable because women could not vote in national political elections. Green and Owens (2003) confirm Barbara Bodichon's insight that a woman can take part in the government of a great empire by buying East India Stock: "Women's involvement in the securities market—the institutional mechanism for the sale and purchase of, especially, government debts—draws attention to their role as 'gentlewomanly capitalists,' participating in imperial expansion by virtue of their position as fund holders" (512).

Women were also active in the governance of joint-stock companies other than the East India Company, representing on average 20% of shareholders. Freeman et al. (2006) argue: "Women's investment in the corporate economy, though not deep was extensive" (287).[9] There was an increasingly positive attitude toward women shareholders beginning in the mid-nineteenth century, which may be traced to historical practices by which "stock companies placed female proprietors, if often only by default, on largely the same constitutional footing as men" (288). In addition to voting in shareholder meetings, women investors could, theoretically, assume leadership roles on shareholder governing boards, though few women took advantage of this. In the late eighteenth century and early nineteenth century, "there were generally few discriminatory or even gender-specific regulations passed by British and Irish stock companies" (Freeman et al. 2009, 106). Proxy voting was offered to women as an alternative to voting in person, a practice, which became widely accepted during the first half of the nineteenth century (106).

Women could attend and vote in shareholder meetings because "the great majority of stock companies placed few, if any, internal regulatory barriers in the way of female proprietors availing themselves of the same rights as their male counterparts" (107). The activities of female shareholders challenge the notion of an emergent separate sphere ideology in the nineteenth century. In their research, Freeman, Pearson, and Taylor found no evidence "that women were driven out of the equity markets by any new ideology that made female investment, or indeed active female participation in stock company governance, unacceptable" (108).

In the mid-nineteenth century, women were silent investors and lenders to real estate development and large engineering projects such as canals, docks, and bridges. Women investors took an interest in the shares traded on the London Stock Exchange, consulting and also directing their financial advisors. Charlotte and Emily Brontë were investors in the 1840s; Elizabeth Gaskell was a shareholder throughout the 1850s; and George Eliot began her investing career in 1860. These authors and investors followed the successes and failures of the government and company shares they held and which supplemented the income they received from their publications, adding to their wealth and their independence. As successful novelists, they were unlike most women, but their behavior as shareholders was typical of women investors who had other earned or inherited sources of income.

Historically, the largest single group of female shareholders invested in the Consols (Green and Owens 2003, 515). *Bradshaw's Guide Through London and Its Environs* (Blanchard 1862), which positively represents London as a financial center (in contrast to many novels), explains the system to potential tourists in a section devoted to the Bank of England: "Herein are paid half-yearly the dividends or annual interest of the national debt. The recipients frequently attend in person, ladies as well as gentlemen, acting as their own agents in the pleasant business of receiving money" (38). By midcentury, Dividend Day was a tourist attraction on which visitors would see "the dexterous celerity with which the business we have indicated is carried on" (39).[10]

Women were such a familiar presence in the City on Dividend Day that the preface to *Bradshaw's Guide* relates an anecdote about two older ladies who went to receive their dividends. Asked about their day in the City of London, one lady replied: "We had a most agreeable ride to the Bank on Thursday, everything looked so lively; and, though we were tossed about over the rough stones, it was amusing to see the variety of people and the numerous carriages; such faces full of business, such evidences of a brilliant commerce—I was quite sorry when we got home again" (2). In contrast, her sister complained: "We were almost jolted to death in that rumbling coach the other day; and it was so hot with the sun shining on it, and we were such a long time, drawl, drawl, throughout Fleet Street and Ludgate Hill, that I thought we should never have reached the end of our journey! I wish we could be saved the trouble of going for our money another time" (2). Although the example is meant as a humorous illustration of "how different minds are affected by the same circumstances" (2), it confirms the familiarity of women entering the City to receive their dividends. Some were exhilarated by the "brilliant commerce"—as Lucy Snowe had been when entering the City in Charlotte Brontë's (1853) novel *Villette*: "The City seems so much more in earnest: its business, its rush, its roar, are such serious things, sights, and sounds. The city is getting its living—the West-end but enjoying its pleasure. At the West-end you may be amused, but in the city you are deeply excited" (49).

Charlotte Riddell had a similar reaction to the money-getting energy of the City and devoted much of her career to chronicling the lives of City businessmen and women in her fiction. Other women, however, wished to avoid the tiresome journey into the foreign territory of the City and preferred simply to collect their dividends rather than lingering to absorb its stimulating atmosphere.[11]

The dividends paid by the Consols, and the numbers of investors in it, hit a historic high in 1815 when the wars with France had created the greatest need for government borrowing and the issuance of new debt. After the war, numbers dipped before beginning to climb steadily for most of the century, always remaining a popular investment for women. In 1840, 40% of all fund holders were female (Rutterford and Maltby 2006b, 122). As late as 1893, an article entitled "Dividend Day" described the ongoing ritual of collecting dividends by emphasizing "the governess element is well represented, pale faces growing paler and more faded year by year, but brightening up in the reflection of the pink dividend warrant" (*All the Year Round* 1893, 462). At this time, the rate on the dividends paid by the funds was decreasing and slipped to as low as 2.5% by 1896, driving more risk-tolerant investors to search for higher paying yields on their capital (Michie 2011, 159). Yet risk-averse investors and low-wage workers like governesses were still dependent on the steady, guaranteed dividend paid by the Consols.

In addition to picking up their dividends, West End women visited the City to consult with their stockbrokers. The *St. James's Magazine* (1863), which was managed by Mrs. S.C. Hall from 1861 until Charlotte Riddell took over in 1868, contains an anonymous contribution called "Secrets of My Office by a Bill-Broker." This fictionalized memoir traces national economic history, including the impact of the Napoleonic wars on British finance and the influence of the Rothschilds—all from the perspective of a lifelong City man. Upon retiring, the narrator rejoices that he will no longer see the annuitant Hannah Leigh, "precisely upon the stroke of twelve on every quarter-day, call for that eternal two hundred and fifty pound cheque" (61): "It was the woman's impudent wont, after receiving the cheque, and waving it in her hand as if it wanted drying, to come unasked into the private office, under pretence of consulting me as to the best security in which to deposit her fast increasing savings,—but never following the advice I gave" (61–2).

Such complaints promote a picture of women investors as annoying busybodies who refuse to take financial advice. Stereotypes dating from the eighteenth century depicted the investing woman as a "vulnerable, adventurous and, by implication, foolish victim" (Freeman et al. 2009, 96). The stereotype evolved from women as dangerous gamblers and speculators in the mid-eighteenth century to naïve victims in the Victorian period (Freeman et al. 2006, 281).[12] In Laurence Oliphant's 1876 *The Autobiography of a Joint-Stock Company (Limited)*, the voice of the company addresses his "fair readers, especially widows and spinsters." He tells us, "I should never have been able to enter upon my fraudulent career had it not been for the powerful support I derived from the trusting contributions of confiding or speculative female investors" (quoted in Poovey 2003, 328).

Historians have also documented the investment activities of individual women within the contexts of their complicated family dynamics throughout the nineteenth century. Janette Rutterford (2013) discusses the case of the heiress Emily Nugent, Lady Westmeath, and the social and economic impact of marital separation for a woman before the Matrimonial Causes Act of 1857 and Married Women's Property Acts later in the century. Emily Nugent (née Cecil) married George Nugent, Lord Delvin, in 1812. She was physically separated from her abusive husband by 1818 and legally separated by 1827. Bitter litigation over money and child custody went on until 1837. While she had been powerless to negotiate her prenuptial settlements and was similarly unable to stop her husband from spending her money, she could, as Rutterford emphasizes, make canny investments of the money she preserved for herself.

She did this with the help of other women, particularly the American Eliza Caton, who had her own investment portfolio and managed investments for her married sisters (138). Analyzing surviving correspondence between the women and Joshua Bates, their advisor at Barring's Bank, Rutterford details their diversified global portfolios. Like George Eliot later in the century, Caton favored Argentine and American railroads, while Emily was excited about her investments in speculative Spanish bonds (139). Rutterford notes the unusually high tolerance for risk of these women in the first half of the nineteenth century and the opportunities offered by the stock market in the midst of other limitations before women's property reform.[13]

Jehanne Wake's *Sisters of Fortune: America's Caton Sisters at Home and Abroad* (2012) tells the story of the four sisters, Marianne, Emily, Louisa, and Eliza (or Bess), who "conducted their lives in a manner quite at odds with traditional accounts of early-nineteenth-century heiresses" (xxi). The sisters' money derived from their mother's family of wealthy Maryland plantation owners, the Carrolls. The initial fortune was made largely in the tobacco trade by their grandfather, who was present at the signing of the Declaration of Independence (8). Unusual for the time, he made sure that his granddaughters had large settlements and kept their fortunes, including the Maryland plantations, in their own hands. The sisters were raised on their grandfather's plantations with their own personal slaves.[14] Richard Caton, their father, was the son of a Liverpool ship captain and slave trader (16). He came as a merchant to Maryland, where he met and married Mary Carroll, but he was never financially successful. His business ventures failed, and he became bankrupt in 1802 and again in 1803 (37–8). His father-in-law paid his debts to prevent his imprisonment and to save the family name and the sisters' marriage prospects.

Marianne and Richard Patterson, her first husband, along with Louisa and Bess, went to England in 1816. Bypassing their father's relatives in Liverpool, they moved in elite London circles, including that of the recently victorious (and married) Duke of Wellington, who fell in love with Marianne. Over the years, Louisa's second marriage made her the Countess of Mornington. After Patterson's death, Marianne married the Duke of Wellington's older brother, making her the Duchess of Leeds. Her husband, Richard Wellesley, however, had squandered most of his own wealth, leaving Marianne to draw on her inheritance to support them in what was ultimately an unhappy marriage.

This transatlantic family history of women investors spans from the late eighteenth century to the mid-nineteenth century and shows the multiple ways in which women exercised their rights to invest globally, even before the passing of democratizing legislation. As Wake shows in specific financial detail, the sisters, "actively managed their fortunes, speculated on the stock-market, and made informed investment decisions" (xxi). Wake and Rutterford each demonstrate that the Catons were part of an Anglo-American network of lady speculators, who used social contacts with other women, such as Charlotte de Rothschild, to gain inside information about politics and finance to make their investments (Wake 2012, 279). Bess Caton managed the finances of her sisters and friends such as Emily Nugent. Wake writes that it was not surprising that the Caton sisters were familiar with "the culture of investment" (275). In addition to his large property holdings, their grandfather had stocks in banks, utilities, and US government securities; while in England, they took tips on American stocks from their mother, who sold her shares in the Bank of New Jersey in 1836 (Rutterford 2013, 138).

As we have seen, historians who have investigated the shareholder records have found reason to challenge the influential thesis that separate sphere ideology curtailed nineteenth-century women's financial freedom. The Catons and Emily Nugent were active in the first half of the century. Emily died after the Matrimonial Causes Act of 1857 but before the Married Women's Property Act of 1870. She and her sisters were not merely passive recipients of dividends; they were speculators: "Unlike longer-term investors, whose surplus capital flowed into the stock markets to finance government debt; foreign loans; the building of canals, turnpikes, railways, and mines; and joint-stock companies throughout the world in return for income, speculators' funds flowed in—and then strategically out again for short-term capital gain" (Wake 2012, 275–6). Questioning the notion of separate spheres, Wake argues: "The sisters and their friends disprove the contention that women possessed neither the knowledge and the inclination nor the surplus capital to be active managers of their wealth and indulge in financial speculations in the early nineteenth century" (276). The Caton sisters were unusual for the knowledge they displayed and for their role as speculators as well as investors.

In the late nineteenth century, a few extraordinary women made headlines for their financial prowess. Alice Cornwell (1852–1932), known as "Princess Midas" or "Madam Midas," was born in Essex. She went to supervise her father's Sulky Gully gold mine in Ballarat in the colony of Victoria, in Australia. In 1887, she returned to London and listed her mine on the stock exchange. She also purchased the *Sunday Times* and ran the paper for five years. It was rumored that she was going to open an office on Wall Street (she did not). She also owned a successful South African diamond mine. Her investments made her enormously wealthy, inviting comparisons to Hetty Green (1834–1916), the "witch of Wall Street."[15] These remarkable cases stand out, but as we have seen, the statistics on women investors who were active in the mid-nineteenth century, between the Catons and Alice Cornwell, establish that women were a crucial presence as investors throughout the nineteenth century.

I offer these examples to prove several points. Throughout the nineteenth century, women from heiresses to authors to governesses invested in the Consols and were especially visible in the City when collecting their semiannual dividends. The story of the nineteenth century is one of industrialization and financialization. A growing middle class had more money to invest; and more diversified options proliferated, adding to those of investing in local businesses. Along with men, upper- and middle-class women invested in banks, domestic and colonial railroads, shipping, docks, foreign bonds, and other global securities. Some wealthy and educated women, like the Catons early in the nineteenth century, took an active hand in successfully managing diversified portfolios, even speculating. Late in the century, a few women in London (Alice Cornwell) and on Wall Street (Hetty Green) were famous or infamous for their remarkable investing talents and wealth. Such cases, and many that fall chronologically in between, illustrate that fewer restrictions were placed on women when it came to investing their money than in virtually any other sphere of public activity, with the possible exceptions of philanthropy and authorship.[16]

This chapter has explored the historical contexts of real nineteenth-century women investors, both ordinary and extraordinary. By the early twentieth century, women were not merely tolerated but embraced and targeted as investors (see Maltby et al. 2011; Rutterford et al. 2011). In 1906, Mrs. Archibald Mackirdy (Olive Christian Malvery) offered investment advice in an article titled "Women in the Money Market" (Malvery 1906–1907).[17] She begins by arguing that Hetty Green is an exception that does not prove women's capacity for investing. Rather, all women need to be better educated about finance. She emphasizes that one does not have to be wealthy to invest. Even five pounds, "might be turned to good account and used as a nucleus for collecting a capital which would yield in time quite a decent income" (42). She observes further: "There is a most astonishing interest in financial matters, which no woman can possibly realize till she has dealt with them personally" (44). What is more, there is an "extraordinary pleasure" in seeing money grow, even an "excitement and joy" in reading the financial columns and watching the fluctuations of the money markets. A century earlier, a few wealthy women, such as the Caton sisters, recognized the thrill of investing; by the twentieth century, a woman could write about that excitement in a popular periodical, encouraging all women to find the practical rewards and the pleasures of taking their investments into their own hands.[18]

Women who invested in the East India Company, domestic, colonial, and foreign railroads, joint-stock banks, foreign bonds or London and Liverpool docks took part in the nineteenth-century cultures of investment. This fact accounts for certain realistic details in Victorian novels, from the reference to stars next to the names of female shareholders in the East India Company in Thackeray's *Vanity Fair* (1847–1848) and *The Newcomes* (1853–1855), through to the various women affected by the collapse of the Britannia Loan, Assurance, Investment and Banking Company, Limited, in Gissing's *The Whirlpool* (1897). More importantly, investing was a form of activity that shaped financial lives, requiring decisions as consequential as the choice of a spouse. Often the choice of how to invest, as of whom to marry, reflected character, specifically the tolerance for risk: three percent consols or 5% mortgages? Should a woman trust her financial advisor or her own instincts and research? When passion and excitement clouded reason, these choices became confusing and dangerous. The discussion of such scenarios in novels by male authors begins in the next chapter and continues in the following case studies, which show the global reach of investments in Victorian literature and culture.

By this point, it should be clear that women had an active, diverse, and visible role to play in the nineteenth-century cultures of investment. The question then arises: How were women investors represented in nineteenth-century literature? Did their appearance in realist fiction, for example, suggest approval and encouragement, reflect reality or criticize and distort their activities? As we might expect, the answer is not simple and to some extent must be approached with the gender of the authors in mind. Phillips (2006) argues that "there was no simple relationship between women's actual economic activity and public representations of them" (19). Robb (2017) makes a similar argument about the

American context, showing that popular accounts of women investors often implied that they were more inept and vulnerable than they, in fact, were. Novels offer a variety of investing types, reflecting multiple, sometimes contradictory, views of women who entered the financial sphere.

Historians often invoke novels in support of their research about women's relationship to their property.[19] Literary critics are more reluctant to make connections between real-life and literary representations. Recent economic literary criticism has been particularly anxious to stress that novels do not represent reality and to detach formal analysis of literary texts from the historical record (Kornbluh 2014; Wagner 2010). Such criticism draws on a tradition of Marxist literary critics, from Terry Eagleton to Frederic Jameson.[20] While fiction is never a simple reflection of reality, the historical contexts, as far as we can know them, contribute invaluably to our understanding of fiction; in turn, fiction supplements, complicates, and deepens our understanding of history.

In the next chapter, we will see that Victorian novels expand and elaborate on what we know about the reality of women's presence as investors. The fictional representations of women investors are often colored by an anticapitalist moral stance, which contrasts with the procapitalist perspective of financial journalism and popular works like *Bradshaw's Guide* (Blanchard 1862).[21] Anticapitalist critiques in fiction, as I argue throughout this book, are strongest in the writings of male authors to whom other professions were open. For middle-class women who did not have access to other business and professional opportunities, investing and publishing were two socially sanctioned means of earning money. Both the documentary evidence provided by realist novels and their ideologically inflected narratives are essential to our overall understanding of how women investors acted and how they were perceived within the larger cultures of investment.

Notes

1. Thackeray to Mrs. Reach, April 5, 1857, from a letter held in the Royal Literary Fund Archive. See Cross (1985).
2. In *Family Fortunes*, Davidoff and Hall (2002) focus on the emergence of the middle class in Birmingham, Essex, and Suffolk between 1780 and 1850. Doe (2009) examines women investors in small port cities. Barker (2006) documents female enterprise in Manchester, Leeds, and Sheffield between 1760 and 1830. Morris (2009) concentrates on women and their property in and around Leeds.

3. For more on this topic in the Early Modern context, see Froide (2017); for the American context, see Robb (2017).
4. Froide (2005) concentrates on Southampton, Bristol, Oxford, and York. See also Bennett and Froide (1999). For a succinct account of histories of women and marriage, see Schaffer (2016, Chapter 1).
5. Phillips (2006) observes that these local borough customs became increasingly rare, and that by the nineteenth century, "only women in the City of London could claim the privilege" (13). See also Barker (2017).
6. These numbers provide some context for the investment returns received by Deborah Jenkyns in the joint-stock bank in Gaskell's *Cranford* (1853a).
7. Froide (2017) confirms this fall off (207–8).
8. For more on the implications of limited liability, see Alborn (1998), Taylor (2006), and Loftus (2009).
9. Company records and quantitative data on women shareholders in joint-stock companies show fluctuations in the number of female shareholders and the percentages of shares held. See also Freeman et al. (2011).
10. Michie (2001) writes: "Increasingly, the safety, convenience, and liquidity of National Debt attracted investors who, in the past, might have placed their funds into Land" (25). Dividend Day was so important that it was printed on yearly calendars. See George Lewes's diary for 1869, in Eisenberg (2015).
11. Aristocratic ladies could avoid the scene by designating an agent to collect their money for them. See Wake (2012, 284–5).
12. Ingrassia (1998) argues that Economic man was feminized (i.e., devalued and feared) in the eighteenth century. By the mid-nineteenth century, women who participated in business and finance were likely to be typed as masculine.
13. For the story of the eighteenth-century heiress Mary Eleanor Bowes's attempts to free herself from an abusive husband (the story upon which Thackeray supposedly based *Barry Lyndon*), see Moore (2010).
14. Wake (2012) details the role of slaves on Carroll's Maryland plantations in the late eighteenth and early nineteenth centuries.
15. For details on Cornwell, see Hobson, Knightley and Russell (1972); for information on Hetty Green, see Robb (2017).
16. For women's participation in politics, see Gleadle (2009).
17. Malvery's novel, *The Speculator* (1907), recounts the adventures of a cross-dressing woman who attempts to pass as a male City speculator. See Henry (2007).
18. The financial journalism that became popular in the second half of the nineteenth century was dominated by men, as indicated in the absence of women in Poovey's (2003) *Financial System*.

19. Rutterford and Maltby (2006a) use Trollope to enhance our knowledge of women's relationship to property. Michie (2011) uses Victorian novels as a "prism to capture contemporary public opinion" (170). Taylor (2006) argues that authors responded "in a spontaneous manner to the events they witnessed, and used fiction in order to try to interpret and make sense of the new economy, for themselves and the public" (15).
20. For an account and analysis of this critical history, see Goodlad (2015).
21. For selections of nineteenth-century financial journalism, see Poovey (2003).

REFERENCES

Alborn, Timothy. 1998. *Conceiving companies: Joint-stock politics in Victorian England*. London: Routledge.
———. 2010. Economics and business. In *The Cambridge companion to Victorian culture*, ed. Francis O'Gorman, 61–79. Cambridge: Cambridge University Press.
All the Year Round. 1893. Dividend day. November, 462–464.
Anderson, B.L., and P.L. Cottrell. 2008. Another Victorian capital market: A study of banking and bank investors on Merseyside. *Economic History Review* 28 (4): 598–615.
Barker, Hannah. 2006. *The business of women: Female enterprise and urban development in northern England 1760–1830*. Oxford: Oxford University Press.
———. 2017. *Family and business during the Industrial Revolution*. Oxford: Oxford University Press.
Bennett, Judith M., and Amy M. Froide. 1999. *Singlewomen in the European past, 1250–1800*. Philadelphia: University of Pennsylvania Press.
Blanchard, E.L. 1862. *Bradshaw's guide through London and its environs*. Repr., London: Conway, 2012.
Brontë, Charlotte. 1853. *Villette*, ed. Margaret Smith and Herbert Rosengarten. Oxford: Oxford University Press, 2008.
Carlos, Ann M., Karen Maguire, and Larry Neal. 2006. Financial acumen, women speculators, and the Royal African Company during the South Sea Bubble. *Accounting, Business & Financial History* 16 (2): 219–243.
———. 2009. Women in the city: Financial acumen during the South Sea Bubble. In *Women and their money 1700–1950: Essays on women and finance*, ed. Anne Laurence, Josephine Maltby, and Janette Rutterford, 33–45. New York: Routledge.
Centenary Book of the Liverpool Stock Exchange 1836–1936. 1936. Ed. Stanley Dumbell. Liverpool: The Exchange.
Chapple, John. 1997. *Elizabeth Gaskell: The early years*. Manchester: Manchester University Press.

Checkland, S.G. 1971. *The Gladstones: A family biography, 1764–1851.* Cambridge: Cambridge University Press.

Combs, Mary Beth. 2005. "A measure of legal independence": The 1870 Married Women's Property Act and the portfolio allocations of British wives. *Journal of Economic History* 65 (4): 1028–1057.

Cross, Nigel. 1985. *The common writer: Life in nineteenth-century Grub Street.* Cambridge: Cambridge University Press.

Davidoff, Leonore, and Catherine Hall. 2002. *Family fortunes: Men and women of the English middle class, 1780–1850,* rev. ed. New York: Routledge.

Dickens, Charles. 1849–1850. *David Copperfield,* ed. Jeremy Tambling. London: Penguin, 2004.

Disraeli, Benjamin. 1880. *Endymion,* vols. 2. London: Longmans & Green.

Doe, Helen. 2009. *Enterprising women and shipping in the nineteenth century.* Woodbridge, UK: Boydell Press.

Eisenberg, Michelle. 2015. George Henry Lewes's 1869 diary and journal: A transcription and annotation of unpublished holographs held at the Beineke Library of Yale University. *George Eliot-George Henry Lewes Studies* 67 (2): 93–226.

Evans, D. Morier. 1859. *The history of the commercial crisis, 1857–58: And the stock exchange panic of 1859.* London: Groombridge. https://babel.hathitrust.org/cgi/pt?id=mdp.39015056023602;view=1up;seq=7. Accessed 5 Apr 2018.

Freeman, Mark, Robin Pearson, and James Taylor. 2006. "A doe in the city": Women shareholders in early nineteenth-century Britain. *Accounting, Business & Financial History* 16: 265–291.

———. 2009. Between Madam Bubble and Kitty Lorimer: Women investors in British and Irish stock companies. In *Women and their money 1700–1950: Essays on women and finance,* ed. Anne Laurence, Josephine Maltby, and Janette Rutterford, 95–114. New York: Routledge.

———. 2011. *Shareholder democracies? Corporate governance in Britain and Ireland before 1850.* Chicago: University of Chicago Press.

Froide, Amy. 2005. *Never married: Singlewomen in early modern England.* Oxford: Oxford University Press.

———. 2017. *Silent partners: Women as public investors during Britain's financial revolution, 1690–1750.* Oxford: Oxford University Press.

Gaskell, Elizabeth. 1853a. *Cranford,* ed. Elizabeth Porges Watson. Oxford: Oxford University Press, 2011.

———. 1853b. *Ruth,* ed. Nancy Henry. London: Everyman, 2001.

Gissing, George. 1897. *The whirlpool,* ed. Gillian Tindall. London: Hogarth Press, 1984.

Gleadle, Kathryn. 2009. *Borderline citizens: Women, gender, and political culture in Britain, 1815–1867.* British Academy postdoctoral fellowship monographs. Oxford: Oxford University Press.

Goodlad, Lauren. 2015. *The Victorian geopolitical aesthetic: Realism, sovereignty and transnational experience*. Oxford: Oxford University Press.

Green, David R., and Alastair Owens. 2003. Gentlewomanly capitalism? Spinsters, widows, and wealth holding in England and Wales, c.1800–1860. *Economic History Review* 56 (4): 510–536.

Henry, Nancy. 2007. "Ladies do it?": Victorian women investors in fact and fiction. In *Victorian literature and finance*, ed. Francis O'Gorman, 111–131. Oxford: Oxford University Press.

Hobson, Harold, Phillip Knightley, and Leonard Russell. 1972. *The pearl of days: An intimate memoir of the Sunday Times, 1822–1972*. London: Hamilton.

Hyland, Peter. 2005. *The Herculaneum Pottery: Liverpool's forgotten glory*. Liverpool: Liverpool University Press.

Ingrassia, Catherine. 1998. *Authorship, commerce, and gender in early eighteenth-century England: A culture of paper credit*. New York: Cambridge University Press.

Kindleberger, Charles P., and Robert Aliber. 2005. *Manias, panics, and crashes: A history of financial crises*, 5th ed. Hoboken, NJ: Wiley.

Kornbluh, Anna. 2014. *Realizing capital: Financial and psychic economies in Victorian form*. New York: Fordham University Press.

Laurence, Anne. 2008. Women and finance in eighteenth-century England. In *Women and their money 1700–1950: Essays on women and finance*, ed. Anne Laurence, Josephine Maltby, and Janette Rutterford, 30–32. New York: Routledge.

Laurence, Anne, Josephine Maltby, and Janette Rutterford. 2009. Introduction. In *Women and their money 1700–1950: Essays on women and finance*, ed. Anne Laurence, Josephine Maltby, and Janette Rutterford, 1–29. New York: Routledge.

Loftus, Donna. 2009. Limited Liability, market democracy, and the social organization of production in mid-nineteenth-century Britain." In *Victorian investments: New perspectives on finance and culture*, ed. Nancy Henry and Cannon Schmitt, 79–97. Bloomington: Indiana UP.

Longmore, Jane. 2008. Civic Liverpool, 1680–1800. In *Liverpool 800: Character, culture, history*, ed. John Belcham, 113–170. Liverpool: Liverpool University Press.

Maltby, Josephine, Janette Rutterford, David R. Green, Steven Ainscough, and Carien van Mourik. 2011. The evidence for "democratization" of share ownership in Great Britain in the early twentieth century. In *Men, women, and money: Perspectives on Gender, Wealth, and Investment*, ed. David R. Green, Alastair Owens, Josephine Maltby, and Janette Rutterford, 184–206. Oxford: Oxford University Press.

Malvery, Olive Christian. 1906–1907. Women in the money market. *The Lady's Realm* 21: 41–45, November–April.

———. 1907. *The speculator: A novel.* London: Werner Laurie.
Michie, Ranald C. 2001. *London Stock Exchange: A history.* Oxford: Oxford University Press.
———. 2011. Gamblers, fools, victims or wizards? The British investor in the public mind, 1850–1930. In *Men, women and money: Perspectives on gender, wealth, and investment 1850–1930,* ed. David Green, Alastair Owens, Josephine Maltby, and Janette Rutterford, 156–183. Oxford: Oxford University Press.
Moore, Wendy. 2010. *Wedlock: The true story of the disastrous marriage and remarkable divorce of Mary Eleanor Bowes, Countess of Strathmore.* New York: Crown Publishers.
Morris, R.J. 2009. *Men, women, and property in England, 1780–1870: A social and economic history of family strategies amongst the Leeds middle class.* Cambridge: Cambridge University Press.
Newton, Lucy A., and Philip L. Cotrell. 2009. Female investors in the first English and Welsh commercial joint-stock banks. In *Women and their money, 1700–1950: Essays on women and finance,* ed. Anne Laurence, Josephine Maltby, and Janette Rutterford, 115–132. New York: Routledge.
Newton, Lucy A., Philip L. Cotrell, Josephine Maltby, and Janette Rutterford. 2009. Women and wealth: The nineteenth century in Great Britain. In *Women and their money, 1700–1950: Essays on women and finance,* ed. Anne Laurence, Josephine Maltby, and Janette Rutterford, 151–164. New York: Routledge.
Phillips, Nicola. 2006. *Women and business: 1700–1850.* Woodbridge, UK: Boydell Press.
Poovey, Mary. 2003. *The financial system in nineteenth-century Britain.* New York: Oxford University Press.
Robb, George. 2009. Ladies of the ticker: Women, investment, and fraud in England and America, 1850–1930. In *Victorian investments: New perspectives on finance and culture,* ed. Nancy Henry and Cannon Schmitt, 120–142. Bloomington: Indiana University Press.
———. 2017. *Ladies of the ticker: Women and Wall Street from the gilded age to the Great Depression.* Urbana-Champaign: University of Illinois Press.
Robson, John, Martin Moir, and Zawahir Moir, eds. 1990. *The collected works of John Stuart Mill.* Vol. 30: Writings on India. Toronto: University of Toronto Press.
Rutterford, Janette. 2013. "A pauper every wife is": Lady Westmeath, money, marriage, and divorce in early nineteenth-century England. *Economic women: Essays on desire and dispossession in nineteenth-century British culture,* ed. Jill Rappoport and Lana L. Dalley, 127–142. Columbus: Ohio University Press.
Rutterford, Janette, David R. Green, Josephine Maltby, and Alastair Owens. 2011. Who comprised the nation of shareholders? Gender and investment in Great Britain, c.1870–1935. *Economic History Review* 64 (1): 157–187.

Rutterford, Janette, and Josephine Maltby. 2006a. Frank must marry money: Men, women, and property in Trollope's novels. *Interfaces* 33 (2): 169–199.

———. 2006b. "The widow, the clergyman and the reckless": Women investors in England, 1830–1914. *Feminist Economics* 12 (1–2): 111–138.

Schaffer, Talia. 2016. *Romance's rival: Familiar marriage in Victorian fiction*. Oxford: Oxford University Press.

Shakinovsky, Lynn. n.d. The 1857 financial crisis and the suspension of the 1844 Bank Act. *BRANCH: Britain, representation and nineteenth-century history*, ed. Dino Franco Felluga. *Romanticism and Victorianism on the Net*. http://branchcollective.org/?ps_articles=lynn-shakinovsky-the-1857-financial-crisis-and-the-suspension-of-the-1844-bank-act. Accessed 5 Apr 2018.

St. James's Magazine. 1863. Secrets of my office, by a bill-broker. VI. December–March, 61–62.

Taylor, James. 2006. *Creating capitalism: Joint-stock enterprise in British politics and culture 1800–1870*. London: Royal Historical Society.

Thackeray, William Makepeace. 1847–1848. *Vanity fair: A novel without a hero*, ed. Diane Mowat. Oxford: Oxford University Press, 2008.

———. 1853–1855. *The Newcomes: Memoirs of a most respectable family*, ed. D.J. Taylor. London: Everyman, 1994.

———. 1945a. *The letters and private papers of William Makepeace Thackeray*, ed. Gordon Norton Ray. Vol. 3: 1852–1856. Cambridge, MA: Harvard University Press.

———. 1945b. *The letters and private papers of William Makepeace Thackeray*, ed. Gordon Norton Ray. Vol. 4: 1857–1863. Cambridge, MA: Harvard University Press.

Wagner, Tamara. 2010. *Financial speculation in Victorian fiction: Plotting money and the novel genre, 1815–1901*. Columbus: Ohio State University Press.

Wake, Jehanne. 2012. *Sisters of fortune: America's Caton Sisters at home and abroad*. New York: Simon and Schuster.

Weiss, Barbara. 1986. *The hell of the English: Bankruptcy and the Victorian novel*. Lewisburg, PA: Bucknell University Press.

CHAPTER 3

Investment Cultures in Dickens, Trollope, and Gissing

We must never intrench upon our capital—never—never!
—George Gissing, *The Odd Women*

George Gissing's *The Odd Women* (1893) opens with Dr. Madden, the fiscally irresponsible widower, confiding to his eldest daughter his intention to take out a life insurance policy to provide for his six daughters. Confident that he has a long life ahead of him, he has neglected to put his financial affairs in order and has failed to educate his daughters in a manner that would enable them to support themselves. The seeds of the sisters' helplessness are sown by the narrow conventionality of their father. His view is that "women, old or young, should never have to think about money" (32). Echoing the language of life insurance policies with their talk of averages and estimates, the narrator observes: "Dr. Madden's hopes for the race were inseparable from maintenance of morals and conventions such as the average man assumes in his estimate of women" (33). That very night, the average man is killed when his horse "stumbled and fell, and its driver was flung head forward into the road" (36). Dr. Madden could not fulfill his intention to take out the life insurance policy, and his daughters find themselves limited to a small inheritance. A male friend conservatively invests the six Madden sisters' £800, and the sisters live off the small income from these investments, left to exist at the lower end of the *rentier* class.[1]

© The Author(s) 2018
N. Henry, *Women, Literature and Finance in Victorian Britain*,
Palgrave Studies in Literature, Culture and Economics,
https://doi.org/10.1007/978-3-319-94331-2_3

After beginning in 1872, Gissing's narrative flashes forward to 1887. Two of the Madden sisters have died and another soon commits suicide, leaving three to manage on the income from £800. Gissing's critique of the bourgeois religion of never touching the principal on investments is evident in the timid spinsters' vehemently held belief, as asserted by Alice: "We must never intrench upon our capital—never—never!" Her sister Virginia responds: "Oh never!—if we grow old and useless—" (44). Virginia repeats this conviction to Rhoda Nunn, her independent friend: "Most happily, we have never needed to intrench upon our capital. Whatever happens, we must avoid that—whatever happens!" (51). Rhoda, seeing that Virginia is starving from the pinching economy that she has been forced to practice, ventures: "But wouldn't it be possible to make a better use of that money? ... Have you never thought of employing it in some practical enterprise?" (51). Virginia, shocked by many aspects of Rhoda's life, "at first shrank in alarm, then trembled deliciously at her friend's bold views" (51).

Gissing was interested in this late nineteenth-century predicament for women—the blessing and the curse of financial freedom. It was a subject he treated in *New Grub Street* (1891), *In the Year of Jubilee* (1894), and *The Whirlpool* (1897). Through his representation of various female types, he explores the very modern problem of how women might support themselves in a world where the high proportion of women to men in the population made marriage less likely than in the past generations. In his bleak social landscape, only the fittest survive and fairytale marriages no longer suffice in the realist novel genre. Pessimistically reflecting on what will become of the Maddens, Rhoda laments to Mary Barfoot, her equally independent friend: "And yet they are capitalists; eight hundred pounds between them. Think what capable women might do with eight hundred pounds" (127). The Madden sisters' lives spiral downward into Virginia's alcoholism and Monica's marriage to an abusive husband. In the end, Monica, estranged from her husband, dies in childbirth. Four out of six sisters are dead, and one baby girl has been born, suggesting only a weak hope for the future.

The opening scenario of *The Odd Women* recalls that of Jane Austen's *Sense and Sensibility* (1811), in which Mr. Henry Dashwood is disappointed with his own inheritance; yet "he might reasonably hope to live many years" and still provide for his wife and three daughters (7). When he dies unexpectedly, the Dashwood women learn that the son from his previous marriage (and his wife) will control the money. Among the differences between the worlds of Austen in 1811 and Gissing in 1893 was the freedom women both did and did not have at the end of the century. Gissing was writing after the Married Women's Property Acts of 1870 and 1882, but in *The Odd Women*, marriage is still a prison; few women could exercise newly conferred financial freedom because of residual bourgeois notions of propriety; spinsterhood still meant poverty; and employment could mean financial independence but threatened to unsex working women. Single women were still "odd," and not all odd women were New Women.[2]

Gissing's work exposes the uneven development of English society by showing the simultaneous existence of conventional, helpless women without the imagination to capitalize on their inheritance and the new potential for female economic independence epitomized in the characters of Rhoda and Mary. Into this mix, he introduces a social climbing heiress who speculates to increase her fortune. Rather than working for a living like Rhoda and Mary, Mrs. Luke Widdowson, the widow of Monica's husband's brother, inherits money from her businessman husband. She consults "an old friend great in finance, and thenceforth the excitement of the gambler gave a new zest to her turbid existence" (Gissing 1893, 137). Her speculations are enough to win her the prize of a second husband with a title and an elevated place in society, though the novel hints that the new marriage is not happy.

Gissing's predecessors in realist fiction who were critical of capitalism—Dickens and Trollope—strongly influenced his work. Their examples illustrate the most familiar types of women investors—both comic and tragic—from a male perspective that tended to be skeptical about women's business skills. They are therefore a useful comparison to the case studies explored in subsequent chapters. The works of Dickens, Trollope, and Gissing also introduce subjects and themes that recur throughout this study in relation to women investors, including life insurance and its links, both explicit and implicit, to the history of slavery—the ultimate commodification of human life—which casts its shadow over British literature long after the abolition of the slave trade in 1807 and of slavery in the British colonies in 1833. The types of women investors Dickens and Trollope established, and the cultures of investment they represented, influenced Gissing's bleak naturalism at the fin de siècle. The works of Dickens, Trollope, and Gissing provide important contexts and contrasts to the writing of women novelists discussed in later chapters.

Charles Dickens—No Money, No Story: From *Martin Chuzzlewit* to *Our Mutual Friend*

In Dickens's novels, married, widowed, and never-married women invest or speculate, either directly or indirectly, in local and global markets. For example, in *Nicholas Nickleby* (1838–1839), Mrs. Nickleby urges her husband to speculate, leading to his ruin. In *Dombey and Son* (1846–1848), the widow Mrs. Pipchin's identity is bound up with her husband's failed speculations in Peruvian mines, leading the narrator to refer to her as the "fair Peruvian Miner" (651). In *David Copperfield* (1849–1850), the strong-willed Betsey Trotwood has £8000 in the Consols. Furthermore, Dickens's novels include many women of business, both admirable and despicable. In *Martin Chuzzlewit* (1842–4), three widows support themselves through their businesses: Mrs. Gamp trades on both births and deaths as a monthly nurse attending pregnant women and as a sick nurse in league with the undertaker; Mrs. Todgers runs a boarding house; and Mrs. Lupin runs an inn. In *Little Dorrit* (1855–1857), Mrs. Clennam carries on the English branch of a company while her husband and then her son manage the branch in China.[3] In *Great Expectations* (1860–1861), the history of how Miss Havisham became a perpetual bride, as told to Pip by Herbert Pocket, involves her not only being jilted but also swindled in a business deal when her fiancé and her half-brother (the son of her father's "private" marriage to a cook) conspired to defraud her. The fiancé convinced her to buy the half-brother's interest in the brewery at an inflated price. After failing to appear for the wedding, the lover and half-brother split the profits (see Walsh 1993).

The complex financial plot of *David Copperfield* (1849–1850), which is tangential to the main story lines, suggests both the strengths and the weaknesses of women investors. Betsey Trotwood, David's aunt and benefactor, is the victim of the villain Uriah Heep's animus toward David. Upon learning that she has lost her money, Betsey provides an account of how she has come to financial ruin. Her strange narrative, delivered in the third person as the "case of Betsey Trotwood," is a parody or caricature of real Victorian global speculation schemes, like those in Peruvian mines. She explains to David and Agnes Wickfield that after investing in landed securities: "First, she lost in the mining way and then she lost in the diving way—fishing up treasure, or some such Tom Tiddler nonsense … and then she lost in the mining way again, and, last of all, to set the thing entirely to rights, she lost in the banking way" (473).

She adds, "But the Bank was at the other end of the world and tumbled into space, for what I know" (473). This story makes no sense at first, but we later find that Betsey has fabricated this image of herself as a reckless speculator in foreign markets to disguise what she thinks has been the incompetence of her advisor, Mr. Wickfield (Agnes's father), and to shield him from blame and Agnes from embarrassment. Betsey relates a fairy tale about a woman losing her entire fortune through fantastical, global investment schemes, and the episode provides what sounds like a self-conscious epigraph for Victorian novels generally: "But there was no more money and there is no more story" (474).

It turns out that Uriah Heep sold Betsey's conservatively invested shares in the Consols and then convinced the confused Mr. Wickfield that it was he who had sold them. In Wickfield's panic over what he thought were his own actions, he paid Betsey her dividends to avoid the revelation that her shares had been sold, a fraudulent practice that we find both in historical records and in novels, such as Gaskell's *Ruth* (1853b). So while aunt Betsey is not a speculator who lost her own £8000, she is an example of both a typical conservative investor and also a female victim of male swindling. When Traddles, David's friend, tells Betsey that he has recovered £5000 of her investment in the Consols, she explains that only £5000 was recovered because she had kept the other £3000 in her own control: "I sold three, myself. One, I paid for your articles, Trot, my dear; and the other two I have by me. When I lost the rest, I thought it wise to say nothing about that sum, but to keep it secretly for a rainy day" (714–15). The novel thus introduces three Betseys: the sister of David who was never born; the imagined, speculating woman of Betsey's imagination; and the actual, financially sensible Betsey.

In addition to representing these and other individual women of business, Dickens's novels establish the preoccupation of midcentury realist novels with critiques of capitalism, greed, and the commodification of human life. Grahame Smith (1968) identifies the social conditions that contributed to Victorian writers' "shocked surprise" at "the emergence of money as a social fact with the widest possible implications for themselves and their society" (62).[4] He argues: "What is new in the nineteenth century is the notion that greed for money lies at the very heart of almost all personal and social evil" (64). Dickens's novels contributed to the critique of this modern condition, joining the outraged voices of Carlyle, Ruskin, Arnold, Marx, and others. Works, such as *Dombey and Son*,

Little Dorrit, and especially *Our Mutual Friend* (1864–1865), reflect the pervasive, penetrating, and systemic influence of money, but this perspective on society begins as early as *Martin Chuzzlewit*. Smith writes: "He saw beneath the anarchic, shapeless surface of his civilization to what seemed to him the controlling principle, the role of money. This alone formed the cement of a society no longer held together by human bonds. And so, in the formation of those fictional worlds that constitute a comprehensive critique of nineteenth-century life, we find money as the force that unites their disparate elements" (221).

To counteract the force of money that Smith describes, Dickens grasps desperately at the power of love. Fairy-tale marriages such as those of Bella Wilfer and Lizzie Hexam at the end of *Our Mutual Friend* express the hope that women will love men for themselves rather than for their money. But, to do this, Dickens must leave the bounds of reality, and the fairy tales are both idealized and dark. Bella must be tricked, deceived, and tested; Lizzie must stand by a man who has had the physical strength (and the class prejudice) literally crushed out of him. Any attempt to wholly dissociate the financial from the domestic realm must take on a fantastic, unreal quality.[5]

What Dickens shared with Thackeray, Trollope, and Gissing was what Smith calls the comprehensive critique of nineteenth-century life, specifically the economic dimensions of human relationships. I do not think any woman wrote a critique of nineteenth-century society to compare with *Vanity Fair*, *Our Mutual Friend*, *The Way We Live Now* (all satirical), or *The Whirlpool*. Rather, for Gaskell's Margaret Hale and Charlotte Brontë's Shirley, inheriting money to invest in a factory is a good thing for the women and for society. Succeeding as a banker is also a positive achievement for Oliphant's Catherine Vernon in *Hester* (1883). When Eliot's heroines give up their fortunes, there is rarely a larger social critique implied. Riddell directs her criticism at specific legislation, such as limited liability and bankruptcy rather than society at large. Furthermore, women wrote some of the most influential procapitalist fiction of the period, including Dinah Craik's *John Halifax, Gentleman* (1856) and Harriet Martineau's *Illustrations of Political Economy* (1834). These are but a few examples, but they serve to identify a gendered divide among Victorian authors.

Dickens's criticisms of greed, materialism, and capitalism generally are often explicit, as in his narrators' denunciations of dollars and shares and in the demise of many a greedy villain, including Jonas Chuzzlewit,

Mr. Carker (in *Dombey and Son*), and Mr. Merdle (in *Little Dorrit*). Other critiques are more implicit or associational and are carried out through representations of institutions within the cultures of investment that affect men and women equally. I want to look briefly at the nature of Dickens's romantic, anticapitalist critiques, focusing particularly on slavery, life insurance, and marriage—institutions that epitomize his society's commodification of human lives.

Martin Chuzzlewit exposes a capitalist mentality that turns familial relationships into matters of property. Claire Wood (2015) writes that "death commodification" is pervasive in the novel (25–6). Jonas Chuzzlewit, the villain, has been raised to view everything as property, including Anthony, his own father, whom he wishes to see "banked in the grave" (106). In the American segment of the novel, Dickens's narrator rails against the American worship of the dollar, emphasizing the materiality of the paper currency: "All their cares, hopes, joys, affections, virtues, and associations seemed to be melted down into dollars" (235). The London plot of *Martin Chuzzlewit* involves the Anglo-Bengalee Disinterested Loan and Life Insurance Company, which fraudulently trades on the reduction of lives to money. In its critique of fraud, the novel satirizes the very idea behind the life insurance business; the perpetrators sell policies indiscriminately then bolt with the money before any claims can be made. The greedy Jonas is drawn into Montague Tigg's insurance scam when he seeks to purchase an insurance policy on the life of his wife (the former Mercy Pecksniff). The implication is that this future murderer of Montague Tigg intends to murder his abused wife and profit from the deed.[6]

The English insurance company plot resonates with the American sections of the novel, which are overshadowed by the existence of slavery and the literal reduction of human lives to property and dollars, a point Dickens explicitly emphasizes when he quotes advertisements for the buying, selling, and capturing of slaves in the last chapter of his *American Notes* (1842).[7] In *Martin Chuzzlewit*, the juxtaposition of the life insurance scam in England and the encounter with slavery in the American section is not accidental.[8] Dickens's critique of life insurance is summed up in the words of Poll Sweedlepipe, the barber, on the reported death of Baily, his friend. Referring to the exposure of the Anglo-Bengalee company, he exclaims: "Their office is a smash; a swindle altogether. But what's a Life Insurance Office to a Life! And what a Life young Bailey's was" (Dickens 1842–1844, 640).[9] Bailey, however, is not dead, and later returns. His near-fatal injury in a vivid coach accident is somewhat ironic given his death-defying antics while driving his master Montague Tigg's private coach, set up as part of the insurance scam, through the streets of London. The horse Bailey drives, the "brother of Cauliflower," is famous for having killed his previous mistress. In this novel particularly, horses are ominously associated with death and are yet another form of life that is reduced to its use-value and monetary worth in English and American cultures represented as driven by selfish motives of profit.

Martin Chuzzlewit is concerned with the commodification of lives in the systems of slavery, life insurance, and marriage. As we will see below, Trollope makes a similar set of associations in *Miss Mackenzie* (1864), which was written during the American Civil War.[10] Dickens may well be criticized for not confronting and more directly condemning slavery in both *American Notes* and *Martin Chuzzlewit*. His characters avoid slave states, as he himself had mostly done during his first trip to America in 1842. Yet in the instances when he does introduce the topic, his language is graphic, and his critique explicit, pointing out that enslaved people are treated like animals. For example, Mark Tapley, in *Martin Chuzzlewit*, encounters a formerly enslaved man in America who has been "shot in the leg; gashed in the arm; scored in his limbs, like pork; beaten out of shape; had his neck galled with an iron collar and wore iron rings upon his wrists and ankles" (Dickens 1842–1844, 242). Certainly, there are degrees of oppression, and nothing can compare with the human slavery that was ongoing in the USA. Within England, however, lesser but still insidious forms of abuse existed, and for Dickens this was epitomized in turning human beings into commodities. Thus, he raises the specter of murdering a wife for the return on her life insurance policy. As we will see, in works such as Gaskell's *Mary Barton* (1848), Eliot's "Brother Jacob" (1864), Riddell's *Mortomley's Estate* (1874b), and Oliphant's *Kirsteen* (1890b), women writers also refer to and encode the history of the slave trade, as well as West Indian and American slavery, to signal the moral problems with capitalism and to draw parallels with abusive systems at work in Britain.[11] But these female voices are not raised against capitalism to the same degree as those of Dickens and Trollope.

Following on *Martin Chuzzlewit*, *Dombey and Son* further explores the commodification of human lives by associating the institutions of slavery, insurance, and marriage. The novel foregrounds global trade as the narrator facetiously pronounces: "The earth was made for Dombey and Son to trade in" (Dickens 1846–1848, 2). The construction of railways in London is crucial to the setting and plot, as is the West Indian trade when Walter Gay is shipped off to represent the firm in Barbados.[12] Seamen like Captain Bunby come to and from Greenland and other exotic places; East India directors and bankers form Mr. Dombey's social set; and one guest is an old lady, "like a crimson velvet pincushion stuffed with bank notes, who might have been the identical old lady of Threadneedle Street, she was so rich" (540). Insurance is also a theme. When Walter's ironically named ship is presumed to have sunk, the villainous manager Mr. Carker comments: "At Lloyd's, they give up the Son and Heir for lost. Well! She was insured, from her keel to her masthead" (387). Cruelly disregarding the death of Walter, or perhaps ambiguously intending a double meaning to *Son and Heir*, Carker taunts Captain Cuttle, Walter's distraught friend: "The under-writers suffer a considerable loss. We are very sorry. No help! Such is life!" (494). In contrast to Poll's declaration on the loss of Bailey, in *Martin Chuzzlewit*—"What's a Life Insurance Office to a Life!"—Carker's callous remark implies: Such is life that we lose property at sea, and the death of an inconsequential lower-class man is nothing as compared with the underwriters' lost investment. In one of Dickens's favorite plot twists, Walter, like Bailey (and John Harmon, in *Our Mutual Friend*), is not in fact dead, but rather returns at the end of the novel very much alive to marry Florence and take her off on his own trading ventures in China.

Considerations of gender are at the heart of this novel in which Mr. Dombey devalues his daughter Florence because she is a girl. From the outset, Mr. Dombey views his first wife as the producer of a son, heir, and future partner. Upon her death, the wet nurse Mrs. Toodles is procured, is renamed Mrs. Richards, and is treated as a mere source of nutrition for baby Paul. In addition to his sympathy for the neglected Florence, Dickens examines the plight of Edith, Mr. Dombey's second wife, who has been brought up by her mother to attract men, much like Miss Havisham brings up Estella in *Great Expectations*. Edith has a bracing self-consciousness of having been purchased by Mr. Dombey, declaring: "There is no slave in a market; there is no horse in a fair: so shown and offered and examined and paraded, Mother, as I have been" (417). Slavery, so present to Dickens from his visit to America, haunts the novel, even when metaphorical and mixed with humor, for example, the "native," vicious Joey Bagstock's berated servant; Toots's enslavement to Florence; Rob the Grinder's enslavement to Carker; and Edith's enslavement to her husband. Edith's reference to real slave markets, recalling Dickens's emphasis on the brutality of the slave market in *American Notes* and using a similar analogy to animals ("horse in a fair"), is the literal touchstone for the metaphoric slaveries of servitude, love, psychological intimidation, and marriage. For Dickens, the pursuit of money is itself enslaving.

At the end of *Dombey and Son*, Dickens seems to relax his critique of capitalism when the previously bankrupt uncle Sol's unspecified investments (presumably related to his West Indian travels) begin to pay off: "They do say that some of Mr. Gill's old investments are coming out wonderfully well; and that instead of being behind the time in those respects, as he supposed, he was, in truth a little before it, and had to wait the fullness of time and the design. The whisper is that Mr. Gills's money has begun to turn itself, and that it is turning itself over and over pretty briskly" (921).

In addition to this seeming approval of money "turning itself over and over," the passive investor Harriet Carker emerges as an unlikely financial heroine when she secretly arranges to keep only a small part of her own and her brother John's inheritance. She wants the bankrupt Mr. Dombey to receive the interest on their investments for the "remainder of his life" (864).

The restored fortune was as sacred to Victorian narrative endings as the happy marriage and was familiar even in Jane Austen's work, for example, when Captain Wentworth helps Mrs. Smith recover her West Indian fortune at the end of *Persuasion* (1818). Most Victorian marriage plots are financial plots but with a variety of outcomes.[13] The failure to recover a fortune could be associated with death, for example, that of Richard and other unlucky Jarndyce heirs in Dickens's *Bleak House* (1852–3). The plot of Charlotte Brontë's (1853) *Villette* involves multiple financial failures, including those of the Brettons; Paul Emmanuel's father; and the father of his fiancée, Justine Marie. M. Paul travels to the West Indies to oversee the restoration of Mme. Walraven's West Indian fortune, but we do not know whether he succeeded in doing so before he dies on the journey back to England, leaving Lucy Snowe, his intended bride, to fend for herself. The opportunity to recover lost family wealth could also be rejected on moral grounds, as in the case of Esther Lyon in *Felix Holt* (Eliot 1866) and Will Ladislaw in *Middlemarch* (Eliot 1871–1872). In Eliot's novels generally, romantic marriage often entails foregoing inherited wealth. In a different plot variation, Mrs. Davilow's property, with its origins in her father's West Indian estates, is lost through financial speculation in *Daniel Deronda* (Eliot 1876), as we will see in Chapter 5.

Over the subsequent years, Dickens's vision became darker, and his social critique more existential. In *Our Mutual Friend*, his last completed novel, the prospect of a restored fortune unites its multiple plots. It also involves secrets and alternative identities like those of aunt Betsey, this time for its hero, John Harmon, a man presumed dead who assumes a new identity in pursuit of his lost inheritance, on the one hand, and a romantic marriage, on the other hand. In this novel, Dickens intones about the traffic in shares, as he had about dollars in *Martin Chuzzlewit*: "Sufficient answer to all; shares. Oh mighty Shares!" (Dickens 1864–1865). This transfer of anger against the worship of the dollar in the 1840s to the worship of shares in 1864 marks larger transformations in the cultures of investment. The development and democratization of more abstract markets trading in shares, rather than in commodities, was a reality that Dickens and Trollope, among others, deplored and satirized in their fiction. *Our Mutual Friend* establishes a global context of South African winemaking in the John Harmon plot. That epitome of bourgeois conventionality, Mr. Podsnap, is employed by Marine Insurance, and the commodification of lives becomes ever more literal—from the fishing of dead bodies out of the Thames to Mr. Venus's taxidermy.

Dickens's financial life provides some historical context for our study of women investors, economic instability, and even fraud. Dickens famously suffered from his father's (John Dickens) debts and financial mismanagement. His extended family, including his father and siblings, continued to be a drain on his income after he became successful.[14] In *Charles Dickens's Childhood*, Michael Allen (1988) notes that in 1785, Elizabeth Dickens, Dickens's grandmother, a servant in an aristocratic household, inherited £450 invested in Consols from her husband, who was a butler to the family. The couple's upwardly mobile son, John, married Elizabeth Barrow. In 1810, Charles Barrow, her father, fled the country after it was discovered that he had embezzled thousands of pounds while serving as the Chief Conductor of Money at the Navy Office in London (18). In 1819, John Dickens borrowed £200, and when he defaulted, it was left to Thomas Barrow, his brother-in-law, to repay the loan. Thomas never recovered the money from John, who was thereafter banished from his home, although Thomas continued to help Charles (Slater 2009, 8). Charles wrote to Fanny, his sister, that their maternal grandmother "never cared twopence about us until I grew famous and then she sent me an affectionate request for five pounds or so" (quoted in Slater 2009, 178).[15] In short, Dickens lived with the knowledge of his family's past financial reversals and with the early childhood trauma of debt. He never stopped feeling pressured by the demands of family members—grandparents, parents, siblings, and then children. His experience was, of course, unique, but worrying about money was something he shared with his fellow authors.

Biographer Victoria Glendinning (1993) documents Anthony Trollope's obsession with money following the experiences of his family in his youth. The miseries of his early life, as recalled in his autobiography, arose from lack of money. Later, he became a "fanatical keeper of accounts": "Money and the efficient management of money were to be central to his feelings of security" (36). His father, like Dickens's father, was inept at managing money, and the family suffered as a result. In his mother, Frances (Fanny) Trollope, Trollope had a model of woman who took control of the family's finances. Like later novelists Riddell and Oliphant, Fanny Trollope was called on to clean up financial messes created by her husband. According to Glendinning, Fanny had £900 a year as well as income from rents in Somerset shared with her sister (58). Her capital of £1300 should have remained, but "something untoward had happened to it" (58). In 1834, before she and her family fled to Bruges in Belgium to avoid her husband's creditors and his imprisonment for debt, she bought an annuity of £250 a year for herself and her daughters (59). It is difficult to say how much Trollope knew of his mother's financial struggles after she returned from her failed attempt to establish a bazaar in Cincinnati and then succeeded with her authorship of *The Domestic Manners of the Americans* (1832) and subsequent novels, but his fiction clearly represents the kinds of financial entanglements faced by women when their husbands and other family members fell into debt.

Fanny had to face the same evasive tactics for avoiding debt that were common in Trollope's novels. Glendinning writes that Fanny's husband "was caught in a web of IOUs and 'bills' which he had signed against loans—bills which could be sold on from hand to hand, the interest rising exponentially until the last in the chain attempted to collect some impossible total from the initial borrower" (58). As a young man, Trollope too experienced the escalation of interest on a loan, a traumatic lesson that was recalled in *An Autobiography* (1883) and fictionalized in

Phineas Finn (1866–1867b). Bad bills also circulate in *Can You Forgive Her?* (1864–1865), *The Way We Live Now* (1875), and *The Prime Minister* (1876). While the experience of seeing the interest rates on bills inflate to fantastic proportions was a staple of Victorian financial plots, Trollope, like Charlotte Riddell, as we will see, drew on personal experience when incorporating such scenarios in his fiction.

It is worth noting that Trollope's wife, Rose (née Heseltine), also came from a family that suffered pecuniary embarrassments, though these befell her father after her marriage. It is unclear how much they may have known about the predicament of Mr. Heseltine, who spent his career working as a banker in Rotherham (South Yorkshire). It was not until 1853, after his retirement, that the bank's losses under his management were discovered. He had also been the director of the Sheffield and Rotherham Railway, and no doubt he was a large shareholder in the company. After the railway share crisis of 1849, he probably used bank funds to cover his own debts, concealing this in the bank's accounts. Glendinning (1993) observes: "Mr. Heseltine was one of the thousands who swindled in a small way in the shadow of George Hudson—millionaire, master-swindler and entrepreneurial genius" (225). Hudson was central to the railway empire and speculation bubbles of the 1840s that lay behind the railway plot of *Dombey and Son*. Heseltine and his second wife fled to Le Havre, France, as the Trollopes had fled to Bruges and John Dickens's in-laws had fled England for the continent.[16] However much Trollope knew about his own family's difficulties, or the later troubles of his in-laws, debt, financial scandal, railway speculation, and bankruptcy were all part of the general mid-Victorian culture, and such scenarios appear throughout his fiction.

Upon her death in 1863, Frances Trollope left Anthony all of her shares in the Joint Stock London Bank (348). These shares, along with his own holdings in the Garrick Club (348) and the Smyrna Railway (453), paid dividends that augmented his income from writing. In 1880, the publishing house of Chapman and Hall, in which Harry, Trollope's son, had been a partner from 1869 to 1873, became a joint-stock company. Trollope was one of the directors, and both he and Harry bought shares (483). Upon Trollope's death, Rose inherited his shares in Chapman and Hall. In his will, Trollope gave his executors, Rose and Harry, "discretion to keep or sell his stocks and shares as they saw fit, but new investments must not be in any companies outside the United Kingdom or its colonies and dependencies" (503). He stipulated that

Harry could make no investments without Rose's written consent. These investments continued to pay, and Rose's investment income in 1896 was £538 (506). Frances and Rose Trollope were among the women investors whose numbers grew throughout the nineteenth century. Taking advantage of joint-stock banks and railroad companies, among other proliferating options, investors had new opportunities and new choices about what to do with their capital. As widows, Fanny turned to stocks and shares to supplement her income, and Rose made investment decisions that would affect her well-being. Overall, Trollope's preoccupation with money in his own family life is registered in his fiction, which includes a notable number of investing women (and men).

ANTHONY TROLLOPE—FROM *MISS MACKENZIE* TO *THE PRIME MINISTER*

In Trollope's *Phineas Finn* (1866–1867b), long before Phineas marries the wealthy Madame Max at the end of its sequel, *Phineas Redux* (1873–1874), he is saved from financial difficulties by what the narrator calls a "wonderful piece of luck" (1866–1867b, 355). Miss Marian Persse, his mother's aunt and "an eccentric old lady" who "thought a good deal of her own money," dies and leaves him £3000 (355). The narrator remarks: "He owed some £500, and the remainder he would, of course, invest" (356). The casual mention of the mundane use to which Phineas will put the "wonderful" inheritance is typical of Trollope. A fantastic yet entirely plausible coincidence occurs but is downplayed by an observation that reflects the common sense of investing. That Trollope casually adds "of course" suggests the established middle-class conventions that Gissing criticized in the Madden sisters' horror of removing their capital from its safe, low-interest investment.

Throughout Trollope's novels, investing is a ubiquitous middle-class practice that is registered alongside unexpected inheritances and sensational speculation plots. He treats commerce, advertising, and investment in *The Three Clerks* (1858) and *The Struggles of Brown, Jones, and Robinson* (1861–1862). His speculators include Dobbs Broughton; George Vavasor; Ferdinand Lopez; and Augustus Melmotte. Among his female characters, single women including Miss Dunstable, Alice Vavasor, and Miss Mackenzie, as well as the widows Mrs. Van Siever, Arabella Greenow, Lizzie Eustace, and Madame Max Goesler are all investing women, although some take a more active role than others in managing their money.

Critics have explored the complex role of women generally in Trollope's novels. Jane Nardin (1989) focuses on the early novels and the formal properties of the romantic comedy. Deborah Morse (1987) concentrates on the later Palliser series, arguing that Trollope subverts the traditional structure of the courtship plot. Josephine Maltby and Janette Rutterford (2006), Elsie Michie (2011), and Jill Rappoport (2016) have examined the topic of women and money in his work. Looking specifically at women investors, we see the mentality of investing money with the expectation of a return, whether that money is invested in the market, in efforts to gain a husband or even in paid companions. Trollope, like other novelists, especially Oliphant, explores the way in which women are both dependent on and independent from their male advisors. In Trollope's fiction, romantic and familial relationships are rarely free from questions of the woman's money.

Phineas Finn and *Phineas Redux* are remarkable for the degree to which women's money underwrites and saves the careers of men. Some women want to give away their money to male friends and family members. In addition to Miss Persse, Aspasia Fitzgibbon is "an old maid, over forty, very plain" (1866–1867b, 78), who unexpectedly inherited £25,000—"a wonderful windfall" (78). She uses the money to live independently and becomes the only member of her family with money. Though she dislikes lending to Laurence, her spendthrift brother, she nonetheless buys the accommodation bill that Phineas has signed for him, negotiating with the creditors to lower the price on the loan. For a second time, Phineas is relieved of his debts by an "old maid," and he is ashamed that Miss Fitzgibbon "found herself obliged to satisfy his pecuniary liabilities" (323). The unexpected intervention of wealthy spinsters is one form of female financial aid offered to the hero. Lady Laura—who uses her independent fortune to pay the gambling debts of Lord Chiltern, her brother—wishes to help Phineas after Chiltern finally repays her. Phineas refuses her money, but his career is ultimately made through the wealth of Madame Max, whom he marries at the end of *Phineas Redux*. In this way, women sustain him financially and blur the boundaries between financial and domestic spheres. Trollope's novels suggest the impossibility of isolating business and finance from familial and romantic relationships.

In life and in fiction, nineteenth-century women who looked after their financial interests were often characterized as bloodthirsty animals. Charles Harper, the cousin of real-life investor Emily Caton, wrote that she was amiable and kind to her family, "but put *money* in view, there does not exist a more unfeeling and remorseless shark" (Wake 2012, 267). Trollope contributed to this stereotyping. In *The Eustace Diamonds* (1872), Mr. Camperdown, the lawyer who pursues Lizzie Eustace in order to recover the Eustace diamonds, remarks that he has dealt with widows who were "quite content to accept the good things settled upon them by the liberal prudence of their friends and husbands—not greedy, blood-sucking harpies" like Lizzie (II:14).[17]

Miss Mackenzie (1864) is Trollope's most concentrated study of a woman and her money. In *An Autobiography* (written in 1875–1876 and published posthumously in 1883), Trollope recalls Margaret Mackenzie, his thirty-six-year-old heroine, as "a very unattractive old maid, who was over-whelmed by money troubles" (123). The narrator observes of Margaret: "Like all other single ladies, she was very nervous about her money. She was quite alive to the beauty of a high rate of interest, but did not quite understand that high interest and impaired security should go hand in hand together" (36). This image of beautiful high interest walking hand in hand with impaired security embodies the inseparability of money and romance in *Miss Mackenzie*. The terms interest, security, and liberty are multivalent. For example, in a conversation about interest rates, one of her suitors asks, "How can I fail to feel an interest about you?" (59–60). Miss Mackenzie has liberty to do what she pleases with her money (13), but her brother takes a liberty with that money, putting it at risk (70).

Margaret Mackenzie lived for years as a nurse and companion to one of her brothers, a civil servant in Somerset House, whose investments have increased the £12,000 he inherited from an uncle. When he dies, he leaves this money, plus a freehold estate paying £600 a year, to his sister, thus initiating her new life of freedom and also of financial and romantic problems. For the first time in what has been a dependent and dreary adult life, she begins to taste independence. The narrator observes, "No power of the purse had been with her—none of that power which belongs legitimately to a wife because a wife is a partner in the business" (25). Despite what we know about the relative power of single women to control their money, Trollope thought they were outside the "business" of marriage, which conferred the only real power in Victorian society. Without husbands to guide them, single women were inevitably overwhelmed by their financial freedom.

Miss Mackenzie is to have a little over £800 a year (13), that is, £600 from the property and £200 on the £12,000 at a rate of about 2%. Her lawyers are looking out for higher paying interest on the money.

When her surviving brother asks her for £2400 to take a mortgage on his oilcloth factory at a rate of 5%—an amount he understood she had "lying about idle" (38)—Miss Mackenzie's first worry is that the lawyers might allow this opportunity to "slip through their hands" (38). Initially tempted to place the money in the three percents, instead "she had gone to work with the figures, and having ascertained that by doing so twenty-five pounds a year would be docked off her computed income," she "now again went to work with her figures" (37). She is thus persuaded to lend her brother the money to buy some property at a rate of 5%: "Mortgages, she knew, were good things, strong and firm, based on landed security, and very respectable" (37). She calculates the difference between receiving 3% in the Consols and 5% on the mortgage, choosing the riskier option because she does not consider lending money to her brother a risk. She also rationalizes the calculation in moral, gendered terms: mortgages are good, strong, firm, and respectable—qualities that would be ideal in a husband. The three percents, in contrast, and as we have seen, are associated with ladies, but ironically would be a safer investment than the strong and firm mortgage. Her brother and Mr. Rubb, his partner, assure her that she cannot do better than 5%.[18]

From the moment of her inheritance, Margaret Mackenzie is negotiating between proposals to invest her money and proposals of marriage. The heroine experiencing freedom, power, and wealth for the first time anticipates Henry James's Isabel Archer in *Portrait of a Lady* (1881) and Gissing's Marian Yule in *New Grub Street* (1891). Like these later heroines, Miss Mackenzie's sense of freedom is complicated by pressures from the men in her family and male suitors who are attracted to that money. In contrast to Dickens, Trollope seems to accept commodification as a fact of life in Victorian culture, and from that assumption, moves on to explore the more subtle dilemmas faced by women contemplating marriage.

Miss Mackenzie's troubles throughout the novel involve her attempts to assess the financial advice she receives from various men and to evaluate their relative sincerity. These problems are related because, as Trollope recognizes, passion for money and romantic passion are often intertwined, even in the mind of the suitor himself. Her cousin, the widower John Ball, lost his chance of wealth when Margaret's brothers inherited the money he had expected would be his. Like Trollope's father, John Ball is a barrister who cannot make a living from his practice and whose great expectations of inheritance are disappointed. His title, estate, and nine children are in peril from his inability to earn money, a calamity that he and his overbearing mother trace back to the loss of the inheritance; they are thus eager for him to marry Miss Mackenzie and recover an albeit diminished fortune they believe rightfully to be their own. John Ball is attuned to percentages and share values. His constant attention to his investments "gave him perhaps five per cent for his capital, whereas he would have received no more than four and half had he left it alone and taken his dividends without troubling himself" (74–5). Despite his own failures as an investor, John schools his cousin on the folly of investing in her brother's company: "My dear Margaret, their word for five per cent is no security. Five per cent is nothing magnificent. A lady situated as you are should never part with her money without security—never: but if she does, she should have more than five per cent" (78).

Mr. Rubb makes it especially difficult for Miss Mackenzie to keep business and romance separate because he employs financial language to seduce her: "Five per cent and first-class security were, she knew, matters of business"; however, Mr. Rubb, "winked his eye at her as he spoke of them, leaning forward in his chair and looking at her not at all as a man of business" (57). Later, he "got nearer to her on the sofa as he whispered the word money into her ear" (107). Mr. Rubb uses sexuality to minimize the news that there is a problem with the mortgage. He asks for her trust, and she agrees to "take her interest without asking for any security for the principal." This is a bad business decision, clouded by familial loyalty. Her brother and Mr. Rubb know that their firm had "no longer the power of providing her with the security which had been promised to her" (70). She has been manipulated and betrayed by her brother and his partner. When she refuses Mr. Rubb's offer of marriage, the narrator comments: "I tremble as I look back upon her danger" (397). Security and danger refer to Miss Mackenzie's money and her person.

Four men court Margaret in one year: Handcock, Ball, Rubb, and Mr. Maguire, the greedy, squinting curate from Littlebath. Employing free indirect discourse, the narrator remarks: "One man had wanted her money to buy a house on mortgage, and another now asked for it to build a church, giving her, or promising to give her, the security of the pew rents. Which of the two was the worst? They were both her lovers, and she thought that he was the worst who first made his love and then tried to get her money" (248). She does lose the money she invested in her brother's business, but what she loses through her loan, she regains when a railway company wants to buy property she now owns (188).[19]

The railway company's purchase of her land is one financial plot twist. Additionally, the discovery of an unlikely legal technicality causes Margaret's inheritance (which had been kept for years by her now deceased brother) to revert to John Ball. In this way, Trollope takes away from Miss Mackenzie what he had briefly given her: freedom, money, and power. She relinquishes financial responsibility with a sense of relief and marries and accepts her cousin's proposal.

John Ball is a guinea pig; that is, for a guinea per meeting, he sits on the boards of various City companies, including the ironically titled Abednego Life Office. While thinking of Miss Mackenzie, he "votes for accepting a doubtful life, which was urged on the board by a director, who, I hope, had no intimate personal relations with the owner of the doubtful life in question" (Trollope 1864, 244). This side commentary by the narrator about the unthinking ways in which human lives are discussed as investments on the board of a life insurance company resonates with the major theme of the inseparability of Miss Mackenzie and her money in the eyes of suitors, including John Ball. As I argue throughout this book, life insurance plays an important role in numerous Victorian novels and stories as an example of how lives have been commodified within a capitalist system. For those taking out a policy, life insurance is a way of mitigating risk, but for investors in the company, accepting a "doubtful life" is the epitome of risk.

Furthermore, like Dickens in *Martin Chuzzlewit*, Trollope implicitly links life insurance with the treatment of women on the marriage market and also with American slavery. A final scene in *Miss Mackenzie* takes place at a great charity bazaar on behalf of the "orphan children of negro soldiers who had fallen in the American war" (354). Trollope says in his autobiography (1883) that he wanted to express his criticism of such ways of raising money, and this he does. But the shadow of American slavery, the commodification of "doubtful lives" in the insurance business, and the conflation of Miss Mackenzie and her money are all related in what Trollope considered to be his failed attempt to produce a novel without love.[20]

This novel goes beyond exposing affective ties as monetary at its root. For Miss Mackenzie, keeping her money safe is keeping herself safe. The freedom to do what she likes with her money is the freedom to do what she likes with herself. For the period of the novel's action during which she has money, Miss Mackenzie has an identity that she previously lacked, which disappears in the end when it turns out the money never was hers. Upon marrying John Ball, she becomes Lady Ball, assuming the name of her overbearing mother-in-law, who has sought to convince her throughout the novel that the money is not hers. The happy marriage ending, which overtook Trollope's attempt to write a novel without any love, is in fact quite dark in its obliteration of the person named "Miss Mackenzie." In this sense, *Miss Mackenzie* raises an existential problem that Trollope would treat later in different forms, especially with the speculators Dobbs Broughton, Augustus Melmotte, and Ferdinand Lopez, who commit suicide: Society has become such that the loss of money amounts to an annihilation of self. In *Miss Mackenzie*, this equation of a person with his or her money is subtly echoed in the minor themes of life insurance and American slavery, two forms of monetizing the value of human life, as Dickens particularly emphasized in *Martin Chuzzlewit*.

Trollope seems to accept the economic basis of marriage as a given, while Dickens is more sentimental, Thackeray more satirical, and Gissing darkly cynical. In their various ways, however, all of these authors are suspicious of the City, representing it as a whirlpool of greedy people striving to make money without working for it.[21] In Trollope's *The Last Chronicle of Barset* (1866–1867a), which followed shortly after *Can You Forgive Her?* and *Miss Mackenzie*, Mrs. Van Siever is the widow of a Dutch merchant who had conducted business in the City (241). In the same type of character sketch that reduced Miss Mackenzie to "an ugly old maid," Mrs. Van Siever is "a weird old woman, so small, so ghastly, and so ugly!" (371). She looks after her money in ways that are mysterious to Clara, her beautiful daughter, who stands to inherit her fortune. As the artist Conrad Dalrymple comments: "Miss Van is to have gold by the ingot, and jewels by the bushel, and a hatful of bank shares, and a whole mine in Cornwall for her fortune" (249). The fortunes of modern heiresses, it seems, are diversified; Lady Glencora's sources of income, for example, also include mines; and Madame Max owns real estate. Clara's anticipated fortune was inherited from her father but is enlarged by her mother—Trollope's most active businesswoman and investor.

With Augustus Mussleboro, a former clerk in her husband's office, and Dobbs Broughton, a businessman enjoying a high social profile, Mrs. Van Siever forms a partnership of moneylenders. Mussleboro and Broughton have offices in Hook Court, off Lombard Street in the City. Broughton is a fraudulent social climber who foreshadows *The Way We Live Now*'s Melmotte, though he never inflates to the same degree.

Addicted to drink and horseracing, he collects the interest from Mrs. Van Siever's loans and gambles them away at the track. He is therefore unable to pay her when she comes to the City looking for her profits. Dobbs hypocritically complains about his partner's grasping ways: "For a downright leech, recommend me always to a woman. When a woman does go in for it, she is much more thorough than any man" (367–8). As we have seen, this characterization of a woman investor as a bloodthirsty animal is consistent with other descriptions of women as sharks and harpies.

Trollope is specific about what Mrs. Van Siever gets from her loans. Dobbs sneeringly comments: "For the last three years she's drawn close upon two thousand a year for less than eighteen thousand pounds. When a woman wants to do that, she can't have her money in her pocket every Monday morning" (368–9). Trollope is reinforcing basic principles of investing that influenced women's decisions. In the nineteenth century, some women, whether governesses, widows, or wealthy wives, liked the regularity of the three percents. Dobbs points out that when a woman is getting over 10% in the unregulated world of money lending, she cannot expect a check like clockwork.

Here again is the question of risk versus security and skepticism about a woman's ability to understand that "high interest and impaired security should go hand in hand together" (Trollope 1864, 36). If Mrs. Van Siever wants over 10% on her loans, she cannot have the regularity of picking up her dividend checks, a ceremony, which, as we have seen, was associated with cautious women investors. Dobbs implies that in their shady business of loan sharking, borrowers have to be squeezed, a practice that Trollope represents when the Jewish creditor Mr. Clarkson pursues Phineas in *Phineas Finn* and also in *The Three Clerks* with Mr. Jabez M'Ruen.[22] According to his autobiography, Trollope was in debt to a moneylender who told him, "Now I wish you would be punctual" (Glendinning 1993, 89). He turned the phrase into a chapter title in *Phineas Finn*, "Do Be Punctual" (Chapter. 21), in which Mr. Clarkson repeats this language, which clearly caught the novelist's ear as an ominous if humorous refrain.

Mrs. Van Siever suggests that women, when given the chance, can be just as successful and just as ruthless as men at making money. Trollope seems to think that Mrs. Van Siever is a woman born with an aptitude for business, as Lady Laura and Lady Glencora are born to politics, though social pressures keep them from realizing their natural capacities. Crossing from the West End into the City and wearing her business dress, the ugly socialite Mrs. Van Siever looks even worse, a physical manifestation of her leech-like behavior. She presses Dobbs for the money he owes her and thus contributes to his financial ruin and bloody suicide when he blows his brains out in the City.

Conclusion

Writing after the deaths of Thackeray, Gaskell, Dickens, Eliot, and Trollope, Gissing explored how the possession of money empowers women and permeates their personal relationships with suitors, husbands, fathers, and children. His career overlapped with that of Riddell, Oliphant, and James, and like them, he confronted the era of the "New Woman." As we saw at the beginning of this chapter, in *The Odd Women*, the unmarried Madden sisters are left to subsist on their invested inheritance and would rather starve than touch their capital, thus showing the absurdity of a deeply internalized bourgeois capitalist ethos. In his harshest critique of financial speculation, *The Whirlpool*, Gissing (1897) suggests that the propensity to reckless speculation is an inherited trait. Women as well as men are ruined by the failure of Benet Frothingham. His widow makes half-hearted reparations to the people impoverished by his speculations, but his daughter, Alma, reenacts the recklessness that led to his overdose of morphia, which he had taken to sleep. In the end, she too dies from an overdose of the fashionable cordial she had been taking for insomnia.

In *The Year of Jubilee* (1894), set in 1887, Gissing shows the extent to which investing had become common with modern women. Beatrice French "understood the nature of investments, and liked to talk about stocks and shares with her male acquaintances" (6). On the other hand, Lionel Tarrant's grandmother squanders the fortune he expected to inherit, "speculating here and there without taking any one's advice" (194). In that novel, Horace takes out a life insurance policy "and straightway used the policy as a security for a loan of five hundred pounds" (236). Upon his medical examination, he learns that he will have to pay more than the usual premium because the exam detected ominously the consumption that will eventually kill him.

In *New Grub Street* (1891), the downtrodden Marian Yule stands to inherit £5000 from her uncle's share in a wholesale stationary business—money she hopes will make her an attractive marriage prospect to the ambitious Jasper Milvain. The narrator describes the immediate effect of this inheritance: "Money is a great fortifier of self-respect. Since she had become really conscious of her position as the owner of five thousand pounds, Marian spoke with a steadier voice, walked with firmer step; mentally she felt herself altogether a less dependent being" (321). But her happiness is soon alloyed by her embittered father's proposal that she invest her money in a new literary journal to be edited by him, a scheme which she views with skepticism: "It would be better if we called it a speculation," said Marian, smiling uneasily. "Name it as you will," returned her father, hardly suppressing a note of irritation and adding: "True, every commercial enterprise is a speculation" (323). She ultimately rejects his proposal, causing an irreparable rift between them.

Money is a fortifier of self-respect but also an object of desire coming between family members. The temporary confidence Marian feels is similar to that of Miss Mackenzie at receiving her inheritance. Gissing's ending is even bleaker than Trollope's, as Marian loses her money and, as a consequence, her lover. Whereas Miss Mackenzie is relieved when she learns that her inheritance has been lost, Marian "fell to the floor in unconsciousness" at hearing of her own loss (406). Her father coldly relates: "Her money is lost. The people who were to pay it have failed" (406). Ironically, the demand for the cash from the uncle's deceased partner's investment in the business in order to pay the inheritance causes the company's failure, and Marian becomes "a prisoner of fate" (456). Marian ultimately receives £1500 of her initial inheritance, which will produce £50 a year. Confessing this outcome to the disappointed Jasper, she wonders at bankrupts who will not pay their debts in full.[23] Jasper is sympathetic, but not sympathetic enough to marry Marian in her reduced circumstances.

The investing women discussed in this and later chapters present a spectrum of fictional types: old and sexless business widows and spinsters like Mrs. Van Siever, Catherine Vernon (in Oliphant's *Hester*), and Deborah Jenkyns (in Gaskell's *Cranford* [1853a]); financially naïve and sexually available women like Miss Mackenzie and Lizzie Eustace; and timid spinsters like the Madden sisters. Elsie Michie (2011) emphasizes that heiresses in nineteenth-century fiction reflect the movement from landed to liquid wealth over the course of the century and that Trollope's new-monied heiresses like Miss Dunstable and Glencora Palliser were inspired by the lives of real people (149). Miss Dunstable's ointment fortune resembles that accumulated by Thomas Holloway (the millionaire) and Lady Glencora would have suggested the coal-mining heiress Lady Frances Waldegrave to contemporary readers.[24] As indicated in subsequent chapters in this book, many characters in realist novels have specific models in public figures or people known to the authors. Yet we do not need to identify real prototypes to see that both real and fictional women investors were a central part of the nineteenth-century cultures of investment. Thinking in terms of local, national, and global cultures of investment helps us to see that public and private spheres, like financial and literary spheres, were not separate but rather overlapping and integrated.

This chapter has shown how realist novelists, particularly Dickens, Trollope, and Gissing, treated fictional types of female investors: married or single, timid or bold, victim or perpetrator. Their novels also explore the broader moral implications of financial situations and relationships. Dickens was a scathing critic of greed and the dehumanizing effects of capitalism, a theme that runs through all of his work and achieves its greatest intensity in the dark vision and fanciful resolutions of *Our Mutual Friend*. Trollope was more likely to assume that marital and other familial relationships would have a financial dimension, but in the 1870s his voice grew louder against particular kinds of finance capitalism, most famously in the sharp satire of *The Way We Live Now*.[25] Gissing, especially after he turned in his later fiction of the 1890s to middle-class rather than working-class culture, offered a cynical and naturalist vision of a brutal social and financial world summed up in his metaphor of the "whirlpool."

The chapters that follow are case studies of women who lived, wrote, and invested in the middle to late decades of the nineteenth century. In these studies, I look at novels from Gaskell's *Mary Barton* in 1848 through Riddell and Oliphant's fiction of the 1890s. As obsessed with economic plots and personal dynamics as those of their male contemporaries, these novels are more likely to acknowledge the potential of investing to improve the lives of women, despite the risks of swindles, panics, or economic depressions. Gender matters because we tend not to think of these authors' financial lives outside the business of literature or to imagine that they had financial agency to purchase shares or invest in companies and real estate. But, as I will show, these successful novelists all participated in various other markets. Their familial and financial networks, including mothers, aunts, uncles, siblings, friends, and husbands, brought them into contact with local and global cultures of investment with London and Liverpool as points of geographical connection among them. These intertwined financial and familial histories shaped their lives and informed their fiction. We now turn to the authors and investors Gaskell, Eliot, Riddell, and Oliphant, whose financial lives were inseparable from the literature they produced.[26]

NOTES

1. "The female 'rentier' investor was an individual that looked for safe investment opportunities, as identified in the nineteenth-century discourse" (Newton and Cottrell 2009, 129). Delany (2002) defines *rentiers* as "those who lived off financial wealth, which gave them higher income than if they invested in land" (125). He observes: "Many of the intellectuals who promoted the rural myth of organic Englishness had no actual ties to the land, but drew their family wealth from banking or finance: for example, William Morris, John Ruskin, Cardinal Newman, G.M. Hopkins and E.M. Forster" (127).
2. Like Riddell and Oliphant, Gissing struggled throughout his life and career with financial problems. James (2003) asserts: "The subject of money preoccupies Gissing more than it does any other novelist in English literature" (1).
3. Çelikkol (2011) argues that the Clennams' business must have involved the opium trade: "The Clennams' and the narrator's reticence about their dealings in China intimates past acts of injustice committed by the family in particular and the nation in general" (126–7).
4. Smith's insights apply to the culture at large. For other classic studies of money in Victorian literature and culture before the advent of New Economic Criticism, see Vernon (1984), Copeland (1995), Reed (1984), Russell (1986), and Brantlinger (1996).
5. For a detailed analysis of financial plot resolutions in Dickens's novels, see James (2003). On Dickens and the failed marriage plot, see Hager (2010).
6. Alborn (2009) writes, "As 'risks' bearing calculable economic values, policyholders were *commodified* lives, simultaneously acting as inalienable subjects and being acted upon as financial instruments" (4). See also Wood (2015).
7. Even the title of his American travelogue—*American Notes for General Circulation*—is a pun on what he saw as the driving force of American society—the dollar.
8. Alborn (2009) argues: "More directly than any other enterprise apart from slavery, life insurance set a price on human life" (11). Baucom (2005) and Armstrong (2012) have explored the cultural implications of

insuring slaves as cargo. Armstrong calls the "culture of slavery" a legacy that "enters our thinking when we insure ourselves" (1).
9. Dickens seems to have been intrigued by Marine Insurance, a subject his father wrote about (Slater 2009, 24). Herbert Pocket aspires to deal in Marine Insurance in *Great Expectations*. Podsnap, in *Our Mutual Friend*, is employed in the Marine Insurance line. Dickens had several insurance policies on his own life beginning in 1838 when he was turned down on suspicion of overworking, despite a letter from his doctor. He satirized doctors employed by life insurance companies in *Martin Chuzzlewit* through the character of Mr. Jobling (see Carlton 1955). In 1859, Trollope paid £60 for a life insurance policy (Glendinning 1993, 256).
10. For Trollope's critique of West Indian and American slavery in *He Knew He was Right* and *Doctor Wortle's School*, see Morse (2013).
11. Other authors incorporate a West Indian plot without necessarily implying a critique of slavery: Jane Austen in *Mansfield Park* (1814) and *Persuasion* (1818), Charlotte Brontë in *Villette* (1853), and Wilkie Collins in *Armadale* (1864–1866). Jane Austen's father was the trustee of a West Indian estate (see Gibbon 1982).
12. For *Dombey and Son* in relation to imperialism, including considerations of gender, see Perera (1990).
13. Michie (2011) establishes the pattern in nineteenth-century plots of a man choosing between a poor woman and a wealthy woman, arguing that the figure of the heiress embodies anxieties about capitalism generally and the vulgarity of wealth specifically.
14. As his children grew into adulthood, Dickens tended to regard his sons as financial responsibilities and burdens. Lillian Nayder (2010), in her biography of Dickens's wife, Catherine, complicates the psychology of his behavior toward his sons. By making arrangements to send them to the colonies, "Dickens saw himself providing a necessary antidote to Catherine's influence" (281).
15. This grandmother lived in Liverpool, and Slater (2009) speculates that Dickens visited her there before leaving for America in 1842.
16. Rose's mother had been killed in a train accident in 1840.
17. In *Is He Popenjoy?*, Trollope satirized feminists, wondering whether women would soon "buy and sell in Capel Court, and have balances at their bankers" (quoted in Glendinning 1993, 452).
18. In *Women and Their Money*, Laurence et al. (2009) write: "With the greater safety of mortgages and loans on personal bonds, the development of the capital market and fall of the interest rate, landowners borrowed on security from land. So women's income derived from land ... was increasingly commuted into securities" (9). Mortgages in particular were attractive to women investors.

19. Charlotte Riddell (1874a) also has the railway company's purchase of land save the day in her story, *Fairy Water*.
20. In Trollope's story, "The Two Generals" (1863), set in Kentucky during the Civil War, the heroine is an heiress and an abolitionist Northern sympathizer; her fiancé and cousin is a general in the Confederate Army. The story considers northern and southern perspectives but ends with a clear denunciation of slavery, remarking of Americans: "May it not be that the beneficent power of Heaven, which they acknowledge as we do, is thus cleansing their land from the stain of slavery, to abolish which no human power seemed sufficient?" (401). For Trollope's views of American slavery, see also his *North America* (1862) and Claybaugh (2011).
21. For an overview of attitudes toward the City and descriptions of novels set in the City, see Michie (2009).
22. Jewish moneylenders also pursue Bertie Cecil in Ouida's popular novel, *Under Two Flags* (1867), forcing him to flee England for Algeria. Dickens personifies moneylenders in the (non-Jewish) Fascination Fledgby, in *Our Mutual Friend* and the Smallweed family in *Bleak House*. As a point of comparison, Trollope's George Vavasor borrows £200 for £40, or a rate of 20%.
23. As we will see, late century novels portray characters that struggle to repay creditors after bankruptcy (or ruin), including Riddell's *Mortomley's Estate* (1874b), Oliphant's *Sons and Daughters* (1890c), as well as those who refuse to do so in Oliphant's *Janet* (1890a). In *Dombey and Son* (1848), Dickens's narrator observes: "It was a world in which there was no other sort of bankruptcy whatever. ... There were no short-comings anywhere, in anything but money" (857). The residents of the Marshalsea in *Little Dorrit* (1855–1857) see "insolvency as the normal state of mankind, and the payment of debts as a disease that occasionally broke out" (73). Hunter (2011) argues that in Victorian novels, bankruptcy functions as a "rhetorical mechanism for promoting social and economic change" (138).
24. Michie (2011) intriguingly suggests "in pointing to historical figures that stand outside the text, his novels allow us to see how even our accounts of history are implicitly shaped by the logic of the fictional marriage plot" (109). For recent revisionist approaches to the marriage plot, see Schaffer (2016) and Hager (2010).
25. O'Gorman (2016) has challenged the standard interpretation of *The Way We Live Now* as hostile to capitalism.
26. Charlotte Riddell died in 1906, and by this time Gissing and James were the only authors considered in this book who were still writing, having inherited the legacy of their realist predecessors' representations of Victorian investment cultures. Citing the second Married Women's

Property Act, Delany (2002) argues: "It is probably no accident that money-marriage is a less popular motif in novels written after 1882 (also the year of Trollope's death). Novelists still engaged by the subject— notably George Gissing and Henry James—had to change their angle of approach" (38). Delany might well have added Riddell and Oliphant to this list.

REFERENCES

Alborn, Timothy. 2009. *Regulated lives: Life insurance and British Society, 1800–1914*. Toronto: University of Toronto Press.
Allen, Michael. 1988. *Charles Dickens' childhood*. New York: St. Martin's Press.
Armstrong, Tim. 2012. *The logic of slavery: Debt, technology, and pain in American literature*. New York: Cambridge University Press.
Austen, Jane. 1811. *Sense and sensibility*, ed. Claudia Johnson. New York: W. W. Norton, 2001.
———. 1814. *Mansfield Park*, ed. Claudia Johnson. New York: W. W. Norton, 1998.
———. 1818. *Persuasion*, ed. James Kinsley. Oxford: Oxford University Press, 2008.
Baucom, Ian. 2005. *Specters of the Atlantic: Finance capital, slavery and the philosophy of history*. Durham, NC: Duke University Press.
Brantlinger, Patrick. 1996. *Fictions of state: Culture and credit in Britain, 1694–1994*. Ithaca, NY: Cornell University Press.
Brontë, Charlotte. 1853. *Villette*, ed. Margaret Smith and Herbert Rosengarten. Oxford: Oxford University Press, 2008.
Carlton, William J. 1955. Dickens's insurance policies. *The Dickensian* 51: 133–137.
Çelikkol, Ayşe. 2011. *Romances of free trade: British literature, laissez-faire, and the global nineteenth century*. New York: Oxford University Press.
Claybaugh, Amanda. 2011. Trollope and America. In *The Cambridge companion to Anthony Trollope*, ed. Carolyn Dever and Lisa Niles, 210–223. Cambridge: Cambridge University Press.
Collins, Wilkie. 1864–1866. *Armadale*, ed. John Sutherland. London: Penguin, 1995.
Copeland, Edward. 1995. *Women writing about money: Women's fiction in England*. Cambridge: Cambridge University Press.
Craik, Dinah Maria Mulock. 1856. *John Halifax, gentleman*. Repr. Peterborough, ON: Broadview, 2005.
Delany, Paul. 2002. *Literature, money and the market*. New York: Palgrave Macmillan.

Dickens, Charles. 1838–1839. *Nicholas Nickleby*, ed. Paul Schlicke. Oxford: Oxford University Press, 2009.
———. 1842. *American notes for general circulation: And pictures from Italy*, ed. Patricia Ingham. New York: Penguin, 2000.
———. 1842–1844. *The life and adventures of Martin Chuzzlewit*, ed. Margaret Cardwell. Oxford: Oxford University Press, 2009.
———. 1846–1848. *Dombey and son*, ed. Alan Horsman. Oxford: Oxford University Press, 1984.
———. 1849–1850. *David Copperfield*, ed. Jeremy Tambling. London: Penguin, 2004.
———. 1852–1853. *Bleak house*, ed. Stephen Gill. Oxford: Oxford University Press, 2008.
———. 1855–1857. *Little Dorrit*, ed. Stephen Wall. London: Penguin, 2003.
———. 1860–1861. *Great expectations*, ed. Margaret Cardwell. Oxford: Oxford University Press, 2008.
———. 1864–1865. *Our mutual friend*, ed. Kathleen Tillotson. Oxford: Oxford World's Classics, 2009.
Eliot, George. 1864. Brother Jacob. In *The lifted veil and brother Jacob*, ed. Helen Small, 3–43. Oxford: Oxford University Press, 1999.
———. 1866. *Felix Holt: The radical*, ed. Fred. C. Thompson. New York: Oxford University Press, 1988.
———. 1871–1872. *Middlemarch*, ed. David Carroll. Oxford: Oxford University Press, 2008.
———. 1876. *Daniel Deronda*, ed. K.M. Newton and Graham Handley. Oxford: Oxford University Press, 2014.
Gaskell, Elizabeth. 1848. *Mary Barton: A tale in Manchester*, ed. Edgar Wright. Oxford: Oxford University Press, 1998.
———. 1853a. *Cranford*, ed. Elizabeth Porges Watson. Oxford: Oxford University Press, 2011.
———. 1853b. *Ruth*, ed. Nancy Henry. London: Everyman, 2001.
Gibbon, Frank. 1982. The Antiguan connection: Some new light on "Mansfield Park". *Cambridge Quarterly* 11 (2): 298–305.
Gissing, George. 1891. *New Grub Street*, ed. Steve Arata. Peterborough, ON: Broadview, 2008.
———. 1893. *The odd women*, ed. Arlene Young. Orchard Park, NY: Broadview, 1998.
———. 1894. *In the year of jubilee*. London: Hogarth Press, 1987.
———. 1897. *The Whirlpool*, ed. Gillian Tindall. London: Hogarth Press, 1984.
Glendinning, Victoria. 1993. *Anthony Trollope*. New York: Random House.

Hager, Kelly. 2010. *Dickens and the rise of divorce: The failed-marriage plot and the novel tradition.* Farnham: Ashgate.

Hunter, Leeann D. 2011. Communities built from ruins: Social economics in Victorian novels of bankruptcy. *Women's Studies Quarterly* 39 (3): 137–152.

James, Henry. 1881. *The Portrait of a lady*, ed. Roger Luckhurst. Oxford: Oxford University Press, 2009.

James, Simon J. 2003. *Unsettled accounts: Money and narrative in the novels of George Gissing.* London: Anthem Press.

Laurence, Anne, Josephine Maltby, and Janette Rutterford (eds.). 2009. *Women and their money 1700–1950: Essays on women and finance.* London: Routledge.

Martineau, Harriet. 1834. *Illustrations of political economy*, 9 vols. London: Charles Fox.

Michie, Elsie. 2011. *The vulgar question of money: Heiresses, materialism, and the novel of manners from Jane Austen to Henry James.* Baltimore: Johns Hopkins University Press.

Michie, Ranald. 2009. *Guilty money: The City of London in Victorian and Edwardian culture, 1815–1914.* London: Pickering & Chatto.

Morse, Deborah Denenholz. 1987. *Women in Trollope's Palliser novels.* Ann Arbor, MI: UMI Research Press.

———. 2013. *Reforming Trollope: Race, gender and Englishness in the novels of Anthony Trollope.* Burlington, VT: Ashgate.

Nardin, Jane. 1989. *He knew she was right: The independent woman in the novels of Anthony Trollope.* Carbondale: Southern Illinois University Press.

Nayder, Lillian. 2010. *The Other Dickens: A life of Catherine Hogarth.* Ithaca: Cornell University Press.

Newton, L.A., and P.L. Cotrell. 2009. Female investors in the first English and Welsh commercial joint-stock banks. In *Women and their money, 1700–1950: Essays on women and finance*, ed. Anne Laurence, Josephine Maltby, and Janette Rutterford, 115–132. New York: Routledge.

O'Gorman, Francis. 2016. Is Trollope's *The way we live now* (1875) about the "commercial profligacy of the age"? *Review of English Studies* 67 (281): 751–763. https://academic.oup.com/res/article-abstract/67/281/751/2451585. Accessed 5 Apr 2018.

Oliphant, Margaret. 1883. *Hester*, ed. Philip Davis and Brian Nellist. Oxford: Oxford University Press, 2009.

———. 1890a. *Janet.* London: Hurst and Blackett, n.d.

———. 1890b. *Kirsteen: The story of a Scotch family seventy years ago.* London: Everyman, 1984.

———. 1890c. *Sons and daughters.* Edinburgh: William Blackwood and Sons (The Margaret Oliphant Fiction Collection). http://www.oliphantfiction.com/x0200_single_title.php?titlecode=sondtr. Accessed 5 Apr 2018.

Ouida. 1867. *Under two flags: A story of the household and the desert*, ed. Natalie Schroeder. Kansas City: Valancourt Books, 2009.
Perera, Suvendrini. 1990. Wholesale, retail and for exportation: Empire and the family business in "Dombey and son". *Victorian Studies* 33 (4): 603–620.
Rappoport, Jill. 2016. Greed, generosity, and other problems with unmarried women's property. *Victorian Studies* 58 (4): 636–660.
Reed, John R. 1984. A friend to Mammon: Speculation in Victorian literature. *Victorian Studies* 27 (2): 179–202.
Riddell, Charlotte. 1874a. *Fairy water: A Christmas story*. London: Tinsley Brothers.
———. 1874b. *Mortomley's estate: A novel*. London: Tinsley Brothers.
Russell, Norman. 1986. *The novelist and Mammon: Literary response to the world of commerce in the nineteenth-century*. Oxford: Oxford University Press.
Rutterford, Janette, and Josephine Maltby. 2006. Frank must marry money: Men, women, and property in Trollope's novels. *Interfaces* 33 (2): 169–199.
Schaffer, Talia. 2016. *Romance's rival: Familiar marriage in Victorian fiction*. Oxford: Oxford University Press.
Slater, Michael. 2009. *Charles Dickens*. New Haven, CT: Yale University Press.
Smith, Grahame. 1968. *Dickens, money, and society*. Berkeley: University of California Press.
Trollope, Anthony. 1858. *The three clerks*, ed. Graham Handley. Oxford: Oxford University Press, 1990.
———. 1861–1862. *The struggles of Brown, Jones and Robinson*, ed. N. John Hall. New York: Carroll & Graf, 1993.
———. 1862. *North America*. London: Chapman & Hall.
———. 1863. The two generals. In *Anthony Trollope: The complete shorter fiction*, ed. Julian Thompson, 385–402. New York: Carroll & Graff, 1992.
———. 1864. *Miss Mackenzie*, ed. A.O.J. Cockshut. Oxford: Oxford University Press, 1992.
———. 1864–1865. *Can you forgive her?* ed. Dinah Birch. Oxford: Oxford University Press, 2012.
———. 1866–1867a. *The last chronicle of Barset*, ed. Sophie Gilmartin. Harmondsworth, UK: Penguin, 2002.
———. 1866–1867b. *Phineas Finn*, ed. Simon Dentith. Oxford: Oxford University Press, 2011.
———. 1872. *The Eustace diamonds*, ed. Helen Small. Oxford: Oxford University Press, 2011.
Trollope, Anthony. 1873–1874. *Phineas redux*, ed. John Bowen. Oxford: Oxford University Press, 2011.
———. 1875. *The way we live now*, ed. Francis O'Gorman. Oxford: Oxford University Press, 2016.

———. 1876. *The prime minister*, ed. Nicholas Shrimpton. Oxford: Oxford University Press, 2011.

———. 1883. *An autobiography*, ed. David Skilton. Harmondsworth: Penguin, 1996.

Trollope, Frances. 1832. *Domestic manners of the Americans*, ed. Elsie B. Michie. Oxford: Oxford University Press, 2014.

Vernon, John. 1984. *Money and fiction: Literary realism in the nineteenth and early twentieth centuries*. Ithaca, NY: Cornell University Press.

Wake, Jehanne. 2012. *Sisters of fortune: America's Caton sisters at home and abroad*. New York: Simon and Schuster.

Walsh, Susan. 1993. Bodies of capital: *Great Expectations* and the climacteric economy. *Victorian Studies* 37 (1): 73–98.

Wood, Claire. 2015. *Dickens and the business of death*. Cambridge: Cambridge University Press.

CHAPTER 4

Elizabeth Gaskell: Investment Cultures and Global Contexts

And don't forget the Kath. Docks dividend.
— Elizabeth Gaskell, J.A.V. Chapple and Arthur Pollard,
The Letters of Mrs. Gaskell

In January 1849, building on the success of her first novel, *Mary Barton* (1848), Elizabeth Gaskell invested £1500 in the St. Katharine Docks, the working docks next to the Tower Bridge and Tower of London. She wrote to Edward Holland, her cousin and financial advisor: "Your proposal about the Cath. Dock Shares seems to both my husband & me a very kind & advantageous one; & we gladly consent to having the £1500 so invested put into the general fund at its present value; and in the division to form part of the moiety which is to be invested for me— to be considered as an investment already made in my behalf in short. I don't know if I have expressed myself sufficiently clearly to shew you that I fully sanction what you propose, but I *do*" (Gaskell et al. 1997, 827). This letter makes clear that the investment in the St. Katharine Docks was to be designated as an investment for Gaskell's own use. Guided by Edward's advice, and investing in conjunction with her husband, she nonetheless emphasizes that the investment is made on her behalf. Despite insecurity about how she has expressed her business directions, she is clear about what is to be done with her money.

Thirteen years later, in 1862, she wrote to Edward to authorize a charitable donation, presumably to be made from her income on investments: "I am sure Mr. Gaskell will most gladly contribute the 5 percent requested to the distress around us, as desired by the Manchester, Sheffield, & Lincolnshire railway Cy and thank you for signing the letter all ready." She adds that she has "a great 'spite' at the Catherine Dock shares, which is not diminished by their diminishing dividend, but I quite agree with you that this is not the time for selling out" (Gaskell et al. 1997, 690). In agreeing with her financial advisor, she shows that she is actively involved in considering every step taken with her money. After providing a receipt for dividends from the St. Katherine Dock and Manchester, Sheffield & Lincolnshire Railway, a postscript requests: "Would you be so kind as to make the enclosed check payable to *me*? Elizabeth Cleghorn Gaskell."[1]

At this time, Gaskell was writing *Sylvia's Lovers* (1863), which is set in the context of the trading network between Greenland whaling and the Yorkshire town of Whitby during the Napoleonic wars. The St. Katharine Docks opened in 1828 and in fact was not profitable when Gaskell made her complaint about their dividends. In 1864, they were amalgamated with the London Docks, famous for importing exotic luxury commodities such as ivory, spices, and coffee. Nor did Gaskell "sell out" after the amalgamation. In August 1865, she wrote to Edward: "Thank you about Kath. Dock,—& thank yr father. There *may* be some good cause for the Shares going up—I missed annual report" (Gaskell et al. 1997, 770). From this letter, we see that she watched the company's fluctuating fortunes with anxious interest and also was in the habit of reading annual shareholder reports.

Gaskell continued to rely on the St. Katharine Docks dividends to the end of her life, especially when she got into financial difficulty after taking out a mortgage for half the price (£1200) of a second house, called The Lawn, in Holybourne, Hampshire, with money lent to her by the publisher George Smith in 1865 (Uglow 1993, 573). The house, purchased without the knowledge of her husband and intended as a surprise for him, would become a financial drain and source of stress while she was at work on *Wives and Daughters* (1864–1865), which Smith was serializing in the *Cornhill Magazine*. In the midst of this late trouble in August 1865, she wrote to Marianne, her daughter, who was helping her to furnish the house at great expense: "By the way are the Kath. Dock dividends due yet? I want them sadly; & *you must want some money I am afraid?*" At the end of the letter, she adds: "*And don't forget the Kath. Docks dividend*" (Gaskell et al. 1997, 936). The dependence of Gaskell and her daughters on the dividends from investments in publically traded companies illustrates the phenomenon I have been describing. Women with earned or inherited capital made informed decisions about how to invest that capital with the expectation of future payments that gave them greater freedom.

Examining such financial transactions and the social networks that supported them expands our understanding of Gaskell's life and fiction by showing the multiple ways in which she was connected to local, national, and global economies. She set her "condition of England," "social problem," or "industrial" novels *Mary Barton* and *North and South* (1854–1855), primarily in Manchester, where she lived from 1832 to the end of her life, and she recalled her childhood in Knutsford (Cheshire) via the rural communities that appear in *Cranford* (1853a), *Ruth* (1853b), "Cousin Phillis" (1863), and *Wives and Daughters*. As Gaskell was always aware, seemingly isolated provincial settings were touched by larger economic events such as banking crises, railroad construction, colonial expansion, and foreign wars.[2] The places she wrote about were also haunted by a troubling economic past, for example, by the history of Britain's slave trade, the Napoleonic wars, West Indian and American slavery, and the American Civil War.[3] Gaskell's personal investments were limited to English companies,[4] and her travel was confined to the British Isles and the European continent, yet her fiction, beginning with *Mary Barton*, is informed by both local and global investment cultures. Transportation networks of steamships and trains, as well as communication networks such as the mail system, supported these cultures.[5]

Critics and biographers have drawn on Gaskell's fiction to extract or deduce facts concerning her early life, about which she rarely spoke as an adult.[6] In terms of her relationship to place, Manchester and Knutsford have attracted the most critical attention, along with considerations of her visits to Wales for sections of *Ruth* and her holiday in Whitby, from which she drew to create Monkshaven in *Sylvia's Lovers*. Clare Pettitt (2012) has written about places Gaskell did not visit, especially America, which her reading of American literature and correspondence with American friends enabled her to imagine.[7] Pettitt argues that Gaskell's novella "Lois the Witch" (1859) investigates "the pain of being estranged from the local by a sudden transition into an incomprehensible global world" (600), and that this perspective became available to Gaskell in her late work because of new communication technology and her correspondence with Charles Eliot Norton and other Americans. The experience that Pettitt identifies as being "estranged from the local by a sudden transition into an incomprehensible global world" (600) is present in Gaskell's fiction as early as *Mary Barton*. Gaskell's sense of England's connectedness to the world at large was influenced by new technologies of communication and transportation, as well as her awareness of economic networks through her family's business dealings and her own investments. The estrangement that Lois feels in the American colonies is foreshadowed in scenes from earlier Gaskell novels, which point particularly to these networks, cultures, and histories.

Gaskell was indirectly connected to global trade and finance through the business dealings of her Holland relatives. As part of a family that traveled and traded around the world, she had a pragmatic, material sense of herself and her world as connected by commercial networks.[8] Particularly important are the letters from her sailor brother and her scattered cousins, who were conducting trade around the globe. This context is reflected in her fiction through her sailor characters like Will Wilson, Frederick Hale, and Charley Kinraid, but also in the cotton and textile trades, the whaling trade, and the local commerce of the fictional Monkshaven (based on Whitby).[9] Furthermore, Gaskell's recognition of the centrality of local and global investments to the lives of both single and married women appears in the financial plots that characterize her fiction and which are pervasive throughout her work. Her awareness of the financial underwriting of commercial ventures through the middle-class practice of investing in docks, shipping, canals, mines, railways, insurance companies and local banks appears directly and indirectly in her fiction, for example, in Thurstan Benson's insurance shares in *Ruth*, Miss Matty's joint-stock bank shares in *Cranford*, and the shipping investments of the Quaker Foster brothers in *Sylvia's Lovers*.

Critics differ in their interpretation of Gaskell's critique of capitalism, going back to Raymond Williams, who in 1958 expressed disappointment in the ending of *Mary Barton*, in which the characters abandon the industrial ills of England by relocating to Canada. Gordon Bigelow (2003) argues that in her later fiction, Gaskell begins "working toward a broader critique of the philosophies and forces of the capitalist market" (144). Patsy Stoneman (2007) writes that her main aim was to "evoke sympathy for the victims of the market" (135). Jo Pryke (2005) contends that *North and South* presents industry as "inspiring and invigorating" but "tainted with greed and selfishness" (555–6) (see also Gallagher 1985; Miller 1994). Josephine M. Guy (1996) has shown that money was as important to the melodramatic events in the second half of *Mary Barton* as to the more realistic plot of the first half. She contends that the cost of living is an "obsessive preoccupation" with Gaskell, leading to "a compulsive description of financial transactions" (579). She argues that, unlike Dickens, Gaskell insists that "moral individuals can still be *economic* agents" (581). In contrast, Felicia Bonaparte (1992) argues that Gaskell is "not interested in the economic ends of things" (141), and that she is more zealous than most Victorian novelists in showing that "money is corrupting" (142). The various interpretations of how Gaskell's novels position themselves with respect to capitalism are not surprising, given that her personal views, and the ideologies reflected in her fiction, are not consistent or coherently formulated.

Gaskell's critique of capitalism is as much covert as it is explicit. Her female characters, including Miss Matty, Faith Benson, and Margaret Hale, deny any knowledge of business—a trait they share with Oliphant's heroines. Gaskell professed ignorance of political economy in the preface to *Mary Barton*, a defensive, somewhat disingenuous claim born of her desire to be politically diplomatic and broadly sympathetic in the novel. Rather than revealing how much she knew about political economy and economic history, she developed a strategy of indirection and allusiveness, which has been recognized by some critics addressing particular novels, but has not been seen as an overall feature of her writing. For example, Alan Shelston (2011) argues that she disguises biographical connections to specific places by fictionalizing them (xii). Bonaparte (1992) claims that Gaskell's work contains a "subversive subtext" that "conceals the secrets that explain her fiction," in which she "encodes the secrets that explain her life" (8). Hilary Schor (1992) argues that *Cranford* "comments on its own status as text, but it does so by indirection, a narrative viewpoint it names as peculiarly female" (84). Elaine Freedgood (2006) sees Gaskell's references to calico as a coded reference to the politics of cotton production, arguing that the very material things that comprise her realism "unravel domestic ideology when we see their history" (64). Stephanie Markovits (2013) observes that while overt signs of the Crimean War may be absent from *North and South*, "reading it in a Crimean context demonstrates how the conflict pervaded the atmosphere of the day—and how novelists shaped their work within this medium" (86). Gaskell never rails against dollars and shares, as Dickens does in *Martin Chuzzlewit* (1842–1844) and *Our Mutual Friend* (1864–1865); instead, she employs a covert method of introducing topics such as the history of the slave trade, American slavery, the Opium Wars, and colonialism generally. Overall, this strategy of allusion means that Gaskell's fiction is even more complex, especially in her critiques of capitalism, than has been previously recognized. Characters look but do not see the history of things such as architecture, art, landscapes, trains, ships, and docks, but those histories are embedded in her representations.

Gaskell's Economic Life

Throughout this book, I argue for the importance of authors' lives—specifically their economic lives within the nineteenth-century cultures of investment—to their writing. Our ability to consider such contexts depends on the traditions of individual life stories that we have inherited. While economic lives are never separate from romantic, filial, political, religious, or literary lives, it is useful to reframe our narratives, especially of women's lives, which are usually told along the lines of a romance or marriage plot.

The writing of Gaskell's life was largely a twentieth-century phenomenon as biographers uncovered evidence that was unknown to her contemporaries. Gaskell died in 1865, but a biographical study, by Mrs. Ellis Chadwick, was not produced until 1910. Despite—or perhaps because of—her own struggles to write *The Life of Charlotte Brontë* (1857), Gaskell did not wish her own biography to be written, and unlike Trollope and Oliphant, she did not write an autobiography. Like Dickens and Eliot, she resented the attempts of biographers to tell her life story. She did not have the equivalent of a John Forster or a Johnny Cross—authorized biographers who could establish a master narrative—and she forestalled future biographers by seemingly explicit instructions to her daughters to destroy her letters.

Chadwick (1910), her first biographer, was able to interview those who knew Gaskell. She sets out to "trace her scenes and characters to their originals" (vii). Conscious of the objections to finding real-life originals for fictional scenes and characters (on the part of critics and Gaskell herself), Chadwick nonetheless insists that "Mrs. Gaskell's novels are founded on fact," and, except for *Sylvia's Lovers*, "those facts came out of her own life, or the lives of her relatives and friends" (8), adding that "few of the originals have been discovered by anyone outside of her family circle" (26). Until the first volume of the Gaskell letters was published in 1966, it was assumed that no full life could be written. The first work to be called a biography was Winifred Gérin's (1976) *Elizabeth Gaskell: A Biography*. The most comprehensive biography is still Jenny Uglow's (1993) *Elizabeth Gaskell: A Habit of Stories*. John Chapple's (1997) *Elizabeth Gaskell: The Early Years* documents her life before she became a novelist. Chapple describes his biography as "a composite history of the circles in which she was brought up, a rich tapestry of friendship and association in which, for example, relations like her uncle Samuel Holland were automatically sustained in a great network of support when economic individualism failed" (5). He adds that his book is "an attempt to recreate the interrelated lives of her family and friends, and the life she lived amongst them up to the time when she dwindled into the wife of the Reverend William Gaskell of Manchester" (5). Chapple resists the inclination to map a traditional marriage plot, so familiar to the Victorian novel, onto the life of his subject, and in this respect, the whole perspective of his unusually close-focused biography is refreshingly original, emphasizing communities, religion, and economics in the life of Elizabeth Stevenson before she "dwindled" into Mrs. Gaskell. Chapple, however, declines to speculate on the relationship between Elizabeth Stevenson's early life and Mrs. Gaskell's fiction. His work, therefore, provides an invaluable resource for critics seeking material for biographically informed literary criticism of that fiction.

In contrast, Uglow's (1993) biography quotes liberally from the fiction, offering literary critical readings in light of biographical information. She notes that clues about Gaskell's early life can be taken from patterns in her fiction—of motherless daughters (as she was) and young men gone to sea (as her brother had). Without reducing characters to originals as Chadwick did in 1910, yet searching for something more specific than patterns, we can see that Gaskell drew heavily on personal experience. She integrates references to real events, people, places, and objects in a manner that is sometimes coded or disguised, so that we should not entirely dismiss Chadwick's claim that "few of the originals have been discovered by anyone outside of her family circle" (26). Gaskell's reasons for this veiled approach to representing the real world in her fiction may have to do with her critical attitude toward historical events generally, or even her criticism of individual people, including members of her family, which she may have wished to disguise.

In addition to what we know about Gaskell's integration of her life into her fiction, I explore the specifically commercial and financial cultures to which her extended family exposed her. These cultures of trade, commerce, investment, and speculation shaped her perspective on England's connections to the wider world. These business cultures contributed to her sense of networks and to the presence of global commodities, peoples, and economies in the local lives of her characters. Her Holland aunts, uncles, and cousins established the context in which she was raised and gave her a familiarity with the ways in which trade, finance, religion, politics, and domestic life were interrelated. Her observations of their lives and her own participation in an investment culture after she began earning money as an author all contributed to a naturalized, though often critical, view of capitalism and to her sense of the economic realities of relationships between her characters.

THE EARLY YEARS

When Elizabeth Stevenson, née Holland, died in 1811, her thirteen-month-old daughter, also named Elizabeth, was sent to live with Hannah Lumb, her mother's sister, in Knutsford in Cheshire. Hannah Holland Lumb had left her allegedly insane husband, Samuel Lumb, in Wakefield shortly after her marriage and before the birth of their only child, Mary Anne (also spelled Marianne). Hannah returned from Wakefield to her family in Knutsford, where she first raised the physically disabled Marianne and then several years later her motherless niece Elizabeth, with the aid of other Holland relatives.

From the time she left her husband, Hannah lived on the dividends she received from £2000 invested in 4% annuities at her marriage (since reduced to 3.5%); she also inherited money at various times from other relatives. For example, Samuel Holland, her father, included her and her siblings in his will, and he also provided a £120 annuity for his widow (Chapple 1997, 100). Hannah's £2000 investment, however, in the days before the Married Women's Property Acts later in the century, belonged to her husband. In his 1804 will, Samuel Lumb left that money to the bigamous second wife and second family he began after Hannah left him, so that inheritance could only be realized after that wife's death (97). All of this made Hannah's economic situation as a woman who was legally married but separated, and then as a widow, extremely complicated, but she still managed to live a comfortable, respectable middle-class life within her Unitarian community.

Marianne was thought to have inherited money from her father when he died in 1805 (Uglow 1993, 12). Marianne died in 1812 at the age of 21, shortly after baby Elizabeth came to live in Knutsford. Until Chapple (1997) corrected the record, it was thought that Marianne died, ironically, when she was on her way to sign a will in Halifax that would have left her money to her mother and Elizabeth, and that her death prevented her money from coming to them (Uglow 1993, 13). Chapple discovered that Marianne did not inherit money from her father; she did, however, receive a legacy from her mother's older sister, Ann Holland, and also from her father's aunt, also named Hannah Lumb (Chapple 1997, 119). Her will was finally proven to leave all of this money to her mother (119–20). These updated facts demonstrate the importance of female economic lives and the degree to which women provided for each other through both inheritances and investments. Chapple observes that Hannah "was certainly in a financial position to take advantage of the growing independence of middle-class women" (101) and that unmarried women in the Knutsford community were often provided for by spinster aunts and childless relations (119). Writing of Hannah's life during the time she was caring for Elizabeth, Uglow (1993) remarks: "Widows and spinsters had to be self-reliant and in the unstable 1820s they were particularly vulnerable" (24).

When Hannah Lumb died in 1837, she left Elizabeth (by then married to William Gaskell and with two daughters to support) an annuity of £80, with half of Hannah's remaining property to come after the death of Abigail, a younger sister, for whom she also provided. When Abigail died in 1847, Elizabeth received the full bequest, which was a welcome addition to her income before she began her career as an author (260). In 1848, Elizabeth published *Mary Barton*; she received a modest £100 for the manuscript and another £100 for the second edition (183). Elizabeth's inheritance and income from writing, together with a legacy received in 1848 by William from Ann Gaskell, a childless paternal aunt, gave the couple enough excess capital to begin investing in the stock market, as will be discussed below (Gaskell et al. 1996, 49).

This brief account of Gaskell's early economic life demonstrates that she was part of a community that involved single women leaving bequests to female and male family members. This female economy, as well as the dependence of women on income from their investments, is reflected in Gaskell's fiction. In *Cranford*, for example, the unmarried Deborah Jenkins leaves her shares in the Town and County Bank to Matty, her sister (also single). At the end of *North and South*, Margaret Hale receives an inheritance from Mr. Bell, her family friend and godfather. This enigmatic character was a bachelor living a retired life as a Fellow at a college in Oxford and quietly buying real estate in Manchester, leaving his fortune to an unsuspecting Margaret. Here, Gaskell exploits the familiar fairy-tale inheritance plot, which was so hard for even realist novelists to resist (e.g., Dickens in *Oliver Twist* [1838], Craik in *John Halifax* [1856], Riddell in *Austin Friars* [1870], and Eliot in *Felix Holt* [1866]). This makes Margaret the landlord of the manufacturer John Thornton and empowers her to offer him money to save his failing factory, leading him in turn to propose marriage in the final scene of the novel. As we will see, commercial and financial transactions on a local, national, or global scale provide both historical context and plot developments in *Mary Barton, Ruth, Cranford, North and South*, "Cousin Phillis," *Sylvia's Lovers*, and *Wives and Daughters*. This economic dimension of Gaskell's fiction is linked to her early experience and intimate exposure to mid-Victorian finance capital.

Hannah Lumb and the Holland family were part of a commercial and cultural network of Unitarians (and former Unitarians) throughout England, Wales, and Scotland. Hannah, whose progressive, antislavery sentiments are documented in Chapple (1997), was in touch with liberal and literate circles that included Liverpool, Newcastle, London, Edinburgh, and Wales (129, 144). Swinton Holland, one of Hannah's brothers, worked in banking and finance in London and was a partner in the firm of Barring Brothers; Edward Thurstan, his son (1805–1875), inherited his father's estate, Dumbleton Hall, in the Vale of Evesham, in Worcestershire, where he became a gentleman farmer and agricultural reformer. Edward provided the Gaskells with investment advice, suggesting they purchase shares in the St. Katharine Docks in 1849. Edward, whose infancy is recorded in his mother's diary, which was published in *Private Voices* (Gaskell et al. 1996), would eventually marry the Gaskells' daughter against his father's wishes.

Hannah's brother Samuel Holland was in business in Liverpool. He was heavily involved in developing the Welsh slate mining trade in the early years of the nineteenth century with his company, Humble, Holland, and Worthington. He also had full or part ownership of forty vessels, thus holding a virtual monopoly on the Penryn quarry's transport between 1801 and 1810 (Elis-Williams 1988, 31). He also imported flint from the south of England, had it ground in Wales, and then exported it to Liverpool, where it was used in the Herculaneum pottery works. Following the War of 1812, Samuel's financial fortunes turned downward, and by 1818 he was nearly bankrupt (Uglow 1993, 620). His son, also named Samuel Holland, took over his slate mine in Plas yn Penryn, in Wales, where his entire family would eventually relocate from Liverpool.

Chapple (1997) writes that the elder Samuel Holland was "a by-word in the family for his speculations" (381). His more successful brother, Swinton, was forced to support him after Samuel senior came close to bankruptcy in 1818, at one time providing £7000 (180). For his part, Swinton took particular care to provide for his own wife and children, on whom he settled £28,000 in the Consols and three life insurance policies (180). Edward later supported his uncle Samuel but put stipulations on the £200 yearly allowance he was given, forbidding him to "speculate" (292).[10]

From June to September 1831, shortly before her marriage, Elizabeth joined her aunt Hannah in Woodside, across the River Mersey from Liverpool, where Hannah had taken a house to be near her relatives. During this stay in Woodside, as recounted in letters, Elizabeth visited Liverpool for sightseeing, shopping, and social events. These months in Woodside and Liverpool were formative, and she recalled her knowledge of the city in *Mary Barton*, in which she describes the city as the location of the assizes (circuit courts), describing its bustling port activity: The "glorious river" is a "glittering highway" and a "mighty mart" (341).

In Newcastle, with its thriving shipping industry and trade in coal, she stayed for two successive winters (1829–1830 and 1830–1831) with William Turner, a Unitarian minister and family friend. She befriended Ann, William's younger daughter. His older daughter, Mary Robberds, was by now married and living in Manchester. Chapple (1997) remarks: "The stay with Ann Turner could not have failed to bring home to her the position of single women" (382). Uglow (1993) notes that in Newcastle, Gaskell also knew a Miss Losh, who ran her father's ironworks, another model of women's involvement in business (61; see also Chapple 1997, 283).

Chadwick, in her search for originals, suggested that Rev. Turner influenced the portrait of Thurston Benson in *Ruth*, a notion further advanced by Uglow (1993, 58). Chadwick (1910) argued that Benson's education of Ruth recalls Turner's education of Elizabeth during her stays with him (148). Chadwick also saw Turner's unmarried daughter, Ann, as a model for Faith, Benson's unmarried sister. Chadwick is the source for the claim that Gaskell spoke of *Ruth* as her Newcastle story "because in it is woven so much of her own life when staying with Mr. Turner and his daughter" (152). She even claims that Sally, the Bensons' servant, is based on Turner's servant. Neither of the two towns represented in *Ruth*, Fordham and Eccleston, can be identified as Newcastle. Shelston (1996) argues that the town of Macclesfield provided the basis for Eccleston. More significantly, he observes Gaskell's unwillingness to be expressly biographical and shows that her method was to mask people and places through fiction. Each of the four settings of *Ruth*—Fordham, North Wales, Eccleston, and Abermouth—"can be associated fairly readily with places that Mrs. Gaskell knew well … In each case, however, she superimposes a kind of fictional disguise, as if reluctant to allow the direct association to be made" (xi–xii). Shelston's reading of Gaskell's method of disguising biographical connections is relevant to her fictional methods in other works, specifically in *Mary Barton*, in which she uses the architectural history of Liverpool's Exchange building and the Nelson Monument to incorporate the subject of slave trading, which she may have been reluctant to address directly.

It is not necessary to be as literal as Chadwick in finding originals for fictional characters to see that Turner and Benson share the trait of generosity to a fault and both fall into financial difficulty as a result.[11] Ann Turner was understandably interested in her family's money, specifically their investments. She wrote to Mary about that money, commenting that their brother William "rather preferred the idea of buying into the funds though the interest would be less because when once done any small sum might be added without additional expense" (Chapple 1997, 379). Chapple writes: "A firm grip upon the money that would enable a single woman to live in a ladylike manner is even more evident in a letter Ann wrote to her father" (379). This letter concerns some New York stock left to Ann by her mother, which her father had sold without her knowledge. Her anxiety in the letter is all for her father, and yet she reminds him: "I know indeed that in her ever kind thoughts for me as unmarried: my Mother once said something of considering this Stock as mine" (380). As a result of the letter, Turner gives Ann three years interest on £1200: "She rather than William Turner junior, now held the investment, and there was to be payment up of the arrears" (Harbottle 1997, 157).

Ann Turner is yet another example within Gaskell's young experience of a woman taking part in discussions about financial investments, specifically shares left to her by her mother. Ann's case is also an example of international investing by early Victorian women; the shares inherited from Ann's mother were in New York companies, the value of which Ann debates with her siblings in comparison with holdings in the funds, often attractive to women investors at this time (see Chapter 1). Gaskell's own investments at midcentury were in English companies, but the St. Katharine Docks especially had a global impact.

The young Elizabeth Stevenson also spent time in London with her father, William Stevenson, who remarried and started a second family after his first wife's death. Although William had published writings on political economy in *Blackwood's Magazine* in 1824, he was not a successful manager of his own money, and he fell into personal financial difficulty. At one point, he was forced to raid his second wife's shares in the Bank of England to cover debts. While it is unclear how much of William Stevenson's debt was the fault of his second wife, Catherine Thomson, and how much was due to his own mismanagement, it is clear that he drew on her investments (part of her dowry), with her consent, and sold £800 worth of stock in 1827 (Uglow 1993, 53). The social life of her father and stepmother in Chelsea may have informed the London sections of *North and South*, as well the portrayal of Molly Gibson's stepmother in *Wives and Daughters*.

All of these experiences in Gaskell's early life show that she was not sheltered or isolated from international trade and commerce. It seems that in the Holland and Stevenson families, and those of their extended connections like the Turners, women were often more sensible about the management of money than the men. Hannah Lumb and her sisters, as well as friends like Ann Turner, took an active interest in the sources of their income. Men, including Elizabeth's father, her uncle Samuel, and her friend William Turner, mismanaged money and suffered financial difficulty. Their examples may have been translated into fiction in the suicide of John Thornton's father due to failed speculations in *North and South* and in the character of Thurstan Benson, the generous but financially naïve minister who is defrauded in *Ruth*. Additionally, the commercial and financial contexts in which Gaskell was raised exposed her to the wide-ranging global networks of trade and investing, even before she moved to Manchester and saw firsthand the effects of economic downturns on factory workers and owners.

Critics Pettitt (2012) and Freedgood (2006) have made important contributions to our understanding of Gaskell's writing in transatlantic contexts. Lee (2010) has shown the influence of American slave narratives on Gaskell's novella *My Lady Ludlow*, her short story "The Grey Woman," and novel *North and South*. Lee argues that *North and South* reflects a transatlantic and global network (97) and that the story of Frederick Hale's mutiny reveals a "transnational environment of trade" (99). She notes that Frederick is the novel's "most direct link between the cotton-producing American South and the cotton-manufacturing British North" (99) and is the "vessel through which Gaskell imports cultural and political debates about industrialization, slavery, and international commerce" (101). He acts as the mediator between "cotton-picking slave and cotton-weaving worker" (103). Focusing on Frederick's narrative, Lee concludes that in drawing on the formal conventions of the slave narrative, Gaskell reimagines England as a global community of mutual dependence (105).

While I agree with Lee's reading of *North and South*, I take issue with the notion that Gaskell's earlier work was strictly provincial and unconnected to the global communities identified in *North and South* (98). *Mary Barton*, *Cranford*, and *Ruth* are as conscious of their place within global networks as is *North and South*. Lee is unconcerned with aspects of Gaskell's life beyond her correspondence with American and other friends relating to slavery. She does not, for example, mention the importance of Gaskell's brother's experiences as a sailor and his travel to India, Burma, and elsewhere to Frederick's narrative, material covered extensively in Chapple's work. As I have been arguing, Gaskell's personal experience placed her within these global networks from an early age, and global contexts are central to her fiction from the start. In Knutsford, London, Liverpool, and Newcastle, Gaskell witnessed the importance of managing money to women and also the reach of trade to America, China, India, and elsewhere. These impressions informed her fiction in conjunction with her later, better known experiences of the Manchester manufacturing economy.

I next focus specifically on *Mary Barton* and *Ruth*, with references to investing women in *Cranford* and the financial plots in *North and South* and *Sylvia's Lovers*. To further develop my reading of Gaskell's novels within the context of her economic life, I introduce forms of financial investment and the role of women investors, including Gaskell herself, into ongoing discussions of her writing within nineteenth-century global networks.

MARY BARTON AND LIVERPOOL

Critics—starting with its publication through to the present—who write about *Mary Barton* as a social problem novel tend to focus on the industrial economy and social structure of Manchester, where most, but not all, of the novel's action is set during the period 1834–1841 (Easson 1993, 429). The representation of working-class life in Manchester is certainly vivid, and the cotton trade on which the textile factories depended was indeed global, encompassing cotton grown in the USA, Egypt, and India, turned into textiles in the north of England, and then exported to the south of England and the rest of the world. The fluctuations of trade that depress the Manchester textile industry in the novel were dependent on international markets. But less attention has been paid to the last section of *Mary Barton* (Chapters 26–34), which is set in Liverpool, where Mary travels by an early railroad line from Manchester to find Will Wilson, the sailor who can provide an alibi and save her lover, Jem Wilson, from conviction for a murder he did not commit. In addition to taking her journey by rail, Mary takes a boat when trying to catch Will's ship, which is awaiting high tide so that it can pass through the sandbanks of the river and head out to sea. Having successfully notified Will that he is needed on land, she later testifies at Jem's trial at the Liverpool Assizes and afterward spends days in a delirium in the home of a local seaman and his wife. These Liverpool scenes are simultaneously realistic and surreal, reflecting Mary's emotional state. For example, in the courtroom, she hallucinates, imagining that everyone there is "all at sea" (385). Having recovered from her illness, she takes a last look at the River Mersey, which seems made of "glittering, heaving, dazzling metal" (412).

Just as the Manchester part of the novel provides observations of the contemporary city, so the Liverpool section comments on that city's distinctive characteristics in the late 1830s and early 1840s. The Liverpool and Manchester Railway had opened in 1830. The Assizes had moved to Liverpool from Lancaster in 1835. A Liverpool Stock Exchange was formed in 1836, although it was not part of the great London Stock Exchange, which is featured in the novel.

These Liverpool scenes are essential to our understanding of Gaskell's perspective on global trade and finance. It is surprising how little attention has been given to the Liverpool sequence and how inadequate some of the historical notes are in critical editions that attempt to explain the specific references to Liverpool landmarks in the novel.[12]

The impassioned public debates on West Indian slavery taking place when the young Elizabeth Stevenson visited Liverpool in 1831 were long past, but the history of slave trading was not forgotten: Liverpool remained associated with slavery in ways that were woven into its very architecture as memorials to both its traders and the abolitionists.[13] Just as Gaskell had to tread lightly when portraying the indifference of Manchester factory owners to the suffering of their workers, so she too had to be careful if she wanted to include the legacy of slave trading and slave owning in her realistic and contemporary representation of Liverpool. Her approach was to integrate these topics in a distinctly coded way. The traces of slavery to which she alludes in *Mary Barton* reveal her thinking about historical memory, urban spaces, and the human tendency to see without comprehending. She does this first through her choice of a name for the ship on which Will Wilson is scheduled to sail from Liverpool.

Will's ship is named the *John Cropper*. Gaskell introduces the name, dwells on and repeats it without providing any clue to its resonance outside of the narrative. From Mary's perspective, it is just a name, signifying nothing. She struggles to remember the name of the ship, placing particular importance on the name: "All at once, when she had ceased to try and remember, the name of Will's ship flashed across her mind. The *John Cropper*. He had named it, she had been sure, all along. He had named it in his conversation with her that last, that fatal Thursday evening. She repeated it over and over again, through a nervous dread of again forgetting it. The *John Cropper*" (247–8).

Who was John Cropper? The name resonates within the context of abolitionist activity in Liverpool. James Cropper (1773–1840) was a Quaker abolitionist who engaged in public debate with John Gladstone on the subject of West Indian slavery. His son—John Cropper (1797–1876)—attended the Anti-Slavery Society Convention of 1840 in London and appears in an 1841 painting of the convention by Benjamin Robert Haydon that is now in National Portrait Gallery in London.

The Cropper family was well connected. John married Margaret Macaulay, the sister of Thomas Babington Macaulay, in 1833. Susanna, Matthew Arnold's sister, married John Wakefield Cropper, John Cropper's son. Harriet Beecher Stowe stayed with John Cropper in Liverpool at Dingle Bank, the family home, when she arrived and when she departed on her first trip to England in 1853. She mentions her visit in *Sunny Memories of Foreign Lands* (Stowe 1854).[14] In naming the ship *John Cropper*, Gaskell was subtly but explicitly gesturing toward the complex history of Liverpool as a slave-trading port and later as a locale of abolitionist activism on the part of businessmen such as William Roscoe and James Cropper and John Cropper. Furthermore, the scene in which Mary stops to look at the Liverpool Exchange building and the Nelson Monument shows Gaskell demanding that both the heroine and the reader look at the symbolism in the architecture and public art of Liverpool and recall its history.

The scene involving the Exchange is remarkable in many ways, not least for what is left out. Mary is rushing to reach Will Wilson's ship to catch him in time to provide testimony that may save Jem, when her guide, Charley, stops her abruptly in a passage that bears repeating: "'If you'll only look up this street you may see the back windows of our Exchange. Such a building as yon is! With 'natomy[15] hiding under a blanket, and Lord, Admiral Nelson, and a few more people in the middle of the court! No! come here,' as Mary, in her eagerness, was looking at any window that caught her eye first, to satisfy the boy. 'Here then, now, you can see it. You can say, now you've seen the Liverpool Exchange'" (340).

Mary can only see the back windows of the Exchange, probably not the front of the building or the monument that Charlie describes. While it remains unclear whether Mary, focused on her mission, ever does distinguish the Exchange from other buildings, Gaskell slows the narrative particularly to highlight the existence of the Exchange and the monument and allows Mary to pass by without any recognition of its significance beyond Charley's civic pride. In narrative terms, it is strange, unresolved, and forgettable to Mary and the reader. But Charley explains that the minute it took her to see the Exchange will make no difference to her quest. It is important to him and to Gaskell that we all stop and look.[16]

By calling attention to the Liverpool Exchange building and the Nelson Monument in front of it, Gaskell forces readers to look at the material evidence of an economy that once thrived as a result of slave trading and—consistent with her perspective on the plight of the Manchester workers—adds a pointed if coded moral dimension to the history of Liverpool particularly and global economies generally. The fact that the allusions are oblique and indirect means that readers may have missed them, and it raises questions about what exactly Gaskell intended to suggest about the mixed moral nature of global trade and finance.

Biographies that touch on Gaskell's Liverpool connections mostly avoid the question of slavery. As we have seen, Gaskell had strong familial ties to Liverpool, and the Hollands had been involved in trade and banking in the city since the mid-eighteenth century. The family of Samuel Holland resided for a time in the Liverpool neighborhood of Toxteth Park before moving to Woodside and then to Wales. When Elizabeth Stevenson visited the family in Woodside from June through September 1831, she wrote to Harriet Carr, her friend, whose father worked for a branch of the Bank of England in Newcastle: "We have had several pleasant sails lately up and down this beautiful river; and I do like Liverpool and the Mersey and the accent & the people very much" (Gaskell et al. 2003, 8). Her personal experiences in Liverpool allowed her to describe its docks and city center in *Mary Barton*. Furthermore, she was close to her husband's sister, Elizabeth, who married Gaskell's own cousin, Charles Holland, and they resided in Liverpool. Gaskell sent her daughter Meta to a school in Liverpool run by Rachel Martineau, the sister of Harriet and James Martineau (Uglow 1993, 270).

In the same letter to Harriet Carr, Elizabeth also wrote: "Oh! How tired I am of the Reform Bill—and my Aunt, and most of my cousins, are quite anti-reformers and abuse Lord Brougham and think him superficial" (Gaskell et al. 2003, 11). This is a somewhat surprising observation considering how Chapple (1997) emphasizes Hannah Lumb's progressive politics and antislavery sentiments. Lord Brougham was a champion of the Reform Act, passed in 1832, as well as the Slavery Abolition Act of 1833, according to which slavery was gradually phased out in the West Indies, with the planters being compensated for their losses. Whatever they may have thought about Lord Brougham personally, Gaskell's Unitarian relations might be expected to hold pro-Reform sentiments.[17] There is neither evidence to suggest that Samuel Holland was directly involved in the slave trade before 1807 or in West Indian slavery before 1833, nor does he seem to have been involved in either the first or the second wave of the abolition movement with fellow Unitarians William Roscoe and William Rathbone III (both discussed below) or the Quakers James and John Cropper.[18]

What is clear from Gaskell's cryptic comment (apart from her being tired of hearing about the Reform Bill) is that she perceived her relatives to be conservative and silently objected to their views. It is worth asking whether her critique of her relatives' politics may have worked its way into her fiction. Specifically, the inclusion of the Liverpool Exchange building and Nelson Monument in *Mary Barton* points to the city's history of slave trading, including the opposition of prominent merchants like John Gladstone to the abolition of slavery in the British colonies up to 1833. Albeit in coded form, it constitutes a critique of the hypocrisy of dissenting businessmen that she would develop in the figure of Mr. Bradshaw in *Ruth*.[19]

The Liverpool Exchange building mentioned in *Mary Barton* has a complicated history. Designed by James Wyatt, it was built from 1803 to 1808 and replaced the old Exchange building, which was built in 1754. The old Exchange then became known as the Town Hall. The original building had combined the civic functions of a town hall with the commercial functions of a commodities exchange and had been constructed with funds provided by prominent Liverpool citizens, many of whom were active in the slave trade. It was adorned with a frieze celebrating global trade with carvings of African and American Indian heads. After a fire gutted the inside of this building in 1795, the interior was renovated but the external façade was retained and expanded. In 1795, abolition of the slave trade was only a few years away, but slavery continued in the West Indian colonies. The new Exchange, as pointed out by Charley, the guide, was constructed opposite the old Exchange (now Town Hall), forming a quadrangle in an area known as Exchange Flags. The Nelson Monument that Charley describes was the first public sculpture in Liverpool. It was unveiled in 1813 and placed prominently between the new Exchange and the Town Hall in the Exchange Flags area.

This unusual monument attracted the attention of many visitors to Liverpool. The sculpture features a naked Admiral Nelson astride a cannon, with a protective guardian angel above and a dead sailor at his feet, a mourning *Britannia*, and a skeleton (or Death) emerging from beneath a flag. Nelson's missing arm is draped with a flag. Charley mentions Nelson and 'natomy, that is, the skeleton, and makes vague reference to "a few more people in the middle of the court." These people include four figures of men in shackles encircling Nelson. William Roscoe (1753–1831), an antislavery campaigner by 1807 (he died while Gaskell was visiting Liverpool), donated money to construct the monument and oversaw its commission to Mathew Cotes Wyatt (son of James Wyatt). Roscoe worshipped at the same Unitarian chapel in Liverpool as Gaskell's relatives. Mary Robberds, her friend, recalls meeting "the celebrated William Roscoe" as well as other abolitionists James Currie and John Yates (Gaskell et al. 1996, 112). Charley stops to point out the statue but refers to the shackled figures simply as "a few more people." It is no surprise that Nelson and a skeleton would impress a young boy more than anguished figures in chains, even though these figures are closest to eye level. It is worth thinking about this example of public art, as well as the Exchange's massive architectural testament to local and global commerce, which Gaskell's characters both see and do not see.

Earlier in the novel, John Barton, Mary's father, had been unable to interpret the art and architecture of London while he was participating in the failed attempt of workers to present the Chartist petition to Parliament. He offers his perspective in Swiftian terms: "They're sadly puzzled how to build houses ... in London ... they've stuck great ugly pillars out before 'em. And some on 'em ... had gotten stone men and women as wanted clothes stuck on 'em" (146). Like her father's account of London, Mary in Liverpool experiences a cognitive dissonance: She looks at any window and cannot care whether or not it is the Exchange. She seems not listen to Charley's childish description of the monument, which recalls her father's uneducated description of London architecture. He marvels that London buildings had "stone men and women as wanted clothes stuck on 'em," while Charley refers to the figure of Death as "'natomy under a blanket." These episodes provide a touch of humor to a relatively humorless novel, but they also raise questions about how knowledge affects seeing. How did Gaskell interpret the buildings and monument in Exchange Flags and how would she expect readers to understand what she had interrupted her narrative specifically to show them?

We can be sure that Gaskell saw these sights on her visits to Liverpool, but she may also have read about their history in contemporary guidebooks that made it clear that Liverpool's pride in the Exchange was high. For example, a popular guidebook, in its 10th edition by 1831, *The Stranger in Liverpool* (Kaye 1831), observes that the Exchange is "one of the principal ornaments of the town, and reflects so much honor on its spirit and liberality" (100). Kaye observes that it is probably "among the finest specimens of Grecian architecture ever created in this country, and, perhaps the most splendid structure ever raised, in modern times, for purposes purely commercial" (103). Calling it a "sumptuous erection" (230), Kaye laments that its situation is "so obscure as nearly to escape all observation, except on the very spot where it is erected" (231). This information—that the building could "escape all observation"—provides some insight into Mary's inability to understand what Charley has asked her to see. Thomas Baines (1852) records the response to the new Exchange by quoting a contemporaneous newspaper account (from the *Billinge's Liverpool Advertiser* on April 11, 1808) of the building's opening: "the beauty and grandeur of the whole structure are now taken in by the eye, and seen with the fullest effect." When it opened, the paper commented: "No place in the world affords so elegant and commodious a situation as this for all the purposes of a public exchange" (536). As for the monument, Kaye describes it in detail, referring to "four emblematic figures of heroic size, in the character of captives, or vanquished enemies" (Kaye 1831, 231).

The interpretation of the chained figures as French prisoners of war is standard, but there is an intriguing alternative to interpreting these naked figures in attitudes of physical and mental pain and anguish, a strange way to represent the nation's treatment of prisoners (four thousand of whom were in Liverpool jails at the time of the monument's construction). Art historian Alison Yarrington (1989) has argued that given Roscoe's role and the timing of the monument's commission in 1807, the chained figures, taken to be French prisoners, also represent African slavery. Roscoe the abolitionist joined slave owners such as John Gladstone in the effort to memorialize Nelson. The presence of slave owners on a commissioning committee meant that any overt, negative reference to slavery was impossible. Yarrington shows convincingly that the figures are "both an allusion to the enchainment of prisoners of war ... and an image of the suffering produced by slavery" (25). But inevitably, "the meaning of the inclusion of the chained slave/prisoners in the Liverpool monument is veiled" (26). Such chained figures appear only in the Liverpool monument and were not a convention of the Nelson monuments that were erected across Britain and the British Empire. She writes: "It is obvious that had there been an unambiguous, open whiggite reference to the slave trade, committee members such as John Gladstone and John Bolton would have objected. However, such references were veiled, concentrating upon the human anguish engendered by slavery, which were open to many shades of interpretation depending on the political sympathies of the viewer" (26). Her explanation helps us to understand how this monument could be so variously interpreted from the time of its erection to the present. Despite its powerful implications, historians of Liverpool have not adopted Yarrington's reading. For example, Terry Cavanagh (1997) includes a detailed description of the monument that does not mention slavery, even though he cites Yarrington's article for other facts. He says simply that the shackled prisoners in "poses of anguish and resignation ... represent Nelson's four great Victories" (52). He is also defensive about the Town Hall frieze: "The themes treated in the frieze are those one would expect from the Exchange Building (the Town Hall's original designation) of a major English sea port, the wealth of which depended upon colonial power and maritime commerce" (74). It is significant, however, that both Herman Melville and Margaret Oliphant interpreted the shackled figures as slaves. Furthermore, in Victorian representations of the statue, the figures come to resemble slaves with African features that are not evident in the statue itself.[20]

Freedgood (2006) argues that the things represented in fiction have historically contextualized meanings that may be lost over the generations. It is her project to recover those meanings for modern readers. In her analysis of *Mary Barton*, she mentions Liverpool briefly as "a city that became a city because of the slave trade and a city that in turn enabled Manchester's rise and growth because of its port and shipping capabilities" (64). She notes that while recovering from illness in Liverpool, Mary is wrapped in checked bed curtains (64), and she teases out the implications of checked curtains and calico in the novel, expanding Gaskell's detailed realism and recovering the history of those material things for our twenty-first-century readings: "Checked cotton was thus a key player in the globalization of textile production and distribution and a critical symbol of the competitiveness of British products in the world marketplace" (64). Taking the argument further, she concludes: "A novel like *Mary Barton* holds in strange (or estranged) trust the extraordinary violence that attended the reorganization of markets in the global economy of the Victorian period" (80).[21]

While Freedgood focuses on commodities or everyday things that are metonymic rather than symbolic, her methodology is useful for thinking about the Liverpool Exchange building and the Nelson Monument— things that may have one meaning at the time of their construction— national glory, civic pride, and commercial supremacy—and another set of meanings for Victorians, and yet a different set of meanings for readers today. The significance of Yarrington's argument is that the symbolism of the statue was veiled, even in 1813. Some meanings can only be recovered (or constructed) today with a retrospective excavation of material histories, such as Yarrington has performed for the Nelson

Monument. Freedgood explains: "I am trying to recuperate meanings that may have attended things for earlier readers; but if such meanings are in fact new, they are also 'already there' in some sense: I could not retrieve them otherwise" (68). Whereas Freedgood has identified textiles as metonyms for the "extraordinary violence that attended the reorganization of markets in the global economy," Yarrington links public monuments glorifying national triumphs to the violence that attended those victories.

My reading of the appearance of the Liverpool Exchange and the Nelson Monument in *Mary Barton* is complicated by the fact that civic buildings and monuments are already laden with intentional symbolic meaning, though that meaning is neither named by the narrator nor recognized by those who see them. To the Liverpudlian boy Charley, the Exchange self-evidently symbolizes Liverpool's power as a center of commerce, and the monument symbolizes British military victory, even if he is not equipped to interpret the figure of the skeleton as Death, but rather just calls it 'natomy. Through his inarticulate pride and insistence that Mary look at these symbolic structures, Gaskell gestures to an interrelated history of violence, commerce, and finance in which her relatives are implicated.

Gaskell chose not to address this history directly, but she could reasonably expect her readers to recognize the overt symbolism of the civic structures of Liverpool—objects passed every day by residents but perhaps not always seen or interpreted. The moment it takes Mary to look at the Exchange is a dramatic pause in the action, and in that moment Gaskell stages a scene of not recognizing what is there to be seen. She explores this psychological state in other works, mainly through the relationships between characters: think of Ruth's dreamy obliviousness to her seducer's intentions, the Holmans' inability to see their daughter Phillis's unhappiness following her abandonment by her lover, or even the failure of mill owners to see the suffering of their workers until it is pointed out to them.

What is the symbolism of the Liverpool Exchange and how is it encoded? In *North and South*, Gaskell (1854–1855) writes that, "men jostled each other aside in the Mart and in the Exchange, as they did in life in the deep selfishness of competition" (418). The "Mart" (where commerce is transacted) and the "Exchange" (where financial deals are transacted) are references to specific places in the Milton (Manchester) of *North and South*, as well as to centers of capitalist competition.

In mid-nineteenth-century England, Exchange buildings were emerging in the industrial towns of Manchester, Bristol, and Liverpool, in addition to London. Gaskell sounds more cynical about this "deep selfishness" in *North and South* than she had in *Mary Barton*, where the tone describing the "mighty Mart" is one of wonder, similar to Charley's awe at the Exchange. Furthermore, Charley points out the Exchange as part of the competition between Liverpool and Manchester, reflecting the implicit rivalry between the two nineteenth-century commercial cities (linked by road, canal, and railway). In *North and South*, Gaskell makes the economic interdependency explicit by showing that the failure of commercial houses, which marks the novel's main crisis, began in Liverpool and moved to Manchester. In *Mary Barton*, however, all of this is implied, and both Mary's and Charley's perspectives are more naïve than Gaskell would expect those of her readers to be.[22]

The original Liverpool Exchange was particularly associated with the slave trade. Ian Baucom (2005) argues that Liverpool is the capital of the long twentieth century in terms of world systems theorist Giovanni Arrighi. Baucom invokes Walter Benjamin's theory of history to argue that the eighteenth-century legacy of slavery was present in the forms—textual or architectural—that endured and persisted through the nineteenth century and into the twentieth. He elaborates the role of the initial Liverpool Exchange building as a "boast of Liverpool's new status as London's financial double" (52), pointing specifically to the "set of African heads, circling that Exchange":

> The slave portraits decorating and surrounding the Exchange speak mutely but eloquently to the origins of this exorbitantly plentiful regime of accumulation. They suggest something else also. Bolstered to the walls of the city's Exchange, casting their frozen glance over a port city that had greater traffic with the "Guinea" coast than it did with the interior of England, these slave heads imply that over the course of the eighteenth century Liverpool was less the island's city than the ocean's, that the economy over which it presided and whose circuits of exchange it regulated was less national than transmarine, that the cycle of accumulation for which its Exchange was an orchestrating pace-of-flows was less British than Atlantic. Any mid- or late-century citizen who failed to appreciate this knowledge had only to examine the façade of the city's Exchange to be reminded. (52)

The eighteenth-century Exchange would only accumulate and store more levels of historical meaning when observed by Victorians.

The African heads on the now Town Hall are so tiny as to be almost invisible from the ground, yet they still wield symbolic power. Anthropologist Jacqueline Nassy Brown (2005) recorded an interview in the 1990s with a black resident of Liverpool: "There's a lot more to be uncovered about Liverpool. You know, like, the Town Hall with all the Black faces. People don't even look for that. Liverpool's got a lot hidden" (166).

Baucom does not carry his analysis of the Exchange through the building's transformations in the nineteenth century—its designation as the Town Hall and the construction of the new Exchange as featured in *Mary Barton*. Given her knowledge of Liverpool, Gaskell was no doubt aware of the building's history and the symbolism of the monument erected between the old and new Exchanges. The characters in *Mary Barton* need only look at the modern Exchange building and the Nelson Monument to be reminded that Liverpool had long been a global port. Gaskell's narrator describes the "glorious river, along which white-sailed ships were gliding with the ensigns of all nations ... telling of the distant lands, spicy or frozen, that sent to that might mart for their comforts and their luxuries" (341).

This description clearly comes from her own observations and perhaps awe at the River Mersey, on which her cousins established trade routes from Wales to Liverpool, and on which she traversed between Woodside and Liverpool with great pleasure. Through her surviving letters from 1831, we know that regattas, commercial ships, recalling those on which her brother sailed as well as steamers in the port strongly impressed her. The river is glorious and the mart is romantic, telling of exotic foreign lands. She does not identify this romantic sea life as led by Will Wilson, the merchant sailor, and her own brother with "the deep selfishness of competition" of capitalism or the history of slavery. Lee (2010) notes that "among the responsibilities of the British navy after the abolition of the slave trade in 1807 was to keep slave ships out of British waters" (101). The captain of Frederick's ship has a history of combating slavers (Gaskell 1854–1855, 107). After all, Gaskell herself invested in docks that facilitated the trade in commodities from cotton, pottery, and mahogany to sugar, tea, coffee, and tobacco as well as the more exotic ivory, tortoise shells, and peacock feathers. In *Mary Barton*, the silently looming Exchange embodies civic pride, the "regime of accumulation" (in Baucom's terms) and the selfishness of competition. The Nelson Monument represents at once war, peace, victory, death, and slavery.

The history of the port, the river itself, and the Exchange building(s) were reminders of the slave trade and the trade in West Indian sugar and North American cotton that depended on slave labor. No one in business in Liverpool before the abolition of the slave trade could keep his or her hands clean of slavery until its total abolition. Wake (1997) notes that even a Quaker abolitionist like William Rathbone III, who refused to supply slave ships, had inherited a fortune and business built on the African slave trade: "It was difficult to remain in business without supplying materials for the African trade" (16). Leading abolitionist William Roscoe, a friend of Rathbone and of Gaskell's uncle Samuel Holland, had business dealings with those involved in the late eighteenth-century slave trade, which would have been impossible for him to avoid (Williams 1897, 155). In fact, Roscoe entered a banking partnership with Thomas Leland, a successful slave trader (160). Gaskell's husband's Unitarian family had made sailcloth in Warrington, no doubt for some slaving ships. In Gaskell's lifetime, slavery was far from an issue of the past. Her cousins' antireform views in 1831 may have included mixed feelings about abolition. Though unequivocally antislavery, the Gaskells had mixed feelings about American abolitionists and declined to support their activities in England.[23]

Gaskell was conscious of capitalism's dubious morality at the same time she felt pride in the advances of modern capitalism. Writing about Gaskell's civic pride in Manchester, Angus Easson (1985) argues: "The power of cotton, the power of wealth and of the individual who possessed it, the political power for good and evil, the new and exciting possibilities, literally the glamour, of Manchester, were to be particularly developed by Gaskell in *North and South*" (705).[24] The enigmatic appearance of the Liverpool Exchange building and Nelson Monument in *Mary Barton* introduces the often-invisible living presence of the past in urban landscapes, a way of signaling social change encoded in the very architecture of the Exchange building and monument sculpture. In so doing, Gaskell draws attention to the circuits of global exchange that produced British prosperity during the Victorian period, inviting, if not directly embracing, a moral critique of capitalism's complicity in slavery.

Gaskell was among many Victorian novelists who employed the rhetorical technique of ekphrasis, a literary description of a visual work of art. As will be discussed in Chapter 7, Margaret Oliphant also represents the Nelson Monument in her novels. And Charlotte Riddell (n.d.)[25] guides her readers through the streets of the City of London by having the narrator of *George Geith* remark: "What story is there that the old walls will not repeat at our bidding? From St Paul's down, each has its own monuments—its own records—its own separate portion of the narrative of ancient days" (3). History encoded in architecture is a theme that Riddell developed in all of her City of London novels. In *Mitre Court* (1885), the house at 5 Botolph Lane (a real house) contains a room with panels painted by the artist Robert Robinson (1635–1706) depicting exotic scenes from around the world. A character observes that there must be a story behind the paintings, "but what that story might be no one can tell" (1:44). Similarly in *Dombey and Son*, Dickens (1848) describes the East India House as "teeming with suggestions of precious stuffs and stones, tigers, elephants, howdahs, hookahs, umbrellas, palm trees, palanquins, and gorgeous princes of a brown complexion" (36). Like these heads of elephants, the Indians and Africans circling the Liverpool Town Hall are remnants from a colonial, slave-trading past teeming on the inside and outside of city buildings, which could be puzzling when encountered by Victorians, but Victorian novelists used these surviving works of art in their fiction as a way of encoding the past into the present.

Gaskell invokes the past of the places where she sets her novels as embodied in the architecture, for example, at the beginning of *The Life of Charlotte Brontë* (1857) and *Sylvia's Lovers* (1863). In the opening chapter of *Ruth* (1853b), she describes "an assize-town in one of the eastern counties" as it was a hundred years ago (1). She proceeds to introduce her thoughts on the relationship between place, social customs, and the formation of character: "The picturesqueness of those ancient streets has departed now," her narrator declares (2). The portrait is one of decline, with ancient families fleeing the influx of commercial people. "So the grand old houses stood empty awhile; and then speculators ventured to purchase, and to turn the deserted mansions into many smaller dwellings, fitted for professional men" (4). The poor orphan seamstress Ruth works in one of these mansions converted into a workplace for the production of dresses for the wealthier classes. Forced to work all night sewing gowns for the Hunt Ball, Ruth looks longingly out of the window at the "mean-looking houses" that signify a decline from "grandeur to squalor," and reflects nostalgically on her own past, "dreaming of the days that were gone" (6). Gaskell carefully parallels the degradation of the town with the downward-class spiral of her heroine, setting her up for the fall to come. Furthermore, Gaskell uses ekphrasis to emphasize the loss of past architectural splendor and personal happiness as Ruth pathetically looks at the painted panels of flowers on the walls of what has become her prison. The narrator remarks: "Surely Monnoyer, or whoever the dead-and-gone artist might be, would have been gratified to know the pleasure his handiwork, even in its wane, had power to give to the heavy heart of a young girl" (8).[26] Here, Gaskell establishes a pattern that Riddell would later adopt of using architectural and artistic remnants to mark socioeconomic changes and create a context of place within which her stories unfold.

WOMEN INVESTORS IN *RUTH*

Global as well as local contexts are important in *Ruth*, Gaskell's second novel. Traveling by coach from Wales to England after having been abandoned by her lover, Ruth Hilton meets a woman who boasts that her sons are "soldiers and sailors, all of them—here, there, and everywhere" (Gaskell 1853b, 111). One is in America, one in Gibraltar, and one is "in China, making tea" (112).[27] Ruth's encounters with the outside world are rare, and this episode situates her private drama in the context of overseas emigration, military actions, and trade in the 1830s and early 1840s. "Making tea" is a euphemism for the business of producing and exporting tea, an industry with implications that the mother chooses not to see. Like Charley looking at the Liverpool Exchange, the mother expresses only pride when talking to a stranger. But we hear in her frivolous comments a description of the mid-nineteenth-century economy and career options for middle-class sons. The theme will become central in this novel about a single mother raising a son.[28] The scene also recalls Gaskell's brother and all the other sailors in her novels. How to raise a son is a major question posed in *Ruth*, in the case both of Ruth's son Leonard, who eventually chooses a medical rather than a business career, and Richard, Mr. Bradshaw's son, who is in training to join his father's business, which, though deliberately vague, combines manufacturing and financial services, a point essential to the novel's financial plot.[29]

Like Gaskell's other novels, *Ruth* (1853b) incorporates money and finance to expand the more focused domestic plot. Several of the minor female characters are investors, including Sally, the Bensons' servant, and Mrs. Bradshaw. The novel also highlights and implicitly criticizes the assumption of male characters that women know nothing about finance.

4 ELIZABETH GASKELL: INVESTMENT CULTURES AND GLOBAL CONTEXTS 113

Richard Bradshaw comments to Jemima, his sister: "Women can't understand the share-market, and such things. Don't think I've forgotten the awful blunders you made when you tried to read the state of the money-market aloud to my father that night when he had lost his spectacles" (276). Following this schooling of his sister, Bradsahw proceeds to "borrow" money from her, and his dismissal of his sister's knowledge while at the same time taking money from her betrays his spoiled and corrupt character. At this point in the plot, the pattern son, whom we know has been deceiving his father about many aspects of his life, may already have forged the documents by which he defrauds Minister Thurstan Benson, a poor clergyman who can least afford the financial blow and whom Bradshaw knows is unlikely to prosecute him. The appearance of the ungrateful and criminal son in *Ruth* foreshadows Oliphant's *Hester* (1883) in which the ungrateful Edward Vernon betrays and defrauds his aunt Catherine, who had welcomed him into the family banking business.

The third volume of *Ruth* focuses on financial matters more than the earlier two volumes, a structure that reverses the order of Eliot's (1860) plot in *The Mill on the Floss*, in which the financial plot dominates the early books and all but disappears later.[30] Particularly prominent are the investments of Benson and his sister, Faith, as details about money concerns become directly relevant. Put under financial pressure by Ruth's loss of her position as governess to Mr. Bradshaw's daughters at £40 per year, Benson must support himself, Faith, Ruth, and her son, Leonard, on his £1000 per year. He also loses a £20 pew subscription when Bradshaw leaves his congregation after learning that Ruth is an unmarried mother rather than a widow. Bradshaw pays his pew rent, but Benson returns it in one of the many instances of refusing gifts in the novel.

At this point of crisis, Sally, the household servant, withdraws her savings from the local bank, insisting that this money was saved from an unwanted salary raise the Bensons gave her eighteen years earlier and which she returns to them with interest. Mirroring the plot of Miss Matty's lost income from a bank failure in *Cranford* (which Gaskell was writing simultaneously with *Ruth*), Sally and Benson discuss the withdrawal of her forty-two pounds, seven shillings, and two pence (Gaskell 1853b, 317). "Banks is not always safe," observes Sally, to which Benson replies, "Still, you know, Banks allow interest." Sally retorts: "D'yer suppose I don't know all about interest, and compound interest too, by this time?" She then reasserts her claim that the money belongs to him (318). While Sally proceeds to frame her will (which she cannot read) and hang it on the wall opposite her bed, the narrator assures us that Benson would only keep the money "as a deposit until he could find a safe investment befitting so small a sum" (318).[31] It is a comic scene at the expense of the uneducated but loyal servant, yet it contributes to the several plot strands involving money and investments. The unmarried, genteel Miss Matty and the unmarried working-class Sally are patronized, but both *Ruth* and *Cranford* show how crucial a single woman's money was to her life, a fact that formed part of Gaskell's consciousness from her early life among single women in Knutsford.

Benson is an investor of his own money as well as Sally's. In the accounting of the Bensons' household income, the narrator tells us, "Mr. and Miss Benson had about thirty or forty pounds coming in annually from a sum which, in happier days, Mr. Bradshaw had invested in Canal shares for them" (308). Benson relies on the professional Bradshaw to invest his money in a relationship of trust. Canal shares would be a typical, safe investment for women and clergymen in the first half of the nineteenth century (see Taylor 2006). While the canal shares are not mentioned again, the plot turns on Bradshaw's illicit sale of Benson's life insurance company shares, displaying Gaskell's particular interest in, and knowledge about, how investments worked, reflecting her own recent investments at the time she wrote the novel.

A technicality of investing turns the plot, again displaying Gaskell's knowledge of investing in shares and the practice of life insurance companies offering bonuses to their investors (see Alborn 2009). Bradshaw's partner, Mr. Farquhar, offers Benson his used copies of the *Times*. In the newspaper, Benson reads a report that the Star Life Assurance Company has declared a bonus on its shares. He wonders why he has not received his bonus, which would have been sent to Bradshaw's office.[32] Farquhar's inquiries to the insurance company lead to the discovery that Benson's shares "had been sold and transferred about a twelvemonth ago, which sufficiently accounted for the circumstance that no notification of the bonus had been sent to him" (330). Bradshaw assumes dismissively that the "unbusiness-like forgetfulness" of the Dissenting minister is to blame: "The idea of forgetting that he has sold his shares, and applying for the bonus, when it seems he had transferred them only a year ago!" (330). Bradshaw's description of Benson might refer to the Rev. William Turner, Gaskell's friend, when remarking: "He is just the man to muddle away his money in indiscriminate charity, and then to wonder what has become of it" (331). Further investigation, including Bradshaw's searching of his son's desk at the firm, reveals that Richard has forged a document selling the shares. Richard cashed in on the sale, even issuing Benson a half-yearly dividend to cover up the deed.[33]

Interestingly, it is also implied that Richard may have illicitly sold the shares of a widow, Mrs. Cranmer. Bradshaw complains about executing Mr. Cranmer's will, indulging in stereotypes about women who meddle in the management of their investments: "I wish old Cranmer would have made any other man his executor. She, too, is always coming with some unreasonable request or other" (332). Such details about matters of women and investment, like this and Richard's assumption of Jemima's ignorance, suggest Gaskell's preoccupation with the subject of women investors while writing *Ruth* and *Cranford*. These scenes reflect common myths about women investors that are carefully inserted and not qualified, so we do not really know whether Jemima could understand shares or whether Mrs. Cranmer's requests were unreasonable because these are the biased views of male characters, who are represented as being particularly sexist.[34]

The revelation of Richard's forgery leads his father to disown him and to urge Benson to prosecute the crime, which the sympathetic minister declines to do. Bradshaw's harsh reaction to the transgression of his son, consistent with his reaction to the revelation of Ruth's sin, creates turmoil in his house.[35] Bradshaw's downtrodden and usually submissive wife visits Benson to beg for her son, revealing details about her own fortune: "I have got some money somewhere—some money my father settled on me, sir; I don't know how much, but I think it's more than two thousand pounds, and you shall have it all. If I can't give it you now, I'll make a will, sir. Only be merciful with poor Dick—don't go and prosecute him now" (340). These details add the dimension of the married woman, who has inherited property but, having deferred to her husband in financial matters, does not know the value of what she owns, a marked contrast to the unmarried Sally's exact knowledge of the money she possesses. Significantly, what both women wish to do with their money is sacrifice it for the sake of a man.

Farquhar, now married to Jemima, Bradshaw's daughter, as well as being Bradshaw's partner in the firm, resolves to speak with the manager of the Star Life Assurance company, named Dennison, a "Scotchman, and a man of sense and feeling" (343). Dennison confirms that Benson signed the certificates, but the signature was forged. Following Richard's injury and recovery from the overturning of the Dover coach on his way home from the continent, Farquhar manages to find him a job in Glasgow.[36] These efforts to save Richard by finding a place for him abroad foreshadow the rallying of respectable businessmen to resolve the problems created by the profligate Austin Friars in Riddell's novel of that name (discussed in Chapter 6), as well as the banishment of Felix Carbury to Germany in Trollope's *The Way We Live Now* (1875) and the absconding of John Vernon and Edward Vernon to the continent after their financial malfeasances in Oliphant's *Hester* (1883).

The financial narrative of *Ruth*, running parallel to other late developments in the novel, including a typhus epidemic, a military victory that revives manufacturing in Eccleston, and an election that brings Ruth's seducer Mr. Bellingham/Donne back to town, is part of the novel's larger conception of global contexts for domestic lives and suggests that we consider those earlier scenes in light of global trade and finance (Henry 2001; Inglis 2015).

The emphasis on life insurance shares in *Ruth* echoes Dickens's life insurance plot in *Martin Chuzzlewit*. Gaskell's awareness of insurance as a business is also evident in *Mary Barton* (1848) when Carson's mill burns down. John Barton observes cynically: "And much Carsons will care, for they're well insured, and the machines are a' th' oud-fashioned kind. See if they don't think it a fine thing for themselves. They'll not thank them as tries to put it out" (54). He is right on this score, as the narrator remarks after the fire: "They were well insured; the machinery lacked the improvements of late years, and worked but poorly in comparison with that which might now be procured" (63). Fire insurance provides a means for the factory owners to improve their equipment, reflecting their lack of concern about the risks to the workers in the fire itself or the layoffs that result while the factory is being refitted.[37]

Critics Ian Baucom (2005), Tim Armstrong (2012), and Eric Wertheimer (2006) have explored the relationship of marine insurance and life insurance with slavery. Armstrong (2012) argues that slavery "occupies a middle position in the progress from insurance on goods to insurance on persons, providing a way of thinking about the value of a life" (16). Wertheimer (2006) discusses the poetry of Phillis Wheatley, identifying a poetic and commercial link that is "inferred from the economy of ship underwriting" and reading her work in light of "the commodification of life and labor that is directly suggested by the conditions of slave economies." Wertheimer notes, "Indeed, for Wheatley especially, slave economies *were* shipping economies" (67). As I argued in Chapter 3, nineteenth-century novels that thematically associate life insurance and slavery, such as *Martin Chuzzlewit* (Dickens 1842–1843) and *Miss Mackenzie* (Trollope 1864), make this connection and offer a continuum of commodified lives, even if the eighteenth-century traces of the origin of insurance and its direct connections with the slave trade have been effaced by time. Gaskell too seems to appreciate the class implications of the insurance market, as Paul Fyfe (2015) has shown. Her recognition that commercial and financial prosperity is dependent on morally dubious institutions and practices such as insurance, slavery, and war complicates her understanding of global economies.

Near the end of *Ruth* (1853b), an offstage British military victory is tied to the local economy. There is great rejoicing in the industrial town of Eccleston because, with this "national triumph of arms, it was supposed that a new market for the staple manufacture of the place would be opened" and revive trade which "had for a year or two been languishing" (354). Gaskell's narrator does not name this military triumph, but from internal evidence we can determine that it is based on the first Opium War with China (1839–1842). The instigation for this war was precisely the languishing trade to which she alludes. Mr. Bradshaw in *Ruth*, like Thornton in *North and South*, presents the case for free trade.

The local is always affected by the global in Gaskell's work, from *Mary Barton* through to her novella "Cousin Phillis" (1863), in which the construction of a branch railway slows because "trade was in a languid state, and money dear in the market" (295). In *Ruth*, trade languishes and in "Cousin Phillis" it is languid. These examples suggest that Gaskell had a mixed attitude toward the legacy of capitalism as symbolized from a Liverpool boy's civic pride in an Exchange building constructed with money from the slave trade to a town's celebration of victory over China that forced the importation of opium on an unwilling government. All wars take their toll, bringing suffering and death but also economic revival. From Nelson's victories to the Opium War to the American Civil War, when Gaskell considers military conflict, she links it to trade and the British economy (see Henry 2001).[38]

As we have seen, Gaskell's Unitarian family members created a network of business connections that made international trade and finance part of her reality throughout her life. Aspects of the global economy appear directly and indirectly in most of her fiction. Her practical experience of economic cycles and global interdependencies (of the Manchester dependence on cotton from the southern American states, for example), rather than theoretical knowledge of political economy, complicated her attitudes toward global politics, especially the American Civil War. It is clear, however, that she did understand free-trade debates and represented them in the arguments of John Thornton and Mr. Bradshaw.

I suggest that Gaskell was fully aware of these morally problematic dimensions of global trade and domestic commerce, but, rather than comment directly, she chose to gesture toward such issues indirectly. Her experiences showed her that few forms of commerce were completely clean, whether they were touched by wars or implicated in slavery. Yet she shied away from taking explicit political positions in her fiction. Gaskell's perspective was never of the telescopic sort for which Dickens and Trollope specifically criticized women in *Bleak House* and *Miss Mackenzie*, respectively. Rather, she saw the local effects of the global economy, and she concentrated her fiction on the local without ever forgetting the global.

LADY INVESTORS IN *CRANFORD*

In Gaskell's *Cranford* (1853a), Miss Deborah Jenkins, guardian of gentility and Johnsonian high culture, is also an independent investor. She made her own decision, against the advice of her advisor (the father of the narrator, Mary Smith), to purchase shares in the Town and County Bank, a joint-stock bank in the town of Drumble (usually thought to be based on Manchester). According to her sister Miss Matty, Deborah was invited to attend shareholder meetings to vote for a director of the company and bought a new hat for the occasion, but she was prevented from attending by a cold. These are the shares that Miss Matty inherits. She too is invited to attend a shareholder meeting: "a very civil invitation, signed Edwin Wilson, asking me to attend an important meeting of the shareholders of the Town and County Bank, to be held in Drumble, on the Thursday the twenty-first. I am sure, it is very attentive of them to remember me" (119–20). Unlike her sister, however, she declines to go, fearing she would be "quite in the way" (120).[39] Mary Smith, the narrator, avows that she does not know much about business, suggesting that she (like the readers) is ignorant of the specifics of her father's business dealings. In a letter, paraphrased by Mary, Mr. Smith asks his daughter whether Miss Matty still retained her shares in the Town and County Bank, "as there were very unpleasant reports about it; though nothing more than he had always foreseen, and had prophesied to Miss Jenkyns years ago, when she would invest their little property in it"—against his advice (128).

This information raises several questions about the plausibility of the plot and suggests an inconsistency in Gaskell's specificity as to monetary sums and her vagueness about finance. If Mr. Smith has acted as the Jenkyns sisters' financial advisor, and they both derived the majority of their income from these shares, why would he need to ask Mary whether Miss Matty still retained them? He would have known the details of Deborah's will, and it seems unlikely that Miss Matty would have sold shares and reinvested in something else without his knowledge. We are not told why Deborah insisted on investing in this bank against his advice. Neither are we told what exactly has come to pass to endanger the bank, nor how Mr. Smith could possibly have prophesied the bank's failure so far into the future. By introducing ominous information about the impending failure of the bank through a letter from Mr. Smith, Gaskell emphasizes both Mary's and Miss Matty's lack of financial knowledge. What should we make of the sensible Deborah's going against the advice of the family friend and advisor on such an important matter? The investment seems to have been a good one for many years, paying an 8% return and supporting, albeit modestly, two genteel ladies and enabling their independence. In this respect, Deborah was a successful investor. Miss Matty tells Mary that Deborah "was quite the woman of business, and always judged for herself; and here, you see, they have paid eight per cent, all these years" (173). While the specifics are vague, it seems possible that Deborah was not wrong to invest the money as she did.

The action of the plot is propelled by a financial crisis in which the bank stops payment, and poor Miss Matty's ruin is one of the central dramatic episodes of *Cranford*. There are other unanswered questions about the circumstances. The failure of the Town and County Bank seems to be an isolated incident, as only those in Cranford who held its notes are affected. It is not a general sweep of failures leading to an economic downturn. We are left with the impression that Deborah's stubbornness many years before in independently investing her money rather than taking the male advice led to Miss Matty's ruin and her coming down in the world, but that place was sustained by Deborah's initial investment; this perspective is that of Mr. Smith filtered through

Mary, who claims to know nothing about business. When Miss Matty analyzes her account books, she determines that the loss will cost her one hundred and forty-nine pounds, thirteen shillings, and four pence a year, leaving her only thirteen pounds per year, which is truly impoverished (126). The man whose five-pound note Miss Matty exchanges for gold sovereigns was not a shareholder but merely a depositor in the bank. Actual shareholders in the Town and County Bank, it seems, were rare in Cranford, and we do not know why Deborah insisted on investing her fortune with this bank or what it was that made Mr. Smith so suspicious of it. It is perhaps simply due to Mary's limited perspective as the narrator that we do not know why Mr. Smith was able to foresee a bad outcome for the Town and Country Bank. Although Gaskell is specific about sums, as she was in *Ruth*, she could be vague about business details. Miss Matty's loss in *Cranford*, which parallels Thurstan Benson's loss in *Ruth*, demonstrates that Gaskell was well aware that single women could be independent investors in joint-stock companies, could attend shareholder meetings, and that their investments could produce mixed results. It is far from certain that Mr. Smith's investment advice would have produced the similar 8% return that the ladies enjoyed during Deborah's lifetime.[40]

Overall, it is clear that Cranford's economy looks outward to the provincial city of Drumble and to the British Empire. Just as Freedgood (2006) examines calico in *Mary Barton*, Kathleen Blake (2009) reads *Cranford* in the context of the textile industry and global cloth economy, arguing: "Gaskell invites us to recognize that little old-fashioned Cranford exists within a large and a changing world and that it gains when it opens itself to wider new connections" (174). The tea in which Miss Matty trades "represents the briskly advancing modern commerce of global, imperial scale, as does cotton" (176). She concludes that Gaskell "links change that is progressive in socio-economic and gender terms to participation in a world-scale, rapidly changing economy of cloth" (178). This expansive worldview continued in *North and South*.

North and South

When Mr. Bell, Margaret Hale's godfather, takes her for a visit to her beloved village of Helstone, near the end of *North and South* (1854–1855), he quips: "I'll give you back safe and sound, barring railway accidents, and I'll insure your life for a thousand pounds before starting, which may be a comfort to your relations" (383). This morbid joke about life insurance, suggesting that Margaret's value to her relations is monetary, may be a hint at what Mr. Bell knows but Margaret does not: He is planning to leave her a fortune in his will. When he dies, she expects two thousand pounds but instead receives forty thousand pounds. Mr. Lennox (her one-time suitor) becomes her legal advisor: "She was so entirely ignorant of all forms of business that in nearly everything she had to refer to him" (411).[41] As it happens, the property that Margaret inherits from Mr. Bell includes that property on which Thornton's mill stands, leading Thornton to refer to Margaret repeatedly as "my landlord"; her friends in London refer to Thornton as her tenant—however, she is not only his landlord but also becomes his creditor and investor.

As Margaret's economic fortunes are rising at the end of novel, Thornton's are falling. Thornton's agent trusted in "a house in the American trade, which went down, along with several others, just at this time like a pack of cards, the fall of one compelling other failures" (423). This is the kind of broad economic downturn in which multiple banks, trading houses, and mills fail—distinct from the single bank failure in *Cranford*.[42] Thornton knows he will fail unless he receives an infusion of cash. He is offered a speculation but refuses to invest because he would be risking the capital of his creditors, not his own. He has been well schooled by Margaret about the ethics of business and investment, and in doing the right ethical thing, he loses an opportunity to profit. His brother-in-law takes the risk and makes an enormous fortune: "No one was considered as wise and far-seeing as Mr. Watson" (426). This use of foresight is ironic because Gaskell implies that Mr. Watson was lucky and then retroactively viewed as farseeing.

"Changes at Milton" (*North and South*, Chapter 10) explains what happened while Margaret was away in London. It begins ironically with a nursery song: "Here we go up, up up;/And here we go down, down, downee!" The chapter is notable for both the specificity and the vagueness of the financial crisis that leads to Thornton losing his money. The narrator is clear that the crisis occurring in Milton (Manchester) is directly tied to the American economy: "Hitherto there had been no failures in Milton; but, from the immense speculations that had come to light in making a bad end in America, and yet nearer home, it was known that some Milton houses of business must suffer" (418). In describing the overall unstable economic climate, Gaskell's narrator notes the close connection between Milton and the nearby port—"for credit was insecure, and the most stable might have their fortunes affected by the sweep in the great neighboring port among the shipping houses" (118). Though not named, the great neighboring port must be based on Liverpool, and this reference places an emphasis on the economic relationship between Manchester, Liverpool, and America.

Mr. Harrison, a minor character, gossips on the streets of Milton that Thornton has spent his profits in extending his business by purchasing new machinery rather than saving his capital. The narrator is disdainful: "Mr. Harrison was a croaker,—a man who had succeeded to his father's trade-made fortune, which he had feared to lose by altering his mode of business to any having a larger scope; yet he grudged every penny made by others more daring and far-sighted" (419). Here, "far-sighted" has a positive connotation of fearlessly expanding business to a larger scope. Capitalism is good, including investment, but the unpredictability of the economy threatens the daring businessmen. *North and South* itself used foresight related to American investments. As discussed in Chapter 2 of this book, 1857 saw an international financial crisis precipitated by the collapse of overhyped US railway and insurance companies, creating a global financial crisis in which Thackeray lost money and which affected the family of Johnny Cross (Eliot's future husband), as we will see in the next chapter.

The ending of *North and South* is an example of the intertwining of economic and romantic plots, which was common in Victorian novels. While there can be no doubt of mutual feeling between Thornton and Margaret, Gaskell introduces money and business into the climactic scene in which they express those feelings, altering the dynamic that existed previously between them. As we have seen in Trollope's *Miss Mackenzie*, and will see in Oliphant's *Hester*, Victorian novelists often constructed courtship or seduction scenes in which the presence of money intensifies romantic passion. It is just when Margaret offers Thornton her money to save his mill that he proposes. Her offer of money results in his offer of marriage in a sexually charged final scene in which her attempts to act as a businesswoman melt into her desire for Thornton and marriage.[43] In this respect, *North and South* conforms to a traditional marriage plot, despite the unconventionality of granting the woman financial power.[44]

Sylvia's Lovers, Gaskell's historical novel, departs more dramatically from marriage-plot conventions. Its economic scope encompasses the whaling trade and small business in the seaport of Whitby, and its global vision reaches to the Middle Eastern theater of the Napoleonic wars with the Battle of Acre. Even as the heroine remains confined to home, the novel nonetheless reinforces Gaskell's conception of the global contexts of local economies and romances.

Sylvia's Lovers

Gaskell never directly represents Unitarian businessmen, yet her interest in the association of religious dissent and capitalism is epitomized in the careers of her Liverpool uncles Samuel Holland and Charles Holland. Mr. Bradshaw in *Ruth* is an obvious example of a dissenting businessman who anticipates George Eliot's Mr. Bulstrode in *Middlemarch* (1871–1872), especially in his hypocrisy. But Gaskell also explored the distinctive culture of Quaker businesspeople in *Sylvia's Lovers* (1863). In her account of the seaport's economy, she begins with the ship owners, the commercial elite of the town, and her narrator recounts how a Monkshaven boy would begin as an apprentice and rise to become a captain when he would "have a share in the venture; all these profits, as well as all his savings, would go toward building a ship of his own" (4). This dimension of the town's investment culture is distinctly male.[45] Furthermore, Gaskell emphasizes that every aspect of life in her fictionalized Monkshaven revolved around the whaling trade, from the women selling their eggs in the market to the shop girl Esther and to the wives and mothers who maintained the households while the whalers were at sea.

Inevitably, an industry grew up around the financing of whaling vessels. The wealthy Quaker brothers John and Jeremiah Foster run a shop in Monkshaven that has been in their family for generations. By the 1790s, the time period of the novel's setting, their business has evolved to include a "primitive bank": "No one asked them for interest on the money thus deposited, nor did they give any" (23). They also lent money (based on the character of the borrower) without asking for interest, and this non-usurious practice is an implied virtue. Their shop assistant, the pragmatic, conventional Philip Hepburn, Sylvia's cousin and one of her lovers, is in every way a contrast to her other lover, the romantic whaling harpooner Charley Kinraid. Philip's capitalist mindset and ambitions to rise socially are accompanied by an obsessive desire to possess Sylvia, who neither has nor wants money, thereby removing any economic dimension from the courtship plot.[46] Yet the novel implies that Philip's desire for Sylvia exists in tandem with his desire for money and his careful working, planning, and investing to accumulate it.

Gaskell generously allowed her capitalists to reform at the end of her novels, including Carson in *Mary Barton*, Bradshaw in *Ruth*, and Thornton in *North and South*. Philip goes further, becoming a heroic figure at the end of *Sylvia's Lovers* when he is given the chance to redeem his act of coercing Sylvia into marriage by lying to her about Kinraid's death. He enlists as a soldier and improbably saves both Kinraid and his own daughter from death before dying himself. This Christian pattern of conversion and redemption for businessmen constitutes a retreat from the critique of capitalism and demonstrates the many ideological ambiguities, even contradictions, in Gaskell's fiction. She seems reluctant to sustain criticism of capitalists or the government. Even her condemnation of impressment, so passionate in the early chapters of *Sylvia's Lovers*, fades away when Kinraid becomes a patriotic soldier despite his traumatic abduction and impressment into naval service.[47]

Final Transactions

Mary Elizabeth Leighton and Lisa Surridge (2013) have written about Gaskell's secret purchase of her second home in 1865. They point out that as a married woman, Gaskell could not purchase property without her husband, although she tried to "assume the legal role of the *femme sole* as she arranged for the purchase, mortgage, and tenancy of The Lawn" (490). Ultimately, she had to submit to forming a trust with Charles Crompton (her son-in-law), Thurstan Holland, and her solicitor William Shaen as trustees (490; Gaskell et al. 1997, 770). Leighton and Surridge show how important this biographical context was for *Wives and Daughters*, which explores the themes of "money, debt and credit in relation to gender" (490). In discussing particularly Molly and Cynthia's process of maturation, which involves confronting and resolving Cynthia's debt to Mr. Preston and learning to understand the appropriate use of credit, they conclude, "Women's personhood is inextricably linked to their active participation in the economy" (490). It is certainly true that at the time she was writing the novel, Gaskell was preoccupied with the practical details of obtaining credit, paying off debts and investing in property. She was also frustrated by the restrictions placed on her by the law. The novel explores legal constraints on male characters through the technicalities of entails and wills, but it is primarily concerned with the moral and psychological facets of small debts, specifically the enormous effect of Cynthia's £20 debt to Preston.

Uglow (1993) points out that *Wives and Daughters* is set roughly from 1827 to 1830, the era of Gaskell's young adult life, and that it represents the nation on the brink of the "the railway age and the penny post, of Catholic emancipation and the extension of the franchise" (580). She views the novel in part as a critique of the values held by that generation, including its sons, "like her own cousins, who were now men of power—merchants, lawyers, landowners, MP's" (580). Uglow notes: "Money had always been a force in Gaskell's novels, but *Wives and Daughters* could almost have been written on banknotes (and in a way it was, for each sheet went to pay for the Lawn and her own move south)" (586). She observes further that Gaskell's personal obsession with money at this time informs her portrait of the era she has recreated: "Land is entailed, lives are insured; we are at the start of an actuarial age" (587). The novel is a return to the bygone village ways of *Cranford*, but like *Sylvia's Lovers*, it is infused with a sense of the interplay between the past and present.

Wives and Daughters is set "before railroads" (249) and roughly in the same pre-Reform Bill years as George Eliot's *Felix Holt* and *Middlemarch*. The inheritance details are almost as complicated as those in *Felix Holt*, which Eliot was writing at the time *Wives and Daughters* was being serialized in the *Cornhill Magazine*. Squire Hamley's estate is entailed so that he cannot even raise cash to make improvements to the land, leading him to quip: "I wish I'd never had any ancestors" (365). Roger, his son, tries to get money to help his father, but finds that his maternal grandfather, who had been a merchant in the city, had "tied up the few thousands he had left to his daughter" in such a way that makes it inaccessible (367). Roger is unable to touch the principal of his deceased mother's inheritance. He thinks that he "might have slipped through all these meshes by insuring his life," but he declines to do so (367). He even consults his grandfather's will, but can find no loopholes. Here again, we see Gaskell thinking about female inheritance, life insurance, and money problems generally.

Gaskell's investment in The Lawn while writing the novel involved her in a complex legal and financial situation. Through this real estate purchase, she confronted the limitations of women investors prior to women's property reform, even though she is clear about her intention of leaving the house to any of her daughters who might remain unmarried at the time of her death (Gaskell et al. 1997, 770). In this respect, Gaskell continued the tradition in which she had been brought up of women financially supporting female family members through legacies of property and money.

In order to finance her purchase and mitigate the debt her husband so deplored, Gaskell needed to rent The Lawn for a period of years before retiring to it. While preparing the house for a prospective tenant, she died there unexpectedly on November 12, 1865, after drinking tea with her daughters. *Wives and Daughters* remained unfinished.

From her earliest years, Elizabeth Gaskell was part of an extended family of businesspeople for whom global commerce was a way of life. The history of this network included shipping and pottery manufacturing in Liverpool, mining operations in Wales, and banking in London. Her fiction encompasses various aspects of the mid-Victorian economy. She is best known for her representations of the nineteenth-century textile manufacturing economy in Manchester, but in both explicit and coded ways, her fiction addressed the eighteenth-century slave trade and whaling industry, as well as the nineteenth-century global trade in cotton and sugar, and local investments in joint-stock banks, canals, and insurance companies. After she became a successful author, she drew on family connections to help her invest in developing transportation systems, including docks in London and railroads in the north of England. The income from these investments helped her to maintain a middle-class life, although the purchase of a second home strained her finances.

These personal experiences informed her perspective on, and critique of, nineteenth-century capitalism in diverse ways. She reflexively disliked greed and offered an alternative model of business in her fiction, epitomized in the conversions of the capitalists Carson, Thornton, and Bradshaw. The only objection she seems to have had to investing—which sustained the fictional unmarried Jenkyns sisters and the unmarried Benson siblings, as well the real women in her early life such as her aunt Lumb and friend Ann Turner—was its risk. The bank might fail, financial advisors might commit fraud, or the dividend might be less than anticipated. Overall, as this chapter has shown, Gaskell's fictional explorations of capital accumulation, together with her personal financial activities, contribute to our understanding of the nineteenth-century cultures of investment.

NOTES

1. The Manchester, Sheffield, and Lincolnshire Railway was formed from the merger of several lines in 1847 and had its headquarters in Manchester, see Dow (1959).
2. Critics have taken various approaches to situating Gaskell's works in transatlantic and global contexts. Lee (2010) argues for the importance of American slave narratives to the structure of Gaskell's fiction. Others have written about commodities such as calico in *Mary Barton* and tea in *Cranford*, see Freedgood (2006) and Miller (1995). In *Figures of Finance Capitalism*, Knezevic (2003) writes that in selling Indian tea, Miss Matty (in *Cranford*) "finds herself at one end of a world-wide system of trade whose incursion the community has dreaded all along" (99).
3. The importance of place in Gaskell is explored in a collection edited by Scholl et al. (2015); for example, Inglis (2015) writes that *Ruth* "depicts a society in transition, one that has not yet grasped the impact on 'remote' communities of the extension of the canal, road and railway networks, innovations in road surfacing, expansion of commercial shipping, increased international trade and military action overseas" (71), and in that same collection, see Mullen (2015). For a discussion of *North and South*, see Markovits (2013).
4. Gaskell discusses the Brontë sisters' investments in the York and Midland Railway from 1846 to 1849 in *The Life of Charlotte Brontë* (1857, 232, 320), emphasizing Charlotte's acumen and foresight as an investor.
5. *Mary Barton* ends with the principle characters immigrating to an idealized Canada. On Gaskell and communication technologies, including the mail system, see Pettitt (2012) and Levitan (2015).
6. D'Albertis (2007) notes that Gaskell's "childhood memories are recounted chiefly through the refracted lens of *Cranford* and *Wives and Daughters*" (16). Foster (2002) writes that Knutsford "partly sources various topographies in her work" (11).
7. Gaskell read Fanny Trollope's *Domestic Manners of the Americans* soon after it was published (Chapple 1997, 391). Pettitt (2012) notes that Gaskell's notion of America in the 1840s was based on images such as those in Dickens's *Martin Chuzzlewit* (605).
8. Moore, Morris, and Scholl (2015) argue: "Gaskell understood her identity in relation to the places she experienced" (1).
9. On sailors in her fiction, see Burroughs (2015), Malton (2018), and Lawson (1999).
10. Another uncle, Henry Holland, became a successful physician in London. He attended the Queen and was knighted. Sir Henry Holland also attended George Eliot's stepson, Thornie Lewes, during the course of his fatal illness in 1869. For George Lewes's journals of 1869, see Eisenberg (2015).

11. Harbottle (1997) questions the myth of Turner's ruinous generosity and discusses his financial relationship with his congregation and with Ann, "a woman who knew what she was talking about in a family who were not financial innocents" (155).
12. The most thorough notes are those of Easson (1993). These notes were reproduced in Wilkes's edited version (see Gaskell 1848).
13. Other debates continued; 1848 was the year France abolished slavery in its West Indian Colonies, a fact relevant to the interpretation of Charlotte Brontë's *Villette* (1853).
14. Gaskell knew another John Cropper, a minister from 1846 at the Unitarian chapel in Stand, a village about ten miles from Manchester (Gaskell et al. 2003, 131). My thanks to Alan Shelston for pointing out the second John Cropper, although I am sure that Gaskell had the abolitionist in mind when she named her ship in *Mary Barton*. Lawson (1999) points out the significance of ship names in *Sylvia's Lovers*.
15. This refers to a skeleton, or perhaps Death, reaching up to Nelson; the monument is discussed later in this chapter.
16. Zemka (2009) observes that characters in *Mary Barton* encounter people on the streets of Manchester, constituting a "momentary perturbation" to the narrative (813). This applies to the Liverpool section of the novel, in which Mary encounters a building and a statue rather than a person. On the streets of Liverpool, both Gaskell and her heroine Mary would have seen black sailors and dock workers.
17. In 1823, a fierce debate took place between John Gladstone and James Cropper in the Liverpool newspapers (Wake 1997, 43). Such public debates carried on until the act abolishing slavery in the colonies was passed in 1833 and would have been ongoing during Elizabeth's visit in 1831.
18. There was at least one branch of the Holland family that was active in the slave trade before 1807. Nehemiah Holland was the captain of a ship that transported slaves to West India; Williams (1897, 240) connects Nehemiah to the Samuel Holland family. Pope confirms that Nehemiah Holland (1713–1786) and his son Francis (1745–1800) were among Liverpool's leading slave merchants from 1750 to 1799.
19. Some of her relatives lost their Unitarian faith during their climb up the social ladder. Gaskell's father and her Uncle Swinton Holland joined the Church of England. Although her Uncle Samuel Holland worshiped at Renshaw Street Chapel with Roscoe, the Rathbones, and other anti-slavery activists, there is no evidence that he or his family members were active in the campaign, so Elizabeth's perception that they opposed reform is revealing (Stange 1984). For the role of daughters in the family business, see Pederson (2004).

20. Armstrong (2012) argues that nineteenth-century statues often reveal "states of bodily torment which in actual experience are unspeakable" (115). In the era of slavery, "labour and pain haunt sculpture" (132).
21. Freedgood's (2006) reading of "negro head tobacco" in Dickens's *Great Expectations* is also relevant, as she finds "a particularly overwhelming horror that cannot be named but only encoded fetishistically in the most apparently negligible of details" (82). Manchester cotton cloth was a key commodity traded for African slaves (Parthasarathi 2011).
22. While little has been published on the role of Liverpool in *Mary Barton*, Alan Shelston discussed this in his unpublished paper, A Tale of Two Cities: Manchester and Liverpool in *Mary Barton*. Twinn (1999) explores the topic in her dissertation. My thanks to Alan Shelston and Frances Twinn for sharing their work with me.
23. On Gaskell and America, including American slavery, see Pettitt (2012), Lee (2010), Henry (2007), and Shelston (2001).
24. Easson also points out that Jem Wilson "works for an engineering firm that sends out its products to the realms of the Czar and Sultan, to Russia and Turkey, those two great autocratic powers, which yet are dependent upon the commercial and intellectual strength of Manchester, so that, in turn, the political power of these great domains is dependent on the democratic, commercial and intellectual power of England. So England is to be seen as a greater Empire than either the Russian or the Turkish, not because of its territorial possessions but because of its economic scope" (704).
25. *George Geith of Fen Court* was originally published in 1865 (and under the pseudonym F.G. Trafford).
26. Jean-Baptiste Monnoyer (1636–1699) was a Felmish painter who specialized in flowers.
27. The phrase "here, there and everywhere" is ubiquitous. For a discussion of its importance in *Little Dorrit*, see Çelikkol (2011, 134).
28. Dickens's son, Charles, was a tea merchant in Hong Kong in the early 1860s. Arthur Clennam, in Dickens's *Little Dorrit* (1855–1857), was in business in China.
29. Gaskell's uncles and cousins tended to follow either medical or business careers.
30. On the structure of the financial plot in *The Mill on the Floss*, see Poovey (2009).
31. Freeland (2003) argues: "Sally violates the logic of economics by arresting the cycle of exchange, unmasking money as a symbol rather than a material reality" (209). More broadly, Freeland claims that Ruth's sexual transgressions become a "critique of the market economy as a whole" because "by refusing to become either a prostitute or a wife ... Ruth breaks down the categories which kept the sexual and market economies working in tandem" (199).

32. For life insurance companies declaring bonuses, see Alborn (2009).
33. Such frauds did actually occur, for example, on the Liverpool Stock Exchange (see Chapter 2) and are also represented in Dickens's *Great Expectations* (see Chapter 3).
34. For the myths versus the reality of female shareholders, see Robb (2009).
35. For the parallels between forgery and illegitimacy in the novel, see Freeland (2003) and Malton (2009).
36. I have argued that from internal evidence we can determine that the setting of the novel is 1830–1843 (Henry 2001, xxxiii).
37. Writing about the risk, loss, and fire insurance in *Mary Barton*, Fyfe (2015) contrasts the insurance market in which middle-class property owners can participate with the lottery-like nature of working-class lives: "She uses the rising social acceptability of insurance to contrast the impoverished and exposed condition of England's working class" (see Fyfe 2015, 119–20). Fyfe also notes that we do not know whether Gaskell had a life insurance policy, as Dickens had (116).
38. Çelikkol (2011, 126) notes that Little Dorrit implies without directly saying that Arthur Clennam may have been involved in the opium trade with China.
39. Miller (1994) argues that "Matty's ethical code can have only theoretical validity in the material circumstances of the mid-Victorian period," but that Gaskell "nonetheless wants to present that theoretical stance as an agent of moral improvement" (154).
40. As discussed in Chapter 2 of this book, bank failures were common plot devices in Victorian fiction. See Reed (1984), Weiss (1986), Alborn (1995), and Hunter (2010, 2011). Acheson and Turner (2011) provide historical context for women investing in joint-stock banks (1825–1870), perhaps helping to explain what seems to Mr. Smith like Deborah's unreasonable willfulness: "bank stock earned higher returns than the overall market thus compensating investors for the downside risk which they faced" (208).
41. Margaret's ignorance is compounded by the secrecy of Mr. Bell's will, which echoes the surprise endings used by Dickens in *Bleak House* and *Our Mutual Friend*, both of which turn on women being intentionally misled about their inheritances by men. It is an interesting historical twist that near the end of her own life, Gaskell concealed her purchase of a new house from her husband, intending to surprise him, as discussed in this chapter.
42. Shelston (2005) speculates that the crisis in America that affects Thornton's business is based on economic conditions of the 1830s. See *North and South* (379, n. 1).

43. Gaskell's own knowledge of finance is compromised here in that she first had Margaret offer Thornton only £1857 and had to amend the sum in the second edition to the more realistic £18,057 (Gaskell 1854–1855, 452).
44. Charlotte Brontë (1849) created a similar scenario of a woman investing in a factory in *Shirley*.
45. Doe (2009) documents the role of women in Whitby's nineteenth-century shipping economy, noting that in 1865 Whitby had "one of the highest percentages of women managing owners" of commercial ships (67). She provides case studies of individual women owners of ships and observes that a woman, Margaret Campion, founded one of Whitby's many banks in 1800 (67).
46. Kinraid, however, ends up marrying Clarinda Jackson, an heiress from Bristol who has £10,000 and whose father was in the "sugar-baking business" (393). According to Molly, Sylvia's former friend, Kinraid "had all her money settled on her, though she said she'd rayther give it all to him" (393). Sugar baking (refining) in Bristol suggests West Indian connections.
47. For the global dimensions of *Sylvia's Lovers*, see Pettitt (2012). For the sea and sailors generally connecting Gaskell's representation of sailors to slavery, see Lee (2010), Greven (2014), Burroughs (2015), and Malton (2018).

References

Acheson, Graeme G., and John D. Turner. 2011. Shareholder liability, risk aversion, and investment returns in nineteenth-century British banking. In *Men, women, and money: Perspectives on gender, wealth, and investment 1850–1930*, ed. David Green, Alastair Owens, Josephine Maltby, and Janette Rutterford, 207–227. Oxford: Oxford University Press.

Alborn, Timothy. 1995. The moral of the failed bank: Professional plots in the Victorian money market. *Victorian Studies* 38 (2): 199–226.

———. 2009. The first fund managers: Life insurance bonuses in Victorian Britain. In *Victorian investments: New perspectives on finance and culture*, ed. Nancy Henry and Cannon Schmitt, 58–78. Bloomington: Indiana University Press.

Armstrong, Tim. 2012. *The logic of slavery: Debt, technology, and pain in American literature*. New York: Cambridge University Press.

Baines, Thomas. 1852. *History of the commerce and town of Liverpool, and of the rise of manufacturing industry*. London: Longman, Brown, Green, and Longmans.

Baucom, Ian. 2005. *Specters of the Atlantic: Finance capital, slavery and the philosophy of history.* Durham, NC: Duke University Press.

Bigelow, Gordon. 2003. *Fiction, famine, and the rise of economics in Victorian Britain & Ireland.* Cambridge: Cambridge University Press.

Blake, Kathleen. 2009. *Pleasures of Benthamism: Victorian literature, utility, political economy.* Oxford: Oxford University Press.

Bonaparte, Felicia. 1992. *The gypsy-bachelor of Manchester: The life of Mrs. Gaskell's demon.* Charlottesville: University Press of Virginia.

Brontë, Charlotte. 1849. *Shirley: A tale*, ed. Margaret Smith, Herbert Rosengarten, and Janet Gezari. Oxford: Oxford University Press, 2008.

———. 1853. *Villette*, ed. Margaret Smith and Herbert Rosengarten. Oxford: Oxford University Press, 2008.

Brown, Jacqueline Nassy. 2005. *Dropping anchor, setting sail: Geographies of race in black Liverpool.* Princeton, NJ: Princeton University Press.

Burroughs, Robert. 2015. Gaskell on the waterfront: Leisure, labor, and maritime space in the mid-nineteenth century. In *Place and progress in the works of Elizabeth Gaskell*, ed. Lesa Scholl, Emily Morris, and Sarina Gruver Moore, 11–22. Farnham, UK: Ashgate.

Cavanagh, Terry. 1997. *Public sculpture of Liverpool.* Liverpool: Liverpool University Press.

Chadwick, Mrs. Ellis. 1910. *Mrs. Gaskell: Homes, haunts and stories.* New York: Stokes, 1910.

Çelikkol, Ayşe. 2011. *Romances of free trade: British literature, laissez-faire, and the global nineteenth century.* New York: Oxford University Press.

Chapple, John. 1997. *Elizabeth Gaskell: The early years.* Manchester: Manchester University Press.

Craik, Dinah Maria Mulock. 1856. *John Halifax, gentleman.* Repr., Peterborough, ON: Broadview, 2005.

D'Albertis, Deirdre. 2007. The life and letters of E.C. Gaskell. In *The Cambridge companion to Elizabeth Gaskell*, ed. Jill Matus, 10–26. Cambridge: Cambridge University Press.

Dickens, Charles. 1838. *Oliver Twist*, ed. Stephen Gill. Oxford: Oxford University Press, 1999.

———. 1842–1844. *The life and adventures of Martin Chuzzlewit*, ed. Margaret Cardwell. Oxford: Oxford University Press, 2009.

———. 1846-1848. *Dombey and son*, ed. Alan Horsman. Oxford: Clarendon Press, 1984.

———. 1852–1853. *Bleak house*, ed. Stephen Gill. Oxford: Oxford University Press, 2008.

———. 1855–1857. *Little Dorrit*, ed. Stephen Wall. London: Penguin, 2003.

———. 1860–1861. *Great expectations*, ed. Margaret Cardwell. Oxford: Oxford University Press, 2008.

———. 1865. *Our mutual friend*, ed. Kathleen Tillotson. Oxford: Oxford University Press, 2009.
Doe, Helen. 2009. *Enterprising women and shipping in the nineteenth century*. Woodbridge, UK: Boydell Press.
Dow, George. 1959. *Great central. Vol. 1: The progenitors 1813–1863*. Shepperton, UK: Ian Allen Ltd.
Easson, Angus. 1985. Elizabeth Gaskell and the novel of local pride. *Bulletin of the John Rylands University Library of Manchester* 67 (2): 688–709.
———, ed. 1993. Introd. to *Mary Barton, by Elizabeth Gaskell*. Halifax: Ryburn.
Eisenberg, Michelle. 2015. George Henry Lewes's 1869 diary and journal: A transcription and annotation of unpublished holographs held at the Beineke Library of Yale University. *George Eliot-George Henry Lewes Studies* 67 (2): 93–226.
Eliot, George. 1860. *The mill on the Floss*, ed. Nancy Henry. Boston: Houghton Mifflin, 2004.
———. 1866. *Felix Holt: The radical*, ed. Fred C. Thompson. New York: Oxford University Press, 1988.
———. 1871–1872. *Middlemarch*, ed. David Carroll. Oxford: Oxford University Press, 2008.
Elis-Williams, M. 1988. *Bangor port of Beaumaris: The nineteenth century shipbuilders and shipowners of Bangor*. Caernarfon, Scotland: Gwynedd Archives.
Foster, Shirley. 2002. *Elizabeth Gaskell: A literary life*. New York: Palgrave Macmillan.
Freedgood, Elaine. 2006. *The ideas in things: Fugitive meaning in the Victorian novel*. Chicago: University of Chicago Press.
Freeland, Natalka. 2003. "Ruth's" perverse economies: Women, hoarding, and expenditure. *ELH* 70 (1): 197–221.
Fyfe, Paul. 2015. *By accident or design: Writing the Victorian metropolis*. Oxford: Oxford University Press.
Gallagher, Catherine. 1985. *The industrial reformation of English fiction: 1832–1867*. Chicago: University of Chicago Press.
Gaskell, Elizabeth. 1848. *Mary Barton: A tale of Manchester*, ed. Edgar Wright. Oxford: Oxford University Press, 1998.
———. 1848. *Mary Barton: A tale of Manchester*, ed. Joanne Wilkes. London: Pickering & Chatto, 2005.
———. 1853a. *Cranford*, ed. Elizabeth Porges Watson. Oxford: Oxford University Press, 2011.
———. 1853b. *Ruth*, ed. Nancy Henry. London: Everyman, 2001.
———. 1854–1855. *North and south*, ed. Angus Easson. Oxford: Oxford University Press, 1998.
———. 1854–1855. *North and south*, ed. Alan Shelston. New York: W. W. Norton, 2005.

———. 1857. *The life of Charlotte Brontë*, ed. Angus Easson. Oxford: Oxford University Press, 2009.
———. 1859. Lois the witch. In *Cousin Phillis and other stories*, ed. Angus Easson, 105–194. Oxford: Oxford University Press, 1981.
———. 1863. Cousin Phillis. In *Cousin Phillis and other stories*, ed. Angus Easson, 259–356. Oxford: Oxford University Press, 1981.
———. 1863. *Sylvia's lovers*, ed. Nancy Henry. London: Everyman, 1997.
———. 1864–1865. *Wives and daughters*, ed. Angus Easson. Oxford: Oxford University Press, 2009.
Gaskell, Elizabeth, Sophia I. Holland, and J.A.V. Chapple. 1996. *Private voices: The diaries of Elizabeth Gaskell and Sophia Holland*. Keele, UK: Keele University Press.
Gaskell, Elizabeth, J.A.V. Chapple, and Arthur Pollard. 1997. *The letters of Mrs. Gaskell*. Manchester: Manchester University Press.
Gaskell, Elizabeth, John Chapple, and Alan Shelston. 2003. *Further Letters of Mrs. Gaskell*. Manchester: Manchester University Press
Gérin, Winifred. 1976. *Elizabeth Gaskell: A biography*. Oxford: Clarendon Press.
Greven, David. 2014. American shudders: Race, representation, and sodomy in "Redburn". *Leviathan* 16 (2): 1–22.
Guy, Josephine. 1996. *The Victorian social-problem novel: The market, the individual and communal life*. New York: St. Martin's Press.
Harbottle, Stephen. 1997. *The Reverend William Turner: Dissent and reform in Georgian Newcastle-Upon-Tyne*. Leeds, UK: Northern Universities Press for the Literary and Philosophical Society of Newcastle upon Tyne.
Henry, Nancy (ed.). 2001. *Introd. to Ruth*, by Elizabeth Gaskell. London: Everyman.
———. 2007. Elizabeth Gaskell and social transformation. In *The Cambridge companion to Elizabeth Gaskell*, ed. Jill L. Matus, 148–163. New York: Cambridge University Press.
Hunter, Leeann D. 2010. *Bankruptcy's daughters: The economics of the new daughter in Victorian literature*. Gainesville: University of Florida.
———. 2011. Communities built from ruins: Social economics in Victorian novels of bankruptcy. *Women's Studies Quarterly* 39 (3): 137–152.
Inglis, Katherine. 2015. Unimagined community and disease in "Ruth." In *Place and progress in the works of Elizabeth Gaskell*, ed. Lesa Scholl, Emily Morris, and Sarina Gruver Moore, 67–82. Farnham, UK: Ashgate.
Kaye, Thos. 1831. *The stranger in Liverpool with plates of the principal buildings and a new and correct map of the town*, 10th ed. Liverpool: Thos. Kaye.
Knezevic, Borislav. 2003. *Figures of finance capitalism: Writing, class, and capital in the age of Dickens*. London: Routledge.
Lawson, Benjamin. 1999. From Moby-Dick to Billy Budd: Elizabeth Gaskell's "Sylvia's lovers". *South Atlantic Review* 64 (2): 37–57.
Lee, Julia Sun-Joo. 2010. *The American slave narrative and the Victorian novel*. New York: Oxford University Press.

Leighton, Mary Elizabeth, and Lisa Surridge. 2013. Evolutionary discourse and the credit economy in Elizabeth Gaskell's "Wives and daughters". *Victorian Literature and Culture* 41 (3): 487–501.

Levitan, Kathrin. 2015. Catching the post: Elizabeth Gaskell as traveler and letter-writer. In *Place and progress in the works of Elizabeth Gaskell*, ed. Lesa Scholl, Emily Morris, and Sarina Gruver Moore, 123–136. Farnham, UK: Ashgate.

Malton, Sara A. 2009. *Forgery in nineteenth-century literature and culture: Fictions of finance from Dickens to Wilde.* New York: Palgrave Macmillan.

Malton, Sara. 2018. Vanishing points: Gaskell, impressment and nineteenth-century cultural memory. *Nineteenth-Century Studies* 28.

Markovits, Stefanie. 2013. *The Crimean War in the British imagination.* Cambridge studies in nineteenth-century literature culture. Cambridge: Cambridge University Press.

Miller, Andrew. 1994. Subjectivity Ltd: The discourse of liability in the Joint Stock Companies Act of 1856 and Gaskell's *Cranford*. *ELH* 61 (1): 139–157.

———. 1995. *Novels behind glass: Commodity, culture, and Victorian narrative.* Cambridge: Cambridge University Press.

Moore, Sarina Gruver, Emily Morris, and Lesa School. 2015. Introduction: Placing Gaskell. In *Place and progress in the works of Elizabeth Gaskell*, ed. Lesa School, Emily Morris, and Sarina Gruver Moore, 1–7. Farnham, UK: Ashgate.

Mullen, Mary. 2015. In search of shared time: National imaginings in Elizabeth Gaskell's "North and south." In *Place and progress in the works of Elizabeth Gaskell*, ed. Lesa Scholl, Emily Morris and Sarina Gruver Moore, 107–122. Farnham, UK: Ashgate.

Oliphant, Margaret. 1883. *Hester*, ed. Philip Davis and Brian Nellist. Oxford: Oxford University Press, 2009.

Parthasarathi, Prasannan. 2011. *Why Europe grew rich and Asia did not: Global economic divergence, 1600–1850.* Cambridge: Cambridge University Press.

Pederson, Susan. 2004. *Eleanor Rathbone and the politics of conscience.* New Haven, CT: Yale University Press.

Pettitt, Clare. 2012. Time lag and Elizabeth Gaskell's transatlantic imagination. *Victorian Studies* 54 (4): 599–623.

Poovey, Mary. 2009. Writing about finance in Victorian England: Disclosure and secrecy in the culture of investment. In *Victorian investments: New perspectives on finance and culture*, ed. Nancy Henry and Cannon Schmitt, 39–57. Bloomington: Indiana University Press.

Pope, David. 2007. The wealth and social aspirations of Liverpool's slave merchants of the second half of the eighteenth century. In *Liverpool and transatlantic slavery*, ed. David Richardson, Anthony Tibbles, and Suzanne Schwarz, 164–224. Liverpool: Liverpool University Press.

Pryke, Jo. 2005. The treatment of political economy in "North and south", ed. Alan Shelston, 547–558. New York: W. W. Norton.

Reed, John R. 1984. A friend to Mammon: Speculation in Victorian literature. *Victorian Studies* 27 (2): 179–202.

Riddell, Charlotte. 1865 [F.G. Trafford, pseud.]. *George Geith of Fen Court*. London: Frederick Warne and Co. nd.

Riddell, Charlotte. 1870. *Austin Friars: A novel*. London: Hutchinson.

———. 1885. *Mitre Court: A tale of the great city*, 3 vols. London: R. Bentley.

Robb, George. 2009. Ladies of the ticker: Women, investment, and fraud in England and America, 1850–1930. In *Victorian investments: New perspectives on finance and culture*, ed. Nancy Henry and Cannon Schmitt, 120–142. Bloomington: Indiana University Press.

Scholl, Lesa, Emily Morris, and Sarina Gruver Moore (eds.). 2015. *Place and progress in the works of Elizabeth Gaskell*. Farnham, UK: Ashgate.

Schor, Hilary. 1992. *Scheherezade in the marketplace: Elizabeth Gaskell and the Victorian novel*. Oxford: Oxford University Press.

Shelston, Alan (ed.). 1996. Introd. to Mary Barton, by Elizabeth Gaskell. London: Everyman.

Shelston, Alan. 2001. Alligators infesting the stream: Elizabeth Gaskell and the USA. *Gaskell Society Journal* 75: 53–63.

——— (ed.). 2011. Introd. to Ruth, by Elizabeth Gaskell. Oxford: Oxford University Press.

Stange, Douglas C. 1984. *British Unitarians against American slavery*. Teaneck, NJ: Fairleigh Dickinson University Press.

Stoneman, Patsy. 2007. Gaskell, gender and family. In *The Cambridge companion to Elizabeth Gaskell*, ed. Jill Matus, 131–147. Cambridge: Cambridge University Press.

Stowe, Harriet Beecher. 1854. *Sunny memories of foreign lands*. Boston: Phillips, Sampson.

Taylor, James. 2006. *Creating capitalism: Joint-stock enterprise in British politics and culture 1800–1870*. London: Royal Historical Society.

Trollope, Anthony. 1864. *Miss Mackenzie*, ed. A.O.J. Cockshut. Oxford: Oxford University Press, 1992.

———. 1875. *The way we live now*, ed. Francis O'Gorman. Oxford: Oxford University Press, 2016.

Twinn, Frances E. 1999. *Half-finished streets, illimitable horizons and enclosed intimacy: The landscapes of Elizabeth Gaskell's writing*. PhD dissertation, Durham University. http://etheses.dur.ac.uk/1161/. Accessed 5 April 2018.

Uglow, Jenny (ed.). 1993. *Elizabeth Gaskell: A habit of stories*. New York: Faber and Faber.

Wake, Jehanne. 1997. *Kleinwort Benson: The history of two families in banking*. Oxford: Oxford University Press.

Weiss, Barbara. 1986. *The hell of the English: Bankruptcy and the Victorian novel*. Lewisburg, PA: Bucknell University Press.
Wertheimer, Eric. 2006. *Underwriting: The poetics of insurance in America, 1722–1872*. Stanford, CA: Stanford University Press.
Williams, Gomer. 1897. *History of the Liverpool privateers and letters of Marque, with an account of the Liverpool slave trade*, 2011. Cambridge: Cambridge University Press.
Williams, Raymond. 1958. *Culture and society*. New York: Colombia University Press.
Yarrington, Allison. 1989. Public sculpture and civic pride, 1800–1830. In *Patronage and practice—Sculpture on Merseyside*, ed. Penelope Curtis, 22–31. Liverpool: Tate Gallery Liverpool.
Zemka, Sue. 2009. Brief encounters: Street scenes in Gaskell's Manchester. *ELH* 76 (3): 793–819.

CHAPTER 5

George Eliot: Money's Past and Money's Future

Went into City. Discussed shares (and a chop) with Johnnie Cross.
(Lewes Diary 17 January 1873; Eliot 1954–1978b, V:368)

At the time of her death in December 1880, George Eliot had accumulated an extensive portfolio of global investments. In addition to shares in US, Indian, and South African railways, she held shares in companies that were closer to home. Like Gaskell, she invested in the St. Katharine Docks and held onto these shares after the company amalgamated with the London Docks in 1864. Her financial advisor throughout the 1870s was John (Johnnie) Walter Cross, whom she married in May 1880. His family had moved from Glasgow to Liverpool, and it was connected to some of the same Quaker and Unitarian networks as Gaskell's Holland cousins, including the families of Rathbone, Benson, and Cropper. The Cross family ties to Liverpool, America, and the West Indies were deep, but William Cross, Johnnie's father, was increasingly involved in banking, and his son followed this line, working first for the family firm in New York before setting up his own business in London.

These previously unrecognized biographical connections between Gaskell's and Eliot's extended families illustrate their intimate involvement in Victorian cultures of investment. The fact that both of their investment portfolios included the St. Katharine Docks and that their writing raised ethical questions about the use to which money was put

© The Author(s) 2018
N. Henry, *Women, Literature and Finance in Victorian Britain*,
Palgrave Studies in Literature, Culture and Economics,
https://doi.org/10.1007/978-3-319-94331-2_5

leads to the question: What, if anything, did they know about the history of the companies in which they held shares? It is possible that they did not know about the controversial construction of these wet docks in London in the late 1820s, which were highly contested at the time. The remarkable construction feat, overseen by Thomas Telford, required the demolition of the medieval church and "hospital" of St. Katharine, which were particularly noteworthy historically for having survived confiscation of church property by Henry VIII, the fire of 1666 and the Gordon Riots in 1780. It also required the defiling of a graveyard, the tearing down of 1,250? houses and tenements and the displacement of 11,300 residents. Many opposed the loss of the buildings and displacement of the population; protests were held and legal suits brought to stop the construction.[1] Developers, investors, and others unsurprisingly saw it as a project in the van of modern engineering and commercial progress. This view prevailed, and the docks were opened in 1828.

The old controversy was not forgotten. Bradshaw (1862) noted when describing the area that even though a population of 11,300 persons had to find habitation elsewhere, it was nonetheless "a highly profitable investment." He wrote, "It is impossible to witness this scene of busy activity without being forcibly reminded that it is to commerce that England owes her pre-eminence in the scale of nations" (68). Henry Mayhew's *Morning Chronicle* articles (see Mayhew 1861) describe the docks in 1845, just before Gaskell purchased her shares in 1849. He provides statistics and analysis of the thousands of men who unloaded the ships and the precarious lives of those waiting to be called to work. Besant (1901) called the St. Katharine Docks, "a needless, wanton act of barbarity" (8). Among twentieth-century historians, Pudney (1975) writes that the St. Katharine Docks was the "greediest and most ruthless and silliest of them all" (62). He claims that the vast dock constructions, which sought to capitalize on the end of the East and West India Companies' monopolies, were neither necessary nor profitable: "Every one of the private companies was doomed in the long run—with a long run of diminishing dividends" (62). Brown (1978) agrees that few of the dock companies "ever paid a satisfactory dividend to shareholders" (62). The clearance of neighborhoods to make way for large construction projects is a familiar story, but as reflected in some histories, the St. Katharine Dock project seems to have been both unethical and unprofitable. Apart from Gaskell's complaint about the St. Katharine Docks diminishing dividend, we cannot say what she or Eliot knew of the history of the docks in which they invested, or whether knowing more would have affected their investment decisions.

In *George Eliot and the British Empire* (Henry 2002), I examined Eliot's investments in Indian railroads, specifically the Great Indian Peninsula Railway, suggesting that even as she was attracted to the guaranteed 5% return on her investment, she had reason to believe that she was contributing to the development of India. This remote and distant feat of engineering in a part of the world she would never visit existed for her as a name on a stock certificate and on dividend checks recorded methodically in her own and George Henry Lewes's diaries. She also read articles about the project in the *Westminster Review* and elsewhere, but her letters give no indication of whether her choice of an initial investment was based on this knowledge or simply on a recommendation of a good, reliable security. As Drummond (2008) has observed, "while dreams of Empire were paramount to the British and key to both British and colonial governments, it was far from being the main motive for Britain's investors" (216).

Living in London, Eliot might easily have seen the St. Katharine Docks in which she invested, but she does not record such a visit. After all, Dickens wrote in *Sketches by Boz*, "One of the most amusing places we know, is the steam-wharf of the London-bridge, or St. Katharine's Dock Company, on a Sunday morning in Summer" (Dickens 1839, 125). Protests over the construction of the docks in 1828 were not part of the research she conducted for *Middlemarch* (1871–1872), which recreates protests over the construction of Midland Railways during the same period. She did, however, own shares in the Midland Railway, which originated in 1832.

This chapter considers the ways in which Eliot's fiction explores the ethics of inherited and invested wealth. In this respect, it builds both on my own work and on that of Dermot Coleman (2014). I take his and my own analyses of her investments further by looking at her fiction's preoccupation with how the present generation negotiates the problem of receiving money that may have been tainted by its past means of accumulation or associations with past dubious behavior, whether illegal or immoral. This question extends to matters of slavery and slave-produced cotton and sugar. Can money, like people, nations, and companies, have a past? Or is the value of money simply what it can do when spent in the present or invested for the future? In keeping with the overall themes of her novels, her fictional treatment of money and investments is more subtle and nuanced than those found in anticapitalist novels by William Makepeace Thackeray, Charles Dickens, and Anthony Trollope. I want to suggest that this complexity was related to her position as a woman who looked to investments as a means to supplement her income from writing. In this way, her work has more in common with the writing about investments and capitalism generally in works by Elizabeth Gaskell, Charlotte Riddell, and Margaret Oliphant than it does with the works of her male contemporaries.

Her own small inheritance from her father was invested and overseen by trustees and Isaac Evans, her brother. In 1854, £1500 of her money was temporarily placed in "the funds" (consolidated government debt), where it would receive only 3% interest (see Chapter 1). She found this lack of control frustrating and wrote to Charles Bray on November 12, 1854, to tell him the trustees had called in £1500 of her money, "which must consequently be placed in the funds until a new investment can be found for it. ... I hope he will think it worth while to get another investment. For a considerable part of my sister's money he gets 5 percent" (Eliot 1954–1978a, II:184). She hoped to get 5% on her own money rather than the 3% paid by the funds.

After she began earning a substantial income from her fiction, she took a great interest in how her money was invested. Starting in the early 1870s, she and Lewes were guided in their investment decisions by Cross. Her late novels, beginning with *Felix Holt* (1866), are concerned with wealth both as a foundation of the class system and as a personal condition and responsibility. In *Middlemarch*, Dorothea has too much, while Will has not enough. In *Daniel Deronda*, Daniel has plenty of money but is disinherited culturally; Gwendolen loses the West Indian fortune made by her grandfather through bad investments and comes to realize through Daniel that she also has little in the way of cultural inheritance.

Whatever she may have known about the Indian railways, London Docks, and other domestic and global investments, Eliot thought about ethical questions in relation to money both in terms of direct personal interactions, as seen in her blackmail plots, and in terms of collective national responsibility and guilt concerning questions of empire and of slavery. The personal crimes of characters like David Faux, Dunstan Cass, and Bulstrode, as well as the implicit or explicit cultural costs to England of slavery in the British West Indies, are a consistent theme in her fiction.

"Brother Jacob" (which was written in 1860 but not published until 1864) is Eliot's most explicit exploration of the West Indian colonies in English culture. It is set in the 1820s and offers a mix of real and fictional places. For example, David Faux leaves from Liverpool to Jamaica and, after failing to make a fortune there, returns to the fictional English town of Grimsworth under a new identity, Edward Freely. David's fantasy of becoming a white prince among "the blacks" (76) in Jamaica and his fascination with sugary confections at home in England make the conditions of sugar's production a coded subtext in the story. Plasa (2009) argues that the text "constantly gestures" toward but "never openly names" slavery (88).[2] "Brother Jacob" is an example of Eliot's indirection, allusion, and intertextuality when treating West Indian slavery, a practice she would use again in *Middlemarch* before addressing it somewhat more directly in *Daniel Deronda*.

The West Indian sugar economy in its various stages throughout the nineteenth century provides historical contexts and subtexts for nineteenth-century novels. Schaffer (2016), pointing to the most famous examples of *Mansfield Park*, *Vanity Fair*, and *Jane Eyre*, argues: "The West Indies did important work in the marriage plot, not just for constraining white femininity against a racialized swarthy passionate other, but also for vocalizing what was wrong with English men, for locating dehumanizing perspectives in a very specific economic practice" (17). As we will see, the sugar-refining business figures either centrally or in passing in works such as Margaret Oliphant's *The Melvilles* (1852), Charlotte Riddell's *The Race for Wealth* (1866), and Elizabeth Gaskell's *Sylvia's Lovers* (1863). In Charlotte Brontë's *Villette* (1853), M. Paul travels to Guadalupe to manage the estate of Justine Marie's mother (Malevola/Mme. Walravens). Details in the novel are vague, but historically slavery existed in the French colony until 1848 (35, 392, 461–62). Later, the West Indies also provide a backdrop for Oliphant's *Kirsteen* (1890a) and *Sons and Daughters* (1890b), as well as in George Gissing's *Will Warburton* (1905). West Indian plantations, in addition to their narrative function in the marriage plot and general cultural significance as a site of sugar production—as a place where British fortunes were made, and as a focus of antislavery campaigns—were sources of income for women investors, many of whom received compensation for the loss of human beings they owned after slavery was abolished in 1833 (Draper 2010).

Where is West Indian slavery in *Middlemarch*, which is an important subtext for both "Brother Jacob" and *Daniel Deronda*? The debates about ending West Indian slavery are certainly not foremost among other political issues of reform in *Middlemarch*. In 1830–1, the abolition of the slavery in the West Indies was ongoing and would be achieved in the Slavery Abolition Act of 1833, following the Reform Act of 1832, which is central to the context of *Felix Holt* and *Middlemarch*.[3] But the cultural reality of abolition movements from the 1807 abolition of the slave trade to the abolition of slavery in the colonies is present in indirect, layered allusions. For example, Mr. Brooke claims to have known the Evangelical abolitionist William Wilberforce in his "best days," presumably when he was working for the abolition of the slave trade in 1807. In an early scene, Brooke asks Mr. Casaubon whether he knows Wilberforce (18). Mr. Casaubon does not know him. This, along with his ignorance of Southey, is an ominous foreshadowing of Casaubon's lack of knowledge about the world outside of his scholarship, a shortcoming that Dorothea discovers only after she has married him.

Without ever mentioning slavery or abolition, Brooke comments: "Well, Wilberforce was perhaps not enough of a thinker; but if I went into Parliament, as I have been asked to do, I should sit on the independent bench, as Wilberforce did, and work at philanthropy" (18). Wilberforce continued working for the abolition of West Indian slavery until the late 1820s and died just days after the abolition bill was passed in 1833. In this way, Eliot introduces abolitionist agitation without directly referring to it, except in Brooke's vague reference to philanthropy. Only once is the reference explicit, which is when Brooke tells Ladislaw: "Only I want to keep myself independent about Reform, you know: I don't want to go too far. I want to take up Wilberforce's and Romilly's line, you know, and work for Negro Emancipation, Criminal Law—that kind of thing. But of course I should support Grey" (430). Brooke characteristically lumps the issue of "negro emancipation" and "criminal law" together with the political reforms championed by Prime Minister Grey, and the mention merely gestures to the existence of these broader concerns.[4] There is no West Indian planter in *Middlemarch* to compare with Fanny Davilow's father in *Daniel Deronda*, though *Middlemarch* offers suggestive allusions to Raffles and his wife as traders in slave-grown American tobacco.[5]

These plot details in *Middlemarch* derive partly from Eliot's research into the era of the first Reform Act, some of which was undertaken for the composition of *Felix Holt*, a novel set just after the passing of that act. William Huskisson, who was run over and killed at the openning of the Liverpool and Manchester Railroad in 1829, is also mentioned in both *Middlemarch* and the famous introduction to *Felix Holt*, which reflects on the transition from stagecoach to railway travel by way of surveying the political climate and geography of the Midlands in particular and the nation in general. The narrator delivers Sampson's (the coach driver) thoughts in a stream of free indirect discourse. He is unsurprisingly bitter about the coming of the railways that will eventually render stagecoaches obsolete.

Eliot had a way of embedding dark aspects of personal and national history in allusions that she might expect her readers to recognize, rather than directly elaborating or commenting on them. This is true of her critique of colonialism, slavery, and economic crimes. In 1869, Rosalind Howard, an acquaintance of Eliot's, recalled a conversation in which Eliot said, "Such things as Overend and Gurney made her very wrathful" (Collins 2010, 67). Perhaps she, like Gaskell, had to tread lightly when it came to questions of how families accumulated their wealth.

THE CROSS FAMILY

By the time she was writing *Middlemarch*, Eliot had specific social and financial connections to global business networks—via her friends, the Crosses—that overlapped with those of Gaskell, Oliphant, and Riddell. Mrs. Anna Wood Cross was the widow of William Cross, a banker who had moved his family from Scotland to Liverpool and finally to London. From 1869 and throughout the 1870s, Eliot and Lewes enjoyed a developing intimacy with Mrs. Cross and her large family of children, including her married and unmarried daughters and her son, Johnnie. The Cross family's business history is relevant here for the ways in which it connects Eliot to the global history of commercial and financial transactions, which were brought into her domestic sphere when Cross took over Eliot's and Lewes's finances and became a confidential friend who probably influenced some aspects of the works Eliot wrote after their meeting, specifically *Middlemarch* and *Daniel Deronda*.

John Walter Cross's family was Scottish, and both his mother's and his father's families were active in the West Indian trade. Robert Cross, an ancestor in Glasgow, founded the "Company of Scotland Trading to Africa and the Indies" in 1694. Anna Cross's Glasgow connections, the Dennistouns, were West Indian merchants.[6] In 1786, James Dennistoun married Mary Finlay. Their eldest son was Alexander (1790–1874), and their eldest daughter was Elizabeth (1787–1857). Elizabeth Dennistoun married John Wood (1779), an import merchant in Glasgow.

The Dennistouns and Woods were in business together, and both had a past history of involvement in West Indian trade. Elizabeth and John's eldest son was William Wood (1808–1894), and their eldest daughter was Anna Chalmers Wood (1812–1878). Anna married William Cross, who was a partner in J & A Dennistoun. The third of Anna and William's ten children was John Walter Cross (1840–1924), who was born near Glasgow on March 12, 1840.[7]

William Cross moved his family to Liverpool in 1846 when he became head of the Liverpool Borough Bank, which the Dennistouns had recently acquired. The bank failed in the financial crisis of 1857, by which time William Cross had moved the family to London to work for Dennistoun, Cross and Co., which also failed as a result of events in 1857 (Wake 1997, 163).[8] This was the financial crisis in which Thackeray lost money on his American investments, as discussed in Chapter 2. After the age of six, Johnnie Cross grew up in Liverpool. The census for 1851 shows his family living in Toxteth Park, which is where Gaskell's Holland relatives lived until 1831. Johnnie was sent to school at Rugby, but following the collapse of Dennistoun, Cross and Co., and his father's financial reversals in 1857, he left Rugby early and gave up any thoughts of a university education. He was sent to New York to join William Wood, his uncle, in the business of Dennistoun, Wood and Co.[9]

According to Wood (1895), in 1860 the family companies included: Dennistoun, Cross and Co. (London); Dennistoun, Wood, and Co. (New York); A & J Dennistoun and Co. (New Orleans); and J & A Dennistoun (Glasgow). By 1861, Cross had become a partner in Dennistoun, Wood and Co. in New York. But following the Limited Liability Act of 1862 in England, connections at the Oriental Bank in London—what Wood calls the "greatest banking institution in the East India and China Trade"—formed a new bank in New York called the British and American Exchange Banking Company Limited (Wood II:347).[10] In 1863, at his nephew Johnnie Cross's instigation, William Wood became the manager of this bank, which would have a board of directors in New York, London, and Liverpool. Cross became the second assistant manager of the branch in New York. The offices were set up at 63 Wall Street. An advertisement announced that the new bank would "sell and buy sterling bills of exchange. ... Commercial credits issued for use in the East Indies, China and Australia" (II:354). William Wood's Uncle John Dennistoun (his mother's brother) wrote to congratulate him and added: "What a grand opening too for Johnnie Cross. We are grieved very much to part with him, but we would not hesitate about advising him to accept it. I wonder what old Cross would say if he only knew what turn things had taken. You and *his* son at the head of a rival establishment, as it were, of the old house—sweetened as the knowledge would be that you were both in receipt of splendid salaries" (352).

In 1865, the new bank changed its name to the English and American Bank, Limited. Following the crash of Overend and Gurney in 1866, Wood notes, 1867 was a disastrous year for English business. The shareholders of the bank voted to dissolve it and the process of liquidation began, overseen by Wood in New York. The winding up was completed in April 1869 (II:361). It was also in April 1869 that George Eliot first met Johnnie Cross in Rome, where he was vacationing with his mother and sisters. Once back in London, Cross acted as an independent agent for the purchase and sale of American securities. The acquaintance with Johnnie Cross proved profitable for the Leweses as he soon began to take a role overseeing their investments, and they were confident in placing their money in his hands.[11]

Cross (1872) published an article titled "Social New York," in *Macmillan's Magazine*. The article provides insight into his life in New York particularly and his social perspective generally. He does not offer any information about his financial activities or his personal life, but he makes a strong case for the greater equality shared by men and women in American society as compared with English society and reflects some enlightened views about women.[12] The article begins with a description of New York as compared with Liverpool: "The fine bay, with its white sails and usually clear blue sky overhead, forming so great a contrast to the Mersey, gives at once to the American bound traveller a comfortable sense of breadth and cheeriness."[13] Liverpool, as his childhood home and the point of departure and entry on his trips across the Atlantic, was a touchstone for Cross, and it was to Liverpool connections that he turned when forming his own company in London.

In 1875, Cross formed a new partnership with Robert Henry [Robin] Benson (1850–1929). Robin was the son of Robert Benson (1814–1875), who moved from Liverpool to Manchester after giving up both his partnership with James Cropper and his Quaker faith. After Robert Benson's death, his company was discovered to be insolvent and bankruptcy was declared. Despite losing money when Robert Benson's company failed, James Cropper, son of John Cropper, and proprietor of the Kendall

Paper Company in Liverpool, offered Robin financial backing to enter business with Cross (Wake 1997, 162). In addition to their Liverpool connections, Johnnie and Robin shared the experience of "surviving family commercial disasters" (163); they had both seen the "shadow side" of City life, but as a new generation of investors, they would become highly successful (164).

The new company, with offices at 38 Cornhill, in London, was small, dealing in American securities for clients who were mainly family members and friends, such as the Leweses. Cross and Benson dealt largely in American railroads, as is reflected in George Eliot's portfolio of stocks in the 1870s. From 1879 on, they specialized in financing the construction of railroads in the American Midwest and were beginning to purchase land in Iowa. Con Benson, Robin's brother, went to Iowa to oversee the establishment of a British community there. The company would become increasingly and profitably invested in this venture, but starting around 1879, Cross was only a sleeping partner.[14] In May 1880, Cross married George Eliot. When she died in December 1880, Benson attended her funeral. Cross retired from the company in 1884 because he had become preoccupied with writing *George Eliot's Life as Related in Her Letters and Journals* (Eliot and Cross 1885).

The Scottishness of the Cross family is not often mentioned in biographies of George Eliot, although Lewes, in a letter to Elma Stuart, referred to "our fervid Scotch friends in Weybridge," the area of Surrey in which they settled (Eliot 1954–1978c, VI:322). Bodenheimer (1994, 256) makes a connection between Eliot's admiration of the Scotch Mrs. Anna Wood Cross and Mrs. Meyrick in *Daniel Deronda*. Bodenheimer also emphasizes the degree to which Eliot longed to be taken in as a family member of the Crosses when she married Johnnie (115). As far as I know, no biographies of Eliot have examined Johnnie's Liverpool connections, including his legacy of West Indian trade and his family's Quaker and Unitarian associates in Liverpool going back to the Bensons, Croppers, Rathbones, Gladstones, and Gaskell's relatives, the Hollands. These connections, however, place Eliot within a new context of business history and investment cultures.

All of this shows the various ways in which Eliot's life intersected with nineteenth-century cultures of investment and commercial and financial networks from the Midlands to Scotland, Liverpool, and London and with links to New York, Australia, India, the Caribbean, and beyond. Like Gaskell, she was connected to these various networks through friends and family, and her ties overlapped with those of Gaskell. The religious ideologies of the Unitarians and the commercial ideology of free trade arose when Eliot was editing the *Westminster Review*. What she chose to do with her own money would eventually be bound up with Cross's business interests, as she became increasingly dependent on him as a financial advisor. She would bring both her research and her personal experience to her fictional representations of these ideologies as manifested in the early nineteenth-century settings of her novels.

Most importantly, her fiction asks fundamental questions about how an individual person's money, especially inherited money, could raise ethical issues related to the origin or associations of that money. Her preoccupation with these matters intensified as her career developed; *Middlemarch* and *Daniel Deronda* explore the separate but related notions of dirty money and tainted commodities. These questions were personal, national, and global. They are epitomized in the history of Liverpool, slavery in the West Indies and in the American South, and also in the very modern problem of how and where to invest money based on knowledge about those investments. Today, we recognize the concept of "ethical" investing with attendant movements calling on institutions to "divest" from perceived unethical companies as a way of applying pressure for change (e.g., to apartheid South Africa in the 1980s, or more recently to fossil fuel companies contributing to global warming). Such concepts were emerging in the eighteenth century with respect to boycotting commodities like sugar, even if they were not yet applied to investments (Sussman 2000). Eliot thought seriously about the ethics of money in her fiction, but, arguably, she used a different measure when balancing (or allowing Cross to balance) her portfolio. The following section will consider problems of money's past (inheritance) and money's future (investments) in Eliot's fiction and in her life.[15]

MONEY'S PAST: DIRTY MONEY IN *MIDDLEMARCH*

Leo H. Grindon's (1882) observation that late nineteenth-century Liverpool was "debased by the slave trade" (11) is relevant to how Victorian authors such as Gaskell, Eliot, Riddell, and Oliphant would have thought about Liverpool as they represented it in fiction, even if their references to that late eighteenth- and early nineteenth-century reality are only indirect, for example, in Gaskell's and Oliphant's invocation of Liverpool's Nelson Monument in their fiction. The debates about ending slavery in the colonies were part of the Reform Bill context, as is evident in references to Wilberforce and Huskisson in *Middlemarch*. Such national issues are played out in the lives of individual characters in Eliot's fiction. Whereas the decisions of Eppie in *Silas Marner* and Esther in *Felix Holt* to reject opportunities for inheriting wealth seem relatively straightforward, in *Middlemarch* and *Daniel Deronda*, money, land, and commodities are freighted with moral baggage, and characters' opportunities to receive money are significantly complicated.

Throughout Victorian novels, characters are distinguished by their attitudes toward money. Some are overly scrupulous about rejecting inheritances perceived to have tainted origins and about paying off debts. Others are entirely pragmatic. Dickens's *Dombey and Son* (1846–1848) offers a good example of two women whose perspectives are at odds on this question. Disgusted with her daughter Alice's rejection of Harriet Carker's money, which is tainted by its association with Alice's seducer James Carker, old Mrs. Brown protests: "Money is money, whoever gives it" (521). This simple philosophy is undeniably true even if spoken by a woman who does not count among Dickens's virtuous poor characters but rather is avaricious and grasping. Attaching a moral narrative to money is an act of imagination; it implies not only a refined moral sense but also moral righteousness. Apart from theft, the law offers no clear criteria for judging the purity of the money or the giver. Fiction steps in to explore these questions, which may relate to the material coins Alice throws at Harriet's feet, an inheritance of dubious origins or the income from investments in morally suspect companies.

In *Middlemarch* (1871–1872), the concept of dirty money is introduced in the history of Will Ladislaw's family: His mother is said to have run away out of horror at the family's disreputable business but also, melodramatically, to pursue a career as an actress on the stage, a profession with its own disreputable associations for women and one of which an upwardly mobile and religious family would have disapproved. Will repeatedly defends his mother's reputation and attributes noble motives to her actions. He states his scruples when refusing Bulstrode's offer of money because he imagines that the money has its origins in a pawnbroker's business—a trade that his mother rejected—that accepted stolen goods in the distant past. Bulstrode says, "I wish to supply you adequately from a store which would have probably already been yours" (585). Here, as throughout the conversation, Bulstrode is painfully careful in his language so as not to imply that there is any legal obligation for him to give Will money that "would have probably already" been his. At the same time, it is strange that Bulstrode, as a banker, should refer to the money as coming from "a store," as if he had saved that very money from circulation all these years, like Silas Marner hid his gold guineas under the floorboards of his cottage. On the one hand, this could be a way to avoid "returning" the money to Ladislaw; on the other hand, Bulstrode may have imagined that a certain sum would eventually need to be paid to someone as reparation for his past wrongs.[16] Will refers to his grandfather's business as "thoroughly dishonorable" (586), and he further tortures Bulstrode by scoffing: "What I have to thank you for is that you kept the money till now, when I can refuse it" (586). The idea of Bulstrode keeping "the money" picks up on the vague notion that the original physical money was somehow kept in a store. Taking money from Bulstrode, in Will's view, would sully his character, even though no one but he, Bulstrode, and Raffles knows about the origins of Bulstrode's wealth. The contradiction is: If Will's mother was so noble that she ran away to avoid association with her father's illegal business practices, how can Bulstrode be blamed for not restoring that money to her after her father's death when he stepped in to marry her widowed mother? Ladislaw's personal myth is that his own mother did not want anything to do with dirty money, and this may be largely a story that Will tells himself to counterbalance the shame of his being the son of an actress.[17]

Perhaps the implication is that the widow Dunkirk, Will's grandmother, had inherited her own money, accumulated before she married Mr. Dunkirk, and which was hers to bequeath to her daughter (and the grandson she imagined). But Eliot does not provide enough detail to validate this speculation, and after her marriage, the dirty and clean money could hardly have been kept separate and would be inextricably mixed in investments, since any money that belonged to the wife belonged to her husband in these early nineteenth-century times. Ladislaw is indignant that Bulstrode did not arrange for his mother to inherit money from his grandmother, but he is insulted that Bulstrode should try to give it back to him thirty years later. Citing as a reason for his rejection of Bulstrode's money that a pawn shop thirty years ago may have received stolen goods traded by men no better than "thieves and convicts" (586), Will is hotheaded and irrational about the question of his mother's past. He also thinks that he cannot accept Bulstrode's money because Dorothea (now in the role as a moral conscience to him) would not approve, and this may be a more important consideration than the actual details of the money's origin. Will reflects that he does not take the money because "it would have been impossible for him ever to tell Dorothea that he had accepted it" (587). Will's line of thinking links him to Dorothea's ethical scruples; yet, we know that Dorothea's reasoning about ethics and inheritance is inconsistent.

In the first chapter of *Middlemarch* (1871–1872), for example, Dorothea reflects on the origins of jewels inherited from her mother, a concept familiar to us in the notion of "blood diamonds," and revived by Eliot in *Daniel Deronda* in which the Grandcourt (or Mallinger) family diamonds are tainted for Gwendolen as if by poison. Looking at her mother's jewels, naïve Dorothea exclaims: "Yet what miserable men find such things, and work at them, and sell them!" (13). What does she mean by miserable and what exactly is her objection: the moral character of excavators, working conditions of miners, or the greed of jewelers? Dorothea's moral objections are jumbled, and she accepts the emeralds and diamonds, leading her sister, Celia (untroubled by scruples) to observe: "Dorothea is not always consistent" (14). This scene establishes an intuitive, reflexive moral sense on Dorothea's part that is not clarified by precise knowledge. In this way, her moral sense foreshadows Will's reaction to the dishonorable origins of Bulstrode's money, linking Will and Dorothea in the similar, idealistic impulses that draw them to each other.

We can take a more objective approach to analyzing the ethical problems introduced throughout *Middlemarch*. Money is not like shabby workmanship, adulterated food, the snake oil sold by Felix Holt's father, or the drugs peddled by Middlemarch doctors—morally dubious products that can do literal harm to people who use them.[18] Money's moral dirtiness is not inherent in the material forms it takes (cash or checks), but rather follows from the human imagination of its history. Eliot is compelled to raise questions about money's past, but it is not clear that she would agree with Will's rash refusal of Bulstrode's offer. The larger question is: How does money, which is already symbolic of value, become doubly symbolic? The money Bulstrode offers Ladislaw would have enabled Will to do many things, including advance his political career. But Will chooses to see this money as the same money accumulated by the pawnbroker thirty years ago, as if it were inherited property with a traceable history. In fact, the money he would have inherited in the first place, or that he might have accepted from Bulstrode, has subsequently been laundered, that is, recirculated, reinvested, spent, and reearned, many times over since then, as Kaufman (2009) points out, through "investments in Middlemarch's bank and hospital" (151). But refusing Bulstrode's offer—as if the money itself were tainted—is in Will's mind the honorable thing to do. The novel makes clear that Will's reaction, however cloudy as to the particulars, is preferable to Bulstrode's introspective, self-justifying reasoning that "profitable investments in trade ... became sanctified by a right application of the profits in the hands of God's servant" (582). But if others should misunderstand and condemn him, then "he was cast out of the temple as one who had made unclean offerings" (582).[19]

For Grandcourt in *Daniel Deronda*, the family diamonds symbolize the continuity of bringing his new wife into that family, but for Gwendolen, they symbolize the scorned, secret mistress Lydia Glasher and her children, who will not be admitted to the family line (and are therefore, like Ladislaw, disinherited). The disinherited Ladislaw throws Bulstrode's money back at him as dirty. To take it would be like Gwendolen taking the diamonds that were poisoned for her by Lydia's imparting information on their history. All of this depends on what characters know about the origins of wealth and commodities. Will does not really know much in factual terms about Bulstrode or his money. Dorothea does not know where her mother's jewels were mined, though Gwendolen knows that Lydia has worn Grandcourt's diamonds and thinks herself entitled to them. Eliot explores the capacity of money and commodities to represent the exchange value they carry, as well as the cultural baggage related to the ethics of their production, exposing the view that money can embody its dirty past as logically incoherent and impractical, if nonetheless admirable.

Certainly, the concept of morally tainted commodities was familiar in the late eighteenth and early nineteenth centuries, for example, in the boycotting of West Indian sugar that was produced with slave labor (see Ahluwalia et al. 1999; Plasa 2009; Sandiford 2000; Sussman 1994). Sandiford (2000) notes: "Slave-produced sugar became the target of a nationwide boycott by the London Abolition Committee in 1791," and recalls the popularity of Wilberforce's pamphlet urging people to refrain from buying West Indian sugar and rum (124). Women particularly were involved in the boycott of this tainted, luxury commodity. Writing in Liverpool in the 1820s, John Gladstone accused James Cropper of trading in slave-produced American cotton, even as Cropper hypocritically opposed the West Indian trade in slave-produced sugar. A boycott is more immediate and direct as a response to the morally objectionable production of a commodity. But the inheritance of property—whether of material objects or laundered capital—is more complex, as the situations in *Middlemarch* suggest. How far back can one trace the taint and still feel its force? Does it extend to the money Bulstrode inherited thirty years ago or the diamond that was mined two or three generations ago? This comes down to a question of contextual knowledge: Money, diamonds, sugar, or company shares do not in themselves betray a morally problematic past, but people imbue them with meaning by giving them a history, which is often inevitably incomplete, inaccurate, and vague.[20]

DANIEL DERONDA: INHERITING AND LOSING A WEST INDIAN FORTUNE

In *Daniel Deronda*, Eliot's narrator is cynical about young men of "our day" for whom "the unproductive labour of questioning is sustained by three or five percent on capital that someone else has battled for" (157). In her critique of the 1870s, "our day" echoes Trollope's critique of unproductive young men in *The Way We Live Now* (1875), though his characters do not engage in such introspective questioning. As we saw in Chapter 3 of this book, Gissing explored the malaise of the late century *rentier* class and probed the question of what women's unevenly developing economic independence meant for more traditional gender roles. The separate spheres that earlier Victorian culture had (not always successfully) sought to maintain were dissolving. In *Our Mutual Friend* (1864–1865), Dickens contrasted non-working men like Mortimer and Eugene Wrayburn with working-class women like Lizzie Hexam and Jenny Wren. In *The Way We Live Now*, Trollope satirically treated the dissolute Felix Carbury, whose mother wrote frantically in an effort to support her son. Gissing carried on this tradition when he portrayed a world in which men were often living on their investments while women were entering the workplace.

In *Daniel Deronda*, Daniel is unsatisfied by the idea of living on the income from capital accumulated, or battled for, by others. In Eliot's portrait of England in the 1860s, we see the beginnings of this unevenness and the conflicts and frustrations that arise from it. Gwendolen gambles recklessly in part out of frustration over not being able to do something more active. She then regrets her recklessness when she realizes she might have carried money back to her mother, who has suddenly lost the income from capital that her grandfather had accumulated. Fanny Davilow represents an earlier generation of helpless femininity and has been dependent on husbands and on investments. Gwendolen wishes to do more but is thwarted in her ambition to become a professional singer by her lack of talent. Mirah Lapidoth, however, is equally eager to support herself and is able to do so both because she has talent and because her social position as a Jewish woman of the working class does not preclude her from earning a living. The Meyrick women are also models of the work ethic, as well as a gentle parody of Alcott's *Little Women* (1868–1869), another nod to *Daniel Deronda*'s American Civil War era setting. The novel represents the struggles of the younger generation of men and women to overcome social pressures: Daniel resists the temptation to live on investments and seeks a meaningful vocation, while Gwendolen, after her investment income is lost, gives in to the forces that lead her to marry, specifically her need to support her mother and family of half-sisters.

In *Daniel Deronda*, the source of the twice-widowed Mrs. Davilow's family fortune was in the West Indies. Gwendolen, her daughter, has "no notion of how her maternal grandfather got his fortune"; she knows that he was a West Indian, "which seemed to exclude further question" (1876b, 17). The idea that this knowledge seemed to exclude further question has a forbidding connotation and suggests that Gwendolen feels intuitively that she should not ask questions about the source of her grandfather's wealth, just as she feels she cannot ask questions about her biological father because of her mother's sensitivity on the subject (17–18).

It is rarely noted in criticism of the novel that her father's superior family disinherited Gwendolen. The failure of the Harleth family to recognize Fanny may have necessitated her remarriage, even despite her independent inheritance from her father. On the one hand, if Gwendolen's mother was forced into an ultimately unhappy second marriage to Captain Davilow because her first husband's family would not acknowledge or support her, then Gwendolen's marriage to Grandcourt to support her mother and half-sisters ironically duplicates her mother's life experiences. On the other hand, Captain Davilow may have been a fortune seeker advancing himself by marrying an heiress, in which case Fanny's second marriage has a parallel with that of her sister Nancy's marriage to the social-climbing Captain Gaskin, who took "orders and diphthong but shortly before his engagement to Miss Armyn" (23). His class origins are well disguised, as no one suspects that his father had "risen to be a provincial corn dealer" (117). The prehistory of the Armyn sisters and their West Indian father is left suggestively vague. We do not know, for example, when Mr. Armyn died or when his daughters came into their money. This prehistory nonetheless has resonances with other aspects of the Gwendolen–Grandcourt marriage plot, emphasizing connections to money that might be considered "dirty" and to ongoing British imperialism and structures of power and dominance at home.[21]

I would like to explore further the details of the West Indian inheritance and its loss through speculation as part of the cultures of investment that Eliot represented in her novels. The pattern of inheriting money made through West Indian trade and losing it through a mid-century financial crisis was familiar to Eliot, specifically through Cross, whose family fortune was lost in 1857 when he was seventeen. In introducing these details of Gwendolen's family history, Eliot gestures toward the profiting from slavery that is inherent in a West Indian fortune in a previous generation with roots going back before the 1833 act abolishing slavery in the colonies. As we have seen, Cross's family money went back to the West Indian trade conducted by Scottish merchants, and while it is unclear whether they were involved in the eighteenth-century slave trade, the Crosses and Dennistouns certainly were involved in trading slave-produced sugar and cotton.

At the time she wrote *Daniel Deronda*, Eliot had become close friends with Anna, Cross's widowed mother, and her grown children. It was to Anna Cross that Eliot wrote a description of Byron's grandniece playing roulette at Bad Homburg, often taken to be the inspiration for Gwendolen's gambling in *Daniel Deronda* (Eliot 1954–1978b, V:312). As we have also seen, while Eliot was writing *Daniel Deronda*, in 1875 Cross formed a partnership with Robin Benson, his old Liverpool connection. The Benson family's money also derived from trade with the West Indies and America. The Benson firm failed as a direct result of the Overend and Gurney collapse, but, significantly, it was the business that failed and not simply a loss of personal investments. Benson's sisters, like the Cross sisters, were affected by their families' financial reversals, and Eliot would have been familiar with these events given her intimacy with the Cross family.

The West Indian origins of Mrs. Davilow's family money are given specificity when we learn that her father owned a plantation in Barbados, a fact Mrs. Davilow reveals during a topical conversation about the free blacks in Jamaica following the Morant Bay Rebellion in October 1865 and subsequent Governor Eyre controversy (279). Watson (2008) argues that this scene "connects plantation life in the West Indies with the world of the English aristocracy (and lesser gentry)" (165).[22] Mrs. Davilow's West Indian inheritance is lost at the start of the novel through Mr. Lassman's "wicked recklessness" (*Daniel Deronda* 1876b, 16) and speculations in "mines and things of that sort" (199). Gwendolen and her family are implicated not only in the culture of restless, rootless middle-class Euro-cosmopolites who frequent watering holes and gambling casinos but also in the global migration of capital from the West Indian sugar trade to speculations in unspecified mines.[23]

Without actually explaining the connections to slavery, Eliot, like Gaskell, develops a theme of women not knowing about the financial and political implications of capital accumulation in the early nineteenth century. Typically, she inserts intertextual allusions into her narrative to reinforce the unspoken connections. For example, Grandcourt's horse is the "beautiful black Yarico," a name that recalls the story of Inkle and Yarico and connects Grandcourt to the English exploiter of a West Indian princess, whom David Faux ironically emulates in Eliot's "Brother Jacob."[24] Later in *Daniel Deronda*, Eliot also encrypts West Indian slavery in the scene of Gwendolen's captivity on the yacht in the Mediterranean when Grandcourt spies "a plantation of sugar canes" and forces her to look at it (575). Gwendolen remembers that "she must try to interest herself in sugar-canes as something outside her personal affairs" (575). The scene comes shortly after the narrator imagines Grandcourt being sent to "govern a difficult colony" and concluding that it was "safer to exterminate than to cajole superseded proprietors" (507). Sugarcane plantations in the Mediterranean cannot fail to invoke the colonial history of sugarcane plantations in the Caribbean, and the language of slavery is invoked to suggest Gwendolen's subjection to Grandcourt both on the yacht and in the marriage generally.[25]

The scene on the yacht enforces the themes of knowing and seeing. Gwendolen does not know much about the sugar plantations of her West Indian grandfather or about the mines in which Grapnel and Co. speculated. The moral dilemma and psychological drama of Gwendolen's plot turn on a different, more personal knowledge of the past, but the moral implications of this sexual past are inseparable from crimes—or more accurately sins—of the national past. Mr. Gascoigne knows about

Grandcourt's mistress, Lydia Glasher, when he urges Gwendolen to marry Grandcourt, but at the time of the marriage (presumably), Mrs. Davilow does not know about Lydia. When Gwendolen is on the verge of accepting Grandcourt's proposal under intense social and financial pressure, she thinks about his relationship to Lydia: "I wish I had never known it!" (248).

Daniel's plot similarly depends on the limits of his knowledge of the past. He is paralyzed because he does not know his own history, and his life changes when he learns about his mother and his Jewish heritage. These are themes that preoccupied Eliot in *Middlemarch*. Raffles brings information to Middlemarch, which alters Bulstrode's life, and the opinions of those who learn what he has to tell, however disreputable he is as a messenger. Just as Gwendolen wishes that she did not know about Lydia because not knowing would make her choice easier, so Will Ladislaw views Raffles' information about Bulstrode's past as "thrust on his knowledge" (Eliot 1871–1872, 587).[26]

Eliot and Gaskell both explore the theme of looking but not seeing, or seeing but not knowing the significance of what is seen. Though the main drama is personal for the characters, these authors also imply that people often fail to recognize the broader historical, national, and global implications of what they see. Even though Gwendolen looks at the sugar plantations to take an interest in something outside the misery of her domestic life, she cannot connect Mediterranean and Caribbean sugarcane plantations, just as Mary Barton cannot know what the Liverpool Exchange and the Nelson Monument symbolize because she is so focused on her mission to save Jem, her lover. Eliot and Gaskell expected their readers to know things that the characters do not, and the force of the moral critique in their respective novels depends on readers knowing more than the characters can recognize about the history of money received for stolen goods, diamonds mined under miserable conditions, sugar cut by slaves, and shares that were speculations in bubble companies.

THE LOSS OF INHERITED PROPERTY

In *Daniel Deronda* (1876b), Mrs. Davilow writes a letter to Gwendolen explaining that their family of women is financially ruined: "All the property our poor father saved for us goes to pay the liabilities" (10). It is interesting that she uses the word "property" rather than money.

Gwendolen repeats this language: "I cannot conceive that all your property is gone at once" (198). The episode recounting the loss of the women's property implicitly invokes the historical context of the setting and the composition of the novel, including limited liability and women's property legislation. The novel is set between October 1864 and October 1866, though the narrative begins in medias res. The action thus falls, for example, between the passing of the Limited Liabilities Act of 1862 (for banks) and the Married Women's Property Act of 1870. The language of the former act is invoked in Mrs. Davilow's phrase "pay the liabilities"; the language of the latter act is invoked when Gwendolen returns to Offendene and is deposited from the train as a "*femme sole*," an irony since she is single but less financially independent than ever (194). The emphasis on "saved for us" suggests that Fanny and Nancy Armyn's inheritance may have been protected from their respective husbands' use by prenuptial settlements, just as the inheritance of the Dodson sisters in *The Mill on the Floss* was protected from their husbands. The money invested through Grapnell and Co. may not have been available to Captain Davilow, Mrs. Davilow's second husband, since her ability to establish her own household at Offendene was "mysteriously" made possible after Captain Davilow's death (17). In this unhappy marriage, the captain assumed his presumed rights to his wife's property, as she laments: "All my best ornaments were taken from me long ago" (233). The comment is surprising because the widow "usually avoided any reference to such facts about Gwendolen's stepfather as that he had carried off his wife's jewelry and disposed of it" (233). Furthermore, the loss of the money seems to cast some suspicion on Reverend Gascoigne, who may have advised his wife and sister-in-law on their investments, even if he did not have direct access to the capital.[27] Whoever was responsible for the loss of the Armyn property, it is not the sisters, who had probably been receiving interest on their capital for years, making this loss of income under mysterious circumstances traumatic for the family. In this respect, the question of married women's property, whether invested wealth or material belongings, is central to the novel.

Critics have recognized parallels between Grapnell and Co. and Overend and Gurney, the wholesale discount house, which became a limited company in 1865 and fell prey to a credit crisis through its own overreaching in railway and other investments (Coleman 2014, 47; Elliot 1876a, 784n1).[28] In May 1866, there was a run on the bank causing its collapse and a larger panic in which more than 200 companies failed or, like Robert Benson and Co., were severely strained.[29] This profile of a major failure with a ripple effect does not match the information Eliot provides about Grapnell and Co. in which the Armyn sisters' private inheritance is invested and which is brought down by the rogue speculations of a particular banker, or for Gwendolen, "Certain persons mysteriously symbolized in Grapnell and Co." (1876b, 132). Telling Gwendolen that she knows "nothing of business," Mrs. Davilow explains that "Mr. Lassmann" meant to gain by speculating and "our money has only gone along with other people's" (199).[30] The speculations were risky but apparently not illegal, so "law can never bring back money lost in that way" (199). While investors in Grapnell and Co. clearly lost money, its failure was not a national crisis leading to the failure of other businesses of consequence in the novel. When Lush tells Grandcourt about the family's reversals, for example, he attributes it simply to "some rascally banking business" that others are not likely to know about (240).

Grapnell and Co. fails in August 1865 in the novel's chronology, wiping out all the capital of its investors. It seems that Grapnell and Co. was not a Limited Liability bank since the investors, including Fanny Davilow, are liable for the losses, recalling Miss Matty's liability in the failure of the Town and County Bank in *Cranford* before the passage of the Limited Liability Act. The type of bank, the historical timing, and the limited impact of the failure all suggest that Eliot did not intend Grapnell and Co. to be exactly the same type of failure as Overend and Gurney, though she may be suggesting that it was an old-fashioned house that retained unlimited liability out of a gentlemanly sense of responsibility, as Overend and Gurney had done up until it desperately tried to raise funds by soliciting more investors, a strategy that failed and resulted in more widespread losses. Rather, with the failure of Grapnel and Co., Eliot self-consciously relies upon a conventional plot device.[31] When Eliot wants to mark time in the novel, she refers to real events like the American Civil War or the Morant Bay Rebellion and does not transmute them into fictional events. Plenty of realist literature after 1866, including Riddell's *Susan Drummond* (1884) and Charles Reade and Dion Boucicault's *Foul Play* (1868), referred directly to the failure of Overend and Gurney with its extensive, national economic consequences. The failure of Grapnell and Co. is generic rather than specifically mimetic. It creates the unlikely conditions for Gwendolen's marriage, and the particular circumstances are left vague, part of the unsettled, dislocated society that Eliot describes.

Eliot's fiction explores questions about inheritance of property with a morally tainted past even when the money has been laundered over a period of decades, reaching back to an era of colonial slavery. In *Daniel Deronda*, she further employs a familiar plot convention to represent the loss of that money through the corruption and gambling-like nature of modern finance. Mrs. Davilow's money should have been invested in the Consols or in the type of securities George Eliot chose in 1860—Indian railways guaranteed by the British Government to pay 5%. The crucial event that sets Gwendolen's plot in motion is an interesting combination of realist detail, literary intertexuality, and social critique. The speculation of Mr. Lassman(n) clearly resonates with the gambling motif (and Eliot had strong moral objections to gambling), but her choice to represent a bank failure that was catastrophic for innocent, but still liable, investors is more subtle than Trollope's portrayal of high finance as fraudulent in his recently published *The Way We Live Now*, which Eliot had read before writing *Daniel Deronda* (Haight 1968, 548). Eliot was an experienced investor by the 1870s, and she knew that investments could be safe. It would be the height of irresponsibility to allow Mrs. Davilow's and her sister's entire fortune to fall into the hands of a speculator, yet this perhaps oversimplified explanation for the firm's failure reflects the generally volatile economy of the 1860s. Our understanding of these events comes from the perspective of Mrs. Davilow, to whom it was probably explained by Mr. Gascoigne, her brother-in-law. No trustee of the money is mentioned. The narrator never intervenes to clarify the circumstances. We do not know if Mr. Lassman(n) is a rogue speculator or was authorized by the house in his mining ventures, the riskiest of investments.

Ultimately, the financial plot in *Daniel Deronda* was not subject to the same standards of realistic accuracy that Eliot famously applied when researching *Romola* (1862–1863), the legal plot of *Felix Holt*, or aspects of Jewish culture in *Daniel Deronda*. Though she might easily have consulted Cross in order to make the incident more realistic, the bank failure belongs to the realm of the coincidental, melodramatic, and traumatic, leaving its specifics unknowable.

"ALL THAT ABOUT THE COMPANIES": MONEY'S FUTURE

Daniel Deronda's opening scenario of middle-class women's lives thrown into chaos when familial money is suddenly withdrawn recalls Austen's *Sense and Sensibility* (1811) and anticipates Gissing's *The*

Odd Women (1893). The situation is pervasive throughout nineteenth-century fictional plots, with many variations, including Austen's *Persuasion* (1818), Eliot's *The Mill on the Floss* (1860a), Gaskell's *Cranford* (1853a), and works by Riddell and Oliphant that will be discussed in later chapters.[32] Eliot actually favored narrative endings in which women voluntarily renounce inherited wealth, as do Eppie in *Silas Marner* (1860b), Esther in *Felix Holt* (1866), and Dorothea in *Middlemarch* (1871–1872). These decisions emphasize the higher values of women who choose love or helping others over personal gain and are more straightforward than the ethical questions implicitly raised about money's dirty past in the case of Bulstrode's fortune or the West Indian origins of Fanny Davilow's inheritance.

In *Daniel Deronda*, the loss of "property" saved by a West Indian planter for his daughters is at once formulaic and consistent with the experiences of those cultures of investment in which Eliot moved late in her career. The money was saved and invested to provide for the future of the Armyn sisters. But for reasons not made clear—greed, impatience, bad judgment, bad information, or some combination of these—the best intentions of the early nineteenth-century West Indian planter were thwarted. As we have seen, Eliot's fiction was often concerned with the history of money's accumulation (Bulstrode's wealth, Mr. Armyn's property), but her own earned income was invested with an eye to the future, even beyond her death.

However satirically she portrayed the Dodson sisters' obsession with their investments and wills in *The Mill on the Floss*, Eliot carefully attended to her own financial legacy. Her will provided for her dependents, specifically Bertie Lewes's South African widow Eliza Lewes and her children. Eliza had the income from £12,000 in trust for her life or until her remarriage. Upon Eliza's death or remarriage, the moiety went to the children, George Henry and Marian Lewes. Eliot also made a bequest of £5000 to Emily Clarke, her niece, and established annuities for life for Mrs. Caroline Bray (£100) and Mrs. Mary Dowling, her housekeeper (£40).[33] Her first major purchase in 1860 had been £2000 worth of shares in the Great Indian Peninsula Railway, which paid 5%. She kept these securities for the rest of her life, and they were part of her extensive portfolio at her death. She specifically requested that the earnings from *Daniel Deronda* be conservatively invested (Eliot 1954–1978c, VI:344). Coleman (2014) notes that the overall return on her investments decreased to 4% by the end of her life, reflecting her cautious investment behavior (47).[34]

Coleman has written about Eliot's investments and published an analysis of her portfolio at the time of her death (Appendix A). He emphasizes that her diversified holdings, especially in American railways, reflect Cross's influence. There is still more to be said about the nature of those investments and the close attention Eliot and Lewes paid to their specific stock holdings, which connected them to the expanding global financial network to which Eliot gestured in her fiction as an integral part of the late Victorian cultures of investment. Both Eliot's and Lewes's journals record the dividends paid from specific investments, intermingled with the most personal of details, including what they were reading, who they met, and, in Lewes's case, the sad details in 1869 of how many drops of morphine he administered to Thornie, his dying son. These investments were made possible almost exclusively by Eliot's income from her writing, though Lewes also notes the dividends he received for his mother and the shares he transferred to Vivian, his nephew, whom Eliot continued to support financially after Lewes's death and to whom she left £1000 in her will.[35]

Even before Cross formed his new company with Robin Benson in 1875, he was investing for Lewes and Eliot, with Lewes handling most of the business correspondence but trusting Cross implicitly to manage the account. On January 17, 1873, Lewes wrote to Cross, "I should be glad if you would invest 2000–2300 £ for me *as you think best*. Whatever you do will be well done in my eyes, so that you need refer nothing to me on this matter" (Eliot 1954–1978b, V:368). In 1873, Lewes's lists of investments began to include more US stocks, including railways in Baltimore (Maryland), Louisville (Kentucky), Nashville (Tennessee), New Jersey, and Philadelphia and Pittsburgh (Pennsylvania), as well as US bonds (368). Three months later, in a letter addressed to "Delightful Nephew," Lewes is more assertive, instructing Cross on April 18, 1873, to sell US bonds and "reinvest the proceeds by some of your American confidences" (402). Taking advantage of Cross's "confidences," and mixing business and social news, he adds: "Yesterday I dined out and met Emerson—delightfully simple creature! I hope you got my cheque." He signs the letter, "Ever your Uncle."

Lewes's diaries continue to reflect the interest he and Eliot took in their investments and to mingle the personal and the financial. In 1875, for example, he records the death of Bertie, his son, in South Africa. The diary also includes a summary of the stocks and shares they held from around the globe, including the Oriental Bank, with which Cross had long associations, and from Russia, South Africa, Australia, India, and various US states (New York, Illinois, Michigan). Lewes and Eliot had long held shares in the London and St. Katharine Docks and the East and West India docks in London; even closer to home, they invested in the Regents Canal, running alongside their house (the Priory, in Regent's Park); and the Commercial docks in Surrey, where they would soon purchase a second house. Income from their investments at this time was around £4000 annually. Reflecting Cross's balancing of the portfolio by 1875, the Louisville and Nashville Railway shares had been sold and investments in Buenos Aires had been added.[36]

After Lewes's death in November 1878, when Eliot was endowing a Studentship for him at Cambridge, she carefully entered her investments in her journal, and she called on Cross repeatedly to discuss financial matters relating to the endowment, but no doubt also to her own future and the provisions after her death. For example, on March 11, 1879, she wrote in her journal: "Johnnie came to discuss investments and brought me a register with all my investments neatly written out. I authorized him to sell San Francisco Bank, Continental Gas, and the American Coupons previously marked to the amount of £5000—to be invested in L. and N.W. Debentures—also U.S. Funded which were about to be paid" (Eliot and Cross 1885, 166). A week later, on March 18, she went to her lawyer at Bloomsbury Square to sign her will and noted, "J.W.C. came, and brought me the account of sales and purchases of stock" (167). Having written what would turn out to be her last published work, *Impressions of Theophrastus Such*, Eliot was putting her financial life in order, and the accounts of sales and purchases of stocks were essential to this planning for the future.

Familial misfortunes such as those suffered by Cross in 1857 and Benson in 1867 and 1875 were a cultural reality, which had a personal face for Eliot, though she had not experienced comparable failures in her own investments. Having written about the devastating consequences for women of poorly invested money, and being so heavily invested herself in a variety of stocks and shares, Eliot made sure to avoid the "wicked recklessness" of financial managers such as the fictional Mr. Lassman(n). As Lewes's letters and Eliot's journals show, their financial relationship with Cross was inherently one of trust and intimacy, and it is no wonder, however much surprise it caused at the time, that financial dependence led to marriage. As discussed in other chapters, financial and personal relationships were often intermingled in the nineteenth-century cultures of investment, and the relationship between women and the financial advisors on whom they depended often involved an affective and/or sexual dimension.[37] Eliot was fortunate in her choice of a financial advisor and husband: Imagine how vulnerable she would have been if Cross had proven anything other than trustworthy and competent.

In analyzing Eliot's investments, which were part of the culture of investment that she inhabited, we may apply some of the same scrutiny to the history of money that she did in her writing. Ethical investing may be a modern concept, but it seems relevant to understanding the contexts of investments made by Eliot and her contemporaries. Naturally, Eliot would not want to invest in a company that she knew produced shoddy goods or was otherwise corrupt. But she invested in so many companies (notably not in mines) that she could not possibly inquire into all their histories and operations. "Moral Swindlers," a chapter in *Impressions of Theophrastus Such* (1879), considers the national implications of fraudulent productions in relation to the modern use of the word "morality." The chapter begins with a conversation "in a time of commercial trouble" about the exposure of a swindler named Sir Gavial Mantrap, "his conduct in relation to the Eocene Mines, and to other companies ingeniously devised by him for the punishment of ignorance in people of small means," and his victims, "the widows, spinsters, and hard-working fathers whom his unscrupulous haste to make himself rich has cheated of all their savings" (129). That Sir Gavial is able to live comfortably on "his wife's settlement of one or two thousand in the consols" is a source of her narrator's outrage, while "Melissa," representing popular opinion, absolves Sir Gavial on the grounds of his good domestic behavior. Reflecting a cynicism about business, Melissa remarks: "Oh, all that about the Companies, I know was most unfortunate. In commerce people are led to do so many things" (130). This leads Theophrastus to rail against those who seek to gain by "supplying bad preserved meats to our navy" (131). He argues that "make-shift work" is "the fatal cause that must degrade our national rank and our commerce in spite of all open markets and discovery of available coal-seams" (134), and that no domestic virtues excuse "a manufacturer who devises the falsification of wares, or a trader who deals in virtueless seed-grains" (135).[38] Eliot had taken a moral stance on the quality of work from the first scene in her first novel *Adam Bede* (1859) and with her idealized Everyman characters Adam, Felix Holt, and Caleb Garth. They are heroes precisely because they embody a doctrine of hard work and care more about the quality of the work they do than what they are paid for it. "Moral Swindlers," following on the Bulstrode plot in *Middlemarch* and the Grapnel and Co. subplot in *Daniel Deronda*, confirms Eliot's opinion about poorly made goods particularly and about business and financial ethics generally.

When it comes to the government securities and private companies in which Eliot invested, we may ask whether she considered anything other than the percentages on the dividends paid. As surviving journals and letters show, Eliot and Lewes were enamored of this profitable game of buying and selling shares. Was it speculating? It certainly was more than passively receiving dividends from money invested in the Consols.[39] As in so many other ways, Eliot and Lewes were on the cutting edge of cultural change. Cross took them to the Bank of England to view the latest technology for measuring gold, a device Theophrastus mentions in "Shadows of the Coming Race" (Haight 1968, 477). Cross also demonstrated to them a new invention called the telephone. Thanks to their young "nephew," their money was invested according to the most modern strategies. Cross's familiarity with US railways in particular meant that Eliot would never invest in the type of fraudulent bubble railways that Trollope satirized in *The Way We Live Now* or the mines that Eliot herself criticized in Sir Gavial Mantrap's Eocene Mines.

CONCLUSION

This chapter began with some background on the history of the St. Katharine Docks in which both Eliot and Gaskell invested. Eliot was familiar with similar controversies over engineering projects dating back to the early construction of railroads when she was still living in Nuneaton and Coventry. The tension between preservation and progress is evident throughout her fiction, for example, in the introduction to *Felix Holt* and in the detailed representation of opposition to the railway in *Middlemarch*. This latter includes the violence threatened to the surveyors by the local workers, who were stirred up by Solomon Featherstone to believe that the railways will threaten their livelihood. The superstitious fear of progress is epitomized in the comment by Mrs. Waule (Solomon's sister) that with trains running through the pastures, "the cows will all cast their calves" and "I shouldn't wonder at the mare too, if she was in foal" (520). The novel, written in the retrospective knowledge of what the railroads have done for the country, comes down on the side of progress, as expressed by Caleb Garth. But Eliot also shows an awareness of the birth pangs of progress, part of the overall context of *Middlemarch*.

Dickens had represented the carnage caused by railway construction to the neighborhood of Camden Town in *Dombey and Son* (1846–1848), and Riddell lamented the destruction of City landmarks attending the construction of railway terminals in *Austin Friars* (1870). Eliot's knowledge of these social and political tensions leads to questions of what she may have thought about the history of the St. Katharine Docks when she invested in these domestic securities, as well as in multiple railroad companies around the globe, even though railroads would not require such wholesale displacement of (mostly uncompensated) residents as did the construction of the docks.

Dorothea might have thought about the miserable men who constructed railways in the USA, India, or South Africa, as she thought about miserable miners when she looked at her mother's jewels. But it is far from clear that Eliot had similar qualms about receiving dividends from companies with controversial histories. If she had thought critically about the companies in which she invested, Eliot might have rationalized along the lines of Deronda's advice to Gwendolen when he urged her to take her inheritance from Grandcourt. He understands that she wants to keep herself "pure from profiting" by her husband's death, but urges her to "let your remorse tell only on the use that you will make of your monetary independence" (657). Daniel's advice is consistent with his own behavior: Having been raised with all the advantages that Mallinger money could provide, he is at this point in the novel relying on his own economic independence to advance the larger social good, specifically in his idealistic scheme of helping Jewish people.

The St. Katharine Docks are a prime example of how commercial interests combined with engineering to transform the landscape of London and the nation in the nineteenth century, a process that fascinated novelists, including Gaskell, Dickens, Eliot, and Riddell.[40] Gaskell represented transformations in landscape and architecture in the opening scenes of *Mary Barton* (1848) and *Ruth* (1853b). Eliot reflected self-consciously on such changes from the destruction of Lantern Yard in *Silas Marner* (1860b) to the coach ride in *Felix Holt* (1866) to the coming of the railway in *Middlemarch* (1871–1872). Riddell particularly was relentless in recording and lamenting alterations to the landscape and architecture. Consider her meditation on the construction of the Cannon Street railway station in the opening chapter of *Austin Friars* or her attribution of new purposes to new buildings (profiting from limited liability) in the first pages of *Mortomley's Estate* (1874). In the latter novel, she also describes the docklands in which Gaskell and Eliot had invested, situating Mortomley's factory between "what is now called Regents Canal and the then unbuilt West Indian Docks" (31).[41] As we will see in the next chapter, reflections on the destruction of the past in the construction of modern cities are central to Riddell's fiction and her sensibility as a novelist. She, like Gaskell and Eliot, had a complex, ambivalent relationship to the advances of modern capitalism, but more than any other novelist of her generation, Riddell had direct experience of business and faced unique ethical choices in her own financial life. Her experiences are reflected in her fiction.

Notes

1. The *Times* [London] (1828) reported these statistics on October 27, and they are widely quoted in subsequent histories. Walter Thornbury (1878) observes: "In no single spot of London, not even at the Bank, could so vivid an impression of the vast wealth of England be obtained as at the docks."
2. As we saw in the last chapter, gesturing to but not naming slavery is also a feature of Gaskell's *Mary Barton* (1848) and *North and South* (1854–1855). In another example of coding and ekphrasis, Eliot (1864) in "Brother Jacob" refers to "Turner's latest style." Kate Flint (1999), in her discussion of sugar in Victorian fiction, calls it a "haunting reminder" of slavery (84). Flint (1999) connects this reference to Turner's 1840 painting, *The Slave Ship*. For a detailed reading of this painting, see Baucom (2005).
3. The bill was passed in 1833 and partial emancipation occurred in 1834, followed by an apprenticeship period and full emancipation in 1838 (Walvin 2001, 264). There was a slave uprising in Jamaica in 1831–1832, which overlaps with the setting in *Middlemarch* (1871–1872).
4. On the cosmopolitan nature of Brooke's connections, see Robbins (2010).
5. Freedgood (2006) argues that "negro head tobacco" in Dickens's *Great Expectations* "encodes" the genocide of aboriginals in Australia (82). Just as Flint (1999) argues that slavery haunts Victorian literature in the form of sugar, so Freedgood contends that colonial atrocities are remembered through tobacco (83).
6. Wake (1997) writes of Cross: "On both sides the family fortunes had originally been made through the West Indian trade" (163). Draper (2010) records that in 1836 the Dennistoun family of Glasgow claimed £6000 in compensation for their Milton estate in Trinidad (132).

7. For a history of Dennistoun, see Baird (1922). For information on Alexander Dennistoun, see *100 Glasgow men* website, s.v. "Alexander Dennistoun," http://www.glasgowwestaddress.co.uk/100_Glasgow_Men/ Dennistoun_Alexander.htm (accessed 5 April 2018); also see Wood (1895). Harris (2000) states that John Walter Cross was born at St. Michael's Mount, in Aigburth, a wealthy suburb of Liverpool that is bordered by Dingle, where the Croppers also lived (71). However, according to Ancestry. com (2005), Liverpool Record Office, Liverpool, England, Reference Number: 283 PET/2/42, his birth record shows that he was born on March 12, 1840, in Barony, Lanark, Scotland. According to the 1851 British Census, he was living in Toxteth Park: see Ancestry.com (2011), Class: HO107; Piece: 2188; Folio: 567; Page: 31; GSU roll: 87195. On Cross's career and investment experience, see Coleman (2014), Wake (1997), Wood (1895).
8. Much of this information about the Bensons and Crosses comes from Wake's (1997) history of the Kleinwort and Benson family companies. Charlotte Riddell named one of her city businessmen Kleinwort in *Mortomley's Estate* (1874).
9. It is unclear exactly how long Cross spent in New York. Wake (1997) says he spent eight years (162); Harris (2000) says that he was there for twelve years. Wood (1895) implies that Cross had moved back to England before the bank closed down in 1868, remarking that his son-in-law joined him at the bank after "John W. Cross went home" (II:355).
10. Eliot and Lewes's portfolio would later include shares in the Oriental Bank.
11. George Robb discovered that the New York City firm of Morton, Bliss and Co. listed R.J. [Robert James] Cross as having $17,000 on deposit in 1886; this was Johnnie Cross's younger brother. From 1878 until 1899, R.J. was a member of Morton, Bliss, as were bankers and bro kers for many leading Republican Party politicians and power brokers of the day. R.J. was also a director of the Manhattan Trust Company and a trustee for several insurance companies. He had a house in Washington Square, in New York City. The dates suggest that he assumed responsibility for the family business in America after Johnnie's return to England (personal correspondence with George Robb, May 20, 2016). See also Leonard (1911, 551).
12. White (1983) refers to Cross's relationships with two women. White may have had access to family letters as a source for this transformation of fact into fiction.
13. Cross (1893) reprinted this article, along with others he had written; Cross (1905) also republished other essays.

14. Benson also invested in railroad and land development companies in the Midwest through his brother, who was based in St. Paul, Minnesota. After Cross retired in 1883, the firm reverted to Robert Benson & Co.
15. For the most comprehensive study of money, economics, and ethics in Eliot's writing, see Coleman (2014).
16. Coleman (2014) observes that in the last year of her life, Eliot held a portfolio of investment valued at £30,000 but "never had more than £1000 in the Union Bank of London" (47). She was not inclined to store money without earning interest.
17. The widow Dunkirk wanted to find her daughter because her son had died and she hoped for a grandson as a "channel" for the property she had inherited both inside and outside of the business (580). After her death, Bulstrode withdrew his capital from the business and "used his hundred thousand" to make himself respectable in a new life in *Middlemarch* (581).
18. Coleman (2014) notes that in Eliot's novels, financial pathology is "rarely identifiable by its transgression of civil or criminal laws" (147). The questions she raises are ethical rather than strictly legal.
19. This passage supports Kaufman's (2009) argument that the origins of the money in *Middlemarch* are distinctly Jewish. She discusses the problem of inheritance, money, and bloodlines in what she calls "a story about a town that attempts to conceal or lose its historical and cultural intimacy with a Jewish past" (155).
20. "It" narratives that trace the life of a thing caught the imagination of Victorian readers. See Plotz (2008), Freedgood (2006).
21. Meyer (1996) and Linehan (1992) each explore the relationship between colonial power and domestic tyranny in Eliot's work.
22. Watson (2008) claims that debates about West Indian slavery in the 1860s recall "an earlier invocation of a united empire in the wake of the American Revolution and the struggle over slavery in the Caribbean in the early nineteenth century" (156). He argues that Eliot's *Felix Holt* engages questions raised by events in Jamaica (e.g., the Morant Bay Uprising), even though "the Caribbean never appears in the novel" (173), and slavery is "displaced from the Caribbean to Turkey" (180). Along with "Brother Jacob," *Felix Holt* in this reading is another instance of Eliot's indirect and allusive approach related to contemporaneous conditions in the Caribbean.
23. There is no indication that the mines were colonial, as Andres (1996, 93) claims.
24. This story originated in an eighteenth-century history of Barbados; see Small (1999). Meyer (1996) notes the significance of the horse's name.

25. McCormack (2015) points out that when Eliot and Lewes sailed from Barcelona to Malaga in 1867, Lewes plucked a stalk of Mediterranean sugar cane, out of scientific interest, and recorded it in his journal (92). She suggests that the reference to the sugar cane plantation in *Daniel Deronda* may be one of the many instances of coded communication with Lewes in Eliot's fiction.
26. For the limits of knowledge in *Middlemarch*, see Welsh (1985).
27. Rosenman (1990) refers to Gwendolen's misfortune as a result of "her uncle's speculation" (186).
28. For details, see Elliott (2006) and Taylor (2006).
29. It is not clear what kind of firm Grapnel and Co. is, but Mrs. Davilow's comments suggest that it was not a "limited" company or bank. The majority of established banks did not adopt limited liability until after 1879 (Acheson and Turner 2011, 210). In considering the reasons women were particularly attracted to unlimited (and therefore riskier) bank investments, Acheson and Turner conclude that the high rate of return was enough to attract even risk-averse investors such as women (226). Johnnie Cross was involved in establishing the first "limited" bank in the USA following the Limited Liability Act of 1862. The English and American Exchange Banking Corporation, however, voluntarily liquidated in 1867 following the collapse of Overend and Gurney (Wood 1895, II:360–61).
30. Eliot's first reference is to "Mr. Lassman," and her second reference is to "Mr. Lassmann," an apparent oversight. In his introduction to *Daniel Deronda*, Newton suggests that Eliot "probably intended 'Lassmann' as it has stronger Jewish associations and Jews were strongly identified with finance and capitalism" (see Eliot 1876b, 697n195). Overend and Gurney was a Quaker establishment.
31. For the novelistic convention of failed banks, see Weiss (1986), Reed (1984), Alborn (1995), Wagner (2010).
32. The theme of a West Indian inheritance appears in Jane Austen's *Persuasion* (1818) via the character of Mrs. Smith, whose West Indian fortune Wentworth helps to recover, and more prominently in *Mansfield Park* (1814). For Austen's own connection to West Indian plantations, see Gibbon (1982). The legacy of West Indian slavery casts a shadow over works such as Thackeray's (1847–1848) *Vanity Fair* (with the West Indian heiress Miss Swartz), and famously in Charlotte Brontë's *Jane Eyre* (1847) and Eliot's "Brother Jacob," *Felix Holt* (1866) and *Daniel Deronda*. The subject is explored further in Chapter 7 as it relates to Margaret Oliphant's *Kirsteen* (1890a) and *Sons and Daughters* (1890b).
33. This information appeared in the *Illustrated London News* and was republished in a notice in the *New York Times* (1881).

34. Eliot also held shares in "Improved Industrial Dwellings," which appears to be a socially progressive investment choice.
35. For Lewes's 1869 journal, see Eisenberg (2015). For the Great Indian Peninsular Railroad, see Kerr (2008).
36. Coleman (2014) breaks down these percentages in his Appendix A.
37. See Henry (2013).
38. Charlotte Riddell's (1866) *The Race for Wealth* treats the subject of food adulteration. For a reading of the novel within the context of Victorian debates about food adulteration, see Stern (2008, Chapter 3).
39. Coleman (2014) notes that Cross's major career move "represented a shift from the principal, proprietary, risk-taking that his work for the family firm of Dennistoun Cross involved, to the advisory, fee-generating nature of the firm he set up with Robert Benson in 1875" (46).
40. Another ethical question arises concerning the exotic commodities traded in the late nineteenth-century activities of the docks including ivory, ostrich feathers, and turtle shells.
41. By this, Riddell must mean the South Docks, which were constructed in the 1860s.

REFERENCES

Acheson, Graeme G., and John D. Turner. 2011. Shareholder liability, risk aversion, and investment returns in nineteenth-century British banking. In *Men, women, and money: Perspectives on gender, wealth, and investment 1850–1930*, ed. David Green, Alastair Owens, Josephine Maltby, and Janette Rutterford, 207–227. Oxford: Oxford University Press.

Ahluwalia, D.P.S., Bill Ashcroft, and Roger Knight (eds.). 1999. *White and deadly: Sugar and colonialism*. Commack, NY: Nova Science Publishers.

Alborn, Timothy. 1995. The moral of the failed bank: Professional plots in the Victorian money market. *Victorian Studies* 38 (2): 199–226.

Alcott, Louisa May. 1868–1869. *Little women*, ed. Valerie Alderson. Oxford: Oxford World's Classics, 2009.

Ancestry.com. 2005. *1851 England Census* [database on-line]. Provo, UT: Ancestry.com Operations, Inc.

———. 2011. *Liverpool, England, Church of England Baptisms, 1813–1906* [database on-line]. Provo, UT: Ancestry.com Operations, Inc.

Andres, Sophia. 1996. Fortune's wheel in "Daniel Deronda": Sociopolitical turns of the British empire. *Victorians Institute Journal* 24: 87–111.

Austen, Jane. 1811. *Sense and sensibility*, ed. Claudia Johnson. New York: W. W. Norton, 2001.

———. 1814. *Mansfield Park*, ed. Claudia Johnson. New York: Norton, 1998.

———. 1818. *Persuasion*, ed. James Kinsley. Oxford: Oxford University Press, 2008.
Baird, James. 1922. *Dennistoun past and present*. http://parkheadhistory.com/surrounding-areas/dennistoun/4308-2/. Accessed 5 Apr 2018.
Baucom, Ian. 2005. *Specters of the Atlantic: Finance capital, slavery and the philosophy of history*. Durham, NC: Duke University Press.
Besant, Walter. 1901. *East London*. New York: Century Company.
Bodenheimer, Rosemarie. 1994. *The real life of Mary Ann Evans*. Ithaca, NY: Cornell University Press.
Bradshaw, George. 1862. *Bradshaw's handbook to London*. Repr. London: Conway, 2012.
Brontë, Charlotte. 1847. *Jane Eyre*, ed. Margaret Smith. Oxford: Oxford University Press, 2008.
———. 1853. *Villette*, ed. Margaret Smith and Herbert Rosengarten. Oxford: Oxford University Press, 2008.
Brown, R. Douglas. 1978. *Port of London*. Lavenham, UK: T. Dalton.
Coleman, Dermot. 2014. *George Eliot and money: Economics, ethics and literature*. Cambridge: Cambridge University Press.
Collins, K.K. (ed.). 2010. *George Eliot: Interviews and reflections*. New York: Palgrave Macmillan.
Cross, John Walter. 1872. Social New York. *MacMillan's Magazine*, 117.
———. 1893. Social New York. In *Impressions of Dante and of the new world*, 266–293. Edinburgh: W. Blackwood and Sons.
———. 1905. *The rake's progress in finance*. Edinburgh: W. Blackwood and Sons.
Dickens, Charles. 1839. The river. In *Sketches by Boz*. 122–128, ed. Dennis Walder. New York: Penguin, 1995.
———. 1846–1848. *Dombey and son*, ed. Alan Horsman. Oxford: Oxford University Press, 1984.
———. 1864–1865. *Our mutual friend*, ed. Michael Cotsell. Oxford: Oxford University Press, 2009.
Draper, Nicholas. 2010. *The price of emancipation: Slave-ownership, compensation and British society at the end of slavery*. New York: Cambridge University Press.
Drummond, Diane K. 2008. Sustained British investment in overseas railways, 1830–1914: The imperial dream, engineers' assurances or an "investment hungry public"? In *Across the borders: Financing the world's railways in the nineteenth and twentieth centuries*, ed. Ralf Roth and Günter Dinhobl, 207–224. Burlington, VT: Ashgate.
Eisenberg, Michelle. 2015. George Henry Lewes's 1869 diary and journal: A transcription and annotation of unpublished holographs held at the Beineke Library of Yale University. *George Eliot-George Henry Lewes Studies* 67 (2): 93–226.

Eliot, George. 1859. *Adam Bede*, ed. Carol A. Martin. Oxford: Oxford University Press, 2001.
———. 1860a. *The mill on the Floss*, ed. Nancy Henry. Boston: Houghton Mifflin, 2004.
———. 1860b. *Silas Marner: The weaver of Raveloe*, ed. Terence Cave. Oxford: Oxford University Press, 1996.
———. 1862–1863. *Romola*, ed. Andrew Brown. Oxford: Clarendon, 1993.
———. 1864. Brother Jacob. In *The lifted veil and brother Jacob*, ed. Helen Small, 3–43. Oxford: Oxford University Press, 1999.
———. 1866. *Felix Holt: The radical*, ed. Fred. C. Thompson. New York: Oxford University Press, 1988.
———. 1871–1872. *Middlemarch*, ed. David Carroll. Oxford: Oxford University Press, 2008.
———. 1876a. *Daniel Deronda*, ed. John Rignall. London: Everyman, 1999.
———. 1876b. *Daniel Deronda*, ed. K.M. Newton and Graham Handley. Oxford: Oxford University Press, 2014.
———. 1879. *Impressions of Theophrastus Such*, ed. Nancy Henry. Iowa City: University of Iowa Press, 1994.
———. 1954–1978a. *The George Eliot letters*, vol. II: 1852–1858, ed. Gordon Sherman Haight, 9 vols. New Haven: Yale University Press.
———. 1954–1978b. *The George Eliot letters*, vol. V: 1869–1873, ed. Gordon Sherman Haight, 9 vols. New Haven: Yale University Press.
———. 1954–1978c. *The George Eliot letters*, vol. VI: 1932–1933, ed. Gordon Sherman Haight, 9 vols. New Haven: Yale University Press.
Eliot, George, and J.W. Cross. 1885. *George Eliot's life as related in her letters and journals*, 3 vols. Edinburgh: William Blackwood and Sons.
Elliott, Geoffrey. 2006. *The mystery of Overend and Gurney: A financial scandal in Victorian England*. London: Methuen.
Flint, Kate. 1999. Spectres of sugar. In *White and deadly: Sugar and colonialism*, ed. Pal Ahluwalia, Bill Ashcroft, and Roger Knight, 83–94. Commack, NY: Nova Science Publishers.
Freedgood, Elaine. 2006. *The ideas in things: Fugitive meaning in the Victorian novel*. Chicago: University of Chicago Press.
Gaskell, Elizabeth. 1848. *Mary Barton: A tale of Manchester*, ed. Edgar Wright. Oxford: Oxford University Press, 1998.
———. 1853a. *Cranford*, ed. Elizabeth Porges Watson. Oxford: Oxford University Press, 2011.
———. 1853b. *Ruth*, ed. Nancy Henry. London: Everyman, 2001.
———. 1854–1855. *North and south*, ed. Angus Easson. Oxford: Oxford University Press, 1998.
———. 1863. *Sylvia's lovers*, ed. Nancy Henry. London: Everyman, 1997.

Gibbon, Frank. 1982. The Antiguan connection: Some new light on "Mansfield Park". *Cambridge Quarterly* 11 (2): 298–305.
Gissing, George. 1893. *The odd women*, ed. Arlene Young. Orchard Park, NY: Broadview, 1998.
———. 1905. *Will Warburton: A romance of real life*. New York: A.P. Dutton.
Grindon, Leo H. 1882. *A history of Lancashire: From earliest times until 1880, incorporating Manchester & Liverpool*. Bolton: Aurora Publishing, 1995.
Haight, Gordon Sherman. 1968. *George Eliot: A biography*. New York: Oxford University Press.
Harris, Margaret. 2000. John Walter Cross. In *The Oxford reader's companion to George Eliot*, ed. John Rignall, 71–74. Oxford: Oxford University Press.
Henry, Nancy. 2002. *George Eliot and the British empire*. Cambridge: Cambridge University Press.
———. 2013. George Eliot and finance. In *A companion to George Eliot*, ed. Amanda Anderson and Harry Shaw, 323–337. Chichester, UK: Wiley Blackwell.
Kaufman, Heidi. 2009. *English origins, Jewish discourse, and the nineteenth-century British novel: Reflections on a nested nation*. University Park: Pennsylvania State University Press.
Kerr, Ian J. 2008. John Chapman and the promotion of the great Indian Peninsula Railway, 1842–1850. In *Across the borders: Financing the world's railways in the nineteenth and twentieth centuries*, ed. Ralf Roth and Gunter Dinhobl, 225–239. Aldershot, UK: Ashgate.
Leonard, John William. 1911. *Who's who in finance*. New York: Joseph & Sefton.
Linehan, Katherine Bailey. 1992. Mixed politics: The critique of imperialism in *Daniel Deronda*. *Texas Studies in Literature and Language* 34 (3): 323–346.
Mayhew, Henry. 1861. *London labour and the London poor: A cyclopaedia of the condition and earnings of those that will work, those that cannot work, and those that will not work*. London: F. Cass, 1967.
McCormack, Kathleen. 2015. Yachting with Grandcourt: Gwendolen's mutiny in "Daniel Deronda". *Victorian Literature and Culture* 43 (1): 83–95.
Meyer, Susan. 1996. *Imperialism at home: Race and Victorian women's fiction*. Ithaca, NY: Cornell University Press.
New York Times. 1881. George Eliot's Will, March 4.
Oliphant, Margaret. 1852. *The Melvilles*. London: Richard Bentley. The Margaret Oliphant Fiction Collection. http://www.oliphantfiction.com/x0200_single_title.php?titlecode=melvls. Accessed 5 Apr 2018.
———. 1890a. *Kirsteen: The story of a Scotch family seventy years ago*. London: Everyman, 1984.
———. 1890b. *Sons and daughters*. Edinburgh: William Blackwood and Sons. The Margaret Oliphant Fiction Collection. http://www.oliphantfiction.com/x0200_single_title.php?titlecode=sondtr. Accessed 5 Apr 2018.

Plasa, Carl. 2009. *Slaves to sweetness: British and Caribbean literatures of sugar.* Liverpool: Liverpool University Press.
Plotz, John. 2008. *Portable property: Victorian culture on the move.* Princeton, NJ: Princeton University Press.
Pudney, John. 1975. *London's docks.* London: Thames and Hudson.
Reade, Charles, and Dion Boucicault. 1868. *Foul play.* Boston: Ticknor & Fields.
Reed, John R. 1984. A friend to Mammon: Speculation in Victorian literature. *Victorian Studies* 27 (2): 179–202.
Riddell, Charlotte. 1866. *Race for wealth*, 2 vols. Leipzig: Benharhd Tauchnitz.
———. 1870. *Austin Friars: A novel.* London: Hutchinson.
———. 1874. *Mortomley's estate: A novel.* London: Tinsley Brothers.
———. 1884. *Susan Drummond: A novel*, 3 vols. London: Bentley.
Robbins, Bruce. 2010. Victorian cosmopolitanism, interrupted. *Victorian Literature and Culture* 38 (2): 421–425.
Rosenman, Ellen. 1990. The house and the home: The family in the "Banker's Magazine" and "Daniel Deronda". *Women's Studies: An Inter-disciplinary Journal* 17 (3–4): 179–192.
Sandiford, Keith A. 2000. *The cultural politics of sugar: Caribbean slavery and narratives of colonialism.* Cambridge: Cambridge University Press.
Schaffer, Talia. 2016. *Romance's rival: Familiar marriage in Victorian fiction.* Oxford: Oxford University Press.
Small, Helen. 1999. Introduction to *The lifted veil and brother Jacob*, by George Eliot. Oxford: Oxford University Press.
Stern, Rebecca. 2008. *Home economics: Domestic fraud in Victorian England.* Columbus: Ohio State University Press.
Sussman, Charlotte. 1994. Women and the politics of sugar, 1792. *Representations* 48: 48–69.
———. 2000. *Consuming anxieties: Consumer protest, gender and British slavery: 1713–1833.* Stanford, CA: Stanford University Press.
Taylor, James. 2006. *Creating capitalism: Joint-stock enterprise in British politics and culture 1800–1870.* London: Royal Historical Society.
Thackeray, William Makepeace. 1847–1848. *Vanity fair: A novel without a hero*, ed. Diane Mowat. Oxford: Oxford University Press, 2008.
Thornbury, Walter. 1878. St. Katherine's docks. In *Old and New London*, vol. 2. London: Cassell, Petter & Galpin, 117–121. http://www.british-history.ac.uk/old-new-london/vol2. Accessed 5 Apr 2018.
Times [London]. 1828. Opening of the St. Katharine's docks, October 27.
Trollope, Anthony. 1875. *The way we live now*, ed. Francis O'Gorman. Oxford: Oxford University Press, 2016.
Wagner, Tamara. 2010. *Financial speculation in Victorian fiction: Plotting money and the novel genre, 1815–1901.* Columbus: Ohio State University Press.

Wake, Jehanne. 1997. *Kleinwort Benson: The history of two families in banking*. Oxford: Oxford University Press.
Walvin, James. 2001. *Black ivory: A history of British slavery*. Oxford: Blackwell.
Watson, Tim. 2008. *Caribbean culture and British fiction*. Cambridge: Cambridge University Press.
Weiss, Barbara. 1986. *The hell of the English: Bankruptcy and the Victorian novel*. Lewisburg, PA: Bucknell University Press.
Welsh, Alexander. 1985. *George Eliot and blackmail*. Cambridge, MA: Harvard University Press.
White, Terence D.V. 1983. *Johnnie Cross: A novel*. New York: St. Martin's Press.
Wood, William. 1895. *Autobiography of William Wood*, 2 vols. New York: J.S. Babcock.

CHAPTER 6

Charlotte Riddell's Financial Life and Fiction

Death is bankruptcy.
—Charlotte Riddell, *Mortomley's Estate*

In 1856, an aspiring author named Charlotte Eliza Lawson Cowan, an immigrant to London from Ireland, published her first novel, *Zuriel's Grandchild* (Riddell 1856). It begins with the story of John Zuriel, a Jewish merchant, who has risen from poverty in the streets of Liverpool to splendid wealth. The plot is set in motion by Zuriel's disinheritance of his daughter when she marries against his wishes. At the end of the novel, Dora, his granddaughter, inherits his fortune and estate. Perhaps most remarkably, Dora and her husband agree to change their last name to Zuriel. Such themes of recovered inheritance and restored Jewish identity anticipate Eliot's *Daniel Deronda* (1876), published twenty years later. Riddell's forgotten novel also shows that the author, who later became known as the novelist of the City and Middlesex, was trained on matters of money and financial instability even before she married the inventor Joseph Riddell, to whose influence critics have attributed her knowledge of business. In tracing her financial life, this chapter recovers aspects of her family history and also introduces new details about business and legal entanglements during her marriage. This biographical context is essential to understanding her unique place in literary history as a female author with an inside perspective on business and finance.

Charlotte Riddell (1832–1906) was at the height of her literary and financial success when her husband Joseph declared bankruptcy in 1871. The hard-earned income that she received from her fiction had been invested in his business of manufacturing and marketing patented stoves. She was active in managing the business, which, like his previous ventures, failed. The writer Wemyss Reid (1905) was surprised to find "this gifted woman, in whose brilliant pages I had found so much to delight me, acting as her husband's clerk, and engaged in making out invoices in the cellar beneath the shop" in Cheapside (141). Entrepreneurial capitalism—the dealings of small businessmen—was what she knew, and this knowledge created a niche for her fiction, which offered an insider's perspective on business and investment cultures that were mysterious to many readers. While her commercial life may have conflicted with her literary life, in terms of both the time it demanded and the social circles from which it excluded her, in fact the two worlds were intertwined. Her life and her writings represent a unique bridge to commercial, financial, and domestic lives, as well as to the economic and the literary spheres of Victorian culture.

Most of the women investors I discuss in this book were able to keep their hands clean from commercial dealings while putting their money to work precisely because of the increasingly common practice of investing in the stock market. Riddell was different. There she was in a Cheapside basement writing invoices. Her husband apparently was a social embarrassment to her literary friends, and yet he was the inspiration for her most enduring and repeated fictional type—the inventor or engineer ensnared in circumstances beyond his control that prevent his financial success. Nevertheless, in 1870 she sued her husband and James Smith, his creditor, in an attempt to retain her own earnings under the Married Women's Property Act (MWPA), and Smith testified that she had told him, "If I imagined she was going to work any more to pay her husband's debts, I was quite mistaken."[1] Despite the tough rhetoric, she did work to pay her husband's debts, turning her observations of business into popular—but also formally innovative and psychologically complex—realist fiction that generated income to pay the bills. That it was a woman who became known as the "novelist of the City" and provided details about company promoting, financial legislation, and shareholder culture is all the more remarkable.

In an era when provincial settings such as Elizabeth Gaskell's Manchester, Anthony Trollope's Barsetshire, Margaret Oliphant's

Carlingford, and George Eliot's Midlands were popular, Riddell made "the City" within the city—the financial heart of London with its life of business and trade—into a province in its own right. Place was important to her; she moved frequently to different addresses in London, Middlesex, Essex, and Surrey, turning every place she lived into settings for her fiction. She also set novels in Ireland, where she was born, and in Liverpool, the birthplace of her mother. Over the course of a career that spanned from 1856 to 1902, she sought to erase the stigma attached to trade through realistic and sympathetic representations of City men that document the history and changing character of the City and its expanding suburbs. She made her reputation through her financial novels, which reflected her belief: "The City is the proper land for younger sons to emigrate to, if younger sons could but be induced to think so" (Riddell 1864, 181). As an emigrant herself, her notion that the financial center of the City of London was a foreign territory to which even aristocratic sons might emigrate is an interesting and original conceit. The movement from country to city or from city to city is crucial to plot development and character identity in her fiction.

Riddell was younger, more prolific and less successful than George Eliot, but their fiction writing careers began at the same time and only after they had moved to London—Riddell from Ireland and Eliot from the Midlands. *Zuriel's Grandchild* was published in 1856, the year before Eliot (1857) began serializing *Scenes of Clerical Life*. Furthermore, the two authors shared a determination to represent common people and a narrative voice that self-consciously commented on the importance of realism in fiction. As we have seen, Eliot explored the themes of financial responsibility and dirty money in both *Middlemarch* and *Daniel Deronda*. Riddell treats the same topics, but does so in more literal and explicit ways, which made one reviewer wonder whether her novels should be reviewed in the columns that are set apart for literature or whether "they would not more fitly receive a notice side by side with the works on foreign exchanges or the currency" (*Saturday Review* 1882). For example, whereas Eliot turned the failure of Overend and Gurney into a generic type of economic failure, Riddell refers to the crisis of 1866 directly—in *Susan Drummond* (1884) and *Mortomley's Estate* (1874c)—viewing it as a watershed of national history.

The differences between Eliot, the most influential of Victorian novelists then and now, and Riddell, who was forgotten even by late twentieth-century feminist critics, are more apparent than their similarities. Nonetheless, contemporary readers noted the connections. A reviewer of Riddell's *City and Suburb* (1861) remarked that it was "a natural fruit" of Eliot's *Adam Bede*, which had been published the previous year (*Saturday Review* 1861, 356). George Henry Lewes (November 1865–February 1866), in his *Fortnightly Review* article, "Criticism in Relation to Novels," made implicit comparisons in Eliot's favor about the responsibility of the critic to judge honestly rather than praise mindlessly the mass of mediocre literature flooding the market. Lewes uses the examples of Mary Elizabeth Braddon's (1865) *Sir Jasper's Tenant* and Riddell's (1865) Irish novel *Maxwell Drewitt* (published under the pseudonym F.G. Trafford). Lewes's criticism of Riddell's realism is harsh: "Without knowing anything of Ireland, I am quite sure that life at Connemara was not like what it appears in these pages" (358). Yet, he insists that he is only holding her work to the highest standards. If his remarks are severe, he writes, "let them be understood as at least implying the compliment of serious criticism" (356).

Three years after Eliot's death and in the shadow of her tremendous influence, Riddell published *A Struggle for Fame* (1883). This self-reflective portrait of an artist compares the novels written by her heroine Glenarva Westley to those of George Eliot. Glenarva, like Eliot and Riddell herself, refuses to tell conventional and therefore marketable love stories: "Where, for example, George Eliot counted her thousands, the *Family Herald* counts its tens of thousands!" (III:55). The comment implies that Eliot may have sold more copies than Riddell, but she never stooped to the level of the *Family Herald*, a weekly magazine of light literature published from 1843 to 1940, and here representing a periodical that pandered to mass-market tastes. Lewes elevates Riddell's work above the "commerce in trash" (November 1865–February 1866, 352) that he sets out to condemn, and his critique of her realism confirms that her social and aesthetic aims were similar to those of Eliot. Her financial subject matter and her pressure to publish for money (Lewes called her writing rushed), however, determined that future critics would not consider her writing in the same category as that of Eliot.

Through events like the crash of 1866 and financial legislation like the Bankruptcy Act of 1869, Riddell situates her characters within national history; their stories also draw on her own life. Rather than representing wars, natural disasters or sensational murders, her novels establish a social context in which commercial and financial networks—local and global economies—shape and determine the fate of ordinary people.

In this respect, she is typical of Victorian realists who are obsessed with money, but she also represents an extreme example of anxieties generated within a modern, uneven capitalist economy encompassing older models of commerce and newer models of finance functioning simultaneously in the City. It is tempting to see her preoccupation with money as a reflex of her unsettled financial times, but the specifics of her life must be considered in order to show how she was at once typical and exceptional. The mixture of fiction and reality in Riddell's novels extends to their autobiographical elements, which are not easily detected because we know so little about her life.

Twentieth-century and twenty-first-century literary criticism of Riddell's work has focused on the City novels, ghost stories, and Irish tales.[2] While there is still much more to say about the City and Irish novels, as well as the ghost stories, this chapter will focus on previously unexplored connections, such as the experiences of her mother's family and her life as a businesswoman, which she fictionalized to generate income to pay her husband's debts. Her family history, her marriage, and her long life as a widow all informed her fiction. Even before she met her future husband, her fiction was focused on money, business, and finance with radical financial insecurity constituting the practical and existential conditions of her characters' lives and identities.

Riddell was uniquely situated among Victorian authors as a participant in both the business and the literary worlds. She endorsed cultures of commerce and investment in which an ethics of economic survival challenged the gentlemanly scruples about trade and finance that characterized her fellow novelists and her reviewers.[3] I have been arguing that women novelists had a more tolerant attitude to, and appreciation of, investing as a means of earning income when other middle-class avenues to wealth were not open to them. Although Riddell often expressed moral objections to corruption and dishonesty, especially in her later work, her perspective on business and finance was more complex than even that of Gaskell, Eliot, and Oliphant precisely because of her personal involvement with the practical details—and actual people—of the Victorian commercial and financial spheres.

One reason the financial lives of Gaskell, Eliot, Riddell, and Oliphant are so interesting is that authorship made them the primary breadwinners in their families, reversing the gender roles of their time. Although they shared ambivalences about capitalism and stressed their place as wives and/or mothers, it is a remarkable fact that these women were not heiresses but rather earners in the literary marketplace and investors of their income. Their support of dependent husbands and children is a scenario that is familiar in middle-class households today, but even now it is still not the norm. Riddell, like all of her author contemporaries, dealt in the business of publishing, but the pressures to maintain her husband's business meant that the trade in boilers and stoves, the legal suits over debts, and the struggles to avoid and then endure bankruptcy became entangled with the ownership of her copyrights as well as her income from writing. Her income was his income; his debts became her debts. While she accepted this as a condition of marriage, she also used whatever modern means she could, especially the court of law, to protect her husband and herself.

Riddell's influence on later realist fiction is greater than has been credited in literary history, though it was recognized in her time. Anne Thackeray Ritchie (1870a) remarked in her "Heroines and Their Grandmothers" (first serialized in *Cornhill Magazine*): "It seems strange as one thinks of it that before these books came out no one had even thought of writing about City life" (403). Riddell's obituary in the September 26 issue of the *Times* (*Times* [London] 1906) asserted that before Riddell: "Commerce had scarcely before been considered a suitable theme, at least in this country, for fiction or the drama." Her determination to represent practical business affairs complemented the realism of Dickens, Gaskell, Trollope, Eliot, Oliphant, and others. Her obituary compared her to Balzac. George Gissing, whose career overlapped with hers and with whom she shared at least one publisher, Richard Bentley (also a publisher of Oliphant), furthered the economic determinism that is evident in her fiction. Unlike the inheritors of the financial novel tradition that she initiated, including the Americans Edith Wharton, Frank Norris, and Theodore Dreiser, her moralizing was attenuated by a personal knowledge of what business was like from the inside.

The critic S.M. Ellis (1931) published *Wilkie Collins, Le Fanu and Others*, in which one of the "others" was Riddell about whom he wrote that she held a "peculiar position as the novelist who could present with pathos the lives and aspirations of City men and make interesting the details and hectic excitements of business affairs, stocks and shares, and Company promoting" (279). Ellis was correct in observing that Riddell's fiction has much to recommend it. Architecturally, socially and financially, she is a historian of the City—recording and lamenting, for example, the encroaching of London suburbs on Middlesex and the destruction of old buildings and their replacement with inferior modern constructions. In an 1890 interview with the *Pall Mall Gazette*, Riddell explained: "I understand men well, I have much in sympathy with them, and I always find them easier to describe than women" (quoted in Ellis 1931, 279). Ellis considered that the subject of commerce and lives of City people accounted for Riddell's success because she found a ready audience among men of business. Furthermore, these popular representations of the London financial world gave her an income when her husband suffered financial ruin. The City, Ellis rightly concludes, was both her "blessing and her bane" (280).

In her most famous and successful novel, *George Geith of Fen Court*, published under the pseudonym F.G. Trafford, Riddell establishes her intention to make business interesting, to show "what trade really is; what an excitement, what a pain, what a struggle, and when honestly and honourably carried out, what a glory too" (97). George Geith is an accountant who tries to erase his past as a clergyman by focusing on his business and its profits. He falls in love with the daughter of Mr. Molozane, his client, an aristocrat who has been ruined by an ill-advised speculation in Cornish mines. Although he loses his own hard-won fortune in a bank failure, George marries and finds happiness with Beryl Molozane. His past comes back to haunt him in the form of an alcoholic wife he thought was dead. He is tried in court for bigamy—so common in the sensation novels of the 1860s—but is acquitted. In the end, Beryl dies and George becomes a successful City magnate.

Five years after Eliot interrupted the narrative of her *Adam Bede* (1859) to assert her realist agenda, Riddell offered a similar manifesto in *George Geith* (1864). Complaining of the governesses, sensitive young men, gold-diggers, emigrants, hunters, and explorers who populated contemporary novels, she laments:

> It is only trade, only that which is the back-bone of England, only that which furnishes heiresses for younger sons; only that which sends forth fleets of merchantmen, and brings home the products of all countries; only that which feeds the poor, and educates the middle classes, and keeps the nobility of the land from sinking to the same low level as the nobility of all other lands has done; it is only this, I say, which can find no writer worthy of it, no one who does not jeer at business and treat with contempt that which is holy in God's sight, because it is useful, and proves beneficial to millions and millions of his creatures. (144–5)

Without specifying names, Riddell's narrator implies that all fiction writers jeer contemptuously at trade and business. She defends trade as essential to the nation and therefore holy. Rather than emphasizing the work ethic of individuals, as most Victorian novelists do, she echoes the standard free-trade discourse of her time by praising the global economic networks that send forth fleets of merchants who bring home the products of all countries.

As she noted, she had a particular affinity with City men, and her arguments for the relevance of their interior and exterior lives to fiction are analogous to Eliot's arguments about the need to include the peasant classes in fiction. In *George Geith*, Riddell writes:

> Every other class has found some writer to tell its tale; but I can remember no book which has described a shopkeeper as a man, or ventured into the debatable middle land, where talent and energy are struggling from morning to night in dingy offices, in dark warehouses, unknown in the world's eye, solely because business has never yet learnt to be self-conscious; because it is in its very nature to work, rather than to think, to push forward to the goal rather than to analyze the reasons which induce it to push forward at all. (97–8)

Although throughout her work she emphasizes the psychological lives of her characters, she is unique in defending the heroism of men who do not analyze their own motives, an insight that works against the grain of much Victorian realism for its refusal to judge such men as inferior socially and intellectually. Her fiction uniquely combines the realist commitment to representing common life with an unapologetically procapitalist stance. Her novels take us into dingy offices and dark warehouses, and her call to represent a shopkeeper as a man anticipates later naturalist novels, such as Gissing's *Will Warburton* (1905).

Novels that incorporate dramatic financial events, such as swindles, crashes, and bankruptcies, have received their share of critical attention. In *Little Dorrit* (Dickens 1855–1857), *Vanity Fair* (Thackeray 1847–1848), *Cranford* (Gaskell 1853), *The Way We Live Now* (Trollope 1875), *Daniel Deronda* (Eliot 1876), *Hester* (Oliphant 1883), and many other works, such events often come down to the greed of men like Dickens's Merdle and Trollope's Melmotte, who are disposed of through the melodramatic convention of suicide. Less evidently suited for dramatic presentation are the everyday lives of honest capitalists and their families who, despite honesty and hard work, are buffeted about by the economy.

In *Austin Friars* (1870), Riddell argues, "The majority of writers who have undertaken to portray business know nothing on earth about it, and know, if that be possible, a trifle less about the men who work hard to keep wife and children above want while they live, and to leave an unsullied name behind them" (235). Furthermore, Riddell's real-life business experience meant that she was affected directly by some of the Victorian era's most significant financial legislation pertaining to limited liability, bankruptcy, and married women's property. To the chagrin of contemporary reviewers of her novels, she often wrote her opinions of such legislation into her fiction in the form of narrative asides and pronouncements. As Poovey (2008) notes, Charles Reade "considered it essential to refer to actual situations and to cite factual information because he wanted to provoke readers to action" (324). Reade's works were therefore hybrid genres that attracted criticism, including that of Margaret Oliphant (325). Riddell's fiction was exposed to the same criticisms.

Riddell's feelings on issues such as bankruptcy and limited liability were passionate. In *The Race for Wealth* (1866b), she writes: "No person who has not studied the statistics of companies can have the faintest idea of the deluge which came upon the earth for its wickedness when once Parliament opened the sluice-gates by doing away with Unlimited Responsibility" (140). In *The Senior Partner* (1882), she was still denouncing the law and the principle that had led to so many company failures, prompting one reviewer to observe that limited liability "fills her mind in much the same way as the Pope of Rome used to fill the minds of anxious Protestants" (*Saturday Review* 1882). A review of *Mitre Court* complains that "there is certainly no excuse for the interpolation in the early part of the book of a whole chapter of invective against the Metropolitan Board of Works, or whatever other person or persons are responsible for the changes in the City" (*Spectator* 1886, 118). The diatribes against limited liability, the Bankruptcy Act of 1869, the Metropolitan Board and tax law, while tedious to some of her more literary-minded critics, spoke to the men and women whose lives were affected by financial legislation and who, forming a core of the commercial middle class, made her novels popular. Her representations of the everyday lives of City people and the impact of financial changes on Victorian society give us a personalized window into an otherwise dry and faceless aspect of Victorian culture.[4]

Robb (1992) argues that during the mid-Victorian period, the values of rugged individualism and free trade meant that "ethical boundaries remained vague" and "many persons in the business community developed private patterns of behavior that were at odds with the professed, public morality" (169). Such persons believed that "success was incompatible with strict integrity" (170). He argues further: "The entrepreneurial culture of Victorian England created generations of businessmen who never told direct lies, or were never caught in criminal acts, but whose minds were inured to 'legal duplicity'" (172). Robb is concerned with big business and large-scale commercial and financial crimes, but his observations are relevant even to small entrepreneurs, and he notes that it was the employees and clerks who often received the harshest legal punishments for their transgressions.

Riddell's fiction is full of petty frauds and crimes, which she judges harshly. In her life, she both observed and participated in similar dubious practices. Her fiction is distinctive because she does not impose her values on those of a compromised business morality, which was necessary for economic survival. As Colella (2016) argues, Riddell offered an "unprejudiced view of commercial society, the democracy of business, and the potential for change inherent in the modern urban environment in which her characters dwell" (86). *George Geith* does not condemn its hero's single-minded pursuit of profit, and *The Race for Wealth* represents food adulterators as otherwise honest businessmen.[5] Riddell charts the same conflict between business and traditional morality that Trollope does in *The Prime Minister* (1876) and *The Way We Live Now*, but she accepts rather than opposing this modern culture of investment.

As far as we know, Riddell never had the excess capital to invest in publically traded stocks and shares, as Gaskell and Eliot did. Rather, she invested her income in her husband's ventures, and she suffered financially throughout her life mainly because of his failures. Her fiction shows a familiarity with company promotion and shareholder politics beyond what the casual, removed investor could have known. From her mother, she probably inherited property in Ireland, which generated income that she tried to protect from her husband's creditors. Above all, her contacts with the business community in the City and her role as an active businesswoman gave her detailed knowledge of investment and finance that is reflected in her fiction, and which amazed her reviewers, who rarely failed to comment, and often complained, about her display of financial knowledge in her fiction. A reviewer of *The Senior Partner* remarked, "The language of debtor and creditor pervades even the love scenes" (*Saturday Review* 1882, 257). This language was the product of direct experience, but she also inherited, through her mother, a remarkable financial knowledge.

THE ECONOMIC LIVES OF ELLEN KILSHAW AND CHARLOTTE RIDDELL

Charlotte Riddell came from a commercial family with a history of dramatic economic uncertainty. Her mother was born Ellen Kilshaw (1794–1856), the daughter of John Kilshaw, a Liverpool merchant, and Eliza Gladding.[6] In 1816, Eliza Kilshaw, Ellen's sister, married John Howe Greene. When the couple moved to Boston, Ellen visited them in 1817, staying for eighteen months. While there, she befriended the family of Timothy and Margaret Fuller, including their young daughter, also named Margaret (1810–1850). Ellen impressed the Fullers as a refined and intelligent English woman and was especially known for her harp playing (see von Frank 2013, 142). As a child, the future author Margaret idolized the older Ellen and later wrote about her with passionate intensity: "My thoughts were fixed on her with all the force of my nature. It was my first real interest in my kind, and it engrossed me wholly" (Emerson et al. 1859, 24).

Before Ellen returned from Boston to Liverpool in 1818, her father's business dealings began to go wrong. The progressive decline of the family seems to have been a combination of the national economic climate, bad decisions related to business partners and failed commercial ventures.[7] This reversal of fortune altered Ellen's life profoundly. On January 16, 1820, Margaret wrote to her father about Ellen: "I love her better and reverence her more for her misfortunes" (Fuller Family Papers).[8] Mr. Kilshaw's business affairs are detailed in a series of letters that Ellen wrote to Mr. and Mrs. Fuller from Liverpool.[9] They are worth recounting briefly because they show Charlotte Riddell's mother's involvement in, and knowledge of, the turbulent economic climate in early nineteenth-century Liverpool. Mr. Kilshaw's experiences, as described in Ellen's letters, read like one of Riddell's novels and add color to the portrait of the Liverpool culture of investment that was shared by Elizabeth Gaskell's Holland relatives, Johnnie Cross's family and Margaret Oliphant's experiences later in the century.

In a letter to Mrs. Fuller dated May 22, 1819, Ellen writes: "You must have heard of the dreadful situation of mercantile affairs in England; we are all in gloom, I believe not a merchant has escaped without some heavy loss. Numberless families who have lived in splendour are unexpectedly reduced to the greatest distress" (Fuller Family Papers). This sudden, unexpected loss is traumatic at the national level, but Ellen's letters give it a personal face.

In a letter received on February 21, 1821, she tells the story of a foreigner with whom her father entered into partnership that ended in disagreement, leaving Mr. Kilshaw in debt. He considered bankruptcy but was persuaded against it by a friend who set him up as a fruit-trader to Smyrna. That investment failed when the price of fruit in Smyrna was greater than expected. This had been the state of the family finances while Ellen was in Boston, causing her to worry about expenses. John, Ellen's brother, traveled to Smyrna, but this venture failed because the price of the fruit they hoped to sell in England dropped from 80 shillings to 42 shillings: "You may be surprised at my knowing so much about mercantile but papa and John found it a relief to their minds to commiserate with us and I was too closely interested to forget any particulars" (Fuller Family Papers). She goes on to relate that her father has resolved to give up selling merchandise and would return to the commission business.[10]

In 1827, after working as a governess, Ellen married James Cowan, a widowed Irish businessman and proprietor of a cotton and flax-spinning mill in what is now Northern Ireland. Ellen was still corresponding with the Fullers in 1835, and her last surviving letter describes a happy life with her son, John, and daughter, Charlotte, who was born on September 30, 1832, at Barn Cottage, Carrickfergus, County Antrim. James Cowan died in 1851. In the *Oxford Dictionary of National Biography*'s entry for Riddell, Charlotte Mitchell states that Charlotte Cowen "had one full brother, and a half-brother and six half-sisters from her father's first marriage. From her childhood her father was an invalid. On his death much of his property went, by her marriage settlement, to the family of his first wife; his widow had an annuity of £100 p.a. with which she and her daughter went to live on a small jointure at Dundonald, Co. Down, the setting for Charlotte's novel *Berna Boyle*."[11] In January 1855, Charlotte and Ellen moved to London, where Charlotte struggled to support them through writing, and eventually succeeded in publishing *Zuriel's Grandchild* with the publisher Thomas

Newby in 1856. That same year, her mother became ill with cancer and died. Soon thereafter, Charlotte married Joseph Hadley Riddell, an inventor and businessman seventeen years her senior.

As mentioned, critics have always assumed that Joseph was the source of Charlotte's interest in business and finance. Even before her marriage, however, Charlotte shared with her mother a surprising knowledge of trade, finance, and the specter of bankruptcy, which haunted her grandfather. Her first novel draws on her mother's past and demonstrates a perceptive sense of social mobility and insider–outsider dynamics. While the portrait of the "little Jewess" Selina Zuriel and Dora, her daughter, in the novel is not explicitly autobiographical, the title and the narrative emphasize the relationship of grandparent and grandchild, not parent and child. Both real and fictional grandfathers, John Kilshaw and John Zuriel, respectively, experienced fluctuations in social standing in early nineteenth-century Liverpool with profound consequences for their daughters and granddaughters.

Zuriel's Grandchild (1856) was published under the pseudonym R.V.M. Sparling. Zuriel, meaning "rock of God" in Hebrew, appears in Numbers 3:35 as the prince of the house of Merari. Riddell associates ancient and modern princes in the first line of the novel: "There was no prouder nor richer man in the length and breadth of Lancashire— county of ancient gentry and merchant princes—than John Zuriel, Esq., of Stor Court" (I:1). This novel might have been forgotten completely had Riddell not republished it under her own name in 1873 after her reputation was established. The motivation for republication was certainly economic; at this time, she was under particularly intense financial pressures and, as we will see, was involved in several lawsuits. The new title she gave the novel, *Joy After Sorrow*, alludes to the New Testament rather than the Old Testament. In John 16:20, Jesus refers to his future death and resurrection: "You will be sorrowful, but your sorrow will turn to joy." Interestingly, Jesus also uses the analogy of a woman going through childbirth as an example of joy after sorrow. Presumably, the less exotic new title was more commercially viable.[12] The life and influence of *Zuriel's Grandchild*, then, went beyond its first publication by an obscure Irish immigrant and justify our paying some attention to its unusual interest in Jewish identity and to the plot devices of disinheritance, debt, bankruptcy, and forgery that characterize Riddell's later novels. Its details of Liverpool and London landmarks and streets also foreshadow her interest in the history and geography of London in novels published from the 1860s through the 1890s. The story begins with the prehistory of John Zuriel in Liverpool; it demonstrates familiarity with locations such as Old Hall and Tithebarn Street (80). It was believed (and is affirmed): "Mr. Zuriel's father had lived and died, so to speak, with a bag on his back, and that the owner of Stor Court himself had, in his juvenile days, awakened with the well-known melody of 'old clo',' the slumbering echoes of many a quiet Liverpool street" (I:2). The narrator expresses some sympathy and admiration for a man whose race had been "burnt to cinders in the fire of adversity" (2). Despite being called "an upstart, a parvenu, and other disparaging names too numerous to mention," he had been restored to what he considered his proper rank (3). Riddell captures the precarious social mobility of her mother's family and of others at the time. Historian Hannah Barker (2017) paints a similarly dramatic picture in the case of Liverpool baker John Coleman, whose "journey from 'tradesman and baker' to 'esquire and merchant'— and back again—is a cautionary tale of the risks and vagaries of urban commercial life in the late eighteenth and early nineteenth centuries. His rise and fall in Liverpudlian society … remind us that the wealth and social status of individuals living in provincial towns during the Industrial Revolution could be extremely changeable" (7). In this volatile economic culture, John Zuriel rises financially as surely as Riddell's grandfather John Kilshaw had descended and as John Coleman rose and fell.

The novel recognizes the need for Jews to abandon their religion in order to advance socially and economically: "After Zuriel senior shuffled off his mortal coil, Zuriel junior shuffled off his parent's religion" (Riddell 1856, I:3).[13] The narrator observes that Zuriel "forsook Judaism but joined no one of the numerous sects into which the church is divided" (I:5). Without actually embracing Christianity, he nonetheless married a Gentile in St. Peter's Church, "situate as every body knows, in the thoroughfare called, because of its close proximity to the sacred edifice, Church Street" (6). Riddell assumes that her audience is familiar to these locations. As noted above, her mother was baptized in St. Peter's, and it seems likely that Jewish peddlers were also part of her mother's memories of growing up in Liverpool.

It is not surprising that Zuriel conceals his Jewish origins in order to advance in the Liverpool business community, but it is unexpected that after making a fortune, and retiring to a country estate outside of the city, he reestablishes his Jewish identity. In a parody of genealogy that is reminiscent of Sir Walter Eliot in Jane Austen's *Persuasion* (1818), as well as the opening of Dickens's *Martin Chuzzlewit* (1842–1844), Zuriel "contented himself with frequently reviewing the rest of his mighty army of Israelitish ancestors" (Riddell 1856, I:4). After all his hard work, hoarding and speculating, he had "leisure and inclination to renew his formerly interrupted acquaintance with his progenitors, or perhaps, indeed, to make acquaintance with them for the first time, and to discover from what great Jewish family he was sprung" (7). Almost twenty years later, in *Mortomley's Estate* (1874c), Riddell similarly mixes biblical and secular language of ancestry and inheritance. In that novel, Bertrand Kleinwort and Henry Werner are Jews of different "tribes": "I should be sorry to insult the memory of any one of the ten sons of Jacob who failed to send down clear title-deeds with his posterity, by suggesting to which of the number Mr. Kleinwort might directly trace his existence, but it certainly was to another brother than he from whose loins sprang the progenitor of Henry Werner" (11).[14]

Riddell's tone is ironic in both novels, but Zuriel's assertion of superior family is a legitimate defense against the nobility who despise but still borrow money from him (Riddell 1856, I:24). The novel offers a perceptive look at the way outsiders who attain wealth in a modern capitalist economy mimic the behavior of the landed gentry and nobility, purchasing land and fashioning a story of noble ancestry.

On his rise from poverty to wealth, Zuriel proves to be a cruel husband to Dorothea, his wife, who dies after bearing Selina, a daughter. After a lonely childhood, the "little Jewess" (79) grows up and is courted by Captain Arthur August Delorme, who tells her father: "My ancestors came over with William the Conqueror." To this, Zuriel retorts: "And mine crossed the Red Sea with Moses" (33). When Selina elopes with Delorme, Zuriel disowns her, leaving her to an impoverished life in London. The father who cuts off his daughter's inheritance is a familiar trope in Victorian novels. Recall Will Ladislaw's grandmother in Eliot's *Middlemarch* (1871–1872). In Riddell, the inheritance involves not only land and money but also Jewish identity, an illustration of how she borrows conventions but also adapts and integrates them to her distinctive agenda. As in the case of Eliot's *Daniel Deronda* (1876), *Zuriel's Grandchild* emphasizes that Jewish identity is something that can be lost and found.

Selina's marriage, like her mother's, turns out badly, and she too has one daughter, Dora. Selina tries to reconcile with her father but is rejected. She dies, leaving Dora at the mercy of Delorme, who has become indebted to a moneylender and usurer named Conroy Bradshaw (Riddell 1856, I:222). Riddell is evenhanded in portraying both Jewish and Gentile men as bad husbands and moneylenders. Delorme bets, borrows, and gambles, eventually forging the name of Lesparde, his friend, on a bill, a criminal act he later regrets. This scenario marks the beginning of Riddell's obsession with bills, debt, lending, and forgery, which would characterize her later novels. Delorme is the husband, hopeless with money and given to fraud, for whom the narrator has sympathy, although Charlotte Cowan could not know that her future marriage would lead to a life of similar petty evasions of creditors. After many twists and turns of plot, Dora marries Lesparde and learns that her grandfather has left his estate to her. The couple inherits Stor Court, and Lesparde agrees to take the name "Mr. Lesparde Zuriel" (III:304), an act that, as noted earlier, restores his wife's Jewish heritage. Riddell employed various conventional comic and tragic endings in her novels. Her tragic endings usually involve the death of the heroine, as in *George Geith* and *Mortomley's Estate*. But, as in the example of *Austin Friars*, this story winds up with a fairy-tale happy ending, justifying the second title she gave to the republished novel: *Joy After Sorrow*.

The novel emphasizes the experience of traveling between Liverpool and London with a kind of awe at modern progress that might be expected from a young woman raised in the Irish countryside. In a passage anticipating Eliot's *Felix Holt* (1866)—in which the narrator remarks that "posterity may be shot, like a bullet through a tube, by atmospheric pressure from Winchester to Newcastle" (5)—Riddell's narrator observes: "For people used to travel on the earth and meet with a good deal by the way; now they seem to speed through the air, and have no leisure to observe anything, for they are scarcely lifted at one station before they are dropped at another" (Riddell 1856, I:115). Perhaps the mother and daughter made this very trip, which Riddell uses as an occasion to reflect on the mental travel of her reader within her story: "As the pen of the novelist has never been anything more than a vehicle to convey the thoughts of the writer and the imaginations of the reader from place to place, and from scene to scene ... I must ... ask the individual who may chance at the moment to be perusing these pages, to travel from Liverpool to London, with no more ceremony nor delay than that caused by closing one chapter and commencing another" (116). Like Eliot, but in her own distinctive way, Riddell consistently demonstrates a fascination with geography as a marker of historical change. She also uses her narrative voice to self-consciously break the narrative frame and compare train travel to the imaginative experience of novel reading.

Zuriel's Grandchild sets the pattern for Riddell's later novels in several ways. It turns life experience into fiction, drawing on local knowledge to give specificity to urban and suburban settings. It is concerned with social mobility in both directions: A Jewish peddler becomes a millionaire through trade and speculation and his daughter falls into poverty when he disinherits her; her daughter in turn descends into debt and is restored to the wealth her grandfather accumulated. Riddell's later novels would be more concerned with fallen aristocrats who take to trade and finance, perhaps reflecting the life (or at least his personal mythology) of her husband.

RIDDELL'S MIDLIFE PROFESSIONAL SUCCESS AND ECONOMIC CRISES

On September 24, 1857, Charlotte Cowan married Joseph Hadley Riddell, an inventor who had called himself variously "civil engineer," "hot water engineer," "boiler manufacturer," and "American stove merchant."[15] In an 1890 interview with Riddell, Helen Black (1906) observes: "Mr. Riddell belonged to an old Staffordshire family, a branch of the Scotch Riddells, of long descent and gentle blood. 'Courageous and hopeful, gifted with indomitable energy,' says his widow, 'endowed with marvelous persistence and perseverance; modestly conscious of talents which ought to have made their mark, he, when, a mere lad, began his long quest after fortune, one single favour from whom he was never destined to receive'" (24).[16] The theme of sons from noble families coming to the City is common in Riddell's novels. In contrast, Austin Friars, named for the London court in which he was rescued as a foundling, fraudulently pretends to be from a wealthy family named Friars. Riddell's fiction thus shows both sympathy for those leaving aristocratic roots behind and skepticism because of the ability to falsify such connections. Ellis (1931) refers to Joseph Riddell's alleged history, noting that Swarston Royal, in Riddell's 1862 novel, *The World and the Church*, is based on Joseph's supposed home, Winsor Green House, in Staffordshire, "where his ancestors had long been established" (277). Existing records, however, do not confirm this story of Joseph's origins.

Recalling his visit to Riddell at her home in Leyton, Essex, in 1873, the aspiring Irish illustrator Harry Furniss remarked: "I believe her husband through some queer way in business was resting somewhere at his country's expense" (quoted in Ellis 1931, 287). Ellis is quick to dismiss Furniss's observation, calling it indefensible and false. Joseph was bad with money, Ellis admits, but "that he committed any malfeasance leading to imprisonment seems highly improbable" (287). To support his position, Ellis cites his correspondence with Arthur Hamilton Norway (1859–1938), who knew Riddell in the late 1880s after her husband's death, and, as we will see, may have been romantically involved with her. Norway, thus, is not a reliable witness to Joseph's life, and while we do not know whether Joseph was imprisoned for debt in the 1870s, records show that he was no stranger to English prisons.

Before he married Charlotte, Joseph had a criminal record, and he displayed a propensity to scheme and to litigate. This was the life into which he initiated his young bride, eventually involving her in further litigations and schemes to avoid creditors that would, on the one hand, undermine her literary successes, and on the other hand, provide material for her fiction. Reviewing several of Riddell's novels—all published under the pseudonym F.G. Trafford—Anne Thackeray Ritchie (1870b), in referring to Riddell's *Too Much Alone*, observes that the novel's hero is a type that "reappears in disguise, and under various assumed names, in almost all the author's subsequent novels" (402). Speaking of this type, she writes perceptively: "Whether he turns his attention to chemistry, to engineering, to figures, to theology, the amount of business he gets through is almost bewildering, at the same time something invariable goes wrong, over which he has no control, not withstanding all his industry and ability, and he has to acknowledge the weakness of humanity, and the insufficiency of the sternest determination to order and arrange the events of life to its own will and fancy" (409). As we have seen, Charlotte was already inclined to draw on life experiences to create fiction, and this pattern would continue throughout her career. Joseph is without doubt the inspiration for a character type described by Ritchie. His story is worth recounting briefly because it relates to Riddell's intimate knowledge of business and investment cultures and because it suggests that she was exposed to a way of thinking about business ethics and values that shaped the distinct perspective of her literary work and put her outside the bounds of middle-class respectability that many Victorian novelists sought to maintain.

In 1835, Joseph was imprisoned for debt. He subsequently sued Mr. Pakeman, his creditor, for wrongful incarceration, probably a stalling tactic to avoid paying his debt of £20. He lost the suit (Court of Exchequer). In 1844, Joseph and William, his brother, were sued for being "insolvent" debtors when they were working as manufacturing chemists and color manufacturers in London (*London Gazette* 1844).[17] In 1849, the brothers were accused of stealing construction materials worth £3 from the coppersmith's factory in Millwall, where they worked. Such petty crimes were serious offenses at the time, often resulting in imprisonment or transportation (see Godfrey and Cox 2013).[18] William was acquitted but Joseph was indicted on two counts of larceny and sentenced to seven years' transportation to Australia. He was twice scheduled to be transported in 1852 (November and December), and twice he was scratched off the ships' lists of criminals.[19]

The story of how Joseph came to evade transportation is a saga in itself. He was convicted on December 26, 1849. On December 31, 1850, he was brought to Portland Prison on the Isle of Portland, in Dorset. In 1852, he began petitioning to be released due to illness. Sixty pages of correspondence survive documenting this complicated process, including a petition signed by friends and the testimonies of medical examiners. His physical malady was scurvy and his mental state was what we would call depression. From the prison's infirmary, Joseph wrote long, sad letters to the secretary of state for the Home Department, begging to be released. On January 3, 1853, he writes that "could your petitioner be restored to liberty, resume his former habits of life as far as his present state will permit be able to mix in cheerful society and to breath his native air, his disease might be palliated if not removed and his life thereby prolonged." Essentially, Joseph argued that if he were not released from prison, he would die.[20]

The amazing result of these petitions was that his transportation sentence was canceled and he was released. While it is unclear how much, if anything, Charlotte knew about her husband's past incarcerations, it is certain that she lived with his depression and his recourse to pleas of illness when he was under pressure, thereby placing on her the burden of managing his debts.

Early in their married life, Charlotte enjoyed success as a novelist, enabling the couple to move from the City to the North London suburbs. Living with them was a paternal widowed aunt, Mrs. Moore, and Joseph's two unmarried sisters. Charlotte Moore was an "annuitant," and Maria and Charlotte Riddell were "fund holders" (Ancestry.com 2005). While her extended family were living on investments, Charlotte wrote numerous popular novels and hosted literary gatherings at her home at St. John's Lodge, Hanger Lane, Stamford Hill.[21]

The height of her success came when she was editing the *St. James Magazine*, which she took over from Mrs. S.C. Hall in 1867.[22] At her home in Hanger Lane, Riddell entertained fellow writers. Ellis (1931) notes that with her editorship of the *St. James*, her "struggle for fame was won" (285). Llewellynn Jewitt, an engraver who contributed to the *St. James*, wrote in his diary for March 11, 1869, that he had a delightful evening dining with Mrs. Riddell (Goss 1899, 235). Arthur Waugh (1931) recounts that Riddell had once been so successful that her publisher gave her "a smart brougham, and an even smarter horse between the shafts." But he adds: "Unluckily what she made by writing her husband lost by patenting impracticable stoves, and she was now a rather sad and disillusioned widow, yet always rich in a certain wistful sympathy" (202). Wemyss Reid (1905), a contributor to the *St. James*, recalled the ornamental nature of Joseph's stoves: "One stove appeared in the guise of a table, richly ornamented in cast-iron; another was a vase; a third a structure like an altar, and so forth. But whatever their appearance might be, they all were stoves."[23]

Most of what we know about Charlotte and Joseph Riddell comes from such reminiscences. It has been recognized that *A Struggle for Fame* (1883) has strong autobiographical components recalling her early life as an aspiring writer. But many of her novels throughout a publishing career that spanned the second half of the century draw on her own experiences, as well as those of people she knew.

As more facts about her life are uncovered, we can see a continued pattern of turning personal experiences into material for her fiction. She produced so much (more than fifty books) that she seemed to fictionalize events as soon as they happened. During her mid-career (1869–1874), her husband's financial problems gave urgency to her literary production as the couple dodged creditors and engaged in various schemes to maximize the money she could obtain from publishers. During this period, husband and wife were embroiled in several lawsuits over money matters. These lawsuits contribute to our understanding of Victorian women's relationship to business and finance. For her, the cultures of investment included litigation over financial matters and national legislative acts. These lawsuits illuminate the desperate, chaotic nature of her life before and after 1871 and show her awareness of the laws that also play a role in her fictional plots.

In August 1870, Joseph Riddell owed the Glasgow boiler manufacturer James Smith £2000. One year earlier, the Bankruptcy Act of 1869 overturned a practice that had been in place since 1841, putting the bankrupt's assets in the hands of a Bankruptcy Court.[24] The new law favored creditors, empowering them to oversee the distribution of the bankrupt's property. Knowing that her assets belonged to her husband, Charlotte took desperate measures to prevent his bankruptcy. She offered Smith the copyrights to seven of her novels: *The Rich Husband* (1858), *Maxwell Drewitt* (1865), *Phemie Keller* (1866a), *The Race for Wealth* (1866b), *Far Above Rubies* (1867), *My First Love* and *My Last Love, A Sequel* (1869). The final copyright offer was to *Austin Friars* (1870), which had just appeared in print. She also offered the rights to *St. James Magazine*. According to Smith, she also offered future earnings from her writing. The Married Women's Property Act was passed in August 1870, the very month she made the promise to Smith. Between August and September 1870, Riddell stalled Smith's claims to collect his debt. Letters were misaddressed and bankers were unavailable. She finally committed her copyrights and other assets to him in September 1870, but settling the debt still depended on future earnings.

In May 1871, Charlotte was mugged on the streets of London as she walked through "the Poultry." She was carrying £300 worth of checks and ten shillings in cash. The *Pall Mall Gazette* of April 29, 1871, reported: "The cheques have all been stopped, and Mrs. Riddell said her actual loss was only 10s." The thief was apprehended, and she identified him in a lineup, later testifying in his trial. As a result, according to the *Pall Mall Gazette* of May 4, 1871, William Bradley was convicted and sentenced to eighteen months' hard labor. The robbery and canceled checks conveniently bought her time to pay outstanding bills.[25]

Rarely failing to translate a significant life experience into fiction, she expressed sympathy for pickpockets in *Mortomley's Estate* (1874c): "It is only the poor wretches who have no brains to enable them to take a higher flight than picking pockets that really suffer" (317). Her narrator imagines a legal judgment: "'You are a hardened ruffian,' says the judge, looking through his spectacles at the pickpocket who has been convicted about a dozen times previously, 'and I mean to send you for five years where you can pick no more pockets'" (317). The narrator asks: "But, then, what about the hardened ruffians who are never convicted, who float their bubble companies and rob the widow and the orphan as coolly as Bill Sykes, only with smiling faces and well-clothed persons?" (317). The reference to *Oliver Twist* is telling; borrowing from art and life, the Artful Dodger and William Bradley are merged into her prototypical pickpocket.

In July 1871, after the mugging, Charlotte leveraged the same copyrights she had promised to Smith in September 1870 (and five more) for a loan from the publisher Henry S. King & Co. The agreement of July 24, 1871, stipulates that the publisher will hold her copyrights for a loan of £285 at 5% interest, and if the loan is not repaid by March 1, 1872, the publisher will keep the copyrights.[26] And yet, the copyrights to seven of the novels had been promised to Smith, who could not have known anything about King, just as King could not have known anything about Smith.

All of these efforts failed to stave off Joseph's bankruptcy, which was announced in the *Times* on September 28 (*Times* [London] 1871). His assets were placed in the hands of the Metropolitan Bank, represented by the accountant George Whiffin. Still, Charlotte realized that she might yet be able to protect her future earnings under the new MWPA, so sometime at the end of 1871, with the help of William Riddell, her brother-in-law, she sued her husband and Smith in an attempt to deny that either of them had any right to her future earnings. It appears that the reason she sued her husband was to establish that under the MWPA, her future earnings belonged to her and could not be absorbed in the debt that he owed to Smith. Given that her brother-in-law was named with her as a plaintiff, it is likely that this was a collaboration among the three of them (Charlotte, William, and Joseph) to ensure Charlotte's future earnings in the coming years—which would be the only income the Riddells could expect. Charlotte's suing for her rights in 1871 lends some irony to Ellis's (1931) conclusion that she was carelessly indifferent to her own rights "by virtue of her Irish insouciance" (266).

In this case, we have only the answer of the defendant, James Smith, to the complaint brought against him by Charlotte Riddell on January 8, 1872. Smith testifies that Charlotte Riddell "is an experienced woman of business and has had for many years extensive business transactions with me ... her husband has never interfered in the business except to sign Bills."[27] He notes that in August 1870, she pledged "her literary abilities" and handed him a "policy on her life."[28] She supplied a covenant committing her copyrights and her entire estate, including future earnings according to the "then state of the law." It is worth noting that the

MWPA gave women the rights to their earnings, including those from literary work and also to any insurance policy on their own lives.[29] We do not have a definitive answer as to the outcome of this trial, but it is possible that the bankruptcy allowed the couple to avoid paying Smith anything beyond the copyrights he had already received (and against which she had borrowed from King).

In February 1871, before her agreement with King, Joseph's bankruptcy or her suit against her husband and Smith, Riddell had signed a contract with the publishing firm of Hurst and Blackett to produce a new, three-volume novel titled *The Little Provincial*, due in sixth months, as well as a three-volume collection of short novels. The contract stipulated that she would not publish or advertise any work with another publisher until she delivered these manuscripts. For this, she received an advance of £400. She entered into the agreement "relating to her separate earnings and under the powers given by the Married Women's Property Act of 1870."[30]

In negotiating this contract, she dealt exclusively with Henry Blackett, but on March 7, 1871, Blackett died. Richard Collinson administered the estate on behalf of Blackett's children.[31] The remaining partners of Hurst and Blackett took the liberty of advertising her forthcoming novel, prompting her to plead illness and ask for an extension. In September 1871, during this grace period, unbeknown to the publishers, Joseph declared bankruptcy and Riddell soon thereafter sued him and Smith.

In May 1872, still waiting *A Little Provincial*, the publishers at Hurst and Blackett saw an advertisement for a new novel by Riddell called *The Earl's Promise* (1873b), to be published by Tinsley Brothers. Riddell explained that this was a different work, which Henry Blackett had verbally agreed she might publish outside the restrictions of her contract with him. She continued to defer her obligation into January 1873, when again the firm of Hurst and Blackett contacted her. She sent Joseph to negotiate with them. He admitted that his wife signed the contract with them to deliver a new novel and cashed the £400 advance, and that she faced a debt to Tinsley Brothers of £1400 (probably also a result of advances taken out on his behalf). He also confessed that she sold Tinsley a novel called *Home, Sweet Home* (1873a) for £750, to be serialized anonymously in *Tinsley's Magazine*, and that she had previously signed an agreement with Tinsley in 1869 to produce four novels. Acknowledging that his wife had breached her contract, Joseph proposed to pay off the £400 debt to Hurst and Blackett through "bills of exchange at 4, 8, and 12 months date with insurance." This offer of bills of exchange is a move typical of Riddell's fictional characters upon finding themselves in financial difficulty.[32] Ever the operator, Joseph proposed alternatively that his wife provides Hurst and Blackett with two novels for the price of £600, applying the £400 already received. The publishers rejected both offers.[33] In any event, as a bankrupt, he would not have had the assets to pay the bills he proposed (10).[34]

It seems between 1869 and 1871, Riddell took advances from two different publishers for the same book (which was never written) and signed over copyrights of the same books to two different parties. Advances and loans from publishers were not uncommon. Elisabeth Jay (1995) observes that Margaret Oliphant treated Blackwood and other publishers essentially as banks (280). But Riddell took advantage of the fact that her two worlds were separate. What was a Glasgow boiler manufacturer going to do with a London journal he had never heard of before it was offered to him? And how would he know if the same copyrights offered to him were also being used to raise cash from a London publisher? Together, Charlotte and Joseph employed various means to exploit the publishing system to their advantage. Such evasions and downright swindles are a feature of Riddell's novels, and her perspective on such dealings is ambivalent, rather than morally outraged, as we might expect from most Victorian realist novelists. In *Mortomley's Estate* (1874c), she reflects that it is unfair for financial swindlers to escape punishment, "and yet I must confess time has destroyed much of my sympathy with the widow and the orphan who entrust their substance to strangers and believe in the possible solvency—for such as them—of twenty per cent" (317). In other words, those who are naïve about financial matters might well expect that canny business people would take advantage of them.

Her novels also explore aspects of domestic deception. *The Race for Wealth* treats both adultery and food adulteration. *Austin Friars* includes the portrait of a pathological liar who makes false claims about his origins, deceives both his lover and his wife and creates a financial disaster that almost ruins his father-in-law. As a fictional type, he foreshadows Ferdinand Lopez in Trollope's *The Prime Minister*—a smooth-talking speculator obsessed with getting at his wife's money. But the more we know about Joseph and Charlotte's behavior as bankruptcy loomed (and Joseph's behavior before he married Charlotte), the more disturbing *Austin Friars* becomes for its possible autobiographical elements.

In April 1873, having rejected their offers to negotiate the £400 debt, Hurst and Blackett sued Charlotte, Joseph, George Whiffin, and another of her publishers, George Routledge and Sons, in order to recover their losses. Testimony in Chancery documents reveals the desperate lengths of evasion, deception, and financial juggling to which Riddell resorted to help pay her husband's business debts and her own debts to publishers. In *Mortomley's Estate* (1874c), she writes, "Our clever financiers always keep a little in advance of the law, as our clever thieves always keep a little in advance of our safemakers" (317). She stayed a step ahead of her creditors, but the Blackett lawsuit finally caught up with her.

During this case, it was revealed that in 1869, Riddell had signed a contract for £500 with Tinsley Brothers to produce four novels, one of which may have been called *A Little Provincial*, the novel she promised to Blackett in 1871. The details of the lawsuit are complicated, but essentially Hurst and Blackett sued to recover their money. They invoked the MWPA to show that, despite Joseph's bankruptcy, Charlotte still owed them either £400 or the novels, and they sued Routledge in the same suit to stop them from publishing the announced Christmas book (*Fairy Water*) until Riddell paid off her debts (one way or the other) to Hurst and Blackett. On October 8, 1873, the court issued an injunction to restrain the publication of *Fairy Water* and ordered that Riddell was not to publish anything until she repaid Hurst and Blackett.[35] Riddell never wrote *A Little Provincial* and never published a book with Hurst and Blackett.[36]

In 1873, however, she published not only two novels with Tinsley Brothers (*The Earl's Promise* and *Home, Sweet Home*) but also two works with Routledge and Sons (*Fairy Water* and *Joy After Sorrow*, the reprint of *Zuriel's Grandchild*).[37] In *Fairy Water* (1874a), Riddell employs the convention of a West Indian plot. Unlike Bertha Mason, Lady Mary Severn is an Anglo Negress who is "acquisitive beyond belief, and impertinent and insolvent beyond description" (178). But Lady Mary becomes increasingly sympathetic as the plot unfolds, and helps to solve a mystery that brings two lovers together. While one could hardly call the portraits of the Jewish John Zuriel or the West Indian Lady Mary realistically developed, they are more than mere racist stereotypes: They are both attempts to balance realism and sensation against a cosmopolitan literary and commercial background. The source of the West Indian money is not explored, but economic connections between England and the West Indies form part of the global networks in Riddell's fiction, such as the sugar refinery in *The Race for Wealth*. It is also rare to have a railway company purchase a family estate just in time to save the family from bankruptcy, as occurs in *Fairy Water* (246), although, as we saw in Chapter 3, Trollope employs a similar twist of financial plot in *Miss Mackenzie* (1865). This strange story, no doubt rapidly written for money, nonetheless offers some interest in the way it combines sensation, racialized characters, and modern economic realities.

The years 1869–1873 were filled with physical, emotional, and financial exhaustion for Riddell, due entirely to Joseph's business transactions. In 1870, she was enjoying a successful career as a novelist and editor, but she was forced to apply all of her earnings to her husband's debts. She lost her journal and her copyrights and was in debt to Tinsley as well as Hurst and Blackett. The Married Women's Property Act cut two ways for her: She was able to claim in one lawsuit that her husband's debts were not hers, but, in the second lawsuit, the plaintiff claimed that the debt to them was her responsibility. Nevertheless, these and the following years were ones of notable literary production. She lost no time in transforming aspects of her personal experience into fiction. In turn, the fiction is illuminated by knowledge of her life.

In 1874, Riddell published *Frank Sinclair's Wife* (1874b) and *Mortomley's Estate* (1874c), both with Tinsley Brothers. A reviewer of *Mortomley's Estate* quipped: "It would scarcely be too much to say that the hero of the story is the Bankruptcy Act of 1869, and the heroine, winding up an estate by liquidation" (*Saturday Review* 1874, 481). The reviewer is correct. The novel is about a bankruptcy and it is obsessed with the Bankruptcy Act of 1869. Barbara Weiss (1986) argues that bankruptcy as represented in Victorian novels "threatened to reveal beneath the obvious prosperity and optimism of the nineteenth century a chasm that imperiled the very reality of the self" (88). In the 1870s, Riddell examined the psychological and material effects of bankruptcy, asking: What happens to a life when society has valued it at less than nothing?[38]

In *Mortomley's Estate* (1874c), as in many of Riddell's works, there is an element of chaos and social disintegration that is experienced rather than analyzed; but the chaos of the lives in this novel reflects not just the fact but also the theme of bankruptcy, whereby a husband and wife are represented as victims stripped of their home, their possessions, their social standing, and their dignity—everything that gave their lives meaning. In the opening pages, the narrator observes:

Death is bankruptcy. Can I say more in its disfavour when writing of a class who hold personal bankruptcy—their own, I mean—a calamity too great to contemplate; who estimate a man's standing, for here and hereafter, by the amount he has managed to rake and scrape together; and who live by swooping down upon his possessions, and selling the house which shelters him, the bed he lies on, the toys his children have played with, the dog he has fondled, the horses he has ridden, the harp his dead mother's fingers have touched? (3)

This and other passages describing repossessed property in *Mortomley's Estate* suggest the intimate pain of bankruptcy. Mortomley's bankruptcy, like that of Joseph Riddell's, is announced in the *Times*. The harp may allude to the one Riddell's mother, Ellen Kilshaw, was known for playing, preserved by her daughter until bankruptcy led to repossession. The fate of the animals too is a poignant reminder of such disruption and poverty. It is not until Dolly Mortomley returns to her ruined home and finds the half-starved family cat that she understands "what our ruin meant to us and to the dumb brutes who had trusted to us for kindness" (296). The mare, Black Bess, descends from being Mr. Mortomley's favorite riding horse to a carthorse and finally to a paltry source of income when she is cruelly sold (332). Perhaps recalling Mr. Whiffin, who oversaw Joseph's estate, Mr. Swanland, the trustee who takes over Mortomley's estate, "was truly the lord of Mortomley, the controller of his temporal destiny, as any southern planter ever proved of that of his slaves" (209–10). Swanland is a major villain in the novel, suggesting Riddell's anger at her own experience.

Even though Riddell later said that she was better at representing men than women, in this novel she removes the bankrupt man from the trials of his family by having him remain an invalid throughout, unable to face reality or his creditors. In this respect, his fate recalls that of Mr. Tulliver in Eliot's *The Mill on the Floss* (1860), who similarly remains unconscious while his debts cause financial trauma to his family. Mr. Tulliver and Tom, his son, epitomize the virtuous but impractical insistence on paying back creditors beyond what is owed after bankruptcy (or insolvency). This practice was well known to Victorians through the real-life case of Walter Scott as well as through numerous fictional examples such as Mr. Dombey, who is "resolved on payment to the last farthing of his means" (Dickens 1846–1848, 862). Characters with similar scruples appear in *Cranford* (Gaskell 1853), *Sons and Daughters* (Oliphant 1890b) and

The Whirlpool (Gissing 1897). In Oliphant's *Janet* (1890a), a wife schemes to prevent her husband from paying his creditors. In Gissing's *New Grub Street* (1891), Marian Yule is the victim of debtors who will not pay. She says: "I should have thought men would wish to pay their debts, even after they had been bankrupt; but they tell us we can't expect anything more from these people" (456). Her suitor, Jasper Milvain, who is about to abandon her, replies: "You are thinking of Walter Scott, and that kind of thing. ... Oh, that's quite unbusinesslike; it would be setting a pernicious example nowadays" (456).

These examples show that debt and bankruptcy were features of Victorian novels and the paying of debts was a moral touchstone for the evaluation of character. Yet, *Mortomley's Estate* is different because of its intensely personal nature, fictionalizing the Riddells' experience of becoming entangled in a bureaucracy, essentially the business, of bankruptcy. It reveals a parasitical economy of people who "swoop down" on the unfortunate victims or "slaves." At the same time, it criticizes corporate promoting and shareholder greed, which drove the unwitting Mortomley—a business naïf and inventor/artist of colors—to this state of insolvency.

Riddell focuses on the bewildered consciousness of Dolly Mortomley, who struggles to survive in a world turned upside down. Rather than defending the honest businessman, as she had done in her novels of the 1860s, here Riddell emphasizes the ways in which limited liability and bankruptcy laws have transformed the financial landscape: Acts of legislation are her villains, and characters like Archie and Dolly Mortomley are victims and prisoners, no better than slaves to these heartless laws. On the one hand, this dark novel must have reflected Riddell's sense that she was losing the struggle to keep afloat financially; on the other hand, she was able to translate these feelings into novels, the sales of which became instrumental to her survival as the couple's only source of income after 1871.[39]

In the 1870s, Riddell's debts and her writing were thoroughly entangled; she was borrowing on her future production, selling her copyrights, suing and being sued, evading, dodging, lying, testifying, and justifying—all the while turning experience into fiction. *A Struggle for Fame* has been viewed as her most autobiographical novel because it is the story of a writer. *Mortomley's Estate*, however, written from the perspective of a woman who has been thrust into a ruthless world of business and debt collection, is equally autobiographical and more immediate. If, as Linda Peterson (2009) argues, *A Struggle for Fame* is structured according to a myth of female authorship established in Gaskell's *Life of Charlotte Brontë*, *Mortomley's Estate* drifts from incident to incident, each diminishing and ultimately destroying its heroine. The events surrounding the writing of this novel show that in the 1870s, Riddell was in no position to stand above negotiating prices for her writing: She was trying to draw money wherever she could, however she could, from everything that she had written in the past and present and would write in the future.[40]

Mortomley's Estate (1874c) is the story of a woman married to a man whose business fails. Dolly came to the marriage with her own small inheritance from a godmother (in the hands of trustees). Upon her marriage, that money was invested in Mortomley's General Chemical Company (Limited), located on St. Vedast Wharf, St. Vedast Lane, Upper Thames Street. That the company is limited reflects Riddell's abiding hatred for limited liability and the irresponsible behavior she thought it encouraged.[41]

When Mortomley, a chemist and color inventor (as Joseph once was), learns that the company is near bankruptcy, he falls ill and slips in and out of consciousness for the rest of the novel. Dolly tries to sort out his business affairs, even preserving his patent on the original color called Mortomley's Blue from exploitation by his cunning creditors. Dolly's efforts to protect her husband's patent function as an allegory for artists' rights, especially when we consider the legal trials Riddell was undergoing to protect her own copyrights at the time. When Mortomley comes out of his coma, he says that no law can take away a man's brains (329). The narrator continues: "Homewood, his business, his house, his furniture, his horses, his carriages, his plant, his connection, Mortomley had yielded without a struggle, but his mental children he would not so relinquish nor would he" (329). Here, Mortomley's defense of his "mental children" seems to merge Joseph's patented stoves with Riddell's own literary output, recalling her testimony that she had no intention of working to repay her husband's debts (although of course she did) and revealing her sense of violation at her own "mental children" being used as pawns in this desperate game.

Like Yorke Friars in *Austin Friars*, Dolly has the obligations of business forced upon her: "The time when she had known nothing about business, when she took no interest in the City ... or the state of trade, seemed like an almost forgotten dream" (115). Just as Yorke asks: "What is to prevent the business being carried on by Y. Friars as well as it was by A. Friars?" (Riddell 1870, 44), so Dolly conducts business as "D. Mortomley" (Riddell 1874c, 294). Women in business favor ambiguously gendered names, as Riddell herself had originally published under the pseudonym F.G. Trafford.

Reflecting Riddell's knowledge of investment, *Mortomley's Estate* is also a story of boardroom drama within a limited liability company. Like people and places, companies have histories in Riddell's novels. Her narrator takes us back to the consolidation of the company with an ironic, nostalgic tone: "When in the palmy days of 'promoting,' long before Black Friday was thought of, while the Corner House was a power in the City, the old and long-established business (*vide* prospectus of the period) of Henrison Brothers was merged into the General Chemical Company, Limited, with a tribe of directors, manager, sub-manager, secretary, and shareholders,—probably no one, excepting Mr. Henrison and his brothers and the gentlemen who successfully floated the venture, was aware that the old and highly respectable house was as near bankruptcy as any house could well be" (91–2). With these seeds of corruption planted, Riddell then takes us forward to the appointment of Mr. Forde as general in command. He means to "send up the dividend to something which should astonish the shareholders," but, in fact, the narrator laments, he "brought down the shares to something which astonished them still more" (94). Just as Mr. Swanland, the trustee, is compared to a southern plantation slave owner, so Mr. Forde is demonized when the narrator observes that he treats the workers in the company like "South Carolina Slaves"—both invocations of American slavery ten years after its abolition (210).[42]

One thread of the plot involves Dolly's money and whether she is liable for her husband's debts. She is accused of hiding that money, so personal responsibility is at the heart of the novel. It is very much a married women's property dilemma. There is a legal question of whether Dolly has a settlement made on her. If a formal settlement had been made, then her money is her own; if no settlement was made, then her money belongs to Mortomley and thus now to Mr. Swanland. When Swanland tries to extract this information from Dolly, she asserts: "We never had separate purses, we never could have. What was his was mine, and what is mine shall of course always be his" (228). Swanland coolly observes that what is his is the creditors, to which Dolly replies: "Then you mean to have my money?" (229). Throughout the novel, Dolly's ignorance plays against her business savvy in preserving her husband's patents and paying off his debts. Riddell's own knowledge is reflected in what Dolly does not know. Dolly asks her lawyer: "What was a settlement—had any been made—was it true ... that if there were no settlement, everything went to the creditors?" (232). Her lawyer informs her that her fortune cannot be saved, and incidentally editorializes: "My unprofessional opinion is that settlements which place a woman in a position of affluence, and consequently provide a handsome income for a man, no matter how reckless or improvident he has been, can scarcely be defended on any ground of right or reason" (233). This conservative stance affirms the idea of coverture and presents a negative view of legal settlements that protect a woman's independent inheritance from her husband.

Dolly does not understand these ethical complexities, as perhaps Riddell herself did not at first when she was faced with the question of whether her own inheritance from her mother was bound up in Joseph's debts. But experience taught her hard lessons, so that by the time she wrote *Mortomley's Estate*, she was able to interject the type of commentary on financial law that troubled her reviewers. For example, she writes: "He who goes into liquidation without first being sure of his trustee, his lawyer, and his committee passes into an earthly hell, over the portals of which are engraved the same words as those surmounting Dante's Inferno" (210).[43] The narrator further condemns the gentlemen "commercial and legal" who "concocted the Bankruptcy Act of 1869, and the other gentlemen of the Upper and Lower Houses who made it law" (210). She warns: "And if any man in business whose affairs are going at all wrong should happen to read these lines ... let him remember liquidation means no appeal, no chance of ever having justice done him, nor even the remote contingency ... of setting himself right in the world" (210). Riddell was probusiness, but she also supported government regulation and regretted the minimizing of government role in overseeing bankruptcies and liquidations, just as she lamented the turn to limited liability.

In the chaotic resolution of the novel, which shows companies, communities, and families to have been dissolved, the two Jewish characters (Bertrand Kleinwort and Henry Werner) epitomize the conventional fates of many a corrupt financier in Victorian fiction: Kleinwort absconds to South America and Werner commits suicide. Mr. Forde sets up shop in Liverpool, living in "an extremely small house situate at Everton" (416). In the end, Dolly gains a cynical wisdom: "I, who have been through it all, tell you any human being who allows sentiment to influence business pays for his folly with his life" (402). Having paid off her husband's debts, Dolly quietly dies in an extraordinary fantasy showing how the woman literally gives her life—having worn it away in work and worry—to pay off her impractical husband's debts (which have become hers).

If *Mortomley's Estate* (1874c) is the domestic tragedy of 1874, *Frank Sinclair's Wife* (1874b) is the comedy, further reflecting the topsy-turvy world in which Riddell found herself in the mid-1870s. It is the story of a husband and wife who switch roles: He stays at home to do domestic duty and she goes into the City to conduct business, leading to bankruptcy. This offers much humor about stereotypical gender roles and also an opportunity for the narrator to remark: "Those were the days before 'Women's Rights' was discussed either privately or publicly" (I:87). The narrator asserts further: "If women think themselves unfairly treated, it is better they should say so in the market-place than beside the domestic hearth; that the question should be decided by the experience of the world, rather than sulked over between husband and wife, father and daughter" (88). But Riddell's sympathy remained firmly with men: "I do not believe the woman ever lived whose imagination enabled her thoroughly to realize the meaning, say, of the single word 'ruin'; and I can scarcely credit that even the virtues of an Act of Parliament will assist her" (I:244). Riddell experienced the material effects of bankruptcy, but they did not humiliate and debilitate her to the extent that they apparently did her husband, who, Riddell claimed, remained an invalid in the years before his death in 1881, as he had been during the years he was in prison.

The new evidence I have introduced about Riddell's lawsuits gives some specific answers to the question of where she learned her business knowledge. Her career lasted so long—almost fifty years—that those who met and wrote about her at the end of her life knew little of the active role she took in her husband's business despite the language, situations, and City settings of her novels. Her diatribes against the Bankruptcy Act of 1869, while tedious to her critics, spoke to the men and women whose lives were affected by financial legislation and who helped to make her novels popular.

Later Life: Debt, Productivity, and Return to Liverpool

After Joseph's death in 1881, Riddell continued to struggle with debt. Ellis (1931) says Riddell considered it a question of honor rather than a legal obligation. She moved from place to place: Addlestone near

Weybridge, in Surrey, London (Lambeth Road) (299); Upper Halliford, near Shepperton (320); and finally to Windsor (327). And she kept writing City novels that entered into the details and mysteries of finance. Her men and women of business worked as insurance officers, fruit merchants, and civil servants auditing taxes. *Susan Drummond* (1884) returns to the Overend and Gurney failure as a watershed of British commercial life—the "wild speculation, the reckless private expenditure, the sudden madness of all classes" that were briefly "stopped by the collapse of '66" (I:84). Like Thackeray, Dickens, Trollope, Gaskell, Eliot, Oliphant, Gissing, Reade, Braddon, and others, Riddell appreciated the dramatic potential of company failures and collapses. Like them, she could assume a moralizing tone when it came to speculation, fraud, and bankruptcy. To these literary conventions, she added her own long experience of nineteenth-century financial instability, encompassing her married life and reaching back to her grandfather's economic losses.

While living in Surrey in the 1880s, Riddell took the young Arthur Hamilton Norway as lodger. With him, she coauthored a novel, *The Government Official* (1887b), drawing on his experience as a civil servant in the Inland Revenue.[44] The novel opens with a description of Somerset House in London from which Selwyn Serle, the young hero, is transferred to an office in Liverpool's Custom House. The rest of the action recalls *Zuriel's Grandchild*, which similarly shuttles back and forth between Liverpool and London. The first volume is concerned mainly with the dreary lives of civil servants in the Inland Revenue Department of Liverpool. The characters, no doubt inspired by Norway's experience, include an alcoholic genius with numbers, a loquacious Irishman named Kelly, and a compulsive gambler and horseplayer named Mr. Gough. The novel displays some interesting insights into the Civil Service and offers an implicit critique about the folly of pensions. As *Mortomley's Estate* entered into the details of bankruptcy law, this novel revels in the details of tax laws and the men who enforce them, seeing a kind of poetry in the very language of the statutes.

Selwyn's boss at Inland Revenue is the aloof Mr. Trosdale, whom Selwyn is surprised to learn is an inventor, specifically of furnaces. The narrator explains that Selwyn is naïve about inventors: "He had never scanned the patent lists, and learned they are as plentiful as blackberries in October" (I:294). Having taken his young assistant into his confidence, Trosdale delivers a self-justifying speech: "I have been considered a visionary enthusiast; I have been assailed with reproaches; in my own household the finest products of my brain have been at best looked upon as the dreams of a lunatic" (I:294). His diatribe sadly recalls Joseph Riddell, the inventor of stoves and furnaces. Trosdale continues: "I have seen my ideas stolen, my plans frustrated, the offspring of my brain coolly appropriated; yet I have never lost courage or heart; and now—now I am going to reap my reward: I have perfected *the* blast furnace of the century—the blast furnace destined to supersede all others—the blast furnace which must make the fortunes of all connected with it" (295). This almost mad inventor mesmerizes the gullible Selwyn. In a tone that is difficult to judge, the narrator remarks: "To many, a blast furnace would have represented nothing. It is not given to everyone to understand the length and breadth, the height and depth of the beauty comprising those two words; but Selwyn had sat at the feet of an enthusiast in such matters" (I:296). As a result of his enthusiasm, and Selwyn's attraction to Madge, Trosdale's daughter, Trosdale convinces Selwyn to invest his inheritance in the furnace of the century.

The autobiographical dimensions of this novel are intriguing. In it, Riddell returns to the Liverpool setting of her first novel and the city of her mother's childhood. She mixes the experiences of her young friend Norway in the Civil Service with the portrait of a character whose pursuits are so similar to that of her deceased husband that she probably would never have written it during his life. The young Selwyn is seduced by the inventor of furnaces in a way that we can only imagine the young Charlotte must herself have been seduced and, in turn, induced to invest her own money in his inventions. The novel does not venture too far into psychological territory and retreats from any profound consideration of her characters' internal lives, but it nonetheless provides some valuable insight into her perspective on Joseph Riddell and lends some irony to Norway's testimony to Ellis that he never heard Riddell speak of her husband as anything other than an admirable, upstanding man.

When another inventor beats Trosdale to the patent, he loses his money. As a result, he and Madge move to Doughty Street in London (a downscale address). Picking up on the theme of gambling, Madge tells Selwyn: "Do you think there are no gamblers save those who spend their nights at the card-table? What are betting men? What are speculators? What are *inventors?*" (II:109). Echoing Riddell's experience of living with a failed inventor of stoves, she laments: "For years we have been going steadily downhill—getting poorer and poorer, dropping lower and lower in the social scale." The novel ends abruptly and happily with the union of Selwyn and Madge.

The same year that she published *The Government Official* (1887b), Riddell also published *Miss Gascoigne* (1887a), which tells the story of a young man and an older woman who fall in love but cannot marry for social reasons. The heroine is an heiress, and the offers made to her, "or rather to her money, were more than she cared to count" (5). She has one suitor, Mr. Holford, who cruelly says that she refuses him only "because you are in love with a boy young enough to be your son—a boy who would laugh the house down if I told him you were so foolish" (221). The young man is in fact willing to take the risk of marrying Miss Gascoigne, but she wisely rejects the proposal. The young man soon marries someone else. The novel anticipates Oliphant's (1893) "A Widow's Tale," a short story on a similar theme.

Miss Gascoigne ends with an example of the ultimate in investor responsibility. The heroine retreats to the south of France after her lover's marriage; however, after a year passes, news arrives of a "frightful colliery accident in the mine whence Miss Gascoigne drew her income." Although she had "no responsibility about or knowledge of the matter, yet within an hour after reading the article she was on her way to England" (260). While the details are left vague, this is an interesting twist, emphasizing how a female investor takes seriously the responsibilities of her investments and actually acts on what she perceives as a moral obligation to help in an accident at the mine that provides her income, even though she has no legal obligation to do so.

After Norway married another woman and exited her life, Riddell continued to struggle and to write. She enjoyed a small revival of attention in 1890 with the interviews in the *Pall Mall Gazette* (Blathwayt 1890) and in Helen Black's *Notable Women Authors of the Day* (1906). In letters published by Ellis (1931), she remarked that the *Pall Mall Gazette* interview contained inaccuracies; yet, these late interviews are the sources of self-perpetuated myths, especially about Joseph Riddell, which I have tried to complicate by introducing the historical records of Joseph's failures. Was he a talented but impractical and unlucky inventor, or a criminal, a financial drain, and a social embarrassment? Probably all of these, but he was also an inspiration for her City novels, though we now know that her family legacy of commercial experience and financial trouble stretched back at least as far as her grandfather, John Kilshaw, in Liverpool, and that even before Charlotte was born, her mother had a surprising knowledge of commercial details and investment cultures.

Prolific as she continued to be in the 1880s, by the 1890s, Riddell was so poor that her musicologist friend A.J. Hipkins applied to Prime Minister Lord Roseberry on her behalf and obtained a £200 grant from the Royal Bounty Fund.[45] Later, J.M. Barrie, with the help of Mrs. Ethel Tweedie, obtained a pension of £60 per year for Riddell from the Society of Authors. In 1900, they also succeeded in winning for Riddell (age 68) a grant from the Royal Literary Fund of £200.[46] Barrie noted in his application that Riddell could no longer write and had no private means. Tweedie added that Riddell supported a paralyzed brother for many years and that this brother had only died four years before.[47] Riddell's economic life encompassed the self-help narrative of getting herself published, years of investing in and managing her husband's stove business, evading debts, enduring bankruptcy, and finally subsisting on charity. Her life does not have the arc of middle-class accumulation that we see in the lives of Gaskell, Dickens, Trollope, and Eliot.

I began this chapter by discussing some similarities between Riddell's realist aesthetic and that of George Eliot. As we have seen, Riddell's novels explore questions of ethics and economics in more practical terms than do Eliot's novels. Though she valued honesty and good character, Riddell was often less troubled by the unethical behavior of the businessmen with whom she sympathized than she was by what she considered the unfairness of national legislative acts, such as those limiting shareholder liabilities and encouraging irresponsible speculation. Her critics complained that such topics were not literary, but by the time of her death, as her obituary in the *Times* noted, the commercial and financial worlds she introduced into fiction had become so accepted and even commonplace that her novels seemed dated: "In the 'sixties' it was the fashion, in English novels and plays, to look down on men engaged in trade. Mrs. Riddell's chief object seems to have been to prove that a man did not lose caste by engaging in business in the City. The point has long since been conceded in English society; and to the present generation, Mrs. Riddell's novels, like the French plays, in which there is a somewhat similar *motif*, of Augier and Sandeau, consequently seem somewhat antiquated" (*Times* [London] 1906).[48] This testimony about the influence of Riddell's abiding project of honoring the business of City men indicates the importance of her work within the history of British—and I would also argue of American—literature. Her contemporaries were better able to see her similarities to French writers than to her fellow Victorian realists; they were not yet able to see the groundwork she was laying for financial novels by Edith Wharton, Frank Norris, Theodore Dreiser, and others.

I conclude with some comparisons between the life and work of Riddell and her contemporary Margaret Oliphant, who is the subject of the next chapter. The Scottish Oliphant and the Irish Riddell were extremely prolific. Both wrote feverishly in response to pressing demands for money that were generated by the debts of others. Both wove their obsessive concern about money into their fiction, although in different ways. Oliphant seems to resist Riddell's model of financial realism by professing her ignorance of finance, maintaining a deliberate vagueness about the types of knowledge Riddell displayed and avoiding the financial details that distinguished Riddell's City novels. Writing about Charles Reade, known for financially themed works like *Hard Cash*, Oliphant argued in October 1869 in *Blackwood Magazine* that copying too directly from life is "bad practice": "Fiction is bound by harder laws than fact is, and must consider *vraisemblance* as well as absolute truth" (quoted in Poovey 2008, 325). Riddell had fewer aesthetic scruples about putting the details of everyday life into her fiction. Yet, this hardly means that her work lacked imagination or literary quality.

Riddell never stopped worrying or writing about money. For her and her characters, money meant life. It is not surprising that her last published novel, *A Poor Fellow!* (1902), written before cancer prevented her from writing more, ends with a financial failure and suicide. As we will see, Oliphant also explored the subject of suicide as a result of financial failure, especially in her late work. Her diary in 1887 laments, "I want money" (Oliphant 1899, 155). Writing beyond the generation of Thackeray, Dickens, Gaskell, Trollope and Eliot, and approaching the *fin de siècle*, Riddell and Oliphant lived remarkable lives of literary productivity and economic anxiety. Their fiction, in distinctive yet similar ways, explores the profound relationship between money and life itself.

Notes

1. *Riddell v. Riddell and Smith* 1871, 11, R133, C16/747, British National Archives.
2. Colella (2016) wrote the first and, so far, only book devoted to Riddell's work. See also R. Michie (2009), Wagner (2010), Henry (2014). For the ghost stories, see E.F. Bleiler; Edmundson (2010), Bissell (2014). For the Irish contexts, see Murphy (2011). For women's writing and *A Struggle for Fame*, see Kelleher (2000) and Peterson (2009). There is a Web site devoted to Riddell's work: http://www.charlotteriddell.co.uk.
3. For the prejudice against City business as a subject for fiction on the part of Riddell's reviewers, see Srebrnik (1994).

4. Taylor (2006) has explored the "persistent and pervasive fear of and hostility to joint-stock enterprises" in Victorian culture (3).
5. For food adulteration generally and in Riddell's *The Race for Wealth* specifically, see Stern (2008).
6. Ellen Kilshaw was born to John and Elizabeth Kilshaw, of Bold Street, on November 18, 1794. She was baptized at St. Peter's Church, Liverpool. See *The Parish of St. Peter, Liverpool* Web site, http://www.lan-opc.org.uk/Liverpool/Liverpool-Central/stpeter/index.html (accessed 20 April 2018).
7. Kindleberger and Aliber (2005) write: "In 1818 and 1819 there were panics on both sides of the Atlantic that were connected in a non-obvious way. The 1819 crisis in Britain followed the collapse of commodity speculation in 1818" (113). For details on the American context of this panic, which has received less attention than other crises, see Rothbard (1962).
8. In *The Letters of Margaret Fuller* (Fuller 1983), editor Robert N. Hudspeth informs us: "The 'misfortunes' suffered by the Kilshaws were the sickness of Ellen's sister and the financial ruin of her father and brother during the Liverpool panic of the time" (95). Matteson (2012) is one of the few scholars to make the connection between Fuller, Kilshaw, and Charlotte Riddell. According to him, "the only surviving letter from Margaret to Ellen is one that was never sent" (37).
9. These letters run from 1818 to 1835 and include Ellen's marriage and the birth of Charlotte. They are preserved in the Margaret Fuller Family Papers (1662–1970), at the Houghton Library, Harvard University, MS AM 1086, vol. 2: 63. I am indebted to Silvana Colella for sharing her images of these manuscript letters with me.
10. Indicating the closeness of the bond, in 1820 Timothy and Margaret Fuller named their fifth child Ellen Kilshaw Fuller.
11. Charlotte Mitchell cites private sources as well as the will and death certificate of James Cowan. See s.v. "Riddell [née Cowan], Charlotte Eliza Lawson [pseud. F. G. Trafford] (1832–1906), novelist." *Oxford Dictionary of National Biography*. http://www.oxforddnb.com.proxy.lib.utk.edu:90/view/10.1093/ref:odnb/9780198614128.001.0001/odnb-9780198614128-e-35748 (accessed 15 Apr. 2018).
12. *Joy After Sorrow* (1873) was reissued in 1892.
13. In the nineteenth century, Liverpool had the second largest Jewish community in Great Britain, after London. For the history of Jews in Liverpool, see Cesarani (2002), Milne (2006), Kokosalakis (1982).
14. See s.v. "Riddell [née Cowan], Charlotte Eliza Lawson [pseud. F. G. Trafford] (1832–1906), novelist." *Oxford Dictionary of National Biography*. http://www.oxforddnb.com.proxy.lib.utk.edu:90/view/10.1093/ref:odnb/9780198614128.001.0001/odnb-9780198614128-e-35748 (accessed 15 Apr. 2018).

In *Mortomley's Estate*, the appearance of German Jewish businessmen in the City after 1870 reflects what Michie (2009) describes as the "somewhat dormant fears" of foreigners and Jews who were moving into the City (79).

15. This information is confirmed in the census records for 1851, 1861, and 1871. For the census of 1861, see Ancestry.com (2005), Class: *RG 9*; Piece: *795*; Folio: *28*; Page: *7*; GSU roll: 542702.
16. In census records, Joseph listed himself as being from Worcester, Moseley (1861), and Warwickshire, Birmingham (1871). Joseph Reddell, his father, is listed as being from Balsall Heath, Moseley, King's Norton, and Worcester and working as a sword cutler at the Royal Hotel, Birmingham.
17. The original spelling of the name seems to have been Reddell. Joseph may have changed it to suggest connections with a prominent family named Riddell. See Proceedings of Old Bailey, *Trial of Joseph Hadley Riddell, William Moore Eclipse Riddell, Theft: Stealing from master, 26 November 1849*. https://www.oldbaileyonline.org/browse.jsp?id=t18491126-87&div=t18491126-87&terms=Joseph_Hadley_Riddell#highlight. Accessed 5 April 2018.
18. Prosecutions for "workplace appropriation" in textile factories would apply to Joseph's case of appropriating building materials (see Godrey and Cox).
19. See Ancestry.com (2007) for Riddell's first and second transport: Joseph Hadley Riddell in the Australian Convict Transportation Registers–Other Fleets & Ships, 1791–1868; Vessel: Dudbrook, Voyage Date: 17 Nov. 1852, Home Office: Convict Transportation Registers, The National Archives Microfilm Publication Class: HO 11; Piece: 17.
20. See HO 18/292: Petitions (65 Items), 1850 Nov. 20–1869 Dec. 17 and 1850 Nov. 20–1869 Dec. 17, MS Crime and the Criminal Justice System: Records from the U.K. National Archives. "HO" 18 Records created or inherited by the Home Office, Ministry of Home Security, and related bodies, Home Office: Criminal Petitions, Series II HO 18/292, at the National Archives, Kew, United Kingdom. These were originally published in *Crime, Punishment, and Popular Culture 1790–1920*. Records are available via the Tennessee Electronic Library, http://tinyurl.galegroup.com/tinyurl/3UJM45 (accessed 20 April 2018). I am grateful to Kat Powell, who solved the mystery of why Joseph was not transported.
21. She wrote about this area in *City and Suburb* (1861) and *Above Suspicion* (1874–1875).
22. This journal ran in various forms from 1861 to 1900. The *Oxford Dictionary of National Biography* (see Note 13) notes that Riddell "edited for some time the *Home Magazine* (which ran from 1856 to 1866) and, from 1867, *St James's Magazine*, of which she was co-proprietor and in which her novel *A Life's Assize* ran from 1868 to 1870." Clarke (1992) establishes that *Home* actually ran from July 1879 to May 1882. On Oliphant's contributions to *Home*, see Chapter 7.

23. Reid (1905) writes: "The literary men who frequented Mrs. Riddell's house were not, I am sorry to say, so respectful to her husband as they might have been. They made it very clear, in fact, that it was the novelist and not the inventor of stoves whom they came to see, and they were impatient when the latter attempted to intrude his views upon them" (143–4).
24. For Victorian bankruptcy, see Weiss (1986), Lester (1995).
25. Proceedings of Old Bailey, *Trial of William Bradley, Theft: Pickpocketing, 1st May 1871*, https://www.oldbaileyonline.org/browse.jsp?id=t18710501-404&div=t18710501-404&terms=william_bradley#highlight, accessed 5 April 2018. See also Pall Mall Budget (1871).
26. This contract is held at the Harry Ransom Center, University of Texas, Austin, and is cited by Peterson (2009) as Woolf Uncat. 4 (265). It is probable that Riddell did repay the loan, although Peterson assumes that she did not.
27. *Riddell v. Riddell and Smith* 1871, 1–2, R133, C16/747, British National Archives.
28. Ibid., 2.
29. The full text of the MWPA is reproduced in Holcombe (1983, 243–6).
30. *Collinson v. Riddell, Riddell, Routledge Brothers, and Whiffin*, 1873, Vol. C16/852 C92 C588778, British National Archives.
31. Hurst and Blackett pressed Riddell, especially because Blackett had died insolvent and intestate. Oliphant was shocked when she learned that Blackett had failed to provide for his family, leading her to take out an insurance policy on her own life (Jay 1995, 281).
32. It was also typical of Joseph. In a letter dated April 3, 1868, Riddell told a Mr. Walford that her husband would "hand him a promissory note" for the £200 they owed him (Harry Ransom Center, University of Texas–Austin, Wolff Collection, Series II, Container 23.7).
33. *Collinson v. Riddell and Riddell* 1873, 7.
34. In his testimony, Joseph pleads illness, denies knowledge of his wife's literary business and claims to have forgotten the content of conversations. *Collinson v. Riddell and Riddell* 1873, 10.
35. National Archives C/33 1199A (2618).
36. On November 12, the court issued an injunction to the sheriff of Middlesex against Joseph and Charlotte for failure to respond to the accusations. There is no evidence of a final judgment in the National Archives. I am therefore inclined to think that the Riddells paid the £400, resolving the case.
37. Riddell told the story of going to Newby to get a copy of *Zuriel's Grandchild* to reprint and the publisher's surprise at learning R.V.M. Sparling was now a famous novelist (Ellis 1931, 280–81).

38. The only critical study of *Mortomley's Estate* appears in Colella (2016), in which she intriguingly analyzes the effects of the bankruptcy in terms of trauma, arguing that "some of the peculiarities of Riddell's fictional writing of disaster can best be explained as expressions of a traumatic kind of knowledge" (202–3).
39. Colella (2016) rightly observes that both Joseph Riddell and Archie Mortomley undergo "liquidation by arrangement," a distinctive form of bankruptcy that became popular between 1869 and 1883, after which it was abolished (187–8).
40. Colella (2016) acknowledges an autobiographical basis for the novel but stresses the aesthetic transformation of life into art. I find it illuminating to emphasize correspondences between the bankruptcies of the Mortomleys and the Riddells.
41. Taylor (2006) provides a context for her sentiments: "Opposition to joint-stock enterprise was widely diffused throughout society and could be found in liberal circles as much as conservative, and in the counting houses as much as in the Commons" (8).
42. Colella (2016) notes Riddell's shift from defending small business to criticizing big business in the late novels, beginning with *Mortomley's Estate* and continuing in works such as *The Senior Partner*, a shift that reflects actual changes in business and investment cultures. For more on the context of family firms, see Taylor (2006), Barker (2017).
43. Weiss (1986) explores the metaphor of bankruptcy as the "hell of the English."
44. Her name was on the contract but the book (1887b) was published anonymously and she only confessed in a letter to Bentley that Norway was the coauthor (Bentley Papers, Vol. LXIII ff341 and ADD MS 46622, 24 April 1885–1 June 1888, British Library). Norway became an important figure in the Irish Post Office and was present during the Sinn Fein Rebellion. Mary Louisa Gadsen, Norway's wife, published *The Sinn Fein Rebellion as I Saw It* (1916). The novelist Neville Shute Norway, their son, emigrated to Australia after World War II. In his *Slide Rule: Autobiography of an Engineer* (1954), he has little to say about his father.
45. Letter to A.J. Hipkins, 1892. Bentley Collection, 2131894, British Library.
46. The details of Barrie and Tweedie's efforts are provided in Kelleher (2000), who did not know about the earlier appeals of Mr. Hipkins. Kelleher also notes that Riddell's story, "Out in the Cold," which appeared in *Handsome Phil and Other Stories* (1899), is about a young woman who wants to become an author but is overshadowed by her father's failure as a writer. The father is awarded a £200 government pension, and Kelleher observes that this is an "uncanny anticipation" (128) of Riddell's future pension; but it is also, once again, an incorporation of her earlier 1894 experience into fiction.

47. Mrs. J.H. Riddell. MS. Archives of the Royal Literary Fund: Archives of the Royal Literary Fund 2573. (n.d.). World Microfilms, Nineteenth Century Collections Online, http://tinyurl.galegroup.com/tinyurl/6P54E7. Web. 23 May 2013. In her memoir, *Thirteen Years of a Busy Woman's Life* (1912), Ethel Tweedie (1862–1940) writes about Riddell and repeats the story of the paralyzed brother. I have found no other evidence of this brother, but he must have been James Cowan, the son Ellen Kilshaw mentions in her letters to the Fullers. Tweedie, an author of travel books and memoirs, knew Riddell well and raised private funds from friends (including W.S. Gilbert and Mrs. Humphrey Ward) to pay Riddell's household bills when she was dying of cancer. Tweedie's own husband had died in 1896 from what she calls "a broken heart" following the financial ruin of his marine insurance business (60). He left her with no money and two children. She supported herself through writing and conservative investing.

48. The French playwrights Émile Augier (1820–1889) and Jules Sandeau (1811–1883) coauthored several works on financial themes.

References

Ancestry.Com. 2005. *1861 England census* [database on-line]. Provo, UT: Ancestry.Com Operations Inc.

———. 2007. *Australian convict transportation registers–Other fleets & ships, 1791–1868* [database on-line]. Provo, UT: Ancestry.com Operations Inc.

Austen, Jane. 1818. *Persuasion*, ed. James Kinsley. Oxford: Oxford University Press, 2008.

Barker, Hannah. 2017. *Family and business during the industrial revolution*. Oxford: Oxford University Press.

Bissell, Sarah. 2014. Reconstructing masculinity in Charlotte Riddell's "The open door", and Rudyard Kipling's "They". *Victoriographies* 4 (1): 62–78.

Black, Helen C. 1906. *Notable women authors of the day*. London: Maclaren and Company.

Blathwayt, Raymond. 1890. The ladies' corner: Lady novelists—A chat with Mrs. J.H. Riddell. *Pall Mall Gazette*, February 18.

Cesarani, David. 2002. Port Jews: Concepts, cases and questions. In *Port Jews: Jewish communities in cosmopolitan maritime trading centres, 1550–1950*, ed. David Cesarani, 1–11. London: Routledge.

Clarke, John Stock. 1992. "Home", a lost Victorian periodical. *Victorian Periodicals Review* 25 (2): 85–88.

Colella, Silvana. 2016. *Charlotte Riddell's city novels and Victorian business: Narrating capitalism*. New York: Routledge.

Dickens, Charles. 1842–1844. *The life and adventures of Martin Chuzzlewit*, ed. Margaret Cardwell. Oxford: Oxford University Press, 2009.
———. 1846–1848. *Dombey and son*, ed. Alan Horsman. Oxford: Clarendon Press, 1984.
———. 1855–1857. *Little Dorrit*, ed. Stephen Wall. London: Penguin, 2003.
Edmundson, Melissa. 2010. The "Uncomfortable houses" of Charlotte Riddell and Margaret Oliphant. *Gothic Studies* 12 (1): 51–67.
Eliot, George. 1857. *Scenes of clerical life*, ed. Thomas A. Noble. New York: Oxford University Press, 1985.
Eliot, George. 1859. *Adam Bede*, ed. Carol A. Martin. Oxford: Oxford University Press, 2001.
———. 1860. *The mill on the Floss*, ed. Nancy Henry. Boston: Houghton Mifflin, 2004.
———. 1866. *Felix Holt: The radical*, ed. Fred. C. Thompson. New York: Oxford University Press, 1988.
———.1871–1872. *Middlemarch*, ed. David Carroll. Oxford: Oxford University Press, 2008.
Eliot, George. 1876. *Daniel Deronda*, ed. K.M. Newton and Graham Handley. Oxford: Oxford University Press, 2014.
Ellis, S.M. 1931. Mrs. J.H. Riddell, "novelist of the city and of Middlesex." In *Wilkie Collins, Le Fanu and others*, 266–335. London: Constable, 1951.
Emerson, Ralph Waldo, William Henry Channing, and James Freeman Clarke (eds.). 1859. *Autobiographical romance in memoirs of Margaret Fuller Ossoli*, repr. New York: Burt Franklin, 1972.
Fuller, Margaret. 1983. *The letters of Margaret Fuller*, ed. Robert N. Hudspeth. Ithaca, NY: Cornell University Press.
Gadsen, Mary Louisa. 1916. *The Sinn Fein rebellion as I saw it*. London: Smith Elder.
Gaskell, Elizabeth. 1853. *Cranford*, ed. Elizabeth Porges Watson. Oxford: Oxford University Press, 2011.
Gissing, George. 1891. *New grub street*, ed. Steve Arata. Peterborough, ON: Broadview, 2008.
———. 1897. *The whirlpool*, ed. Gillian Tindall. London: Hogarth Press, 1984.
———. 1905. *Will Warburton: A romance of real life*. New York: A.P. Dutton.
Godfrey, Barry, and David J. Cox. 2013. *Policing the factory: Theft, private policing and the law in modern England*. London: Bloomsbury.
Goss, W.H. 1899. *The life and death of Llewellynn Jewitt. With fragmentary memoirs of some of his famous literary and artistic friends especially of Samuel Carter Hall*. London: Henry Gray.
Henry, Nancy. 2014. Charlotte Riddell: Novelist of the city. In *Economic women: Essays on desire and dispossession in nineteenth-century British culture*, ed. Lana L. Dalley and Jill Rappoport, 193–205. Columbus: Ohio University Press.

Holcombe, Lee. 1983. *Wives and property: Reform of the married women's property law in nineteenth-century England*. Toronto: University of Toronto Press.
Jay, Elisabeth. 1995. *Mrs. Oliphant, "a fiction to herself": A literary life*. Oxford: Clarendon Press.
Kelleher, Margaret. 2000. Charlotte Riddell's "A struggle for fame": The field of women's literary production. *Colby Quarterly* 36: 116–131.
Kindleberger, Charles P., and Robert Aliber. 2005. *Manias, panics, and crashes: A history of financial crises*, 5th ed. Hoboken, NJ: Wiley.
Kokosalakis, N. 1982. *Ethnic identity and religion: Tradition and change in Liverpool Jewry*. Washington, DC: University of America Press.
Lester, V.Markham. 1995. *Victorian insolvency: Bankruptcy, imprisonment for debt, and company winding-up in nineteenth-century England*. Oxford: Oxford University Press.
Lewes, George Henry. November 1865–February 1866. Criticism in relation to novels. *Fortnightly Review* 3: 352–361.
London Gazette. 1844. The court for relief of insolvent debtors. Vol. I, Part 1: 1071.
Matteson, John. 2012. *The lives of Margaret Fuller: A biography*. New York: Norton.
Michie, Ranald. 2009. *Guilty money: The city of London in Victorian and Edwardian culture, 1815–1914*. London: Pickering & Chatto.
Milne, Graeme J. 2006. Maritime Liverpool. In *Liverpool 800: Culture, character, and history*, ed. John Belchem, 257–310. Liverpool: Liverpool University Press.
Murphy, James H. 2011. The Irish book in English, 1800–1891. In *The Oxford history of the Irish book*, ed. James H. Murphy, vol. IV. Oxford: Oxford University Press.
Norway, Neville Shute. 1954. *Slide rule: Autobiography of an engineer*. New York: Ballantine.
Oliphant, Margaret. 1883. *Hester*, ed. Philip Davis and Brian Nellist. Oxford: Oxford University Press, 2009.
———. 1890a. *Janet*. London: Hurst and Blackett, n.d.
———. 1890b. *Sons and daughters*. Edinburgh: William Blackwood. The Margaret Oliphant Fiction Collection. http://www.oliphantfiction.com/x0200_single_title.php?titlecode=sondtr. Accessed 5 Apr 2018.
———. 1893. A widow's tale. *Cornhill Magazine*, July–September. The Margaret Oliphant Fiction Collection. http://www.oliphantfiction.com/x0200_single_title.php?titlecode=widtal. Accessed 5 Apr 2018.
———. 1899. *The autobiography of Margaret Oliphant: The complete text*, ed. Elizabeth Jay. Oxford: Oxford University Press, 1990.
Pall Mall Budget. 1871. "Law and police": *The Pall Mall Budget: Being a weekly collection of articles printed in the Pall Mall Gazette from day to day: With a*

summary of news, vol. VI, March 31–September 29, 1871. London: Pall Mall Budget.
Peterson, Linda H. 2009. *Becoming a woman of letters: Myths of authorship and facts of the Victorian market.* Princeton, NJ: Princeton University Press.
Poovey, Mary. 2008. *Genres of the credit economy.* Chicago: University of Chicago Press.
Reid, Sir Wemyss. 1905. *Memoirs of Sir Wemyss Reid: 1842–1885*, ed. Stuart J. Reid. London: Cassell and Company.
Riddell, Charlotte. [R.V.M. Sparling, pseud.]. 1856. *Zuriel's grandchild: A novel*, 3 vols. London: Thomas Cautley Newby.
———. 1858. *The rich husband: A novel of real life*, 3 vols. London: Skeet.
———. 1861. *City and suburb.* London: Skeet.
———. [F.G. Trafford, pseud.]. 1864. *George Geith of fen court.* London: Frederick Warne.
———. [F.G. Trafford, pseud.]. 1865. *Maxwell Drewitt.* London: Tinsley Brothers.
———. 1866a. *Phemie Keller: A novel*, 3 vols. London: Tinsley Brothers.
———. 1866b. *Race for wealth*, 2 vols. Leipzig: Bernahard Tauchnitz.
———. 1867. *Far above rubies: A novel.* London: Tinsley Brothers.
———. 1869. *My first love* and *my last love, a sequel.* London: Tinsley Brothers.
———. 1870. *Austin Friars: A novel.* London: Hutchinson.
———. 1873. *Joy after sorrow.* London: Tinsley Brothers.
———. 1873a. *Home, sweet home.* London: Tinsley Brothers.
———. 1873b. *The earl's promise: A novel.* London: Tinsley Brothers.
———. 1874a. *Fairy water: A Christmas story.* London: Tinsley Brothers.
———. 1874b. *Frank Sinclair's wife, and other stories*, 2 vols. London: Tinsley Brothers.
———. 1874c. *Mortomley's estate: A novel.* London: Tinsley Brothers.
———. 1874–1875. *Above suspicion: A novel.* London: Tinsley Brothers, 1875.
———. 1882. *The senior partner*, 3 vols. London: R. Bentley and Son.
———. 1883. *A struggle for fame*, 3 vols. London: R. Bentley and Son.
———. 1884. *Susan Drummond: A novel*, 3 vols. London: Bentley.
———. 1887a. *Miss Gascoigne: A novel*, vol. 1. London: Ward and Downey.
———. 1887b. *The government official.* London: R. Bentley.
———. 1892. *Joy after sorrow.* London: Hutchinson & Co.
———. 1899. Out in the cold. In *Handsome Phil and other stories*. London: F.V. White.
———. 1902. *Poor fellow!* vol. 1. London: F.V. White.
Ritchie, Anne Thackeray. 1870a. Heroines and their grandmothers. In *The writings of Anne Isabella Thackeray*, 400–408. New York: Harper & Bros.
———. 1870b. *The writings of Anne Isabella Thackeray.* New York: Harper & Bros.

Robb, George. 1992. *White-collar crime in modern England: Financial fraud and business morality, 1845–1929*. Cambridge: Cambridge University Press.

Rothbard, Murray N. 1962. *The panic of 1819: Reactions and policies*. New York: Columbia University Press.

Saturday Review. 1861. Review of "City and suburb." October 5, 356.

———. 1874. Review of "Mortomley's estate." October 10, 481.

———. 1882. Review of "Senior partner." March 25, 375.

Spectator. 1886. Review of "Mitre court." January 23, 118.

Srebrnik, Patricia Thomas. 1994. Mrs. Riddell and the reviewers: A case study in Victorian popular fiction. *Women's Studies: An Inter-disciplinary Journal* 23 (1): 69–84.

Stern, Rebecca. 2008. *Home economics: Domestic fraud in Victorian England*. Columbus: Ohio State University Press.

Taylor, James. 2006. *Creating capitalism: Joint-stock enterprise in British politics and culture 1800–1870*. London: Royal Historical Society.

Thackeray, William Makepeace. 1847–1848. *Vanity fair: A novel without a hero*, ed. Diane Mowat. Oxford: Oxford University Press, 2008.

Times [London]. 1871. Court of bankruptcy, Basinghall-street, Sept. 27. September 28, 9.

———. 1906. Obituary of Mrs. J.H. Riddell, September 26, 8.

Trollope, Anthony. 1865. *Miss Mackenzie*, ed. A.O.J. Cockshut. Oxford: Oxford University Press, 1992.

———. 1875. *The way we live now*, ed. Francis O'Gorman. Oxford: Oxford University Press, 2016.

———. 1876. *The prime minister*, ed. Nicholas Shrimpton. Oxford: Oxford University Press, 2011.

Tweedie, Mrs. Alec. [Ethel B., pseud.]. 1912. *Thirteen years of a busy woman's life*. London: John Lane.

von Frank, Albert J. 2013. Margaret Fuller and antislavery: "A cause identical." In *Margaret Fuller and her circles*, ed. Brigitte Bailey, Katheryn P. Viens, and Conrad Edick Wright, 128–147. Durham: University of New Hampshire Press.

Wagner, Tamara. 2010. *Financial speculation in Victorian fiction: Plotting money and the novel genre, 1815–1901*. Columbus: Ohio State University Press.

Waugh, Arthur. 1931. *One man's road: Being a picture of life in a passing generation*. London: Chapman and Hall.

Weiss, Barbara. 1986. *The hell of the English: Bankruptcy and the Victorian novel*. Lewisburg, PA: Bucknell University Press.

CHAPTER 7

Margaret Oliphant, Women and Money

I don't understand business.
—Margaret Oliphant, Hester

In her autobiography, Margaret Oliphant laments her husband's failed attempt to establish a business restoring stained glass windows for which she had supplied the capital: "We neither of us, I suppose, knew anything about business" (Oliphant 1899, 63). Francis Oliphant's experiences trying to manage the men who worked for him struck her forcefully. Although she had been "brought up with a high idea of the honour and virtue of working men," she was soon "cruelly undeceived": "I do not think I have ever got over the impression made upon me by their callousness and want of honour and feeling" (65). Her fiction reflects this transformation in her sensibilities. The novels she wrote before this disillusionment with working men focused on the mistreatment of laborers, apprentices, and clerks by heartless, greedy employers. After her husband's financial failure and death in 1859, she developed a preoccupation with middle-class financial entanglements generally and women's relationship to the financial sphere particularly. The narrators and female characters throughout her fiction deny any knowledge of business; yet finance, speculation, and wise investment are staples of her plots.

© The Author(s) 2018
N. Henry, *Women, Literature and Finance in Victorian Britain*,
Palgrave Studies in Literature, Culture and Economics,
https://doi.org/10.1007/978-3-319-94331-2_7

In contrast to Thackeray, Trollope, Dickens, the Brontës, Gaskell, and Eliot, Oliphant never accumulated enough money to invest in stocks and shares. Her autobiography reflects on her inability to save money (117). In addition to investing in her husband's business, however, she invested in real estate to provide a stable home for her extended family, maintaining a house in Windsor, where she raised her children and wrote her autobiography (see Jay 1995, 214). *Hester* and *Kirsteen* are the most famous of her financial novels, and rightly so for their unique creation of psychologically complex female business heroines. But other novels show women to be competent managers of their inherited investments. Reading her works along side those by Gaskell, Eliot, and Riddell reveals another dimension to our exploration how women's financial lives and writing shaped Victorian cultures of investment.

This chapter tracks developments in Oliphant's writing about money, finance, and investment over the course of her long career. Whereas Riddell's personal experiences transformed her from a defender of small businessmen to a critic of corporate greed, distinct but similar pressures transformed Oliphant from a defender of the working class to an appreciator of investment opportunities even in the midst of corruption. I examine Oliphant's novels of the 1850s, moving on to discuss her later fiction, including *In Trust: The Story of a Lady and Her Lover* (1881–1882), *Hester* (1883), "Queen Eleanor and Fair Rosamond" (1886, first published in serial form in *Cornhill Magazine*), *Kirsteen: The Story of a Scotch Family Seventy Years Ago* (1890b), *Janet* (1890a), *Sons and Daughters* (1890c) and *The Ways of Life* (1897; a collection that includes two previously published short stories, "Mr. Sandford" [1888] and "The Strange Story of Mr. Robert Dalyell" [1892]). I place these works within the context of her personal financial struggles as well as within the larger contexts of global trade and finance to show their intertextual conversations with other fictional works published in the second half of the nineteenth century.

In 1890, Oliphant wrote the publisher William Blackwood to ask whether he could send her a copy of a magazine, "a little gossiping affair called *Home* which belonged to and was edited by Mrs. Riddell the novelist."[1] Oliphant recalls that Riddell had "got into rather a miserable position several years ago, and Annie Thackeray and I laid our heads together to get her up a Christmas number of this little magazine without expense" (quoted in Clarke 1992, 86). This letter confirms that Oliphant knew Riddell and was one of the authors that rallied around her when she was in a particularly miserable financial position.

These extraordinarily prolific authors, whose careers spanned the second half of the nineteenth century, were inevitably in conversation with each other.[2] Oliphant's envy and resentment toward George Eliot is well known from comments in her autobiography, in which she complains that Eliot's financial success and domestic comfort allowed her to produce great art. Riddell does not appear in Oliphant's autobiography, but Oliphant's repeated insistence in her work that she knew nothing about business, as well as her vague treatment of financial details, suggests that she was reacting against the display of financial knowledge that characterized Riddell's fiction. Even in *Hester*, the novel that features perhaps the boldest representation of a female banker and investor, the narrator makes repeated disavowals of knowledge. With respect to making a fortune in a few hours, she writes: "The present writer does not pretend to be able to inform the reader exactly how it was ... but he did so" (177). Describing a stock exchange "coup," the narrator remarks: "To furnish the details of this operation is beyond the writer's power, but the three young men understood it, or thought they understood it" (246).

In contrast to Riddell, Oliphant's work was rediscovered in the late twentieth century and continues to receive sustained attention. Many critics of Oliphant's work have focused on narrative patterns and concluded that Oliphant resisted fictional conventions. Merryn Williams (1986) established that Oliphant disliked ending her plots with marriages (54). D.J. Trela's (1995) important collection of essays is titled *Margaret Oliphant: Critical Essays on a Gentle Subversive*. Clare Pettitt (1999) argues that Oliphant refused to conform to the formulaic self-help narratives as epitomized in Dinah Craik's *John Halifax, Gentleman*. Tamara Wagner (2010b) argues that Oliphant self-consciously rewrites the standard plot of financial speculation, especially those of sensational fiction. Elsie Michie (2011) shows that Oliphant rejects the familiar Victorian marriage plot in which the male suitor chooses the poor woman of virtue over the vulgar wealthy woman. Patricia Johnson (2010) argues that in *Hester*, Oliphant undercuts the typical romance plot. While the subversive thesis has lost some of its power through overuse, critics who highlight Oliphant's financial plots add to our appreciation of her role as a financial novelist (see Johnson 2010; Michie 2013; Wagner 2010a).

I am less interested in arguing that Oliphant was subversive either politically or aesthetically than in showing how thoroughly saturated her work is with the subject of money generally and women's negotiation of the financial sphere particularly, including the surprising ways in which they manage their money. Probing further into her lesser-known fiction and financial life, I demonstrate the distinctive ways in which she understood the economic basis of society and asked existential questions about the relationship between the possession of money and life itself.

Biographer Elisabeth Jay (1995) observes that Oliphant was more interested in domestic stories and families than in extended social and financial networks (198) or dealings in high finance (215). While it is true that Oliphant tended to place family dynamics and psychological analysis at the center of her stories, as did most realist novelists, she, like Gaskell, Eliot, and Riddell, had knowledge of social and financial networks, specifically those that connected Scotland, Liverpool and London. Oliphant's worldview was influenced by Liverpool and its distinctive position as a global seaport and cradle of nineteenth-century financial institutions, such as marine and life insurance, and also as a city with a history of slave trading, an economy once tied to West Indian slavery and extreme wealth inequality. This knowledge is reflected in her work. A focus on the contexts of finance will provide new perspectives on writing about women and money in Oliphant's work, specifically, its insistence on the inseparability of the domestic and financial spheres.

Oliphant's Financial Life

Margaret Oliphant Wilson was born at Wallyford, in Midlothian, Scotland, in 1828 and moved with her family first to the village of Lasswade, outside Edinburgh, and then to Glasgow, where Francis Wilson, her father, worked for the Royal Bank. In 1838, the family relocated to Liverpool. Between 1838 and 1852, she lived first in Everton, a community of Scottish and Welsh immigrants. Later the family moved to Woodside across the River Mersey from Liverpool (where Gaskell had visited her relatives in 1831).[3] After marrying her first cousin Francis Oliphant in Woodside in 1852, she and her husband moved to London. Her parents followed her there, while Frank, her brother, who had also married a cousin, remained in Woodside.

She and her family thus followed the same trajectory as that of Johnnie Cross, moving from Scotland to Liverpool to London. In fact, the Wilson family was living in Liverpool at the same time as the Cross and Wood families, although Francis Wilson's position as clerk in the Export Department of the Excise Office at the Custom House, not as an independent businessman, makes it unlikely that his daughter socialized in the same set as the Crosses. Her career began in Liverpool, and her life there is a touchstone by which to compare her later perspectives on class, business, and finance.

Historian Graeme J. Milne (2006) observes that the wives and daughters of Liverpool businessmen "worked to bind the mercantile elite together through marriages, cultural patronage, and membership in philanthropic organizations" (297). Oliphant's representation of Liverpool culture in "Queen Eleanor and Fair Rosamond" (1886) demonstrates her awareness of the role women played by bringing money into the business community. In the story, Mrs. Lycett-Landon is valuable to her husband, a wealthy Liverpool cotton broker, not only as a wife and mother but because "she had money enough to help him in business and business connections in the west of Scotland (where the finest people have business connections), which helped him still more" (58). This is the generalization of a type clearly familiar to Oliphant, even though she observed this segment of society as an outsider. Mr. Lycett-Landon's firm has "houses" in Glasgow, Liverpool, and London. The type accurately describes families that were part of close-knit business communities characterized by intermarriages in which the women brought capital and connections to their unions.

As Gaskell had done in *Mary Barton* (1848) and was doing in *North and South* (1854–1855), Oliphant called attention to industrial poverty and the working class in her early novels, which included negative portrayals of Chartism. *John Drayton* (1851) and *The Melvilles* (1852) are set in Liverpool. As Pettitt (1999) notes, these novels belong to the industrial novel genre but differ from it in important ways that reflect Oliphant's unique perspective as a Scottish Presbyterian who was skeptical of oversimplified narratives of self-help.[4] As I have mentioned, in her early novels she was concerned with questions of class inequality, and in *The Melvilles*, for example, she criticizes the way wealthy merchants exploit their clerks, paying them less than subsistence wages (or paying nothing for apprentices) even as those same merchants congratulate themselves on charitable subscriptions that enhance their social reputation. Later, her critical lens shifts, as in "Queen Eleanor" and *Janet*, to the more privileged problems of the upper-middle class. The economic challenges faced by women remained a constant throughout her career and define her contribution to writing about women and the cultures of investment.

Like all of the novelists discussed in this book—Thackeray, Dickens, Trollope, Gaskell, Eliot, Riddell, and Gissing—albeit in differing degrees, Oliphant experienced a drain on her finances due to the behavior of family members. Her attitude toward money and the financial plots of her later novels reflect this personal experience. As we have seen, Thackeray's family money was lost through Indian speculations followed by his own bad investments in the 1850s. Dickens's father was famously insolvent, and his children as well as his relatives became a constant strain on his considerable income from writing. Trollope's father mismanaged his money, escaping creditors by fleeing to Belgium and leaving Fanny, his wife, to support the family through her writing. Gaskell's father experienced financial reversals, and she struggled with overextended finances to the end of her life. Eliot's brother-in-law went bankrupt, causing Eliot great anxiety before she attained success as a novelist, after which she assumed the burden of supporting G.H. Lewes's sons, legal wife, and extended family. Riddell's life was dominated by the business failures and bankruptcy of her husband. Jay (1995) notes connections between Oliphant's life and that of Mrs. Humphrey Ward, whose husband "squandered his wife's earnings in speculative art purchases" and her son "declined into a drag on family fortunes" (45).[5]

As these examples demonstrate, Oliphant's troubled financial life as a nineteenth-century middle-class novelist was not unique. She was subject to the same instabilities of the capitalist economy, which led to so many bankruptcies and the same problems of helpless dependents as many of her contemporaries. She was, however, unusual in being a single mother trying to raise and educate an extended family, including her two sons and, following her brother Frank's bankruptcy, his son and two daughters, and eventually Frank himself. She also supported their alcoholic brother, Willie, by arranging a life for him with friends in Rome. Her autobiography demonstrates the degree to which her husband's early death, the profligate behavior and illnesses of her brothers, and the inability of her sons to support themselves despite expensive educations drove her to earn an income through writing.

Certainly, she would have written regardless of her financial situation, but she would never know what she might have accomplished had she not been pressured to write for money. Her autobiography planted the seeds for future speculation that she had sold her work at the expense of her art (see D'Albertis 1997). She laments that her works were never as successful as those of Eliot, Trollope, Dinah Craik, or Mary Elizabeth Braddon (Oliphant 1899, 91, 157). She was bitter about what she considered to be her lack of financial success and her inability to negotiate strenuously for higher pay (102). Jay (1995) describes some of her complex negotiations with publishers over the years, including at least one lawsuit (285).

Success, inevitably, is relative, and thanks to her steady employment reviewing for *Blackwood Magazine* and the popularity of her Carlingford novels, she was better placed financially than Riddell, although never as well off as Eliot. Like Riddell, Oliphant was involved in extraliterary business activities through her husband's business, which consumed her literary earnings during their marriage (Jay 1995, 63). Her novels are characterized by financial plots that involve not only the stories of wills and inheritance—so ubiquitous in Victorian fiction—but also banking, limited liability, trusts, insurance, investment, and speculation. She emphasized the importance of family relationships, often self-consciously relegating financial matters to the background. But her fiction raises such issues as the morally degrading effects of the West Indian slave economy in her historical novel *Kirsteen* and the morbid fact that the families of suicides were unable to collect on life insurance policies (e.g., *At His Gates*; "Mr. Sandford"; "Mr. Dalyell").[6] Like George Eliot, she was interested in the ethical problems posed by the supposedly "dirty" origins of wealth, and she explored these problems as experienced primarily by the privileged few and especially by self-entitled sons (e.g., *Sons and Daughters*).

Oliphant's fiction incorporates aspects of the genre that Riddell helped to establish, the "City" novel of finance, although Oliphant never provided the same level of specificity about business transactions.[7] She wanted to consider the reverberations of finance on families and women in particular, whereas Riddell often focused on men, aspiring inventors, or businessmen who were estranged from their families. The patterns in their respective novels emerge from their life experiences. Riddell and her husband had no children, but Oliphant's children defined her personal life. Oliphant's plots explore the role of familial networks and intermarriages in business and finance and reflect a different social reality from that of Riddell. Nevertheless, the narratives of the lone engineer or inventor making his way in London and the narrative of the family business are both essential in defining the Victorian financial novel genre and cultures of investment.[8]

OLIPHANT AND LIVERPOOL

During the time that Oliphant lived in Liverpool (1838–1852), she observed the extremes of poverty and wealth that characterized the city from the vantage point of the Scottish immigrant community in Everton and from the perspective of the lower-middle classes. In her autobiography, she recalled that there was great distress in Liverpool (Oliphant 1899, 58). Both her father and brother Frank worked as clerks, a notoriously underpaid profession. Her life there encompassed the "hungry forties," when a depressed national economy, Corn Laws restricting free trade, immigration in the wake of the Irish famine and a cholera epidemic all contributed to poverty. Though she may not have understood the larger picture at the time, she participated with Willie and Frank, her older brothers, in charitable activities to help the poor by distributing coal.[9]

These were the mean streets of Liverpool, where Mr. Earnshaw found the boy Heathcliff in Emily Brontë's *Wuthering Heights* (1847).[10] The religious communities conducted charitable efforts to relieve the poor and the merchants lobbied for repealing the Corn Laws. William Wood, Johnnie Cross's uncle, was a vice president of the Liverpool Anti-Monopoly Association. He describes a meeting of the group in January 1843 in the Music Hall that was attended by prominent businessmen, including Charles Holland (Elizabeth Gaskell's cousin) (Wood 1895, I:329). While the men were meeting indoors, fifteen-year-old Margaret Wilson was collecting petitions in the streets of Liverpool on behalf of a women's anti-Corn Law campaign (Oliphant 1899, 61).

In an extensive review titled "Modern Novelists Great and Small," published in May 1855 in *Blackwood's Magazine* (Oliphant 1855b), Oliphant discusses Gaskell's recently published *North and South* and comments: "The popular mind seems to have accepted *Mary Barton* as a true and worthy picture of the class it aims to represent" (560). There is an implied critique and perhaps a resentment that her own representations of working-class life had not been as influential, but she also shows a grudging respect for what Gaskell has achieved in impressing the "popular mind."[11]

Oliphant's own *John Drayton* (1851), published three years after *Mary Barton*, is the story of economic distress among the working class of Liverpool. Oliphant does not attempt to provide specific economic reasons for the depression, though Chartism is vaguely represented as a false hope for larger economic solutions. The hero, trained as an engineer, loses his job when the foundry where he works building iron ships closes because the men who own it, Mr. Hardman and Mr. Power, dissolve their partnership. At the same time, his lover emigrates to America with her family, and his parents across the Mersey in Cheshire face poverty when his father is no longer able to work. Following the loss of his job, John has come down socially from being a skilled mechanic and is forced to look for work as a cotton porter, hoping to be called for minimal daily wages. He suffers the humiliation of watching the activities of the city's commercial and financial center, where great wealth is made and from which he feels excluded. From the perspective of Drayton, the workingman, Oliphant portrays the traders conversing on the Exchange Flags of Liverpool and operating with profit as their chief motive. Like Gaskell, Oliphant highlights the indifference of the wealthy to the plight of starving families around them. The "silken women" of Liverpool go "sweeping into those luxury shops" and the "merchant-men" think of the "present speculation, or profit, or brokering" without care of the unemployed men congregating nearby (II:82–3).

The Exchange building and Nelson Monument, to which Gaskell cryptically alludes, are at the physical center of this wealth inequality. Oliphant makes an explicit connection between the chained figures surrounding the monument and the cotton traders in the area:

> It is Tuesday again, and John stands at the corner of the square where the Liverpool merchants congregate. It is a paved quadrangle, and has heavy buildings and cloisters round it; and in the centre is a mystic statue called to Nelson, surrounded by disconsolate chained figures of bronze, who weep, no one can tell you why. Within the cloisters, through doors carelessly swung open, and at great dusty windows, you see long vistas of men and newspapers, for yonder are the Exchange reading-rooms; and out in the square they are thronging thick as bees, and as you pass you hear them talk of cotton, and commissions, and percentages; and great and small—the old man who is a *millionaire*, and the young man who pants and wrestles to become one—are bound to each other like the mystic slaves around their Nelson's monument, with stony chains of profit and interest; and the thoughts of every soul turn on a golden pivot, and to make money, there, is the chief end of man. (85–6)

This scene of men gathering for work was common in Liverpool at mid-century. Beckert (2014) describes the thousands of workers assembled and waiting for work on the Liverpool docks at this time (200).

The Liverpool Exchange Building and the Nelson Monument were central to Liverpool's civic identity and were powerful symbols of its economic history. Rather than relying on the reader's knowledge to supply an interpretation of the monument, as Gaskell had done, Oliphant highlights the mystery surrounding the monument's figures. It is her interpretation that the chained figures "weep," and—implying that her narrator has asked—she notes pointedly that "no one can tell you why." Her narrator persists in calling the figures "mystic slaves" and, furthermore, equates their bondage to the "stony chains of profit and interest" by which those working in the Exchange are bound. Referring to the wealthy, she calls the statue "their Nelson's monument," stressing that the military hero and his monument do not belong to the disenfranchised poor.

This passage seems like an elaboration of precisely what Gaskell could not say about the same monument and building three years earlier in *Mary Barton*: the "disconsolate figures in chains" are slaves and that their placement in the Exchange Flags across from the great Liverpool Exchange building, which impressed Oliphant as it did Gaskell, might be connected to the activities of commerce and finance that were ongoing long after the abolition of the slave trade in 1807 and the abolition of slavery in the colonies in 1833. Slavery, however, plays virtually no role in the rest of the novel, in which Drayton finds work in London and then on a steamer traveling back and forth between Liverpool and Boston, via Halifax, where he discovers his love and returns with her to Liverpool. He eventually finds work in a new foundry, and the novel ends happily with the family comfortably established.

Published shortly after *John Drayton*, *The Melvilles* (1852) also mentions the Exchange building and the Nelson Monument in cryptic fashion. Mrs. Melville and her son first enter the city to seek employment for him. Their meeting with a merchant in "a dingy street near the Exchange" is unsuccessful (I:34). Furthermore, walking from their home in Everton to Liverpool, the widowed and now impoverished Mrs. Melville and her daughter go in search of sewing work. The narrator mentions the suburban nature of Everton, once a separate village now being incorporated into the sprawl from Liverpool. The women encounter "the sudden heathen beauty of this great building" and the "graceful pillars of the portico" (72). Describing the city, Oliphant uses the second-person voice, habitual in her early works, to bring the reader into the visual tour. This building is clearly the Exchange, which is "opposite the pediment with its inarticulate sculpture" (72): "You hear music, do you say, just now, as you stand here in the broad day, vainly trying to discover what the story is which that sculptured pediment means to tell" (72). As with *Mary Barton* and *John Drayton*, *The Melvilles* illustrates how the Nelson Monument and its chained figures embody a story of Liverpool's past. The weeping, mystic slaves from *John Drayton* have become for the narrator an inscrutable, inarticulate sculpture meaning to tell a story that the universal "you" tries "vainly" to discover and interpret. The emphasis is on sound, voice, and history—if only the statue's figures could speak.

Like *John Drayton*, *The Melvilles* is a story of poverty and of families desperately attempting to survive in seemingly impossible economic circumstances characterized by gross wealth inequality. This time, not only a son but also a sister and their mother strive to gain employment. Between *John Drayton* and *The Melvilles*, Oliphant's interest has turned to female characters. She writes: "To endure to be useless is the hardest fate of woman" (58). The Melville women receive small payment for their sewing from a Quaker shop while the son, formerly a medical student in Edinburgh, seems unqualified to enter business, and various merchants and cotton brokers refuse to employ him. Ironically, the wealthy businessman who denounces the deceased Mr. Melville, his clerk, for not having a life insurance policy, dies leaving no provisions for his own family. The issues that preoccupy Oliphant here are oddly prescient of her own future predicament as a widow whose husband leaves her in debt and the mother of sons who are educated but unemployed and unemployable. As we will see, the importance of life insurance as a means of supporting dependents following the death of the family breadwinner became a theme in her life writing and late fiction.

Oliphant's first novel (1855a) was entitled *Christian Melville* (written ten years before it was published). She made no attempt to connect the separate Melville families that appear in her two novels, but clearly the name was important to her. *Christian Melville* is set in "one of the largest towns in England" (1). Though not named and only vaguely described, this town is certainly based on Liverpool, the only English town in which Oliphant had lived and the location of two of her subsequent novels. She refers, for example, to "Change, 'where merchants most do congregate'" (245), that is, the Exchange Flags mentioned in *John Drayton* and *The Melvilles*.

However poorly constructed this first attempt at writing a novel may be, *Christian Melville* nonetheless represents the economic and social nexus of Scotland, Liverpool and America, which constituted Oliphant's family experience and would inform her future literary efforts. As this novel shows, before she attempted to write her "condition of England" novels dealing with the Liverpool working class, Oliphant was interested in the family legacies and intermarriages of the merchant middle class. Christian Melville is the eldest daughter of a wealthy merchant who is partner in the firm Rutterford and Melville (21). At one point, her father enjoys the credit for a successful speculation (164). James, her brother, marries the daughter of his father's business partner and enters the firm. Halbert, Christian's brother, attends the University of Edinburgh, but is seduced into alcoholism and atheism by a satanic friend. He travels by ship to America, stereotypically represented as a primal forest, where he converts back to Christianity and then returns to Liverpool just in time to save his youngest sister from marrying his diabolical friend. The plot is overwrought, but its representation of commercial and financial networks between Scotland, Liverpool, and America makes it an important precursor to Oliphant's later, better developed fiction.

The Melvilles displays a characteristic emphasis on the superiority of the Scottish families from which the characters descend. Mrs. Melville is from the Greenlees of Greenlee, and it is her wealthy brother, an Indian "nabob," who returns to Liverpool and helps his widowed sister's family when he learns of their poverty. Miss Greenlees broke with her relatives to marry Mr. Melville, but she retains pride in her family as well as that of her husband, referring to "those reverend Melvilles who have been honored for generations as preachers of the Word" (I:78).[12]

Oliphant's early novels demonstrate her ambivalence about Liverpool and aspects of its capitalist culture. Her narrator in *The Melvilles* describes the unsavory neighborhoods frequented by sailors and the pestilent streets inhabited by Irish immigrants who work in the "sugar house." She writes, "The street overflows with human creatures—overflows with noise, with sin, with everything impure," yet the sun is "gleaming on the beautiful river, whose uses, beneficent as they are, have collected so much evil on its banks" (III:30). She appreciates the river's beauty, and her reference to its "beneficent" uses reflects her general approval of the trade that drove the city's economy. Down by the docks, "there are perhaps in Liverpool places more debased than this; there is none which can boast more of the *appearance* of evil" (III:272). While the novel invokes Christian morality through terms such as "evil" and "sin," its political concerns are more prominent. Throughout *The Melvilles*, Oliphant emphasizes the notion that merchants are unjust to the working class in general and to their lower-middle-class clerks in particular. Once Hugh Melville has been able, through the patronage of his uncle, to receive his medical degree from Edinburgh, he is emboldened to tell his former employer, Mr. Renshaw, that Liverpool is "benevolent but not just" (III:48). Hugh says contemptuously that to "buy in the cheapest market and sell in the dearest" was the "grand palladium of civilization and trade" (49–50). The commercial proverb of buying in the cheapest market and selling in the dearest was a favorite phrase of Oliphant's to encapsulate what she disliked about capitalist practices.

Oliphant left Liverpool after her marriage in 1852, but she remained tied to the city through her brother's family in Woodside and through her memories of a formative period in her life. These early impressions shaped her later, financially themed work. She next moved to London and financed her husband's business, the failure of which resulted not only in her disillusionment with workingmen but also her economic troubles. Frank Oliphant's unexpected death in Italy (where the family had moved for his health) conferred upon her the new identity as a widowed mother left with nothing but debts and her ability to write. As we will see, her subsequent writing put questions of women and money—inheritance, business, speculation, and investment—at the center of novel after novel.

"Your Money or Your Life": Oliphant's Later Fiction

Oliphant provides us with extensive information of her financial life in her autobiography, which reflects on the challenges she faced when writing to support herself and her relatives. But her interest in finance went beyond her personal experience, and her fiction tracks developments within the larger cultures of investment, becoming increasingly concerned with more complex financial institutions, instruments, and practices, such as banking, investing, speculating, and insurance. Wagner (2010b) notes that Oliphant's novels "began to feature financial themes in the 1860s" and that her "first explicit foray into financial plots" was "The Stockbroker at Dinglewood" (1868) (72). It is evident, however, from her description of the Exchange building and Nelson Monument in *John Drayton*, and even earlier in her representation of the commercial classes in *Christian Melville*, that the lives of financiers and other millionaires attracted her attention as subjects for fiction when she first began writing, even if she did not develop financial (as opposed to commercial) plots until the 1860s.

As we have seen, mid- and late Victorian fiction is preoccupied with money generally, and financial plots became pervasive as the financial lives of Victorians became more complicated and the shareholding economy was democratized. In her role as a reviewer of contemporary literature, Oliphant was particularly attuned to what fellow novelists were writing. But she manages her plots, characterizations, and moral dilemmas over money in distinctive ways. Perhaps she was reacting not only against Riddell's novels but also against the centrality of business and finance in novels by Trollope, Reade, and others when she asserted that she knew nothing about business and had her female characters deny knowledge of trade, entails, and other economic matters.

In the nineteenth century, denying knowledge of business was a coded way of establishing femininity, on the one hand, and confirming artistic integrity, on the other hand. Despite her personal disavowals of business knowledge and her relegation of financial details to the background of her domestic plots, Oliphant was as obsessed as other Victorian novelists with exploring the influence of contemporary financial conditions on the lives of her characters. She went even further in entertaining the notion that money was inseparable from life itself. Her exploration of the notion that money is life echoes similar themes in Trollope's *The Last Chronicle of Barset* (1866–1867), Dickens's *Our Mutual Friend* (1864–1865), and Riddell's *Mortomley's Estate* (1874).[13]

Levine (2014) has written about the impossibility (or at least improbability) of reading all 150 items in the Oliphant bibliography: "Most of us have neither world enough nor time to do that" (232). Among literary critics, Jay (1995) stands out in her masterful knowledge of the entire body of Oliphant's works. What follows is an analysis of a representative selection of Oliphant's writing about the complex, multifaceted dimensions of the cultures of investment, which permeated familial relationships and troubled the very souls of her characters. In her attitude toward the investment cultures that she represented, Oliphant demonstrates a unique balance of the practical and the philosophical. Her later fiction offers various geographical settings, as well as variations on financial plots, themes, and moral dilemmas. Yet continuities can be identified, including the Liverpool–London nexus and a concern with women and money. The "grievances of women," as Williams (1986, 151) notes, preoccupied her particularly in the 1880s. Oliphant also poses moral questions about inherited wealth and financial decisions reminiscent of those explored in Eliot's fiction. In this respect, these late works further extend and enrich our exploration of writing by and about women in local investment cultures and their connections to global economic networks, particularly as related to America and the West Indies.

Oliphant's *In Trust: The Story of a Lady and Her Lover* (1881–1882), first published in serial form in *Fraser's Magazine*, offers a good example of a novel that engages with many of the questions we have been exploring about women and money, by responding to the plot devices of other Victorian novels. The scenario is established with an opening conversation between Mr. Mountford and Anne, his daughter: "My dear, the case is as plain as noonday: you must give this man up" (1). Mr. Mountford disapproves of Anne's suitor and threatens to cut off the legacy bequeathed to her by her deceased mother but left in his control. If she marries in defiance of his wishes, he will leave the money instead to Rose, her half-sister, the child of his second marriage. Thus, the daughter's dilemma: the money or the man; or as Anne puts it to the family lawyer: "Your money or your life" (210). The story includes familiar aspects of Oliphant's novels and Victorian novels generally, including heiresses, second marriages, and entailed estates. It recalls works such as Oliphant's *The Greatest Heiress in England* (1879) and anticipates her novel *Hester* (1883), in which women investors figure and money is a form of psychological and material power. The basic plot line of a father disinheriting his daughter echoes Henry James's *Washington Square* (1880), first published in the *Cornhill Magazine*, and likely read by Oliphant. The characters compare Heathcote Mountford, the heir to the entailed estate, who also falls in love with Anne, to Mr. Collins in Austen's (1813) *Pride and Prejudice*. In addition to Austen and James, there are allusions to Eliot's (1871–1872) *Middlemarch* in Anne's interest in reforming cottages on the estate and in the relationship between the sisters, idealistic Anne, and practical Rose. But the novel is more than the sum of these parts and influences; Oliphant's plot twists and psychological insights give it a distinctive character in its treatment of women and money.

Anne indulges in romantic fantasies about how money means nothing compared to true love: "Money! What had money to do with it" (Oliphant 1881–1882, 79). She elaborates: "Had Shakespeare been rich? No Money! That would be the best way to make a life worth living" (81). This ability to disregard the importance of money, as Oliphant often implies, is a privilege available only to the wealthy few. Anne's suitor, Cosmo Douglas, is "nobody," a young barrister given a gentleman's education by a father who is a managing clerk in a solicitor's office in London (90). Cosmo is unconnected to any established Douglas family. Oliphant would use the name Douglas again in *Kirsteen*, in which the degraded Douglas family has a name but no money. Cosmo's situation allows Oliphant to muse ironically about the inherent unfairness and hypocrisy of valuing a man solely by his family connections, which she believes persists in British culture. To Cosmo, "as troublesome and unpleasant a position could not be conceived—to have all that makes a gentleman … yet upon close investigation to be found to be nobody" (97). The characterization of this prejudice is broad but not quite comical. It is even more exaggerated than that of Emily Wharton's father in Trollope's *The Prime Minister* (1876), another novel in which the father objects to the daughter's marriage because the suitor comes from unknown antecedents. But Oliphant is less sympathetic than Trollope to the father's prejudices and is more sympathetic to the suitor without actually absolving him of his financial motive in marrying an heiress. Here, the father's stubbornness is mysterious, whereas in *The Prime Minister* it is Emily's stubbornness that mystifies the reader.

In Trust (1881–1882) is not one of Oliphant's best novels, but it is representative. Although padded with dialogue, it at times goes straight to a disturbing psychological truth about marital relations, probing the inseparability of economic and affective ties through a narrative voice that is unobtrusive and insightful.[14] When Mr. Mountford intimates to his second wife that he may disinherit Anne and leave his money to Rose, her daughter, she immediately begins to calculate what this would mean for her daughter, holding this fantasy of her husband's death in tension with her love for him: "Thus the two sat within a few feet of each other, life-long companions, knowing still so little of each other" (118). The novel is also interesting for the tension it sets up when the father does in fact change his will and disinherit Anne, rendering her powerless between the father's ability to control her economic well-being and her uncertainty about Cosmo.

In a twist of plot, Mr. Mountford dies suddenly in a riding accident when his horse steps into a rabbit hole and falls on him. Death by horse accident is a plot device Oliphant used in works over the decades (from *Harry Muir* in 1853 to "Mr. Sandford" in 1888), as we will see. Mountford's will reveals that he has left his money "in trust" to Anne for Rose when Rose comes of age, a bitter punishment for Anne. Cosmo fails to appear for the funeral but maintains close relations with Anne, all the while knowing that he cannot marry a woman without money. Anne throws herself into her new role as trustee. Mr. Loseby, the family lawyer, explains: "You will have to administer the whole, and watch over the money, and look out for the investments" (281). Of course, Anne says, "I don't know anything about it" (281). Nonetheless, she embraces her duties: "I shall be a kind of land-steward with a little of the stock-broker in me, now" (281). In yet another twist, Rose betrays the family's trust by reading a sealed letter from her father, which she is not supposed to read until her twenty-first birthday. Finding that the property will revert to Anne as long as she does not marry Cosmo, Rose first tries to get Cosmo to marry Anne and then lapses into a state of frustration and anguish at the thought of her own future loss. Meanwhile, Heathcote, Anne's cousin, renews his suit, and her business skills become a metaphor for their potential marriage partnership. Anne says, "I will ask Rose to appoint me her land agent"; Heathcote replies, "I will appoint you mine" (459). The notion of "in trust" is simultaneously legal and moral. Rose ultimately offers Anne half the inheritance, and the grateful Anne never learns the truth of the letter that would have left her the whole amount. Showing that Oliphant did not always subvert the conventional marriage plot, the novel ends happily with Anne marrying Heathcote and Rose marrying the younger son of the clergyman in the parish.

Published just one year later, Oliphant's *Hester* takes the notion of the female money manager further and refuses the happy marriage ending of *In Trust*. *Hester* is unique in Oliphant's body of work particularly, and in Victorian fiction generally, for imagining a woman as the head of a bank, as well as of an extended family. It goes further than *In Trust* in exploring a woman's ability to manage money. Because of its daring premise, its probing exploration of gender roles and the centrality of its financial plot, it has attracted a substantial amount of critical attention (see Hunt 2014; Johnson 2010; Michie 2011; Poovey 2008; Wagner 2010a). *Hester* was an experiment that Oliphant did not repeat, yet it marks a transition to a less familiar fiction that imagines an even darker relationship between money, identity, life, and death as mediated by the financial institutions of insurance, banks, and family firms. In the later works, such as "Queen Eleanor" and *Sons and Daughters*, she continues her interest in family businesses, the most literal embodiments of intertwined financial and affective lives.

Hester (1883) examines the strange relationships between the matriarch Catherine Vernon and a collection of relatives who depend on her financial support. Money permeates every aspect of these family ties, but the situation also carries an implicit, larger argument about the distorting effect of charity and welfare upon their recipients, illustrating in microcosm the collective sense of entitlement and resentment that follows from dependency. In the novel's prehistory, Catherine Vernon saves the family bank after reckless speculation by her cousin, John Vernon, almost ruins it.[15] She does so by applying her natural business skills and also by supplying her own inherited wealth to keep the bank solvent. Long established as the head of the bank as the novel's main action begins, she has managed to keep it prosperous and respectable—a portrait of a powerful female banker that is unprecedented in Victorian fiction.

Catherine is unmarried and thus childless, but she has groomed Edward, her nephew, to take her place at the bank. She has treated him as a son, even if displaying an oppressive and jealous hold over him that perhaps offers insight into Oliphant's own powerful feelings about her sons, who remained financially dependent on her throughout their lives. When Hester, her cousin (the daughter of the miscreant John Vernon), comes with her mother to live in Catherine's compound and receives Catherine's charity, the girl is ignorant of the past and resentful of Catherine's power. The novel tells the story of how Hester comes to understand the weight of the past (her father's misdeeds), the achievements of Catherine (whose strength she shares), and her own identity as the inheritor of these conflicting legacies. But, first, she must navigate a terrain of multiple suitors, including, most dangerously, Edward, her cousin, who rebels against Catherine and tries to seduce Hester in his plot to speculate heavily with the bank's funds. He is motivated less by greed than a vindictive animosity against the woman who has kept him under her control and the institution that represents her power.

Hester offers a critique of speculation commonly found in novels of the late Victorian period. Like other deluded speculators, Edward is intoxicated by the prospect of wealth without work and succumbs to the gambler's mania. At one point, the narrator observes that he "had reached a point of excitement at which the boundaries of right and wrong become so indistinct as to exert little, if any, control over either the conscience or the imagination" (341). Edward describes his secret financial ventures to a horrified Hester as throws of the dice: "Chance is everything in business—luck, whatever that may be: so that gambling words are the only words that come natural" (407). For Oliphant, as for many Victorian novelists, this slippage from respectable investing into reckless speculation represents the worst side of modern capitalism.[16] Taking a sensational, sexualized tone, such passages show that love of money and erotic love are entwined in ways confusing to the woman who wants to remain free of both money and sex.

In addition to sex and marriage, Oliphant explores the complexity of gender roles in relation to modern finance. The manliness of the business world attaches to women who are naturally capable and even gifted at conducting business, but who succeed at the price of their femininity. In *Hester*, it is left to the women to manage the business affairs that have been bungled by importunate men. The story is one that reflects Oliphant's own life, not only because a woman has stepped in where men failed to support an extended family but also by the repetition of generational history. The alcoholism and gambling of Oliphant's brothers were repeated in the lives of her sons, whom she guarded jealously, later wondering whether she had somehow unintentionally contributed to their bad behavior. Similarly, in the novel, the bad behavior of Hester's father is repeated in Edward.[17]

In *Hester*, Oliphant uses the history of a family firm to examine the way modern capitalism still incorporated older dynastic models, with sons succeeding fathers and daughters given in marriages to create strategic business alliances. Oliphant was not part of a business dynasty, but while living in Liverpool, both she and her brother Frank married first cousins. In *Hester*, the young Catherine Vernon was disappointed in not marrying her cousin John, and Edward Vernon's first choice of a bride is his cousin Hester. In the end, having left the bank in ruins, Edward elopes spontaneously with Emma, Roland's sister, a distant cousin who benefits when the fleeing criminal's new speculations pay off. Here, as in many of Oliphant's fictional communities, kinship, sexuality, money, and business interests are completely intermingled.[18]

Hester has inherited Catherine's common sense, ambition, and family loyalty. She has always had "something of the boy in her" (77), and when lamenting her powerlessness to help her impoverished mother, she asks herself why she was not born a man (82). For much of the novel, she is kept ignorant and told, "Do you think a man *ever* talks to women about these things? Oh, perhaps to a woman like Catherine that is the same as a man" (404). After saving the bank a second time, and placing "everything she had in the world in the common stock" (446), Catherine tells her young relative: "A few years' work, and you would be an excellent man of business, but it can't be" (492). It is not clear to Hester or to the reader why it "can't be." Catherine's death and Hester's declaration that she will never marry raise the possibility that she might find her way to a business career. After all, *Kirsteen*, Oliphant's later novel, represents a woman who succeeds in business. Hester recognizes that business is a form of art and that women, as well as men, might be gifted in this sphere, given the right opportunities. Oliphant avoids a happy marriage ending, but her own ambivalence keeps her from turning Hester into a business heroine, as Catherine was called on to be twice in her life. Although some detractors call Catherine a man, and the dependent relatives despise her, she is nonetheless a role model for Hester, pointing the way to economic and social power for women of the next generation.

In the stories Oliphant wrote immediately after *Hester*, money becomes inseparable not only from sex and marriage but also from life itself. In 1871, Oliphant was shocked to learn that Henry Blackett, her friend and publisher, had died without making provisions for his family, leading her to take out an insurance policy on her own life (Jay 1995, 281). The theme of an apparently wealthy man dying with no savings or life insurance occurs in Oliphant's fiction as early as 1852, long before her own husband died leaving her and their children in debt. In *The Melvilles* (1852), the merchant Mr. Waldrop cruelly remarks to Mr. Melville's widow and son, "The money he spent in sending this young man to college would have much more than sufficed for a life insurance" (1:47). His insensitive accusation raises a question that Oliphant would take seriously later in life after her unproductive investments in her sons' educations contributed to her own poverty and concerns about their future after her death. Is it better to invest the little money you have in your children's education or in a life insurance policy to provide for them in case of your death? Like the scene from *In Trust*, in which Mrs. Mountford calmly contemplates the money Rose will inherit upon her husband's death while he is confiding his plans to her, so the monetary value of individual lives becomes darkly central to Oliphant's stories of the 1880s, when the technicalities of life insurance policies affect the actions of husbands in financial distress.

The reality of what Timothy Alborn (2009) calls "commodified lives" (4) in the nineteenth-century history of life insurance touches on problems explored by Baucom (2005) and Armstrong (2012) in relation to the insurance of slaves as cargo in the eighteenth century. Both discuss the Zong massacre and the ensuing legal trials involving Liverpool ship owners and slave traders as the epitome of the modern commodification of lives in the expanding life insurance industry traced by Alborn. Oliphant's fiction of the late 1880s returns to Liverpool in "Queen Eleanor," addresses the abuses of West Indian slavery in *Kirsteen*, and invokes the postslavery economy of the West Indies in *Sons and Daughters*. At the same time, she used life insurance as a vehicle to reflect existentially on the value of a life in *The Ways of Life*, as she would in her own autobiography. Whereas in *Martin Chuzzlewit*, Dickens (1842–1844) showed that the relatively young life insurance business might prey on the fears of a vulnerable public, by the time Oliphant wrote "Mr. Dalyell" (1892), life insurance had become so established that characters worry about the ethics of cheating the insurance company.[19]

Like Oliphant's *John Drayton* and Riddell's *Zuriel's Grandchild* (1856) and *The Government Official* (1887b), "Queen Eleanor and Fair Rosamond" (1886) shuttles back and forth between Liverpool and London. It embodies in microcosm many of Oliphant's preoccupations at this time, and its representation of Liverpool suggests just how far Oliphant had moved in the 1880s from the subjects that interested her thirty years earlier, even though the story itself is set "thirty years ago" (57). Mr. Robert Lycett-Landon is a fifty-year-old businessman (the son of a Scottish laird) who undergoes a midlife crisis arising from his boredom with his respectable career, wife, and family of six children. Told by a narrator from the perspective of the wife, whom he abandons to bigamously marry a much younger woman in London, the center of action is the psychological crisis following Mrs. Lycett-Landon's discovery of her husband's betrayal and her obsession with protecting her children from the knowledge of their father's crime.[20]

After establishing her awareness of commercial and familial networks in Scotland and Liverpool in the opening pages, Oliphant typically disavows her knowledge of commerce, remarking on the family business of Lycett, Landon, Fareham, and Co.: "I think they were cotton-brokers, without having any very clear idea of what that means" (59). This comment, although characteristic, seems disingenuous since she represented multiple cotton brokers in *The Melvilles* and certainly did know what that meant. As we have seen, the repeated denials of financial knowledge were rhetorically important to asserting her status as an artist and distancing herself from the works of Riddell, Charles Reade, and others who cluttered and compromised their art with too much commercial and financial information.

The attitudes of Liverpool residents toward their city and toward London are highlighted throughout the tale. Whereas Oliphant's Liverpool in the early 1850s had been the site of poverty, working-class agitation and the shadow of slavery, the city of the 1850s—presented from the perspective of the 1880s—is staid, dull, and conventional. The respectable middle-class family moves from Liverpool across the River Mersey, not to "bustling Birkenhead" (10) but to "Rockferry" (79) (or Rock Ferry), a desirable area further upriver that was developed in the second half of the nineteenth century.[21] In an extended lyrical passage, the narrator describes the sight of Liverpool from across the Mersey when "darkness hid everything that was unlovely in the composition of the great town and its fringe of docks," concluding that "there are, and were, few things so grand, so varied, so full of interest or amusement as the Mersey at night" (59). She appreciated the sublime beauty of the river, which "slave of commerce as it is and was, was then a very noble sight" (60). With the phrases "are, and were" and "is and was," Oliphant emphasizes the historical setting of the story and strikes a nostalgic note when recalling the city of her youth. Drawing on her knowledge of Liverpool, she seeks in this story to capture its distinctive civic pride and its provincial mentality—the conflicted way in which the city viewed itself and was viewed by others. Mr. Lycett-Landon "felt a little scorn at those who did not see how fine the Mersey was," although his wife and children "patronized the town" and called it vulgar (60).

Oliphant also describes the perspective of Liverpool residents in relation to the prevailing mentality of businessmen in London, a class that she would later treat in *Sons and Daughters*. While the internal lives of businessmen are not her primary concern in this story, she shifts our perspective to Liverpool and away from the representation of London businessmen, found, for example, in Dickens, Trollope, and Riddell. After becoming alarmed at her husband's prolonged disappearances in London, supposedly to take care of business there, Mrs. Lycett-Landon and Horace, their son, go in search of him. They enter the City to inquire at his office. The narrator observes, "In Liverpool it must be allowed the City was not thought very much of. It had not the same prestige as the great mercantile town of the north. The merchant princes were considered to belong to seaports, and the magnates of the City had an odour of city feasts and vulgarity about them" (76). Whereas Londoners look at the visitors from Liverpool as provincials from the country, the narrator reminds us of the reverse snobbery in Liverpool.

In J.M. Barrie's (1898) introductory note to *A Widow's Tale*, the volume in which the serialized "Queen Eleanor" was republished, he says that the story would be better if one could "pitchfork the son out" (viii). But Horace is precisely the vehicle through which Oliphant contrasts the concern with business and moneymaking to the mother's heroic sacrifices. Reflecting what Oliphant assumed to be the values of the Liverpool merchant class and its sons, in contrast to the London merchants who turned their sons into gentlemen, as in *Sons and Daughters*, Horace is obsessed with the business. He "contemplated the likelihood of becoming a very rich man, and raising the firm into the highest regions of commercial enterprise, with pleasure and a sense of power which is always agreeable" (Oliphant 1886, 61). Ignorant of his father's second marriage and anxious about his father's disappearance, he frustrates and patronizes his mother by putting the family firm and his own career ahead of her domestic troubles. He confesses that even his father's illness would not be as bad as compromising the firm's credit: "I mind nothing so much as the credit of the house" (103). Here, as in so many of Oliphant's stories, the son is ungrateful and dismissive of his mother. While Horace's concern about himself is thoughtless and juvenile, the story seems to affirm a separate sphere mentality. Yet, what the story actually shows is the inseparability of domestic and business spheres. As she does with the family bank in *Hester*, Oliphant here suggests that there can be no distinction between economic and domestic life where family businesses are concerned.[22]

Horace hopes that his father has not speculated on "those new bubble companies" (103). He tells his mother, "Ladies have such a different way of looking at things," and "It is always the personal you dwell on" (104). His mother momentarily considers pretending to the world that her husband has lost all of his money, thinking that speculation would be a respectable cover for his bigamy. Instead, after meeting Rose, the unsuspecting mistress/second wife, and confronting her husband, she returns to Liverpool to live down the scandal and raise her children alone. Ultimately, the catastrophic financial events that turn the plots of so many Victorian novels are mentioned, only to be dismissed: "A great bankruptcy with many exciting and disgraceful circumstances followed soon after, and the attention of the community was distracted" (111). In this story, bankruptcy does not affect the main characters and is an ironic aside about the public's distracted attention and the lure of sensational events befalling others, perhaps even a commentary on her own use of the sensational financial plot in *Hester*. In the end, Horace becomes a "prince of commerce" and his disgraced father creeps back to his first wife from time to time, just to learn what has become of his children.

Oliphant would soon introduce a different sensational element to stories exploring the monetary value of a life through insurance plots. *The Ways of Life* (1897) is a collection of two previously published novellas, "Mr. Sandford" (1888) and "The Strange Story of Mr. Robert Dalyell" (1892), both originally serialized in the *Cornhill Magazine*. In the former, a man resists committing suicide because it would deny his family the benefit of insurance: "The only thing that came uppermost was the thought of the insurances, and of the thousand pounds for each which the children would have" (1888, 106). In the latter, Robert Dalyell, a wealthy businessman, covers up his financial failure and defrauds the life insurance company by faking his own death, leaving Frank, his upright son, to feel shame at the idea of the fraud. Just as Horace felt the greatest family disgrace would be to damage the company, so Frank is more concerned about the fraud perpetuated on the insurance company than he is with his father's sacrifices on his family's behalf. In her diary entry for Christmas night 1887, Oliphant describes writing Mr. Sandford "chiefly to give a little outlet to the miserable sensations which I must not express otherwise" (Oliphant 1899, 205). She provided a reflective introduction to *The Ways of Life*, using the metaphor of the "ebb tide" to describe midlife and the approach of death, topics that resonate in the stories. The piece is also a statement of her artistic realism and the importance of representing "all the paraphernalia of common life" (1897, 14). She writes: "Death is illogical, and will seldom come at the moment when it is wanted, when it would most appropriately solve the problems of what is to be done after." For example, she asks: "Why did not Napoleon die at Waterloo?" (17).

Mr. Sandford is an artist. At age 60, he recognizes that the historical genre of painting in which he excels has become obsolete and can no longer sell in the current market.[23] Like Oliphant, he begins to fantasize that his family would be better off if he were dead. The narrator reflects: "A man cannot die when he wishes it, though there should be every argument in favor of such an event, and its advantages most palpable. ... We live when we should do much better to die, and we die sometimes when every circumstance calls upon us to live" (Oliphant 1888, 112). Sandford contemplates suicide, but realizes that this would preclude his family's collecting on his life insurance: "And then another practical thought, more tragical than any in its extreme materialism and matter-of-fact character—it would vitiate the insurances!" (115). In a remarkable narrative of wish fulfillment, he is injured in a coach accident and dies. Sandford's family collects on his insurance and on the profits from his paintings, which ironically become valuable after his death. Clearly, this is a bitterly personal story about the monetary value to which the parent's life is reduced, as well as the failure of the public to value the artist's work during his life. Its companion story takes up similarly dark and bitter themes, putting a different twist on the problem of suicide and life insurance.

"The Strange Story of Mr. Robert Dalyell" (Oliphant 1892) describes the prosperous main character, of Yalton, outside of Edinburgh. His family is comfortable, Fred, his son, is well educated, and his wife "declared constantly that she knew nothing of business" (173). Coming from the landed class, he is not exactly a businessman but is the director of both a railway company and an insurance company. He becomes a bankrupt through vague speculations but keeps this information from his family. Instead, he goes one day from the city to the coast at Portobello to take a swim. But he does not return, leaving his wife in a state of anxiety, especially because she does not receive the habitual telegram from him, which she obsessively awaits.[24] Soon a pile of clothing is found on the beach. Eventually a body is found and the family accepts that Mr. Dalyell has drowned in a tragic accident. Despite his financial reversals, suicide is ruled out and the family collects on the insurance. This gives the bachelor Pat Wedderburn, a family friend and Edinburgh lawyer, some ethical qualms, but without evidence of a suicide, he ignores his suspicions and even proposes marriage to the widow. Only the old family servant, Janet (a name Oliphant would soon use again in *Janet*), keeps suspicion alive. A gothic figure, she haunts the house and finally confronts the unsuspecting son and heir, already disturbed by his mother's remarriage. Janet arranges a meeting between the son and his supposedly drowned father, but the meeting is a disaster. The father leaves in disgrace, wishing he had never obliterated his identity in order to allow his family to collect on the life insurance. Fred agonizes that his father was "not a shameful suicide to cheat the insurance companies as his son had once feared— but a still more shameful survivor, having cheated them, having saved his family and cleared his name by the most dreadful, the most false of frauds, the most tremendous of lies" (297). In an uncanny repetition, Robert Dalyell wanders away, rejected from his home, and goes swimming in the ocean. This time, he is drowned.

As with "Mr. Sandford," this tale shows Oliphant perfecting the surprise, ironic ending of the modern short story. Both stories offer variations on the theme of how insurance puts a price on life, encouraging breadwinners to measure their worth in dollars; their expectation of insurance payments after their deaths even robs them of the free choice of suicide. In these stories, the insurance company owns the lives of their clients; or, as Oliphant herself sometimes felt, her family owned not only her money but also her life.

"A Stain upon the Planter's Fortune": Oliphant in 1890

In her diary in 1888, Oliphant wrote: "During September wrote a short story, two numbers, for Blackwood (pot boiler), called *Sons and Daughters* and began *Kirsteen*" (Oliphant 1899, 209). Just as she seemed preoccupied with life insurance and suicide in the stories discussed above, so in 1888 she continued writing about women and business, as she had in *Hester*. She was also notably interested in West Indian sugar plantations and fortunes made by Scottish and English men there. The two works may profitably be read together for Oliphant's perspective on these aspects of investment cultures in the late 1880s. I will begin with the historical novel *Kirsteen* and conclude the chapter with the "pot boiler" *Sons and Daughters*, which is set in Oliphant's present.

Kirsteen (1890b), considered one of Oliphant's finest works, sets a story of daughters reduced to their exchange value in marriage against the backdrop of West Indian slavery, the Napoleonic wars, and East Indian imperialism.[25] It returns to an era that left its traces on Victorian England in the form of memorials to national victory, such as the Nelson Monument in Liverpool, and the economic networks epitomized in that city's "sugar houses"—all explored by Oliphant in her novels of the 1850s, nearly forty years earlier. It is the story of the Scottish Douglas family, long fallen from its historical place as "lairds" of Drumcarro into a state of proud poverty. In the novel's prehistory, Neil Douglas, having grown up poor but with a sense of superior blood, travels to Jamaica, where he earns just enough money to return to Scotland and purchase a house on what was once Drumcarro land. In the novel's chronology, he would have been in Jamaica roughly in the 1780s. When the novel opens, toward the end of the Napoleonic wars, his third son is being sent off to India thanks to the father's network of connections. The daughters are neglected and viewed as worthless by the narrow-minded patriarch and his feeble, psychologically abused wife. The community perceives Douglas, or Drumcarro, as he now has the right to be called, as an "auld slave-driver" (32), brutalized by his time in the West Indies. Oliphant's narrator is simultaneously graphic and skeptical about this belief: "At that period there were fortunes for the making, attended however by many accessories of which people in the next generation spoke darkly, and which still, perhaps, among unsophisticated people survive in tradition, throwing a certain stain upon the planter's fortunes. Whether these supposed cruelties and horrors were all or almost all the exaggerations of a following agitation, belonging like many similar atrocities in America to the Abolitionist imagination, is a question unnecessary to discuss" (32). There is a strange refusal by the narrator to validate the assumptions and rumors about Drumcarro specifically and events in the West Indies in general. Drumcarro is clearly a brutal man, but fortunes made through West Indian slave labor involve what the narrator euphemistically calls "accessories" and "supposed" cruelties and horrors. The "following agitation" is a reference to abolitionist agitation in England. In the novel's temporal setting, the abolition of the slave trade in 1807 has recently occurred and the abolition of slavery in the colonies lies in the future (1833). But the narrator writes with hindsight of abolition in America (1864) and states that "atrocities" there were exaggerated. In a further, somewhat confusing twist, she observes that the critics of Drumcarro imagine him to be tormented by dreams of "flogged women and runaways in the marshes pursued by him" (32). Yet, after introducing these disturbing images, the narrator condemns Drumcarro as "neither tender-hearted nor imaginative, and highly unlikely to be troubled by the recollection of severities which he would have had no objection to repeat had he the power" (32). The people of "the next generation," then, are viewed as overly imaginative and tenderhearted, while the former slave driver seems callous and cruel by nature. In short, the narrator is oddly noncommittal, preferring to judge both the slave driver and his overzealous critics. It is only later, when Drumcarro commits murder, that he experiences flashbacks to his slave-driving days.

The novel explicitly associates sugar consumption in Scotland with its production in Jamaica, suggesting that people in 1814 made this connection readily. Miss Eelen, the wealthy maiden aunt of the Douglas family, remarks that Drumcarro probably does not want sugar in his tea: "No doubt you've had plenty in your time in yon dreadful West Indies where you were so long." She also refers to "those meeserable slaves!" (68). Through Drumcarro, Oliphant also raises the issue familiar throughout the nineteenth century and made in her own "condition of England" novels of the 1850s: Workers in England were perhaps even more oppressed than West Indian or American slaves. In *John Drayton* and *The Melvilles*, she had used slavery as a metaphor for the "chains of profit" in her description of the slaves surrounding the Nelson Monument in front of the Liverpool Exchange Building. Drumcarro responds to Miss Eelen's remarks about the slaves: "There's few of them would change places, I can tell ye, with your crofters and such like that ye call free men" (68). Oliphant presents this viewpoint, but it is unclear whether she sympathizes more with the tyrannical father's position or that of Miss Eelen. From the distance of the narrative voice, we can only be sure that, rightly or wrongly, there is a "stain on the planter's fortune" (32), recalling the implied taint on West Indian fortunes, from Brontë's *Jane Eyre* (1847) to Eliot's *Daniel Deronda* (1876).

Eventually, Drumcarro goes too far in his tyranny over his family, and his free-spirited daughter Kirsteen runs away rather than marry an old man of her father's choosing. Like Yorke Ford in Riddell's *Austin Friars* (1870), who is running from a similar fate, Kirsteen flees to London and turns to business. Just as *Hester* went furthest among Oliphant's works in imagining a woman at the head of a financial institution, so *Kirsteen* is distinctive for representing a woman who succeeds as a "mantua maker"—rising from a shop assistant to partner in the business to independent entrepreneur. She is, in this respect, a virtual female John Halifax or George Geith. Kirsteen uses her wealth to redeem the Douglas family and its property, although her family, like Catherine Vernon's family, only resents her financial support, and she is placed in a masculine but, nonetheless, socially accepted role of a wealthy, single woman with a large house in Edinburgh.

Running parallel to the theme of slavery and stained money is that of art. The connection between business and art preoccupied Oliphant during the late 1880s. Kirsteen is first awakened to the art she will pursue when Miss Macnab, a dressmaker, comes to make the dresses for her and her sister before attending the ball of the local lord. The fact that Miss Macnab is an artist impresses the young Kirsteen, and the narrator observes: "The mind of the artist is always the same whatever his materials may be" (Oliphant 1890b, 53). In "Mr. Sandford" (as in *At His Gates*), the artist is a painter. In *Hester*, the genius for business inherited by Catherine Vernon is likened to the special gift, which produces "a fine picture or a fine poem" (Oliphant 1883, 5). In *Kirsteen*, the art is clothes making as well as business. The novelist self-consciously reflects on the presence and predicaments of these artists. Oliphant expressed regret in her autobiography that she was never free enough from money worries to see what she might have accomplished in her writing; she was always pressured and her work suffered. Her recognition of art in many forms, including business, suggests that she did not make an absolute separation between the aesthetic and the financial spheres, and for her, writing was never separate from earning money.[26]

Following *Kirsteen*, Oliphant published *Janet*, which offers variations on the themes of paying back creditors and the legacy of ill-gotten money. As a partial rewriting of *Jane Eyre*, Janet is the governess and her employer, Mrs. Harwood, has a madman—her husband—hidden in an unused wing of her home in St. John's Wood, London. Liverpool replaces Jamaica as the primal scene of financial crimes committed by Mr. Adolphus Harwood, a speculator who fled his losses in Liverpool and supposedly died in Spain. Referring to the financial scandal, the narrator characteristically insists on her ignorance: "The money matters of the house in general were cleared up, though I cannot explain how, having small knowledge of such subjects" (151).

Mrs. Harwood had rejected "any quixotic notion of giving up what she had for herself and her children to satisfy the creditors of her husband" (151). The narrator notes: "Some people think differently on such matters, but Mrs. Harwood had never wavered in her determination, and in general her conduct was at least not disapproved by her friends, who thought her an excellent woman of business and as full of integrity and steadiness as her husband had been the reverse" (151). Her decision not to pay off her husband's creditors contrasts to other real and fictional examples of bankrupts and their spouses sacrificing to pay such debts in Dickens's (1846–1848) *Dombey and Son*, Eliot's (1860) *The Mill on the Floss*, and Oliphant's *Sons and Daughters* (1890c). Furthermore, as we have seen, Charlotte Riddell's life was overshadowed by the need to pay off debts, and this image of the indebted author goes back to the example, well known to Oliphant, of Sir Walter Scott. Her tone in *Janet* is cynical when she implies that good business means not repaying debt.

After Mr. Harwood's speculations in Liverpool, "where failures and ruin are commonplace matters such as occur every day" (Oliphant 1890a, 152), the supposed widow and her children relocate to St. John's Wood, where "any little episodes that had happened in Liverpool or in the wilds of North Wales were totally unknown" (152). But the husband (now mad) who perpetuated the unspecified scheme has actually been kept in the house attended by a male servant and is, ironically, fixated on the fantasy of paying back his creditors. He is discovered ultimately with the help of Janet, who spends most of the novel fending off two unwanted lovers. She ends up marrying a former suitor, the much older Dr. Harding, who has known her all her life and now has a practice in Liverpool.

Coincidentally, when the doctor arrives to rescue Janet from her claustrophobic life in the house, it turns out that he had known the Harwoods in the past and was fully aware of the secret financial scandal. Once he sees the madman, however, he decides to let the secret rest. In the end, Mrs. Harwood gets away with the money she has kept by not repaying creditors and hiding her guilty husband. No one, therefore, is ever punished for the financial wrongs committed by Mr. Harwood, and the desire to repay creditors becomes the echo of a madman's ramblings. "As for Janet, the little governess, the wife of the great Liverpool doctor" (319), she becomes "the best-dressed woman in the north of Lancashire, which is saying a great deal" (320). In this way, Oliphant minimizes her financial plot and ends on a trivial note of fashion. Overall, the novel is noteworthy for reversing the gender roles of Jane Eyre (Rochester is Mrs. Harwood, Bertha is Mr. Harwood) and for turning Liverpool into the structural equivalent of Jamaica.

Included in Oliphant's thinking about money, inheritance and morality in the late 1880s and early 1890s was the state of the West Indies, past and present. Published in the same year as *Kirsteen*, *Sons and Daughters* (1890c) is characterized by ambiguous—even contradictory—views about class, particularly the merchant class of the previous generation—wealthy and established in Harley Street in London—which educated its sons to be gentlemen and its daughters to be ladies. The patriarch of the story, Mr. Burton, nonetheless expects Gervais, his son—educated at Eton and Oxford (like Oliphant's sons)—to enter his firm in the City. Unsurprisingly, Gervais objects to this long-established plan. He takes an impractical, self-justifying and idealist moral high ground, saying that he does not wish to work because he would be taking jobs from those who need them more than a rich man's son. This sets up a generational conflict and also a problem for the son's prospects for marriage to the daughter of another wealthy businessman who lives nearby on Harley Street. While Gervais has wealth to throw away, Madeline, his fiancée, has less power but also more respect for what her merchant father has earned for the family. She turns out to be an unexpected, heroic investor in the vein of Catherine Vernon.

I conclude my analysis of Oliphant's work with this novel because, on the one hand, it brings together so many of the themes, social conditions, and cultural preoccupations discussed throughout this book, including moral critiques of capitalism and wealth tainted by West Indian slavery. On the other hand, it illustrates the role of women using investment opportunities to ensure their own security as well as to rescue the men in their lives from financial ruin. It epitomizes what I have been arguing was a fundamental difference between men and women in the nineteenth-century cultures of investment: the critique of business and finance as a male privilege that even middle-class women could not afford and which women authors such as Oliphant found hypocritical. Gaskell, the Brontës, Eliot, and Riddell all appreciated investment, even of inherited wealth, as a means by which women could find independence. This sensitivity to the position of women is reflected in their writing, which constitutes a counter tradition to the canonical, anticapitalist novels by their male contemporaries, and complicates our understanding of writing about business, finance, and the cultures of investment in Victorian literature.

Like *In Trust, Sons and Daughters* (1890c) begins in medias res with dialogue between a parent and child that sets up the story's main themes and dilemmas: "Then you will not take the share in the business, which I have offered you?" (1). Gervais declines his father's offer to join him as a partner in the City firm, proposing instead that he live on his father's wealth. In contrast to Horace in "Queen Eleanor," who is intent on becoming a "merchant prince," the Eton- and Oxford-educated Gervais affects lofty ideas that appall his father and his future father-in-law. He is disgusted with trade and profit: "Paying in the cheapest market and selling in the dearest is not an axiom for me" (31).[27] Madeline, in contrast, appreciates that the comforts and advantages that she and Gervais enjoy come from the business activities of their fathers. She introduces the idea of tainted money and pursues the ethical implications of his complaint about business: "If it is so bad that you will not follow it, shouldn't we give up all we have? For it is purchased in the same way" (31). Evading the question, Gervais can only protest, "Our grandfathers did things in a better way" (32).

These vague gentlemanly scruples and Gervais's lack of a profession make his marriage impossible. Under pressure from Madeline's father, therefore, he agrees to travel to the West Indies to assess the value of his own father's neglected, unprofitable plantation there and arrange for its sale, invoking the scenario of Charlotte Brontë's (1853) *Villette*. In agreeing to take on this job, he understands that he might keep the profits from the sale of the property and marry Madeline. Oliphant had written about West Indian slavery in *Kirsteen*, published in the same year as *Sons and Daughters*, but set back during the late eighteenth century when slavery still existed in the colonies. *Sons and Daughters* (1890c) confronts the controversy over the postabolition condition of black labor when Madeline urges Gervais to go and see about the property, arguing hopefully that he may be able to "throw some new light upon the subject of emancipation ... if you could only find some means of rehabilitating Quashee, Gervais! And making him a human possibility again" (74).[28]

In a narrative thread that is left hanging until the end, we learn that Madeline has £10,000, which, as her father observes, her "wise aunt" left her. Madeline assures him that she has done with it "only what Mr. Mentore has advised me to do" (59). It is clear that she has money inherited from a female relative, which is now in her own hands to invest under advisement from a trusted mentor.

While Gervais is away for many months settling the West Indian plantation, his father takes another partner, the son of a clerk whom Gervais himself had recommended for the position. Gervais learns belatedly that this business decision has led to the ruin of his father's company because the young partner made irresponsible speculations. As is common in Oliphant's stories, the difficulties and delays of communication, whether via mail or telegram, are essential to the plot. On his way back to England, Gervais is shocked to read of his father's bankruptcy in a newspaper, the details of which Oliphant left typically vague: "Great

Panic in the City—the failure of the old established firm of Burton, Baber & Co" (85). This is the type of calamity that distracts society in "Queen Eleanor," but here it shocks Gervais to his core. Consistent with her notion in *Hester* that business talent is an inherited trait, Oliphant's narrator comments that "the fire of commercial blood" is raised in him (95).

Gervais's reaction to his father's bankruptcy settlement poses many of the ethical questions with which Oliphant and other Victorian authors were so preoccupied, even if it does so in muddled form. The creditors have been paid off at fifteen shillings on the pound and are satisfied with that. But Mr. Burton has managed to save the Harley Street house for Gervais and all the West Indian money has been kept out of the settlement. The privileged son's refined morality is engaged, and he insists on reopening the legal case and repaying all the creditors in full from his West Indian profits. This leaves him with nothing but the house. Oliphant seems ambivalent about his scruples in paying off all creditors, showing that, while morally admirable, it is entirely impractical, an example of bad business leading to financial problems for himself and Madeline.

As if by magic, however, Gervais finds that £10,000 have been credited to his account. He can only conclude that his father, who has now disappeared, has sent the money, and he feels qualms about receiving it, believing that his father somehow kept back wealth that might have been used to pay the creditors. At Madeline's insistence, he nonetheless accepts the money, on which they live modestly after their marriage. The plot then takes a fantastical turn. While Gervais and Madeline are vacationing in the Lake District, they catch a glimpse of Mr. Burton, who has remarried and started a new family. Here, Oliphant reprises the theme of the secret second family that she had used in "Queen Eleanor." Confronting his father, Gervais learns that he did not send the £10,000. He leaves his father at peace in his new life and tells Madeline about his discovery. She confesses that she provided the money, left to her by her aunt and carefully invested by her, thereby enabling their marriage. Despite the specter of deceit between spouses, the story ends happily, the woman's inheritance from a female relative saving the day. Commenting on this story, Jay (1995) aptly observes that Madeline has "made wise investments" and that "not only do private investments seem in no way tainted by their connections with either commerce of 'speculation,' but women are able to put the care of their loved ones above abstract codes of behavior" (205). The plot is an interesting variation on the ending of *Janet*, in which the woman saves the family by not paying her husband's debts. Mrs. Harwood in that tale is successful but ruthless, hardly an admirable heroine. Those authors who did not experience crushing debt (Gaskell and Eliot) tended to admire the ethos of paying off debt, whereas Riddell and Oliphant were more sympathetic to the need of preserving the family, even if creditors went unpaid.

In this novel of the 1880s, Madeline epitomizes the view of capitalism that I have been arguing was characteristic of many nineteenth-century women, including authors: it is very fine to disdain the profit motive when you are a man with multiple careers open to you. For women with fewer options, however, investment is empowering and may be the only way to obtain desired ends. *Sons and Daughters* (1890c) bears this out perhaps more simply and clearly than any other work explored in this study. Madeline (of course) "knew nothing of trade" (34) and had done only what Mr. Mentore advised; yet she is proud of her commercial family, whereas her overeducated lover is disdainful and impractical. The story, in this respect, is an allegory. Many male authors took a moral high ground (like Gervais) and earned high fees for their writing while preserving the opportunities for earning salaries in other professions. Many women authors, in contrast, appreciated the value of investing as one of the only ways to enhance the money they inherited (like Madeline) or that they earned through their writing.

The authors whose cases we have examined—Gaskell, Eliot, Riddell, and Oliphant—were as critical of greed and corruption as their male contemporaries. But in the fiction they published, ranging from *Mary Barton* in 1848 through Oliphant's *A Widow's Tale* in 1898, they could not without hypocrisy launch wholesale condemnations of a capitalist system that allowed them (and their heroines) to benefit by putting money out to work for them. Their financial plots and the various moral dilemmas involving the inheritance and investment—the past and the future—of wealth, which they explored in their fiction, are thus remarkably complex, showing the inseparability of domestic and public spheres and of literary and financial spheres within the Victorian cultures of investment. As this and previous chapters have shown, their attitudes toward, and representations of, Victorian financial cultures were inextricable from their own financial lives and from a broader social context in which women investors were a vital part of the global economy and Victorian literature.

Notes

1. Clarke (1992) reconstructed information about the contents of this short-lived periodical and describes the Christmas number for 1880, which included pieces by Margaret Oliphant, Dinah Mulock Craik, Anne Thackeray Ritchie, Laurence Oliphant, and Riddell herself, all friends of Oliphant.
2. Jay (1995) writes that Oliphant published, "ninety-eight novels, fifty or more short stories, twenty-five works of non-fiction, and over three hundred articles" (5).
3. Williams (1986) identifies the specific addresses where the Wilsons lived 1839–1849 (5).
4. These novels were originally published under Oliphant's brother's name. See Clarke (1981).
5. Bourrier (2011) has contested the idea that male family members constituted a drag on women authors' finances. Writing about Oliphant's friend and fellow novelist Dinah Mulock Craik, she traces the myth that Craik's brother, Benjamin Mulock, was a strain on his sister's finances to its source in Oliphant's obituary of Craik. While Benjamin Mulock was in Australia, his sister managed his British bank account for him, at one point purchasing £90 of stock on his behalf (180). In 1857, he went to work as an engineer in Liverpool, where the Mulocks had relatives.
6. Life insurance plots overlapped with bigamy plots in sensational fiction in the 1860s and 1870s. For examples, see McAleavey (2015, 3).
7. For Oliphant's rewriting of financial plots that were typical of sensation fiction, see Wagner (2010b).
8. There are exceptions to this generalization among the novelists' many works: Riddell's *Zuriel's Grandchild* (written under a pseudonym) is explicitly about family dynamics, and Oliphant's Kirsteen is a Riddell-like hero who leaves her family behind to pursue her fortunes in London.
9. From her autobiography (Oliphant 1899), we learn that Oliphant's parents supported the Reform Bill of 1832 when she was still a child in Scotland, and that her mother in particular was something of a radical in politics.
10. Eagleton (1995) argues that Heathcliff was Irish. Crowley (2012) calls this "nonsense," claiming that Heathcliff's gibberish was a form of Liverpool dialect later called "scouse" (xi).
11. Gaskell mentions Oliphant's work when recommending potential English novels to a French translator in 1855. She refers to "Mrs. Margaret Maitland" [*sic*] and "Merkland," but does not know the name of the author (Gaskell et al. 2003, 128). If she knew the Liverpool novels, she could not have associated them with the author of *Maitland* and *Merkland* because they were attributed to William Wilson.

12. The names of Oliphant and Melville are linked historically through their Scottish origins, and there is a Melville–Oliphant tartan. (See Clan Oliphant, http://www.clanoliphant.com/ancientlands, accessed 22 April 2018.) In "The Strange Story of Mr. Robert Dalyell," Oliphant (1892) mentions Melville Street in Edinburgh.
13. Schaffer (2011) writes that Oliphant's work suggests that the credit economy had led to the "radical dehumanization of human life" (166). For the Victorian association of money with life and death, see Gates (2014), Weiss (1986). For suicide in financial novels, see Wagner (2010a), Henry (2009).
14. D'Albertis (1997) suggests problems with the psychological depth model when judging the quality of Oliphant's novels. Many twenty-first-century critics have been more interested in the sociological than the psychological dimensions of her fiction, although Levine (2014) has argued that Oliphant's fiction "explores consciousness with the subtlety and intricacy that the apparently easy lucidity of her style can disguise" (233). Levine also mentions the "quite modernist tendencies to explore the minds of her characters in the form of free indirect discourse" (234).
15. The setting is the country town of Redborough. By way of contrast, the narrator observes: "In Manchester and Liverpool, where they turn over a fortune every day, perhaps this large habit of sowing money about does not matter. People there are accustomed to going up and down. Bankruptcy, even, does not mean the end of the world in these regions" (Oliphant 1883, 9).
16. It is worth noting that in another plot line, Roland Ashton, a distant relation, is a responsible stockbroker, so that the novel's criticism is reserved for speculation rather than investment, per se.
17. For heredity in *Hester*, see Hunt (2014).
18. For cousin marriages, see Corbett (2008, 2013).
19. As we saw in the discussion of Gaskell's *Ruth* (1853), in Chapter 4, insurance companies offered investment opportunities for women and ministers.
20. For the bigamy plot in Victorian novels, see McAleavey (2015). Oliphant was straightforward about middle-age passion and midlife crises, here considered in a man. In *The Mystery of Mrs. Blencarrow* (1889), a woman experiences a similar passion. For Riddell's treatment of middle-age passion in *Miss Gascoigne* (1887a), see Chapter 6.
21. This was the neighborhood where Hawthorne lived during his time as American Consul.
22. For family businesses, including in Liverpool, see Barker (2017).
23. *At His Gates* (Oliphant 1872) involves an artist who dabbles in finance with disastrous consequences, a failed suicide attempt, and an ironic ending, which functions as an allegory for the novelist's art.

24. Oliphant's fiction makes extensive use of the telegram, a technology that transformed the possibilities for the exchange of knowledge in plots. Describing how the news of her sister-in-law's Jeanie Wilson's death arrived by means of a telegram and interrupted what had been a happy family party that included Jeanie's son, Oliphant writes: "It was a like a scene in a tragedy" (Oliphant 1899, 131).
25. The contexts of war and imperialism and Oliphant's conceptualization of time and history in relation to Scott's *Waverley* are explored by Michie (2013).
26. Schaffer (2011) examines Oliphant's treatment of the credit economy in *Phoebe, Junior*. She argues that for Oliphant, the marketplace "altered and superseded craft and craft values" (145), noting that women's craftwork does not appear in the novel, which turns rather on the forgery of an accommodation bill. Her sense that Oliphant was coming up against an emerging aestheticist movement is confirmed in the role of artists in these later works. Schaffer also observes that in the mingling of her household and professional writing duties, Oliphant "did not experience separate spheres" (148).
27. Many authors quote this maxim as an indication of what they disliked about capitalism, including Ruskin, Trollope, and Carlyle (1850). For Oliphant and Carlyle, see Jay (1995, 208).
28. The reference to "Quashee" may have been common shorthand for West Indians, but it also inevitably invokes Thomas Carlyle's use of this name and a negative interpretation of the effects of abolition, first articulated in his "Occasional Discourse on the Negro Question" (1849).

References

Alborn, Timothy. 2009. *Regulated lives: Life insurance and British Society, 1800–1914*. Toronto: University of Toronto Press.

Armstrong, Tim. 2012. *The logic of slavery: Debt, technology, and pain in American literature*. New York: Cambridge University Press.

Austen, Jane. 1813. *Pride and prejudice*, ed. James Kinsley. Oxford: Oxford University Press, 2004.

Barker, Hannah. 2017. *Family and business during the Industrial Revolution*. Oxford: Oxford University Press.

Barrie, J.M. 1898. Introductory note. In *A Widow's tale and other stories*. The Margaret Oliphant Fiction Collection. http://www.oliphantfiction.com/fiction_works/A_Widows_Tale.pdf. Accessed 5 Apr 2018.

Baucom, Ian. 2005. *Specters of the Atlantic: Finance capital, slavery and the philosophy of history*. Durham, NC: Duke University Press.

Beckert, Sven. 2014. *Empire of cotton: A global history*. New York: Alfred A. Knopf.
Bourrier, Karen. 2011. Dinah Mulock Craik and Benjamin Mulock. *Prose Studies* 33 (3): 174–187.
Brontë, Charlotte. 1847. *Jane Eyre*, ed. Margaret Smith. Oxford: Oxford University Press, 2008.
———. 1853. *Villette*, ed. Margaret Smith and Herbert Rosengarten. Oxford: Oxford University Press, 2008.
Brontë, Emily. 1847. *Wuthering heights*, ed. Ian Jack. Oxford: Oxford University Press, 2009.
Carlyle, Thomas. 1849. "Occasional discourse on the Negro question." *Fraser's Magazine*. Project Gutenberg. http://central.gutenberg.org/articles/occasional_discourse_on_the_negro_question.
Clarke, John Stock. 1981. Mrs. Oliphant's unacknowledged social novels. *Notes and Queries* 28 (5): 408–413.
———. 1992. "Home," a lost Victorian periodical. *Victorian Periodicals Review* 25 (2): 85–88.
Corbett, Mary Jean. 2008. *Family likeness: Sex, marriage, and incest*. Ithaca, NY: Cornell University Press.
———. 2013. Cousin marriage, then and now. *Victorian Review* 39 (2): 74–78.
Crowley, Tony. 2012. *Scouse: A social and cultural history*. Liverpool: Liverpool University Press.
D'Albertis, Deirdre. 1997. The domestic drone: Margaret Oliphant and a political history of the novel. *Studies in English Literature 1500–1900* 37 (4): 805–829.
Dickens, Charles. 1842–1844. *The life and adventures of Martin Chuzzlewit*, ed. Margaret Cardwell. Oxford: Oxford University Press, 2009.
———. 1846–1848. *Dombey and son*, ed. Alan Horsman. Oxford: Oxford University Press, 1984.
———. 1864–1865. *Our mutual friend*, ed. Kathleen Tillotson. Oxford: Oxford University Press, 2009.
Eagleton, Terry. 1995. *Heathcliff and the great hunger: Studies in Irish culture*. London: Verso.
Eliot, George. 1860. *The mill on the Floss*, ed. Nancy Henry. Boston: Houghton Mifflin, 2004.
———. 1871–1872. *Middlemarch*, ed. David Carroll. Oxford: Oxford University Press, 2008.
———. 1876. *Daniel Deronda*, ed. K.M. Newton and Graham Handley. Oxford: Oxford University Press, 2014.
Gaskell, Elizabeth. 1848. *Mary Barton: A tale of Manchester*, ed. Edgar Wright. Oxford: Oxford University Press, 1998.
———. 1853. *Ruth*, ed. Nancy Henry. London: Everyman, 2001.

———. 1854–1855. *North and south*, ed. Angus Easson. Oxford: Oxford University Press, 1998.
Gaskell, Elizabeth, John Chapple, and Alan Shelston. 2003. *Further letters of Mrs. Gaskell*. Manchester: Manchester University Press.
Gates, Barbara. 2014. *Victorian suicide: Mad crimes and sad histories*. Princeton, NJ: Princeton University Press.
Henry, Nancy. 2009. "Rushing into eternity": Suicide and finance in Victorian fiction. In *Victorian investments: New perspectives on finance and culture*, ed. Nancy Henry and Cannon Schmitt, 161–181. Bloomington: Indiana University Press.
Hunt, Aeron. 2014. *Personal business: Character and commerce in Victorian literature and culture*. Charlottesville: University of Virginia Press.
James, Henry. 1880. *Washington Square*, ed. Andrian Poole. Oxford: Oxford University Press, 2010.
Jay, Elisabeth. 1995. *Mrs. Oliphant, "a fiction to herself": A literary life*. Oxford: Clarendon Press.
Johnson, Patricia. 2010. Unlimited liability: Women and capital in Margaret Oliphant's *Hester*. *Nineteenth-Century Gender Studies* 6 (1): 1–14.
Levine, George. 2014. Reading Margaret Oliphant. *Journal of Victorian Culture* 19 (2): 232–246.
McAleavey, Maia. 2015. *The bigamy plot: Sensation and convention in the Victorian novel*. Cambridge: Cambridge University Press.
Michie, Elsie. 2011. *The vulgar question of money: Heiresses, materialism, and the novel of manners from Jane Austen to Henry James*. Baltimore: Johns Hopkins University Press.
———. 2013. History after Waterloo: Margaret Oliphant reads Walter Scott. *ELH* 80 (3): 897–916.
Milne, Graeme J. 2006. Maritime Liverpool. In *Liverpool 800: Culture, character, and history*, ed. John Belchem, 257–310. Liverpool: Liverpool University Press.
Oliphant, Margaret. 1851. *John Drayton*. London: Richard Bentley. The Margaret Oliphant Fiction Collection. http://www.oliphantfiction.com/x0200_single_title.php?titlecode=johndr. Accessed 5 Apr 2018.
———. 1852. *The Melvilles*, 3 vols. London: Richard Bentley. The Margaret Oliphant Fiction Collection. http://www.oliphantfiction.com/x0200_single_title.php?titlecode=melvls. Accessed 5 Apr 2018.
———. 1853. *Harry Muir: A story of Scottish life*, 3 vols. London: Hurst & Blackett. The Margaret Oliphant Fiction Collection. http://www.oliphantfiction.com/x0200_single_title.php?titlecode=harrym. Accessed 5 Apr 2018.
———. 1855a. *Christian Melville*. London: David Bogue. The Margaret Oliphant Fiction Collection. http://www.oliphantfiction.com/x0200_single_title.php?titlecode=cmelvl. Accessed 5 Apr 2018.

———. 1855b. Modern novelists great and small. *Blackwood's Magazine* 77: 554–568.

———. 1868. The stockbroker at Dinglewood. *Cornhill Magazine*, September. The Margaret Oliphant Fiction Collection. http://www.oliphantfiction.com/x0200_single_title.php?titlecode=stockb. Accessed 5 Apr 2018.

———. 1872. *At his gates: A novel*. New York: Scribner, Armstrong.

———. 1879. *The greatest heiress in England*, 3 vols. London: Hurst and Blackett, 1880.

———. 1881–1882. *In trust: The story of a lady and her lover*, 3 vols. London: Longmans, Green, 1882.

———. 1883. *Hester*, ed. Philip Davis and Brian Nellist. Oxford: Oxford University Press, 2009.

———. 1886. Queen Eleanor and Fair Rosamond. In *A Widow's tale and other stories*, 57–114. Edinburgh: William Blackwood and Sons, 1898.

———. 1888. Mr. Sandford. In *The ways of life*. London: Smith Elder, 1897.

———. 1889. *The mystery of Mrs. Blencarrow*. London: Spencer Blackett. The Margaret Oliphant Fiction Collection. http://www.oliphantfiction.com/x0200_single_title.php?titlecode=mrsblc. Accessed 5 Apr 2018.

———. 1890a. *Janet*. London: Hurst and Blackett.

———. 1890b. *Kirsteen: The story of a Scotch family seventy years ago*. London: Everyman, 1984.

———. 1890c. *Sons and daughters*. Edinburgh: William Blackwood and Sons. The Margaret Oliphant Fiction Collection. http://www.oliphantfiction.com/x0200_single_title.php?titlecode=sondtr. Accessed 5 Apr 2018.

———. 1892. The strange story of Mr. Robert Dalyell. In *The ways of life*. London: Smith Elder, 1897.

———. 1897. *The ways of life: Two stories*. London: Smith, Elder & Co. The Margaret Oliphant Fiction Collection. http://www.oliphantfiction.com/x0300_series_and_themes.php?categcode=waylifbk&cattype=Collection&descrip=The%20Ways%20of%20Life%20(1897).

———. 1898. *Queen Eleanor and Fair Rosamond in a widow's tale*. Edinburgh: William Blackwood.

———. 1899. *The autobiography of Margaret Oliphant: The complete text*, ed. Elizabeth Jay. Oxford: Oxford University Press, 1990.

Pettitt, Clare. 1999. "Every man for himself, and God for us all!" Mrs. Oliphant, self-help, and industrial success literature in "John Drayton" and "The Melvilles". *Women's Writing* 6 (2): 163–179.

Poovey, Mary. 2008. *Genres of the credit economy*. Chicago: University of Chicago Press.

Riddell, Charlotte. [R.V.M. Sparling, pseud.]. 1856. *Zuriel's grandchild: A novel*. London: Newby, Thos. Cautley.

———. 1870. *Austin Friars: A novel.* London: Hutchinson.
———. 1874. *Mortomley's estate: A novel.* London: Tinsley Brothers.
———. 1887a. *Miss Gascoigne: A novel,* vol. 1. London: Ward and Downey.
———. 1887b. *The government official.* London: R. Bentley.
Schaffer, Talia. 2011. *Novel craft: Victorian domestic handicraft and nineteenth-century fiction.* Oxford: Oxford University Press.
Trela, D.J. 1995. *Margaret Oliphant: Critical essays on a gentle subversive.* Selinsgrove, PA: Susquehanna University Press.
Trollope, Anthony. 1866–1887. *The last chronicle of Barset,* ed. Sophie Gilmartin. Harmondsworth, UK: Penguin, 2002.
———. 1876. *The prime minister,* ed. Nicholas Shrimpton. Oxford: Oxford University Press, 2011.
Wagner, Tamara. 2010a. *Financial speculation in Victorian fiction: Plotting money and the novel genre, 1815–1901.* Columbus: Ohio State University Press.
———. 2010b. "Very saleable articles, indeed": Margaret Oliphant's repackaging of sensational finance. *Modern Language Quarterly* 71 (1): 51–74.
Weiss, Barbara. 1986. *The hell of the English: Bankruptcy and the Victorian novel.* Lewisburg, PA: Bucknell University Press.
Williams, Merryn. 1986. *Margaret Oliphant: A critical biography.* New York: St. Martin's Press.
Wood, William. 1895. *Autobiography of William Wood,* 2 vols. New York: J.S. Babcock.

CHAPTER 8

Conclusion

I can't bear to hear you talk in that early Victorian way.
—George Gissing, The Whirlpool

The accepted presence of investing women in novels at the end of the Victorian period aligns with their increasing numbers in reality. Novels of the 1880s and 1890s feature women investors as a matter of course. An aspect of Sue Bridehead's modernity in Hardy's *Jude the Obscure* (1895), for example, is that after inheriting money from a would-be lover, she invested it in a "bubble scheme, and lost it" (182). More notable than women who lose, however, are those who win through their investments. Beginning with Oliphant's Catherine Vernon in *Hester* (1883), we see the emergence of the woman as financial hero. The title character of Riddell's *Miss Gascoigne* (1887) rushes to the scene of an accident at a mine in which she had invested. Madeline Burton in Oliphant's *Sons and Daughters* (1890) compensates for the financial failure of men by wisely investing her personal fortune. In Gissing's *In the Year of Jubilee* (1894), Beatrice French starts her own women's clothing business with a distinctly new shrewdness about investing. Grant Allen's *Miss Cayley's Adventures* (1899) is a picaresque of female entrepreneurial ventures. In the new century, Olive Christian Malvery's *The Speculator* (1908) presents a woman who cross-dresses to become a trader on the

© The Author(s) 2018
N. Henry, *Women, Literature and Finance in Victorian Britain*,
Palgrave Studies in Literature, Culture and Economics,
https://doi.org/10.1007/978-3-319-94331-2_8

stock exchange (where women were not allowed). This was the culture from which spectacularly successful real women financiers such as Alice Cornwell and Hetty Green emerged. Overall, the *fin de siècle* saw an acceleration of women's (and men's) investing activity, which had been steadily growing throughout the century.[1]

Financial independence was an aspect of the New Woman in fact and fiction, but as I have shown in the preceding chapters, active and passive investing characterized women's lives throughout the nineteenth century, and women investors appeared in Victorian fiction frequently enough to constitute recognizable types. Furthermore, investing women authors wrote works that complicate ethical questions about modern capitalism and contributed centrally to what I have been calling the nineteenth-century cultures of investment—the overlapping domestic and public, as well as the literary and financial spheres—in which familial and affective lives were inseparable from larger economic conditions and personal financial decisions. Tracing their financial lives individually and collectively, from the community of women who raised Elizabeth Gaskell in the 1820s and 1830s through to those who financially supported Charlotte Riddell in her final years of poverty at the turn of the century, we can see both continuity and change.

Late Victorian novels are self-conscious about their modernity. Beyond their references to new technologies (telegrams, lifts) and commodities (bicycles, cigarettes), these novels display proto-modernist attitudes toward art and finance. The enigmatic Sybil Carnaby in Gissing's (1897) *The Whirlpool*, having just lost the money from her investments in Benet Frothingham's failed company, refers to her husband as "rather early Victorian," prompting the narrator to remark that by this term she was "wont to signify barbarism or crudity in art, letters, morality or social feeling" (54). Alma tells her stepmother: "I can't bear to hear you talk in that early Victorian way. Art is art, and all these other things have nothing whatever to do with it" (248). Gissing's lament about the feminized culture in the latter part of Victoria's reign is attended by a sense of inevitability about women's involvement in the world of finance. In the fiction of the 1890s, we find a middle ground between early Victorian culture, with its unrealized ideological ideal of keeping the domestic and public spheres separate, and the Modernist ideal (again, not realized) of keeping art separate from the market. At times, this latter distinction came at the expense of realist novelists writing in the tradition of Oliphant, Riddell, and Gissing, such as Arnold Bennett and John Galsworthy, who were criticized by Virginia Woolf for being "materialists" in her essay "Mr. Bennett and Mrs. Brown" (1923).

One fictional type—the daughter of the financier—tracks these changes into the twentieth century.[2] Kept remote from her father's business, Florence Dombey (Dickens 1846–1848) provides a soothing domestic escape for him after his financial ruin; Marie Melmotte (Trollope 1875) discovers after her father's death that she has inherited his gift for speculation; Alma Frothingham (Gissing 1897) channels the reckless ambition of her father into a musical career, taking both professional and sexual risks. Joseph Conrad's *Chance* (1913) is more formally experimental than these earlier works but is nonetheless faithful to literal details. In that novel, Flora de Barral's name and residence with a governess in Brighton recall Florence Dombey. Flora behaves in a similarly reckless way to her disgraced father, who is imprisoned for his financial misdeeds and upon his release becomes Flora's responsibility. Her suicidal thoughts appear early in the novel, but it is only at the end that we realize her father too had long been contemplating the suicide that he ultimately commits.[3] Undine Spragg in Edith Wharton's *The Custom of the Country* (1913) inherits her father's reckless, speculating ways and indirectly drives her first husband to suicide after his financial ruin.[4]

It may be that this interest in inherited traits, apparent as early as Oliphant's *Hester*, reflected the saturation of the culture with Darwinian ideas. Viewing the financial world as a struggle for existence was characteristic of late-century naturalism in British as well as American and French literature. The assumption that the financial world is one in which the fittest survive distinguishes Gissing, Hardy, Conrad, and Wharton from earlier Victorian writers and constitutes a new way to explore how familial dynamics are inseparable from financial conditions.

As Paul Delany has shown, Modernist writers sought to distance themselves and their art from the sources of their *rentier* income. While this may seem hypocritical, it signified a new way of thinking about the ethics of investing. T.S. Eliot expressed scruples about investing that never would have occurred to George Eliot, writing in "The Idea of a Christian Society" (1939) that he was, "by no means sure that it is right for me to improve my income by investing in the shares of a company" (quoted in Delany 2002, 128). Eliot and Gaskell were excited about the performance of their company shares, whereas *rentiers* like Woolf, T.S. Eliot, E.M. Forster, and Wharton could take their investments for granted and indulge in moral critiques of their class. Forster, for example, initiated a debate about the ethics of investing in South African diamond mines (140), harkening back to Dorothea's passing concern about the "miserable men" who find jewels in George Eliot's (1871–1872) *Middlemarch*, a novel that explores the morality of accepting money with a tainted (that is, criminal) past. In Forster's *Howard's End* (1910), the popularity of foreign investments, such as those pursued by the Schlegel sisters, is linked to the new, polluting automobile. Whereas in *The Whirlpool* and *Miss Cayley's Adventures*, characters invest in bicycle factories, by 1906 investors were turning to motorcar factories and to the plantations that supplied rubber for automobile tires (Michie 2011, 167). The economy developed unevenly, and Gissing's *Will Warburton* (1905) shows that West Indian sugar production was still a relevant issue, as it had been in novels throughout the nineteenth century.[5]

The American Edith Wharton was strongly influenced by British realist fiction, adapting and developing themes that are evident especially in Trollope and Gissing. In her *The House of Mirth* (1905), for example, Lily Bart becomes the victim of her financial advisor, who pretends to invest her money in the hope of receiving sexual favors, a scenario that had been suggested in *The Whirlpool* (see Collinson 1980). Lily sinks into poverty and, like Alma in Gissing's *The Whirlpool*, dies by taking an overdose of a sleeping drug, while the financiers in the novel live on unpunished. This plot marks a contrast to the convention of suicidal financiers in fiction by Dickens, Trollope, and Gissing and revived by Conrad in *Chance*. Rather than completely demonizing the financier, Wharton acknowledged that finance could be an art, an idea developed more fully in her contemporary and fellow American Theodore Dreiser in *The Financier* (1912).

I have sought to establish that representations of women investors in fiction tracked the presence of real women investors in the culture. Far from suggesting that novels are simply transparent reflections of reality, however, I have provided detailed analyses of lives and writings—texts and contexts—to reveal the distinctly individual responses of specific authors to broader economic climates as well as their personal financial lives. While focusing on the particular, it is also possible to generalize, especially along the lines of gender. Nineteenth-century female authors, disenfranchised in so many ways, embraced the opportunities that were open to them, and invested their money as and how they could, turning their financial experiences and observations into subtle treatments of ethical problems raised by the financial revolution that characterized their age. Later, women with more social advantages and fewer social disabilities could take investment for granted and begin to criticize not just greed but the subtle implications of relying on invested wealth. Hence, we see that Wharton has more in common with Trollope and Gissing than with Gaskell, Eliot, Riddell, and Oliphant. It is hard to imagine Wharton writing a novel with a business heroine like Catherine Vernon in *Hester* or a business hero like Riddell's (1864) *George Geith*. Yet, the ending of *The House of Mirth*, in which Lily nobly sacrifices all the money she has to repay a debt, is not unlike the ending of Riddell's (1874) *Mortomley's Estate*, in which Dolly dies after seeing her husband's creditors paid. Existential questions about the relationship between life and money appear as a constant in suicidal financiers (Merdle, Melmotte, Lopez, Frothingham, and De Barrel) and their suicidal daughters (Alma, Lily, and Flora). Late in their careers, both Oliphant and Riddell also explored how a man could be driven to suicide due to financial losses.

What I hope this book has accomplished is a reorientation of how we think about economic history, placing women at the center of a narrative of capitalist development that has traditionally kept them on the margins. It has shown that female novelists who were also investors incorporated their life experiences in their fiction and resisted the reflexive critique of capitalism that characterized the work of their male contemporaries. Additionally, I have emphasized the importance of geographical place, bringing the port of Liverpool to the forefront of a literary history from which it has been excluded for a variety of complicated reasons, including its slave-trading past and reputation for unscrupulous commercial activity.

In the early twentieth century, articles offering advice for investing women, such as Malvery's "Women and the Money Market" (1906–1907), were becoming more common. Today, the female investor remains a category apart, and financial journalists continue to ask what women investors want (Holland 2015). The Teacher Insurance and Annuity Association of American (TIAA) investment company maintains a special website called Woman2Woman, which offers advice for ordinary women from successful female investors.[6] Various studies of women's investing behavior have been conducted, such as Pershing's "Women and Investing White Paper" (Liersch 2014). Occasional articles in the *Wall Street Journal* (see Ryzik 2016) and other financial papers continue to address the topic. Books by media personality Suze Orman, such as

Women and Money (2010), along with her website, target women investors and their specific concerns. Some articles even refer to the work of historians, providing a perspective on women's past as investors to help illuminate the present (see Gerner 2016).

Within twenty-first-century popular culture, owning a modest portfolio of shares or an invested retirement account has become so ubiquitous as to be invisible and not worth mentioning. The trust fund baby, one of today's terms for the *rentier*, is a familiar type. But the female speculator still remains rare. The film *Equity*,[7] as noted in Chapter 1, is distinctive for its portrayal of women investors unapologetically pursuing financial gain but encountering the entrenched sexism that still characterizes the financial world they seek to enter. It is significant that women investors financed this film.

As I have shown, women investors have a history distinctively interwoven into the history of all other aspects of Anglo American cultures, including the domestic and the familial. From the beginning, investing was an activity that was open to women because no one thought to exclude them. The mentality of putting money out to work, so central to modern capitalism, was a way not merely to make more money but also to provide for others through extended financial networks, including dependent women who had no other means of support. I have emphasized that investing was a means of independence for nineteenth-century women at the same time that it made them dependent on a volatile economy. Whether women were, or are, more averse to risk remains a topic for debate, as does the question of whether the average woman is any less financially literate than the average man. With more people investing than ever, we would do well to remember and learn from the experiences of nineteenth-century investors and to recognize that women have played an important role as participants in, as well as critics and chroniclers of, the financial system we have inherited.

NOTES

1. See Rutterford et al. (2011), Maltby et al. (2011), Michie (2011). Michie (2011) notes changing attitudes toward investors starting in the 1890s: "Increasingly this perception of wise investment in shares was coming to the fore especially when conducted by or on behalf of women" (176).
2. For daughters and bankruptcy in mid-Victorian fiction, see Hunter (2011).

3. The St. Katharine's Dock, in which Eliot and Gaskell invested, appears Conrad (1913). The unnamed first-person narrator recounts the experience of Charles Powell, the hero, explaining: "At that time the Marine Board examinations took place at the St. Katharine's Dock House on Tower Hill and he informed us that he had a special affection for the view of that historic locality" (16). Today, St. Katharine's Dock, like the Albert Dock in Liverpool, has been developed into luxury apartments and shops.
4. For suicidal financiers, see Henry (2009). For Wharton and Wall Street, see Knight (2016).
5. For sugar production in *Will Warburton*, see Villa (2000).
6. Woman2Woman, https://www.tiaa.org/public/offer/insights/W2W (accessed 23 April 2018)
7. *Equity*, directed by Meera Menon (2016, Broad street Pictures).

References

Allen, Grant. 1899. *Miss Cayley's adventures*. London: G. Richards.
Collinson, C.S. 1980. "The whirlpool" and "The house of mirth". *Gissing Newsletter* 16 (4): 12–16.
Conrad, Joseph. 1913. *Chance: A tale in two parts*, ed. Martin Ray. Oxford: Oxford UP, 1986.
Delany, Paul. 2002. *Literature, money and the market*. New York: Palgrave Macmillan.
Dickens, Charles. 1848. *Dombey and son*, ed. Alan Horsman. Oxford: Clarendon Press, 1984.
Dreiser, Theodore. 1912. *The Financier*, ed. Larzer Ziff. New York: Penguin, 2008.
Eliot, George. 1871–2. *Middlemarch*, ed. David Carroll. Oxford: Oxford University Press, 2008.
Forster, E.M. 1910. *Howard's end*, ed. David Lodge. New York: Penguin, 2008.
Gerner, Marina. 2016. How can we get more women investing? *Money Observer*, April 6. http://moneyobserver.com/our-analysis/how-can-we-get-more-women-investing. Accessed 5 Apr 2018.
Gissing, George. 1894. *In the year of jubilee*. London: Hogarth Press, 1987.
———. 1897. *The whirlpool*, ed. Gillian Tindall. London: Hogarth Press, 1984.
———. 1905. *Will Warburton: A romance of real life*. New York: A.P. Dutton.
Hardy, Thomas. 1895. *Jude the obscure*, ed. Cedric Thomas Watts. Orchard Park, NY: Broadview, 1999.

Henry, Nancy. 2009. "Rushing into eternity": Suicide and finance in Victorian fiction. In *Victorian investments: New perspectives on finance and culture*, ed. Nancy Henry and Cannon Schmitt, 161–181. Bloomington: Indiana University Press.

Holland, Kelley. 2015. What women investors want. *Consumer News and Business Channel*, March 5. https://www.cnbc.com/2015/03/05/what-women-investors-want.html. Accessed 5 Apr 2018.

Hunter, Leeann D. 2011. Communities built from ruins: Social economics in Victorian novels of bankruptcy. *Women's Studies Quarterly* 39 (3): 137–152.

Knight, Peter. 2016. *Reading the market: Genres of financial capitalism in gilded age America*. Baltimore: Johns Hopkins University Press.

Liersch, Michael. 2014. *Women: Investing with a purpose. Why women investors may need a different approach to reach their goals*. Pershing. https://www.pershing.com/_global-assets/pdf/women-investing-with-a-purpose.pdf. Accessed 5 Apr 2018.

Maltby, Josephine, Janette Rutterford, David R. Green, Steven Ainscough, and Carien van Mourik. 2011. The evidence for "democratization" of share ownership in Great Britain in the early twentieth century. In *Men, women, and money: Perspectives on gender, wealth, and investment, 1850–1930*, ed. David R. Green, Alastair Owens, Josephine Maltby and Janette Rutterford, 184–206. Oxford: Oxford University Press.

Malvery, Olive Christian. 1906–1907. Women in the money market. *The Lady's Realm* 21 (November–April): 41–45.

———. 1908. *The speculator: A novel*. London: Werner Laurie.

Michie, Ranald. 2011. Gamblers, fools, victims or wizards? The British investor in the public mind, 1850–1930. In *Men, women and money: Perspectives on gender, wealth, and investment 1850–1930*, ed. David R. Green, Alastair Owens, Josephine Maltby, and Janette Rutterford, 156–183. Oxford: Oxford University Press.

Oliphant, Margaret. 1883. *Hester*, ed. Philip Davis and Brian Nellist. Oxford: Oxford University Press, 2009.

Oliphant, Margaret. 1890. *Sons and daughters*. Edinburgh: William Blackwood and Sons.

Orman, Suze. 2010. *Women & money: Owning the power to control your destiny*. New York: Random House.

Riddell, Charlotte. 1864 (F.G. Trafford, pseud.). *George Geith of Fen Court*. London: Frederick Warne and Co., n.d.

———. 1874. *Mortomley's estate: A novel*. London: Tinsley Brothers.

———. 1887. *Miss Gascoigne: A novel*, vol. 1. London: Ward and Downey.

Rutterford, Janette, David R. Green, Josephine Maltby, and Alastair Owens. 2011. Who comprised the nation of shareholders? Gender and investment in Great Britain, c.1870–1935. *Economic History Review* 64 (1): 157–187.

Ryzik, Melena. 2016. Where women run Wall Street. *New York Times*, July 11, 24, https://www.nytimes.com/2016/07/24/movies/equity-women-wall-street.html. Accessed 6 Apr 2018.

Trollope, Anthony. 1875. *The way we live now*, ed. Francis O'Gorman. Oxford: Oxford University Press, 2016.

Villa, Louisa. 2000. The grocer's romance: Economic transactions and radical individualism in "Will Warburton". *Gissing Journal* 35 (2): 1–19.

Wharton, Edith. 1905. *The house of mirth*, ed. Martha Banta. Oxford: Oxford University Press, 1994.

———. 1913. *Custom of the country*, ed. Stephen Orgel. Oxford: Oxford University Press, 1995.

Woolf, Virginia. 1923. Mr. Bennett and Mrs. Brown in *Virginia Woolf: Selected essays*, ed. David Bradshaw. Oxford: Oxford UP, 2008.

Index

A
Alborn, Timothy, 20, 29, 46, 77, 114, 130, 171, 245
Alcott, Louisa May, 155
Allen, Grant, 267
America, 2, 9, 18, 60, 61, 78, 87, 98, 112, 121, 127, 129, 130, 139, 156, 169, 209, 233, 236, 239, 251
American Civil War, 60, 87, 117, 155, 160
Anderson, B.L., 34
Architecture, 8, 15, 31, 90, 100, 101, 104, 110, 111, 167
Armstrong, Tim, 77, 116, 129, 245
Austen, Jane
  Mansfield Park, 78, 143
  Persuasion, 62, 162, 192
  Pride and Prejudice, 239
  Sense and Sensibility, 54, 161

B
Bank of England, 7, 15, 36, 38, 97, 102, 166
Bankruptcy, 7, 17, 34, 58, 65, 79, 95, 147, 180, 182, 184, 187, 190, 191, 199–211, 214, 218, 219, 230, 248, 256, 257, 260, 272
Barker, Hannah, 20, 46, 192, 219, 260
Barrie, J.M., 214, 247
Baucom, Ian, 77, 108, 109, 116, 168, 245
Bennett, Arnold, 268
Benson, Robert (Robin), 147, 156, 163, 172
Bentley, Richard, 184, 263
Besant, Walter, 140
Black, Helen, 195, 213
Blackett, Henry, 201, 244
Blackwood's Magazine, 97, 232
Blackwood, William, 226
Blake, Kathleen, 20, 21, 120

278 INDEX

Bodenheimer, Rosemarie, 148
Bodichon, Barbara, 4, 37
Bonaparte, Felicia, 89
Bourrier, Karen, 259
Braddon, Mary Elizabeth, 14, 182, 211, 231
Brontë, Charlotte
  Jane Eyre, 9, 143, 171, 252–254
  Shirley, 58, 131
  Villette, 9, 39, 62, 78, 128, 143, 256
Brontë, Emily, 10, 12, 38, 232
  Wuthering Heights, 232
Brown, Jaqueline Nassey, 109

C
Canada, 9, 88, 127
Capitalism, 2, 3, 9, 11, 12, 14–16, 20, 55, 57, 58, 60, 62, 76, 79, 88–90, 92, 109, 110, 117, 122–124, 126, 127, 142, 168, 171, 183, 243, 258, 261, 271, 272
  critiques of, 10, 255
  and women, 2, 11, 14–16, 18, 19, 32, 78, 268
Carlos, Ann M., 36
Carlyle, Thomas, 10, 261
Carr, Harriet, 102
Cavanagh, Terry, 105
Chadwick, Mrs. Ellis, 90, 91, 95, 96
Chapple, John, 35, 91–96, 102, 127
Checkland, S.G., 35
China, 9, 56, 61, 77, 98, 112, 117, 129, 130, 146
Clarke, John Stock, 217, 226, 259
Colella, Silvana, 19, 21, 188, 215, 216, 219
Coleman, Dermot, 17, 19, 21, 141, 159, 162, 169, 170, 172
Collins, K.K., 145
Collins, Wilkie
  Armadale, 78
Collinson, Richard, 201
Commodification of human lives, 59, 60, 71, 77
Conrad, Joseph, 21, 269, 270, 273
Consols (3% consolidated annuities), 6, 7, 10, 12, 21, 33, 36–39, 43, 44, 56, 57, 63, 69, 95, 161, 165, 166
Cornwell, Alice, 42, 43, 46, 268
Cottrell, P.L., 34
Cowan, James, 190, 216, 220
Craik, Dinah Mulock, 58, 94, 227, 231, 259
Cropper, James, 100–102, 128, 147, 153
Cropper, John, 8, 100, 102, 128
Cross, John Walter (Johnnie), 11, 17, 139, 145–148, 169, 171, 189, 228, 232
Cross, Mrs. Anna Wood, 145, 148
Cross, William, 139, 145, 146
Cultures of investment, 4, 10, 12, 15, 30–32, 34, 44, 45, 55, 59, 63, 76, 90, 126, 139, 148, 156, 162–164, 198, 226, 229, 231, 237, 238, 255, 258, 268

D
D'Albertis, Deirdre, 127, 230, 260
Dalley, Lana, 13
Davidoff, Leonore, 4, 5, 45
Delany, Paul, 20–22, 77, 80, 269
Dennistoun family, 168
Dickens, Charles
  David Copperfield, 36, 56
  Dombey and Son, 9, 16, 56, 62, 78, 79, 111, 150, 167, 254
  Great Expectations, 56, 61, 78, 129, 130, 168

Little Dorrit, 3, 16, 56, 57, 59, 79, 129, 186
Martin Chuzzlewit, 16, 56, 58–61, 63, 71, 72, 78, 90, 116, 117, 127, 193, 245
Nicholas Nickleby, 56
Oliver Twist, 94, 200
Our Mutual Friend, 3, 16, 58, 61, 63, 76, 78, 79, 90, 130, 154, 238
Doe, Helen, 7, 34, 45, 131
Draper, Nicholas, 7, 20, 143, 168
Dreiser, Theodore, 184, 214, 270
Drummond, Diane K., 141

E
Eagleton, Terry, 45, 259
Easson, Angus, 99, 110, 128, 129
East India Company, 5, 7, 15, 16, 37, 44
Ekphrasis, 110, 111, 168
Eliot, George (Mary Ann Evans)
 Adam Bede, 182, 185
 "Brother Jacob", 143, 157, 168, 170, 171
 Daniel Deronda, 9, 17, 63, 142–145, 148–150, 152–158, 161, 162, 166
 Felix Holt, 142, 144, 150, 161, 162, 166, 167
 Impressions of Theophrastus Such, 164, 165
 Middlemarch, 9, 10, 17, 141–145, 149, 150, 154, 158, 162, 166, 167
 The Mill on the Floss, 10, 17, 159, 162, 205
 Romola, 161
 Scenes of Clerical Life, 181
 Silas Marner, 150, 162, 167
Eliot, T.S., 269

Ellevest, 1
Ellis, S.M., 184, 195, 198, 200, 210, 212, 213, 218
Equity (film), 1, 2, 18, 19, 22, 272, 273
Ethical questions, 3, 139, 142, 162, 257, 268
Ethics of investing, 269
Evans, D. Morier, 11, 29
Everton, 209, 228, 232, 234

F
Family networks, 4, 7, 17, 76, 148
Finance, 6, 11–13, 15, 18, 19, 30, 31, 33, 40, 42, 43, 46, 55, 67, 76, 77, 88, 92, 94, 99, 101, 107, 112, 116, 117, 119, 126, 131, 161, 171, 179, 183, 188, 191, 195, 198, 211, 215, 225, 226, 228, 229, 231, 234, 237, 238, 243, 255, 260, 268, 270
 cultural history of, 4
Financial crisis, 1, 29, 30, 119, 121, 122, 146, 156
Financial cultures, 4, 31, 34, 92, 258
Financial knowledge, 11, 119, 188, 227, 246
Financial lives, 7, 14–16, 19, 31, 44, 76, 183, 226, 238, 258, 268, 270
Forster, E.M., 18, 22, 77, 269
Forster, John, 90
Freedgood, Elaine, 89, 98, 106, 107, 120, 127, 129, 168, 170
Freeman, Mark, 7, 34, 36–38, 40, 46
Froide, Amy, 2, 6, 20, 33, 46
Furniss, Harry, 196
Fyfe, Paul, 117, 130

G
Gagnier, Regenia, 13

Gallagher, Catherine, 13, 21, 89
Gaskell, Elizabeth Stevenson
  Cranford, 16, 87–89, 94, 98, 113, 115, 118–121, 125
  "Cousin Phillis", 87, 94, 117
  Life of Charlotte Brontë, The, 90, 111
  "Lois the Witch", 87
  Mary Barton, 85, 87–89, 93–96, 98–100, 102, 103, 106–110, 116, 117, 120, 124
  North and South, 87, 89, 94, 97, 98, 107, 108, 110, 117, 120–122, 124
  Ruth, 87, 88, 94–98, 103, 111–113, 115–117, 120, 123, 124
  Sylvia's Lovers, 86–88, 90, 94, 98, 111, 122–125
  Wives and Daughters, 86, 87, 94, 97, 124–126
Gaskell, William, 91, 93
Gérin, Winifred, 91
Gissing, George
  New Grub Street, 16, 54, 69, 74, 206
  Odd Women, The, 16, 53, 54, 74, 161
  Whirlpool, The, 3, 16, 44, 54, 58, 74, 205, 268, 270
  Will Warburton, 143, 186, 270, 273
  Year of Jubilee, In the, 54, 74, 267
Gladstone, John, 35, 100, 103, 105, 128, 153
Gladstone, William, 35
Glasgow, 29, 116, 139, 145, 146, 168, 169, 199, 202, 228, 229
Gleadle, Kathryn, 5, 21, 34, 46
Global networks, 3, 8, 9, 15, 97, 98, 203
Gore, Catherine, 14
Great Indian Peninsula Railway, 141, 162
Green, David, 6
Green, Hetty, 43, 46, 268

Grindon, Leo H., 149
Guy, Josephine M., 89

H
Hall, Catherine, 4
Hall, Mrs. S.C., 40, 198
Hardy, Thomas, 267, 269
Harris, Margaret, 169
Herculaneum pottery works, 35
Hipkins, A.J., 214, 219
Holland family, 94, 128
Home (magazine), 217, 226
Hurst and Blackett, 201, 203, 204, 218
Hyland, Peter, 35

I
Insurance, 7, 8, 15, 18, 20, 29, 53, 55, 59–61, 71, 72, 74, 77, 78, 88, 95, 114, 116, 117, 121, 122, 125, 126, 130, 169, 201, 202, 211, 218, 220, 228, 231, 235, 237, 242, 244, 245, 248–250, 259, 260
Ireland, 9, 179, 181, 182, 188, 190

J
James, Henry, 69, 80, 239
  Portrait of a Lady, 69
  Washington Square, 239
Jay, Elisabeth, 202, 228
Jewitt, Llewellynn, 198
John Cropper (Ship), 100, 101
Johnson, Patricia E., 227, 241
Judaism, 179, 192

K
Kaufman, Heidi, 153, 170

INDEX   281

Kelleher, Margaret, 215, 219
Kilshaw, Ellen, 189, 205, 216, 220
King, Henry S., 200
Klaver, Claudia, 13
Knight, Peter, 12, 19, 21
Krawcheck, Sallie, 1
Kreisel, Deanna, 13

L
Laurence, Anne, 13, 20, 34, 37, 67, 78
Lee, Julia Sun-Joo, 21, 98, 109, 127, 129, 131
Leighton, Mary Elizabeth, 124
Levine, George, 238, 260
Lewes, George Henry, 141, 142, 145, 148, 182
Life writing, 4, 19, 235
Limited liability, 14, 46, 58, 159, 160, 168, 171, 187, 206–209, 231
Liverpool, 8, 9, 17, 29, 31, 34, 35, 41, 44, 76, 78, 94–96, 98–112, 117, 122, 123, 126, 128–130, 135, 139, 143, 145–149, 153, 156, 158, 169, 179, 181, 189, 191, 192, 194, 209–213, 216, 228, 229, 232–237, 239, 243, 245–248, 250, 252–254, 259, 260, 271, 273
Liverpool and Manchester Railway, 34, 99
London, 8, 17, 29–31, 34, 35, 38, 41, 43, 44, 46, 59–61, 63, 76, 85, 86, 94, 97, 98, 100, 104, 108, 110, 121, 126, 127, 139–142, 145–148, 164, 167, 168, 179, 181, 184, 190, 191, 193–195, 197, 199, 202, 211, 212, 228, 229, 231, 234, 237, 239, 240, 245–247, 252–254, 259
Longmore, Jane, 34
Lumb, Hannah, 92–94, 97, 102

M
Maguire, Karen, 36
Maltby, Josephine, 7, 13, 20, 37, 39, 43, 47, 67, 78, 272
Malvery, Olive Christian, 43, 267, 271
Manchester, 9, 17, 31, 34, 45, 86, 87, 91, 94, 95, 97–101, 106, 107, 110, 118, 121, 126–129, 147, 180, 260
Married Women's Property Acts, 7, 15, 40, 92
Marx, Karl, 10
Matteson, John, 216
Mayhew, Henry, 140
McCormack, Kathleen, 171
Melville, Herman, 106, 260
Michie, Elsie B., 13, 67, 75, 227
Michie, Ranald, 21, 36, 39, 215, 217, 270
Midlands, 9, 31, 145, 148, 181
Miller, Andrew, 89, 130
Milne, Graeme J., 216, 229
Mitchell, Charlotte, 190, 216

N
Nelson Monument (Liverpool), 8, 96, 101, 103, 106, 107, 109, 110, 149, 158, 233, 234, 238, 250, 252
Newton, K.M., 171
Newton, Lucy, A., 35, 36, 77
Noble, John Ashcraft, 12
Norris, Frank, 184, 214
Norway, Arthur Hamilton, 196, 211

O
Oliphant, Francis (Frank), 225, 228, 237
Oliphant, Margaret Wilson
  At His Gates, 231, 253
  Autobiography, 225–227, 230, 232, 237, 245

Christian Melville, 235, 238
Hester, 226, 227, 239, 241–244, 247, 248, 250, 252, 257
Janet, 226, 229, 249, 253, 254, 258
John Drayton, 229, 232, 234–236, 238, 245, 252
Kirsteen, 226, 231, 240, 244, 245, 250, 252–254, 256
Melvilles, The, 229, 234–237, 244, 246, 252
"Mr. Sandford", 226, 231, 241, 248, 250, 253
"Queen Eleanor and Fair Rosamond", 226, 229, 245
Sons and Daughters, 226, 231, 242, 245–247, 250, 254–256, 258
"Strange Story of Mr. Robert Dalyell", 226, 248, 249
Ways of Life, The, 226, 245, 248
Widow's Tale, A, 247, 258
Overend and Gurney, 145, 147, 156, 159, 160, 171, 181, 211
Owens, Alastair, 6, 7, 33, 37, 38

P
Pall Mall Gazette, 185, 199, 213
Pearson, Robin, 7, 34, 36, 37, 40
Peterson, Linda, 21, 206, 215, 218
Pettitt, Claire, 87, 88, 98, 127, 129, 131, 227, 229
Poovey, Mary, 11–13, 40, 46, 47, 129, 187, 215, 241
Pryke, Jo, 88

R
Rappoport, Jill, 13, 67
Rathbone, William III, 102, 110
Reade, Charles, 160, 187, 215, 246
Reed, John, 12
Reid, Wemyss, 180, 198, 218

Riddell, Charlotte (Charlotte Cowan)
Austin Friars, 187, 194, 199, 202, 207
Fairy Water, 203, 204
Frank Sinclair's Wife, 204, 210
George Geith, 185, 186, 188, 194
Government Official, The, 211, 213
Joy After Sorrow, 191, 194, 203
Maxwell Drewitt, 182, 199
Miss Gascoigne, 213
Mitre Court, 187
Mortomley's Estate, 181, 193, 194, 199, 202–206, 208–211
Race for Wealth, The, 187, 188, 199, 202, 204
Senior Partner, The, 187, 188
Struggle for Fame, A, 182, 198, 206
Too Much Alone, 196
Zuriel's Grandchild, 179, 181, 190, 191, 193, 195, 203, 211
Riddell, Joseph, 179, 195, 198, 199, 205, 212, 213, 219
Ritchie, Anne Thackeray, 184, 196, 259
Robb, George, 2, 7, 30, 44, 46, 130, 169, 188
Roscoe, William, 101–103, 105, 110, 128
Royal African Company, 7, 36
Russell, Norman, 12, 46, 77
Rutterford, Janette, 7, 13, 20, 37, 39–43, 47, 67, 78, 236, 272

S
Sandiford, Keith, 153
Schaffer, Talia, 46, 79, 143, 260, 261
Schmitt, Cannon, 12, 13
Schor, Hilary, 89
Scotland, 9, 94, 145, 148, 169, 228, 236, 245, 251, 252, 259
Scott, Sir Walter, 205, 254

INDEX   283

Separate spheres, 4, 5, 20, 42, 154, 261
Shakinovsky, Lynn, 29, 30
Shelston, Alan, 89, 96, 102, 128–130, 259
Shute, Neville, 219
Slavery, 7–9, 15, 18, 55, 59, 60, 71, 72, 77–79, 87, 90, 98, 100, 102, 103, 105, 106, 108–110, 116–118, 128, 129, 131, 141–145, 149, 150, 156, 157, 161, 168, 170, 171, 208, 228, 234, 245, 246, 250–253, 255, 256
Slave trade, 55, 60, 87, 90, 102, 103, 105, 106, 108–110, 117, 126, 128, 144, 149, 156, 234, 251
Smith, George, 11, 86
Smith, James, 180, 199, 200
Speculation, 3, 10, 42, 55, 56, 63, 65, 66, 74, 75, 92, 95, 97, 121, 151, 156–158, 160, 161, 171, 185, 195, 211, 214, 216, 225, 227, 230, 231, 233, 236, 237, 242, 243, 247, 249, 254, 256, 257, 260, 269
Srebrnik, Patricia, 215
St. James Magazine, 198, 199
St. Katharine Docks, 8, 11, 85, 86, 94, 97, 139–141, 164, 166, 167
Steinbach, Susie, 5
Stern, Rebecca, 21, 172, 216
Stowe, Harriet Beecher, 100
Stuart, Elma, 148
Surridge, Lisa, 124

T
Taylor, James, 7, 34, 36–38, 40, 46, 47, 114, 171, 216, 219
Thackeray, William Makepeace, 10, 11, 13, 15, 21, 29, 31, 45, 46, 72, 74, 122, 142, 146, 211, 215, 226, 230
Newcomes, The, 3, 16, 30, 44
Vanity Fair, 16, 44, 58, 143, 171, 186
Tinsley Brothers, 201, 203, 204
Trela, D.J., 227
Trollope, Anthony
Eustace Diamonds, The, 68
Last Chronicle of Barset, The, 16, 72, 238
Miss Mackenzie, 16, 60, 68, 71, 72, 117, 118, 122, 204
Phineas Finn, 65–67, 73
Phineas Redux, 66, 67
Prime Minister, The, 3, 65, 202, 240
Way We Live Now, The, 3, 16, 18, 58, 65, 72, 76, 79, 116, 154, 161, 166, 186, 188
Trollope, Frances, 65
Domestic Manners of the Americans, 64, 127
Turner, Ann, 95–97, 126
Tweedie, Ethel, 214, 219, 220
Twinn, Frances, 129

U
Uglow, Jenny, 86, 91, 93, 95, 97, 102, 125

V
Vernon, John, 12, 116, 242

W
Wagner, Tamara, 21, 45, 171, 215, 227, 237, 241, 259, 260
Wake, Jehanne, 7, 41, 42, 46, 68, 110, 128, 148, 168, 169

Ward, Mrs. Humphrey, 220, 230
Watson, Tim, 157, 170
Weiss, Barbara, 13, 30, 130, 171, 204, 218, 219, 260
Wertheimer, Eric, 116
West Indies, 9, 35, 62, 102, 139, 142–144, 149, 155, 156, 203, 239, 245, 251, 252, 254, 256
Westminster Review, 141, 149
Wharton, Edith, 18, 184, 214, 269, 270, 273
Whiffin, George, 200, 203, 205, 218
White, Terence De Vere, 169
Williams, Merryn, 128, 227, 239, 259
Wilson, Francis, 228
Wilson, William (Willie), 259
Women
   authors, 2, 4, 8, 9, 14, 15, 255, 258, 259
   businesswoman, 55–57, 72, 122, 183, 188
   critique of capitalism, 16, 62, 88, 89, 110, 124, 271
   financial independence, 2, 18, 32, 55, 268
   heiresses, 43, 72, 75, 184, 185, 239
   investors, 2, 3, 5, 6, 8, 13, 15, 16, 18, 31, 32, 34, 36, 38, 43–45, 55, 56, 66, 67, 73, 76, 78, 97, 98, 115, 125, 143, 180, 239, 258, 267, 268, 270–272
   married, 2, 6, 7, 14, 15, 33, 34, 56, 88, 93, 159, 187, 208
   single, 6, 33–36, 55, 66, 68, 93, 95, 114, 120
   widows, 6, 7, 10, 30, 33, 35, 40, 56, 66, 68, 73, 75, 93, 165
   representations of, 8, 15, 45, 270
Wood, Ellen, 14
Wood, William, 146, 232
Woodside, 95, 102, 109, 228, 237
Woolf, Virginia, 22, 269
Wyatt, James, 103
Wyatt, Mathew Cotes, 103

Y

Yarrington, Allison, 105, 106

Z

Zemka, Sue, 128

CPSIA information can be obtained
at www.ICGtesting.com
Printed in the USA
LVHW05*1910041018
592416LV00009B/417/P